THE EXISTENTIAL AND ITS EXITS

Literary and philosophical perspectives on the works of beckett, ionesco, genet and pinter

Bloomsbury Academic Collections: English Literary Criticism

This carefully chosen selection of 56 classic works of literary criticism comes from the archives of Athlone Press, one of the most distinguished publishers of English criticism in the period 1950–2000.

The volumes in the collection cover all periods and styles of literary criticism, from Beowulf to Pinter, and include works of literary theory as well as studies of specific periods, writers or works. Authors include Herbert Grierson, Barbara Hardy, Christopher Norris, George Kane, EMW Tillyard, Patricia Ball, Geoffrey Tillotson, David Holbrook, and John Sutherland.

All titles are issued in cased bindings as complete facsimile editions; ebook versions are also available.

Titles in English Literary Criticism are available in the following subsets:

English Literary Criticism: General Theory and History
English Literary Criticism: Pre–1700
English Literary Criticism: 18th–19th Centuries
English Literary Criticism: 20th Century

Other titles available in English Literary Criticism: Pre-1700 include:

Aldous Huxley: A Study of the Major Novels, Peter Bowering
Dylan Thomas: The Code of Night, David Holbrook
Sylvia Plath: Poetry and Existence, David Holbrook
The Irish Drama of Europe from Yeats to Beckett, Katharine Worth
The Filibuster: A Study of the Political ideas of Wyndham Lewis, D. G. Bridson
The Literary Criticism of T.S. Eliot: New Essays, David Newton-De Molina
Theory and Personality: The Significance of T.S. Eliot's Criticism, Brian Lee
T.S. Eliot: Mystic, Son and Lover, Donald J. Childs

THE EXISTENTIAL AND ITS EXITS

Literary and philosophical perspectives on the works of beckett, ionesco, genet and pinter

L. A. C. Dobrez

BLOOMSBURY ACADEMIC COLLECTIONS:
English Literary Criticism – 20th Century

BLOOMSBURY
NEW DELHI • LONDON • OXFORD • NEW YORK • SYDNEY

First published in India 2017
First published in 2013
This edition published in 2013 by Bloomsbury Publishing plc

Bloomsbury Academic
An imprint of Bloomsbury Publishing Plc
Bloomsbury is a registered trade mark of Bloomsbury Publishing Plc

This title published with permission from Bloomsbury Publishing Plc
50 Bedford Square, London, WC1B3DP, UK

Bloomsbury Academic Collections
ISSN 2051-0012

British Library Cataloguing-in-Publication Data
A catalogue record for this book is available from the British Library.

ISBN: 978 93 86606 83 9
10 9 8 7 6 5 4 3 2 1
For sale in the Indian subcontinent only

Bloomsbury Publishing India Pvt. Ltd
Second Floor, Building No. 4
DDA Complex LSC, Pocket C – 6 & 7
Vasant Kunj, New Delhi 110070
www.bloomsbury.com

ISBN: 9781472536150 (Bloomsbury Academic Collections: English Literary Criticism – 20th Century)
Entire Collection ISBN: 9781472535412
(Bloomsbury Academic Collections: English Literary Criticism)

Library of Congress Cataloging-in-Publication Data
A catalog record for this book is available from the Library of Congress
Printed and bound in India

The Existential and its Exits

L. A. C. DOBREZ

The Existential and its Exits

Literary and philosophical perspectives on the works of BECKETT, IONESCO, GENET & PINTER

THE ATHLONE PRESS · LONDON

ST MARTIN'S PRESS · NEW YORK

First published 1986 by The Athlone Press Ltd
44 Bedford Row, London WC1R 4LY
First published in the United States of America in 1986
by St Martin's Press, Inc., 175 Fifth Avenue, New York, NY 10010

Published with the assistance of the
Faculty of Arts, Australian National University

British Library Cataloguing in Publication Data
Dobrez, L.A.C.
The existential and its exits : literary and philosophical perspectives on the work of Beckett, Ionesco, Genet and Pinter.
1. Literature, Modern—20th century—History and criticism
I. Title
809'.04 PN771
ISBN 0–485–11282–5

Library of Congress Cataloging in Publication Data
Dobrez, L. A. C. (Livio A. C.)
The existential and its exits.
Includes index.
1. French literature—20th century—History and criticism. 2. Philosophy in literature. 3. Existentialism in literature. 4. English literature—20th century—History and criticism. 5. Beckett, Samuel, 1906– —Philosophy. 6. Ionesco, Eugène—Philosophy. 7. Genet, Jean, 1910– —Philosophy. 8. Pinter, Harold, 1930– —Philosophy. I. Title.
PQ307.P47D63 1985 842'.914 85–2168
ISBN 0–312–27502–1

Typesetting by Inforum Ltd, Portsmouth
Printed in Great Britain by Redwood Burn, Trowbridge

Contents

Acknowledgements

The Author and Publishers thank the following for permission to use material previously published:

The editors of *Southern Review* (University of Adelaide) for

"Samuel Beckett's Irreducible", *Southern Review*, VI, no. 3, 1973

"Beckett, Sartre and Camus: The Darkness and the Light", *Southern Review*, VII, no. 1, 1974

"Beckett and Heidegger: Existence, Being and Nothingness", *Southern Review*, VII, no. 2, 1974

"Jean Genet: Solitude and the Sartrean Look", *Southern Review*, X, no. 2, 1977

"The Murderer and the Saint: Sartrean Relationships in the Work of Jean Genet", *Southern Review*, X, no. 3, 1977

"The Image and the Revolutionary: Sartrean Relationships in the Work of Jean Genet", *Southern Review*, XI, no. 1, 1978

Macmillan London Ltd for

"To end yet again: Samuel Beckett's Recent Work", in *Transformations in Modern European Drama*, ed. Ian Donaldson (London, 1983).

Thanks are due to John Calder Publishers and Grove Press for permission to quote from Samuel Beckett's *Molloy, Malone Dies, The Unnamable* (London, 1959), and to John Calder for permission to quote from Eugène Ionesco's *Notes and Counter-Notes* (London, 1964). They are also due to the Humanities Research Centre at the Australian National University under whose auspices this book was completed.

Introduction

> It might seem strange that opinions of weight are found in the works of poets rather than philosophers. The reason is that poets wrote through enthusiasm and imagination; there are in us seeds of knowledge, as [of fire] in a flint; philosophers extract them by way of reason, but poets strike them out by imagination, and then they shine more bright.[1]
>
> DESCARTES

> Out of long-guarded speechlessness and the careful clarification of the field thus cleared, comes the utterance of the thinker. Of like origin is the naming of the poet . . . The thinker utters Being. The poet names what is holy.[2]
>
> HEIDEGGER

Descartes and Heidegger and, if it comes to that, a great many other philosophers, have put forward the compelling case for a connection between the activities of poet and thinker, artist and philosopher. Descartes, whose significance in a discussion of more or less contemporary writing and philosophizing will be apparent as we proceed, senses the fundamental unity in seeming diversity of literary and philosophical creativity. Heidegger, whose work is central to the concerns of this book, is even more insistent: poet and thinker trace their diverse inspirations to a common source. Of course we are bound to acknowledge that the relation of supposedly distinct disciplines like literature and philosophy is problematical, though it may well be less so in the present context, which is that of modern existential thought. After all, whereas a great deal of traditional philosophizing tends to begin with the thinking subject and so to develop along epistemological lines, existential philosophy, on which the present argument will focus, has in various ways sought to begin with the subject as existing, that is, as involved in a particular situation, and so to develop along ontological lines. Consequently, a number of existential thinkers have emphasized that if philosophy is to speak for the man of feeling and action as well as for the one who contemplates and reasons it must take the form of a literary philosophy, even of philosophic art. Figures as diverse as Sartre and Gabriel Marcel chose to embody their concepts in novels or plays or both. Kierkegaard, whose work anticipates central features of twentieth-century existential approaches, wrote treatises whose form is nearer to literature than to philosophy. Heidegger, as already noted, went to some trouble to underline his spiritual kinship with the poet. In the case of a loosely-termed existentialist such as Camus, art and philosophy go hand in hand, although here philosophy certainly takes second place.

At any rate, it does not seem necessary to insist too strongly on the distinction between the two disciplines in a book whose aim is to comment on the work of Beckett, Ionesco, Genet and Pinter in relation to the thought of Sartre, Heidegger and others. To say this is by no means to open the door to the facile application of philosophical generalities to the analysis of literature. On the contrary, it becomes more important than ever to conduct the analysis with a detailed precision generally lacking in writing on the subject. For this reason Beckett, Ionesco, Genet and Pinter have been examined not as a group but as individual artists, each with a unique vision and manner. Likewise, the philosophers have been approached with a rigour which is not usual in literary criticism. In short, parallels between writer and philosopher have been based on a very particular, and literary, study of the writer and, at the same time, on a detailed and comprehensive study of the philosopher from a philosophical point of view. The result is an enquiry into what Beckett, Ionesco, Genet and Pinter have in common which attempts to get underneath the generalizations about absurdity and the void and to compare essential rather than general qualities of these writers with equally fundamental qualities of the thought of Heidegger and Sartre. Of course we are not dealing with philosophic "influences" on the art of Beckett, Ionesco, Genet and Pinter: it is more a question of a shared *Weltanschauung*, a concept which allows for differences as well as sameness.

In parable form, the historical and cultural background to the argument of this book might be expressed as follows: like the human subject in one of those awe-inspiring canvases painted by the German Romantic, Caspar David Friedrich, a man encounters a landscape of monumental proportions, whose every vista offers seemingly unlimited possibilities for exploration and discovery; he chooses a promising path only to realize that it quickly leads to constantly narrowing spaces and, in the end, to a single cell in which, inexplicably, he finds himself imprisoned. He is now a king whose domain has been taken from him, and who, like Richard II, hammers out extraordinary conceits, anxious to people the solitary wilderness with imagined beings, dreaming of ways in which – to paraphrase Shakespeare – vain weak nails might tear a passage through a hard world of prison walls. This is the situation of the nineteenth-century European, the Romantic whose unbounded expectations in every sphere from the political to the metaphysical suffer drastic diminution in the course of a hundred years. In literature and philosophy, the shift takes us from Wordsworth's panoramic lookout on the peak of Snowdon to one of Samuel Beckett's cells for the condemned, from the heady intellectual visions of the Idealists to the spare cogitations of more cautious thinkers. The present work does not seek to chart this complex historical metamorphosis, only to provide some perspectives on it on the basis of a study of four major contemporary writers in relation to modern existential thought, chiefly that of Heidegger and Sartre. In the process, philosophy may be expected to shed light on literary phenomena and, in some respects, literature may be expected to clarify philosophical issues.

One further point must be made in this introduction. The use of philosophical language in literary criticism raises some difficulties. I have avoided the term Existentialism, since it appears to restrict the discussion to French thinkers of the postwar, and to speak rather of existential philosophy. In addition, I have capitalized the noun Existence whenever it is used in a technical sense in order to reduce the possibility of confusion. A capital letter also seems necessary in the case of the Absurd or Heideggerian Being, though not in that of Sartrean being.

I The Beckett Irreducible

1 Beckett: the Reduction

> But when the object is perceived as particular and unique and not merely the member of a family, when it appears independent of any general notion and detached from the sanity of a cause, isolated and inexplicable in the light of ignorance, then and then only may it be a source of enchantment.[1]
>
> BECKETT

Beckett is loth to reveal himself to the public. Only rarely has he submitted to an exposure of his views and consequently his comments to Georges Duthuit, published in 1949 as *Three Dialogues*, have a special significance. The discussion with Duthuit possibly represents the most expanded version of the Beckett aesthetic in existence (it is very brief). Actually it does not deal directly with Beckett's own work but with that of the contemporary painters Tal Coat, Masson and Bram van Velde. Beckett quickly dismisses the first of these. Artists like Tal Coat "never stirred from the field of the possible, however much they may have enlarged it" (pp.102–3). Tal Coat's is art "on the plane of the feasible" (p.103). Of course Duthuit protests: What other plane is there?

> B: Logically none. Yet I speak of an art turning from it in disgust, weary of its puny exploits, weary of pretending to be able, of being able, of doing a little better the same old thing, of going a little further along a dreary road.
>
> D: And preferring what?
>
> B: The expression that there is nothing to express, nothing with which to express, nothing from which to express, no power to express, no desire to express, together with the obligation to express. (p.103)

Missing the import of this, Duthuit proposes Masson as a painter who ought to fulfil Beckett's requirements: Masson, after all, "speaks . . . of painting the void" (p.109). But Beckett's reaction remains unfavourable. "In search of a difficulty", he comments, "rather than in its clutch. The disquiet of him who lacks an adversary." (p.109) It is still the plane of the feasible, the possible, "the malady of wanting to know what to do and the malady of wanting to be able to do it" (p.110).

Duthuit, on his guard, finally suggests Bram van Velde. Beckett now approves. Here, at last, is

> the situation . . . of him who is helpless, cannot act, in the event cannot paint, since he is obliged to paint. The act is of him who, helpless, unable to act, acts, in the event paints, since he is obliged to paint. (p.119)

The plane of the possible is now transcended. We are no longer in "the domain of the feasible" where "the much to express, the little to express, the ability to express much, the ability to express little, merge in the common anxiety to express as much as possible, or as truly as possible" (p.120). Duthuit suddenly grasps the odd implications of the argument:

> D: One moment. Are you suggesting that the painting of van Velde is inexpressive?
> B: (A fortnight later) Yes.
> D: You realize the absurdity of what you advance?
> B: I hope I do. (pp.120–1)

An obvious objection to Beckett's position is promptly supplied by the logic of convention: if one paints one must be expressing something, even if only the impossibility of expression. Beckett rejects this way out of the difficulty as an *a priorism* with no force of proof. Art need not express anything.

Duthuit politely treats the matter as an avant-garde joke. "Try and bear in mind", he tells Beckett, "that the subject under discussion is not yourself, not the Sufist Al-Haqq, but a particular Dutchman by name van Velde, hitherto erroneously referred to as an *artiste peintre*" (p.123). Of course Beckett's argument is outrageous. If van Velde's art is inexpressive, it is not "painting". And indeed Beckett is not prepared to say what it is in what appears as an obliteration of the category of Universals:

> For what is this coloured plane, that was not there before. I don't know what it is, having never seen anything like it before. It seems to have nothing to do with art, in any case, if my memories are correct. (p.126)

In spite of the clowning, we are being asked to consider seriously an art which is strictly non-relational and so not art at all, an artist who does not express himself, who does not express anything, and so is not really an artist. According to Beckett, the history of art may be represented as a prolonged attempt to avoid the disquieting conclusion that there is no intelligible connection between the artist and his world, between the act of painting and its result. We are left then with a frankly dualist view, with an unrelated particular which, for reasons unknown, manages to subsist. Bram van Velde does not paint, yet the result is there for all to see, an act "of him who, helpless, unable to act, acts, in the event paints" (p.119). Duthuit can only regard such a stand as illogical. A world in which terms of relation are either not there at all or at least unavailable cannot subsist, it is inconceivable. The world exists as world only by virtue of connections, ideas, Universals. A door is meant to be opened and shut. If it cannot be related in this way to the being who is able to manipulate it, it is not a door as van Velde's picture is not a picture. It is doubtful that we may even say of this door, as of this picture, that it exists. For after all that which *is*, without being anything, can only be *nothing*. The door not a door made of wood not wood from a tree not a tree, the door, which is not anything else apart from the door which it is not, cannot subsist. The idea of the inexpressive, the non-relational, implies not only something unusual: it implies the impossible. And this is exactly what Beckett means: van Velde's art is not on the plane of the feasible, it *is* an Impossible, a saying-nothing in the strictest sense, a something whose existence is inexplicable, since it is nothing at all.

Despite the difficulties of this point of view, Beckett has no qualms about referring the whole discussion to his own work:

> There are many ways in which the thing I am trying in vain to say may be tried in vain to be said. I have experimented, as you

> know, both in public and in private, under duress, through faintness of heart, through weakness of mind, with two or three hundred. (p.123)

Clearly, and from the start there could be no doubt of this, van Velde's predicament and Beckett's are identical. Nor can we dismiss this as avant-garde contempt for "message" or as a Beckett version of *l'art pour l'art*, least of all as a literary joke. Beckett has seriously committed himself to the most difficult task ever resignedly undertaken in the history of art. He has been obliged to say nothing many times over. The present argument attempts, in so far as it is possible, to discuss this fact while remaining on Beckett's own ground, that is, it attempts a criticism that in its own way will reproduce Beckett's obsession with the particular, the non-relational, examining the Beckett void without naming it in other than negative or analogical terms, circling repeatedly around the hole in order to map its outlines much as Dionysius the Areopagite delineated his unknown by the method of negative theology. In this way it avoids the uncomfortable, indeed irrelevant choice of viewing Beckett either as a nihilist or as a humanist in disguise.

These initial chapters are concerned primarily with the subject matter of Beckett's art. In the light of what has already been said, though, it is evident that the only subject available to an art of saying nothing is nothing itself. Moreover, this "nothing" will not mean silence, quite the opposite. In spite of Wittgenstein's famous dictum, Beckett will not give up writing. He will treat nothing not as non-existent but as impossibly *there.* In other words it is not a question of not speaking but of speaking in such a way that nothing is expressed and that what is expressed is nothing. But the full significance of this obscure task cannot be made obvious at once. To begin with it is necessary to note that Beckett does not and could not begin at this extreme point. Rather, his work represents a gradual movement towards it. I have termed this movement towards a negative point, a particular object, the Beckett Reduction. From his early work in the thirties to his latest in the present, for over fifty years of writing, Beckett has made his way to this end product, to an Irreducible which is left as a *sine qua non*, a barely-something-almost-nothing, an impossible being-nothing. This Irreducible is his single subject, though it should be added that in the process of eliminating everything, a great deal may be included.

An early hint of the Reduction is already apparent in 1931, in Beckett's essay on Proust. Beckett is not discussing his own work, which scarcely exists at this stage, and *Proust* is primarily an excellent piece of literary criticism. At the same time, its relevance to Beckett's output over the fifty years following it means that *Proust* is rightly treated by many as an oblique Beckett manifesto. In it we read:

> The only fertile research is excavatory, immersive, a contraction of the spirit, a descent. The artist is active, but negatively, shrinking from the nullity of extracircumferential phenomena, drawn into the core of the eddy.[2]

This assertion is first put into practice in *Dream of Fair to Middling Women* (unpublished) and in *More Pricks than Kicks* (published in 1934), where the Beckett character appears for the first time. Belacqua, whose name relates him to the indolent Florentine encountered by Dante in canto four of the *Purgatorio*, is weary of life and of society, the nineties aesthete on his last legs, Stephen Dedalus with a "new lease of apathy".[3] "Temporarily sane" (p.88) he dreams of suicide but opts instead for a death of love in the enticing arms of Ruby Tough. After a series of strange *amours* he dies once and for all because of a surgical mistake. His one aim in life has been what is termed in *Proust* "the wisdom of all the sages, from Brahma to Leopardi" (p.18), to desire nothing, to suffer patiently the inexplicable burden of an individual life. Doing nothing, wanting nothing: the Reduction has begun and while it has not been taken very far – while Belacqua remains a relatively conventional creature in a social world – its direction has been clearly indicated.

In *Murphy* (published 1938), the Reduction is more properly in focus. The hero of this tragicomedy reincarnates Belacqua as an exile in London who traverses the greater part of the novel in flight from other people. Murphy is a modern mystic who likes nothing better than to remove his clothes, tie himself to a rocking chair with seven scarves and rock himself into oblivion. Solitude and the luxury of doing nothing are essential to his success. Unfortunately, he attracts the interest of the extravagant Miss

Counihan and of a number of other characters who pursue him until he manages to find refuge as a male nurse in the Magdalen Mental Mercyseat. Here the "seedy solipsist"[4] is among his own. Murphy's is a movement inwards that necessitates an ascent towards the goal of emotional indifference, of ascetic detachment from all everyday concerns: "in the beautiful Belgo–Latin of Arnold Geulincx: *Ubi nihil vales, ibi nihil velis*" (p.124).

Beckett's interest in the seventeenth-century Cartesian Geulincx takes us to the centre of the Reduction which so far has been only vaguely glimpsed. The key is chapter six of the novel where, as Beckett explains, "it is most unfortunate, but the point of this story has been reached where a justification of the expression 'Murphy's mind' has to be attempted" (p.76). In justifying it, the author has recourse to any philosophy that will serve so that chapter six becomes a hilarious confusion of Descartes, Spinoza, Geulincx, Leibniz, Berkeley and Samuel Beckett. Murphy's mind, we are told, "pictured itself as a large hollow sphere, hermetically closed to the universe without" (p.76). Like the hero's suit which "admitted no air from the outer world" and "allowed none of Murphy's own vapours to escape" (p.53) it is a closed system, a Leibnizian "windowless" monad. We are not to conclude, however, that Murphy is an Idealist of the Berkeleian or any other kind. On the contrary: "There was the mental fact and there was the physical fact, equally real if not equally pleasant" (p.76). Murphy's mind exists beside Murphy's body, and independently of it:

> . . . Murphy felt himself split in two, a body and a mind. They had intercourse apparently . . . But he felt his mind to be bodytight and he did not understand through what channel the intercourse was effected . . . He was satisfied that neither followed from the other. He neither thought a kick because he felt one nor felt a kick because he thought one. (p.77)

The relevance of the Geulincx dictum is clear. If there is no intelligible relation between mind and body, only a mysterious intercourse over which Murphy has no control, there can be no question of Murphy effectively intervening in extra-mental affairs. The only solution is an attitude of indifference to all that is not mind: *ubi nihil vales, ibi nihil velis*. We are in Beckett's version of the Occasionalist world.

Descartes, whose presence is felt from beginning to end in Beckett's work, based his entire philosophy on the body–mind distinction. While he believed in the interaction of spirit and matter, of spiritual and extended substance, and thought he had found the inconceivable point of interaction in the pineal gland, he acknowledged its problematical nature. Later Cartesians gave up the problem as insoluble. Since mind and body are distinct there can be no intercourse between them. If I desire to walk it is not this desire which moves my legs but the continued intervention of God. Of course my wanting to walk and my walking coincide, but only because God wills to synchronize them. Thus my desire to walk becomes the "occasion" of God's fiat to render the human carcass operative, to breathe life into a dying animal. This is the view of Geulincx and also of another seventeenth-century philosopher, Nicolas Malebranche. In the Leibnizian world what happens is not unlike Occasionalism. Since the monads – those units to which all things are ultimately reduced – are indeed "windowless", all intercourse between them is ruled out. In order to explain what appears to be an interconnection Leibniz postulates a harmony pre-established by God. The monads are like so many clocks wound to run parallel to each other, synchronized in every detail yet always separate. Thus the world appears as a complex machine, each part geared to cooperate in the general motion. Murphy's Occasionalism is more radical than the Leibnizian harmony, though, and Murphy's world, like that of Geulincx, is an immense correspondence of activities, a series of miraculous meetings in which the participants can never touch. Where Geulincx is able to have recourse to a deity to keep things from disintegration, moreover, Murphy is helpless. For him no such principle of cohesion is available. What remains is *pure* Occasionalism, a creation unique to Beckett, infinitely subdivided into incompatible parts. Murphy walks by a series of coincidences. When he wants to walk he *hopes* that, following its own obscure mechanisms, his body will move, which it may well do if he is lucky. In view of this, Murphy wisely expects nothing from it, grateful for any incidental cooperation. As Neary suggests to him early in the novel: "I should say your conarium has shrunk to nothing" (p.8). The conarium is Descartes' pineal, the legendary point at which thought and matter, soul and body, unite. But it is not only the body–mind connection which is threatened. Every act of Murphy is an unknown and takes place in an Occasionalist vacuum. No sustained human relationships are possible, nor is Murphy equipped to cope with social structures. Beckett has reduced the human being to solitude and, since action cannot take place without a degree of coordination, to impotence.

It is evident that a world whose units are not held together but merely juxtaposed is not only unintelligible but also impossible. That which is without relation to anything else can only be nothing at all. We recall the painter who is not a painter and the work of art which is not art. The Duthuit interview took place eleven years after the publication of *Murphy*, yet it is revealing to see how far the Beckett Impossible is already explicit in the first novel. Murphy, even more than Belacqua before him, is himself like van Velde's picture: a living anomaly. The full force of this emerges when we consider the nature of Murphy's mind. Murphy, in his dissatisfaction with what is external to him, deliberately seeks greater solitude and peace within himself in a withdrawal to the sphere of the *cogito*. It is an ascesis which combines the Cartesian movement with the Spinozan three-stage ascent to the Intellectual Love of God or, in this case, to the "*amor intellectualis quo Murphy se ipsum amat*" (p.76). Strapped to his mystical armchair, Murphy moves inwards, passing through the three zones of the mind; first, the one in which he is able to *think* the external world ("here the whole physical fiasco became a howling success" (p.79)), second, the one in which images recede ("here was the Belacqua bliss" (p.79)), and, finally, the one in which there is no individual thought at all. Here Murphy does not act but joins the ceaseless activity of life, participates in an endless motion without himself making any move. We have reached the core of Murphy's mind and, not surprisingly, a new universe, this time a mental one, in the process of falling apart. Murphy's deepest being is that of "a point in the ceaseless unconditioned generation and passing away of line" (p.79). Of course the relation between point and line is analogous to that between mind and body, between Murphy and society: it is a non-relation, a philosophical Impossible. Murphy's innermost mind, like Murphy as a whole, is an inconceivable particular, connected to

Murphy's more superficial mental processes by pure coincidence. The inner world disintegrates in the same way as the outer world. We are reminded of a form of Occasionalism which goes beyond even that of Geulincx: that of Malebranche. For Malebranche, not only is the connection of body and mind dependent on God, but the activities of the mind itself require a deity. The mind receives its ideas not from what is outside it but from God so that all its knowledge is a knowledge of things in God, and all its intellectual operations take place in the context of a continuing divine activity. Murphy's mental processes, of course, do not stem from any such principle of harmony. They take place only by an extraordinary coincidence, by a miracle all the greater for its having no divine source. And at the very core of Murphy's mind is the point where the great mystery has its source, the true Murphy, "matrix of surds" (p.79).

This final reference requires amplification since it provides an added perspective on all that has been said so far. Beckett's monadism, as already observed, leads to an impossibility. To make the point Beckett appeals to the image of the Pythagorean "surd". This question has been treated by Hugh Kenner in his book *Samuel Beckett, A Critical Study*, but it is worth restating. The Pythagoreans found that the square roots of certain numbers could be expressed only by approximations. In the particular case of the triangle formed by the diagonal of a square, for example, the relation of diagonal to side could not be given in terms of a simple number. Any figure which, like Pi, could be extended to infinity was termed an "irrational" and regarded as a mystery not to be offered to the uninitiated. Neary, one of Murphy's pursuers and a Pythagorean, speaks of one Hippasos "drowned in a puddle . . . for having divulged the incommensurability of side and diagonal" (p.36). The "irrational" number or surd was also termed an *alogon*, that is, an "unnamable" by the Greeks. Without commenting at this point on the obvious reference to Beckett's later novel we may note that Murphy himself is the *alogon*, the irrational that will properly fit no scheme, in Beckett's first novel. In short, Beckett's Occasionalism and his appeal to the Pythagorean concept are simply two aspects of a single concern. Murphy has an "irrational" heart (p.6); at his birth his voice alone among "millions of little larynges cursing in unison at that particular moment . . . was off the note" (p.52). Murphy is the great misfit, the number which has no definite mathematical identity, the impossible particular, like van Velde's painting. If his world is falling apart in an Occasionalism without God, then the individual object in it remains suspended in non-relation, an unintelligible fact, cut off from every outside cause – in Murphy's case from society, from the body and, ultimately, from his own mental activities – by an impenetrable mystery. At the limit of its reduction such as entity can only be a zero, but a zero that subsists, and so in the deepest sense an irrational *alogon*: an unnamable. In *Murphy* the Reduction is not taken to its limit. We know that Murphy is a continuing miracle. For all that, he maintains contact with the outside world to the very end. Having found a perfect image of his ascetic ideal in the "higher schizoids" (p.125) inhabiting the Mercyseat asylum, he gazes for a brief instant at his own impossible being after his chess game (an endgame, naturally) with the lunatic Mr Endon. Murphy sees his own reflection in the other's eyes, themselves oblivious of Murphy, and recognizes his existence as an irrational mirrored in the unseeing eyes of a madman – as if a nothing could exist only as a reflection off the face of the void.

It is clear that an important reduction of reality to essentials has been initiated in this early novel. Social relationships, friendship, love, concern for life, for activity, are cut down to a minimum. As if that were not enough, Murphy himself is further reduced, first by a questioning of the body–mind connection, then by a questioning of all connections within the mind. Murphy has increasingly abandoned the ways of the body for those of the mind only to discover that the objective solitude of social existence is matched by the absolute particularity of the mind within the mind. The Mr Endon episode, among others, focusses attention on the central concern of the novel: what remains when all that is incidental is questioned, when human reality is reduced in every respect? What remains is the object, never attained, of Murphy's search and also the subject of Beckett's novel: the Irreducible which subsists when an inexorable Occasionalism has removed its links with all that is not it, the Beckett *alogon*, the impossible fact, the being-nothing that is Murphy.

The Irreducible is announced in *Murphy*. In the novels which follow, it is more closely examined. *Watt*, written during the war although unpublished till 1953, deals with another search.

Whereas Murphy sought the darkness, however, Watt seeks the light. Not unexpectedly he fails completely and moves, though unwillingly, in the same direction as his predecessor. The theme of the book is purpose, value, meaning; Beckett is tackling the same issues as before but in this case from a predominantly epistemological point of view. The Reduction here is to unintelligibility. Watt makes a mysterious journey to join the household of a Mr Knott. After a stay he is ready to leave. He learns nothing about Knott, going as ignorant as he came, ejected from the Kafkaesque situation of the place and for an unknown reason, alone, broken in spirit. Watt is pathetically cut off from others, a state of affairs which he does not accept with Murphy's eagerness. His one relationship, with the one-breasted fishwoman Mrs Gorman, is severely limited ("The irony of life . . . That he who has the time should lack the force, that she who has the force should lack the time!")[5] and he ends his time at the house in the total desolation of his solitude and impotence beside the inhuman Knott:

> Dis yb dis, nem owt. Yad la, tin fo trap . . . Od su did ned taw? On. Taw ot klat tonk? On. Tonk ot klat taw? On. Tonk ta kool taw? On. Taw ta kool tonk? Nilb, mun, mud. (p.166) (*To be read backwards.*)

Two men stand side by side, unable to communicate, dumb, numb, blind. The Watt (what) question receives only a negative answer: Knott.

More alone than ever in this Shandean and Joycean world, Watt begins to lose contact with the outside world, not, like Murphy, by a deliberate process of ascesis but in confused despair. The incident of the Galls begins with piano-tuners visiting Mr Knott's and ends with Watt's failure to extract any significance from the event which "developed a purely plastic context, and gradually lost, in the nice processes of its light, its sound, its impacts and its rhythm, all meaning, even the most literal" (p.69). So it is with the problem of the unnamable pot: "For Watt now found himself in the midst of things which, if they consented to be named, did so as it were with reluctance" (p.78). Jacqueline Hoefer, whose mistake regarding the specific influence of Wittgenstein on *Watt* has unduly obscured the partial validity of her thesis, has seen this as a satire of British empiricism.[6] Certainly it provides an image of the collapse of a Newtonian system of relations, of a scientific approach to reality in general, but with an Occasionalist bias. There are no universal laws governing reality in *Watt.* Man is stripped of all his achievements in the sphere of perception, of reason, of language and the result is a Reduction to epistemological chaos. In effect we witness the disintegration of Watt's mind, a fulfilment of the prophecy of *Murphy*. It is as if the mind, as in the system of Malebranche, required supernatural assistance in order to function and as if this assistance were no longer forthcoming. Watt fails to explain the Galls until his very memory of a sense-perception is cast into doubt:

> . . . were there neither Galls nor piano then, but only an unintelligible succession of changes, from which Watt finally extracted the Galls and the piano, in self-defence? (p.76)

In this extraordinary tangle of Beckett and David Hume what emerges is that distant reflection of continental Occasionalism present in the British philosopher. Of course Hume does not deny the validity of the concept of causality; he merely argues that we cannot demonstrate necessary connections between matters of fact. If A is frequently followed by B we may say that A "causes" B although we cannot prove it. Watt's is a world where items are juxtaposed without apparent interaction, where reality, composed of a mass of sense-perceptions, is undeniable in so far as it is *there*, in so far as *something* is there, but remains in the final analysis what Coleridge termed an immense heap of little things. Nothing exists to hold together the fragments of a world. The unifying power of the mind has failed and so perception itself becomes a game of hit and miss. Watt struggles earnestly to cope The concern with series as an explanation for a given event, the concern with possibilities, with logical alternatives and patterns, shows how desperately and ridiculously he attempts to salvage the scraps of experience. Only a few examples can be cited here. There is the attempt to discover a pattern in the croaking of the three frogs, or to explain the rhythm of life at Knott's or to obtain the key to Erskine's room or to unravel the mystery of Knott's left-over food which requires a series of dogs to eat it stretching to infinity and a series of members of the (mythical) Lynch family to keep those dogs also stretching to infinity. The result of Watt's conjectures is, of course, inevitably negative. The principle of causality has been reduced to absurdity: once we postulate Z as caused by Y we must postulated Y as caused by X and so on, ad infinitum. Likewise, the principles of logic (themselves based on an idea of necessary connections) are demolished. As in *Murphy* a wedge has been driven between mind as knowing subject and world as object of knowledge, as well as between one mental operation and another. Watt, therefore, is certain neither of his interpretations of facts nor of his processes of interpretation.

But this does not mean absolute chaos, at least not in one sense. I may doubt all, said Descartes, except my doubt. Watt is certain of one thing: that one thing is certain. He does not know exactly what that thing is. Nevertheless, it is there, the one thing which remains when all else is questioned. Perhaps there were no Galls, no piano. Perhaps there is no Knott household and no Knott (the name suggests it), no food left over, no dog, no Lynch family, no Watt even. But, if we may quote from *Endgame, something* is taking its course, otherwise there would be no perplexity. Thus the question – What? – reappears from the ashes and, phoenix-like, the protagonist is reborn. Things, as in *Murphy*, are impossibly fragmented and yet they exist. Events after all "happen", albeit magically, since without inter-connections, without some degree of order, nothing can happen. But because there is no order, only chaos, what *does* happen can only be nothing, a non-event, an *alogon* like Murphy and Watt or the negative Mr Knott. In short, an Irreducible remains when all else is destroyed and that Irreducible is a kind of nothing. Arsene's magnificent expression of this truth, anticipating Lucky's speech in its inspired confusion, comes early in the novel, as he describes an obscure fall of sand, from one pile to another:

> Where was I? The change. In what did it consist? It is hard to say. Something slipped. There I was, warm and bright, smoking my tobacco pipe, watching the warm bright wall, when suddenly somewhere some little thing slipped, some little tiny thing. Gliss-iss-iss-STOP! I trust I make myself clear. (p.41)

Arsene's slip of sand is that impossible non-event which is a fact, like the brute fact of Watt and of his coming to and going from Mr Knott's or like the fact of Murphy's nothingness in the eyes of the lunatic Mr Endon. From different points of view Beckett returns obsessively to the same Irreducible.

In the Belacqua stories and *Murphy* Beckett approaches his Irreducible with hesitation born of uncertainty. It is a search conducted casually, even offhandedly by a jaded, *accidia*-ridden hero, heir to the languor of the *fin de siècle* through the intercession of James Joyce. It is true that beneath the mask of unconcern Belacqua and Murphy suffer, in short, that theirs is a voyage through *reality*, not fantasy. But the tone of the early work is playful, it distances the reader from the harshness implicit in the narrative. *Watt* marks Beckett's turning-point, and Deirdre Bair is surely right when she views it as the novel of Beckett's breakdown during the war.[7] Of course *Watt* is comic, as indeed is much of what is to follow. The comedy, however, is of a deeply serious kind, not incompatible with panic. In the war years Beckett abandons those delicately ironic, though biting, displays which were a legacy of Aestheticism. After *Watt*, he writes as one who has a goal clearly before him, with absolute concentration and seriousness. At this point we could say that the search for an irreducible is out in the open.

Mercier and Camier (unavailable in English until 1970) looks forward as well as back in portraying a pair of misfits wandering aimlessly in a setting of disintegration imaged in the bicycle which goes to pieces. The real line of development, though, is in the stories – Beckett's first significant French work – which are available in English as *Four Novellas* (1977). These were written around 1945 and in each case the subject, in the solipsist tradition of Belacqua and his successors, has come of age, clearly recognizable as the Beckett tramp. "First Love", "The Expelled", "The Calmative" and "The End" are superb, but in the present context they must be regarded as a prelude to the trilogy, possibly Beckett's finest work, written in the original French between 1947 and 1949. Here the Reduction is taken to its conclusion and Beckett offers for the first time a direct portrait of the Irreducible. The process of reduction moves forward in each novel as it did in each of the short stories. Molloy, Malone and others, *alogons* in an already long line, are brought closer and closer to a negative point. Molloy begins his ascent to the source of things on a bicycle. But he loses that and has to go on foot. Then a leg gives way and he limps. Then the other leg gives way also. Finally, Molloy crawls along the ground towards an obscure goal which may be his mother or, again, may be Murphy's "matrix of surds". He is utterly alone, separated from everyday normality by a bad memory and an inability to conform to the rules of decency. His communication with his mother is limited to tapping messages on her skull:

> One knock meant yes, two no, three I don't know, four money, five goodbye. I was hard put to ram this code into her ruined and frantic understanding, but I did it, in the end.[8]

Actually Molloy is recalling all of this. From the start of the novel he is confined to a bed in a small room, waiting to die, and his tale recapitulates the events which have led him to this. In a sense he has reached the source of things, the small womb-like room, image of the sphere of mind, but this fact is not evident as yet. "It is in the tranquillity of decomposition that I remember the long confused emotion which was my life" (p.25): Molloy's poetic recollection reveals a life of decay, of failure of mind and body, body alienated from mind, mind alienated from body, of escape from society. It is the prophecy of Lucky come to pass: "I listen and the voice is of a world collapsing endlessly . . ." (p.40).

Malone Dies, the second novel of the trilogy, consolidates gains made so far. Malone, another Molloy at the end of his wanderings, is bedridden, telling vaguely autobiographical stories as death approaches. The Reduction is recapitulated. Malone's story is of Saposcat (*requiescat in pace?*), later called Macmann, son of man, a tramp much like Molloy but bereft of even the latter's rudimentary purpose, who crawls, or rather rolls, in the rain across an interminable plain. But Malone's plight is more austere than that of his hero. If Sapo–Macmann is a stranger in society, Malone in his little room is utterly alone; if Macmann cannot walk properly, the other cannot walk at all. Whereas Molloy's possessions dwindle, after the loss of his bicycle, to the famous sixteen sucking stones in his pockets, Malone, who wishes to make an inventory of his few goods, can only manipulate them to the extent he can draw them to his bed with a stick. The stick is a last relic of civilization and its manipulation of nature by means of machines, the other pole of Kenner's triumphant Cartesian centaur. But one day the stick is lost, and Malone's dry comment "sine qua non, Archimedes was right"[9] sums up the situation. The end of the stick, the running down of the Cartesian machine, is also the end of the body. Murphy's dream of a mind which is bodytight is in the process of realization:

> I am naked in the bed, in the blankets, whose number I increase and diminish as the seasons come and go. I am never hot, never cold. I don't wash but I don't get dirty . . . What matters is to eat and excrete. Dish and pot, dish and pot, these are the poles. (p.188)

Malone waits indifferently for the end. His senses are failing; he sometimes wonders if he is not already dead or if the area to which he is restricted is not in fact his own skull. Towards the end of the novel even the dish–pot activity slows down to a stop when his dish is no longer filled with food. The Macmann story, running parallel to Malone's – it is clearly the story of a younger Malone – now reaches its inevitable resting-place: a lunatic asylum. Here a brief and grotesque idyll is permitted with the ageing Moll, Macmann's nurse. But Moll dies and the tale is interrupted, unfinished, by Malone's disintegration:

> never anything
> there
> any more (p.289)

It would seem that the Reduction could go no further, since *Molloy* and *Malone Dies* realize fully the Occasionalism of *Murphy* and *Watt*. But the true Beckett *alogon*, the Irreducible at the heart of Belacqua, Murphy, Watt, the tramps of the *Novellas*, Molloy, Moran, Malone and Macmann, is reached only in the final novel of the trilogy, aptly named *The Unnamable*. Like its predecessors, the Unnamable is the teller of a story which seems to recapitulate its own disintegration and this time the story carries even the austerity of Malone's situation a little further. Its subject is a tramp called Mahood, no longer walking but orbiting, a crippled puppet "coming to the end of a world tour",[10] back to his family whose rotunda is as the centre of a circle to his own circumferential travels. Mahood, orbiting, illustrates perfectly the obsessive inward movement of the Reduction:

> I must have got embroiled in a kind of inverted spiral, I mean one the coils of which, instead of widening more and more, grew narrower and narrower and finally . . . would come to an end for lack of room . . . unless of course I elected to set off again at once in the opposite direction, to unscrew myself as it were, after having screwed myself up to a standstill . . .
> (pp.318–19)

But the return journey never eventuates in Beckett and the next time we see Mahood he is stuck in a jar, like the later Winnie of *Happy Days* in her pile of sand, or Nagg and Nell of *Endgame* in their bins, totally immobile and speechless.

The final phase of the Reduction takes us to the teller of the story, the Unnamable. To begin with, its situation appears to be analogous to that of a foetus in the womb or of a corpse in the grave. The body is almost gone. The Unnamable lies in the Belacqua posture favoured by all of Beckett's characters, or again, perhaps, in "the shape . . . of an egg, with two holes no matter where to prevent it from bursting", or as "round, solid and round" (p.307). This raises the possibility of atomistic motion: "But do I roll, in the manner of a true ball? Or am I in equilibrium . . .?" (p.308). The possibility is rejected: "No, once and for all, I do not move" (p.294). It looks as if the Unnamable is motionless within a restricted space, at its very centre, knowing nothing of its situation, seeing and hearing very little, utterly indifferent: "They say I suffer like true thinking flesh, but I'm sorry, I feel nothing." (p.356). It is alone or almost so, surrounded by orbiting tramps with whom it does not communicate: "To tell the truth I believe they are all here, at least from Murphy on . . ." (p.295). Inaction, solitude, indifference: the situation is similar to that presented in the original French *Texts for Nothing*, written shortly after. With the body's dissolution, the material world has disappeared and only mind remains.

Indeed the space inhabited by the Unnamable represents Malone's room shrunk to the dimensions of a skull – "the inside of my distant skull where once I wandered, now am fixed, lost for tininess, or straining against the walls . . ." (pp.304–5). It has all been an adventure of the mind, from Murphy onwards, and in *The Unnamable* and the *Texts for Nothing* this adventure has been traced to its source: the voice of consciousness. This voice, cut off from all else, suspended in an unknown, endlessly continues its stories of Manhood, its statements about itself. It takes the Reduction as far as it can. In the course of the novel it demolishes methodically its own constructions. It spoke of a space, of a round body, of tramps in orbit. Now it denies all of these statements: "Nothing has ever changed since I have been here" (p.296). Tramps, material objects, space, sound, light – all are figments of the imagination, attempts to attenuate the harshness of the Reduction:

> There, now there is no one here but me, no one wheels about me, no one comes towards me . . . these creatures have never been, only I and this black void have ever been. And the sounds? No, all is silent. And the lights . . . must they too go out? Yes, out with them, there is no light here . . . Nothing then but me, of which I know nothing, except that I have never uttered, and this black, of which I know nothing either . . .
> (p.306)

Systematically, the voice rejects the protagonists of the earlier novels: "All these Murphys, Molloys and Malones do not fool me. They have made me waste my time . . . speak of them when . . . I should have spoken of me and of me alone" (p.305). The same renunciation is made in the *Texts*. In each case the voice disclaims any relationship with the tramps, its "delegates" (p.299), creatures who stood in its place but who bore no essential relation to it. Where Murphy sought to leave the sphere of matter behind, to withdraw into that of mind, the movement is now reversed, or rather viewed from the other side: the mind disclaims its connection with the material–spiritual entity known as Murphy, or Molloy or Malone or Watt.

Yet it would be a mistake to suppose that we are at the end of the line. "Nothing then but me, of which I know nothing", explains the voice in a passage just quoted, "*except that I have never uttered*" (my italics). The voice is not its own master. It too is a kind of "delegate" for someone else. The Unnamable, which stands *behind* the voice, denies its identity with the voice through the voice itself: "I seem to speak, it is not I, about me, it is not about me" (p.293). Beckett's subject is the silence one stage removed from the voice, "voice that speaks, knowing that it lies. . . It is not mine, I have none, I have no voice and must speak, that is all I know . . ." (p.309). This is the situation of van Velde who, unable to paint, paints. The Unnamable exists as a mind-within-the-mind, like Murphy's third level of inwardness, a point within consciousness which is so particular, so irreducible, that it can have no links with the outside, even with the very voice of consciousness which expresses it. The Unnamable cannot be any of the things said of it: as the ultimate *alogon*, the very essence of all incompatibles, it must be conceived as a negative, an impossible negative which cannot be dismissed because, like the Beckett characters, it exists, it is a non-event which *happens*, a being-nothing that is *there*. Its presence is felt behind every Beckett work but it is at this stage openly the subject of concern. In a sense, of course, it was always that, as the mysterious source of things sought by Murphy meditating in his room or observing the cells of the Mercyseat lunatics, avoided unsuccessfully by Watt in his rearguard struggle to remain in the world of normality, sought once more by Molloy looking for his mother, by Malone waiting for the end, by Macmann in his asylum, by Mahood orbiting towards his family. *The Unnamable* was written at the time of the Duthuit interview and in its light the latter falls easily into place. Beckett has gone from the Occasionalist disintegration of the material and the spiritual to the realm of mind. After that he has reduced the mind itself to bare consciousness, to the voice within a skull, a counterpart of the earlier image of a man within a room. Finally, he has reduced the voice of consciousness to the silent, negative presence which is the very soul of consciousness. It is the end of the Reduction and the Irreducible has been explicitly revealed in an extraordinary seesaw of assertion and negation.

We cannot underestimate the agony which accompanies and colours every stage of this revelation. In the thirteen sections of *Texts for Nothing* its unfolding impact is minutely charted, beginning, impossibly, with an exhausted end: "Suddenly, no, at last, long last, I couldn't any more, I couldn't go on."[11] On his face in the mud, the tramp recalls images of the past, only to be dismissed by a voice which in the same breath dismisses itself: "nothing has stirred, no one has spoken" (p.86). As panic-stricken as Watt, the voice vainly tries to identify itself. It *wills* to *be*, complete with skull and sex (indeterminate). Clutching at straws, it wills itself a "crony" (p.83), a whole existence for two, complete with newspapers:

> The sport of kings is our passion, the dogs too, we have no political opinions, simply limply republican. But we also have a soft spot for the Windsors, the Hanoverians, I forget, the Hohenzollerns is it. Nothing human is foreign to us, once we have digested the racing news. (p.84)

After this bow to the grand humanist tradition, however, a single paradoxical fact remains: these lives belong to anyone but the subject. In the opening of the fourth text, Beckett's cry is as moving as Rilke's in the first lines of the *Duino Elegies*:

> Where would I go, if I could go, who would I be, if I could be, what would I say, if I had a voice, who says this, saying it's me? (p.87)

There is on the face of it only one way to go. Squirming, the voice returns to its creation, a human being, "carcass in God's image and a contemporary skull" (p.104). Immediately it rejects this identity in disgust: "enough vile parrot I'll kill you" (p.104). From being a man waiting in a railway station, it turns into a Parisian beggar. But it is not the beggar either; while he begs silently outside a cafe or the Metro, *it* begs "in another dark, another silence, for another alm" (p.111). Finally it metamorphoses into a student, the young Beckett, in whom it also fails to recognize itself. In the thirteenth text the voice too is painfully discarded:

> . . . no one feels anything, asks anything, seeks anything, says anything, hears anything, there is only silence . . . there is silence, and there is not silence, there is no one and there is someone . . . And were the voice to cease quite at last, the old ceasing voice, it would not be true, as it is not true that it speaks, it can't speak, it can't cease. And were there one day to be here, where there are no days, which is no place, born of the impossible voice the unmakable being, and a gleam of light, still

> all would be silent and empty and dark, as now, as soon now, when all will be ended, all said, it says, it murmurs. (pp.135–6)

These tortured rhythms represent, as well as anything from *The Unnamable*, Beckett's wrestling with the overwhelming presence of the nothing which is his Irreducible. Even the groans are not self-identical, but the property of an Other: "*it* says, *it* murmurs". Who this Other is, neither the trilogy nor the *Texts* can say. It is, nonetheless, what Beckett has been concerned with from the very beginning, the source, the mother, the one reality: an "unmakable being".

On the whole critical discussion of Beckett's writing has failed to focus on this obscure creature. Where the direction of Beckett's movement has been noted it has been viewed as a search for Self, for the mystery of human identity. But the language and the concepts of psychology are inappropriate in what must be regarded as a properly philosophical context. For the purpose of the present argument Kenner's insistence on Beckett's obsessive interest in the Cartesian *cogito* is more relevant. It is clear that, if we refer Beckett's work to the seventeenth-century philosophers, what I have termed the Reduction may be viewed as an illustration of methodical Cartesian doubt applied to the entire sphere of human reality and coloured at the same time by a Stoic ethic of resignation derived from Spinoza or Geulincx. Likewise, the end product of the Reduction may be viewed as the *cogito*, the one thing beyond doubt, or, again, as the true Leibnizian monad, the ultimate, indivisible unit of existence. But there are obvious limitations to this interpretation of Beckett and they follow from what has already been said about the nature of the Unnamable. Beckett's Irreducible, after all, denies identity with the *voice* which in speaking unfolds the sequences of the novel. The Irreducible is that which is *beneath* consciousness, not consciousness itself. Descartes' *cogito*, for all its unlikeness to matter, is conceived as a thinking substance, a *res*, a thing. The Leibnizian monad, though immaterial, is also a substance. But Beckett's subject is nothing at all, a being utterly negative, impossible to define. Thus Beckett's Cartesian Reduction, his Occasionalism and his monadology point in a direction which is uniquely Samuel Beckett, towards something that is not a thinking presence but, if we may distort Kierkegaard's phrase, passionate absence.

From the perspectives provided by the novels it is not difficult to trace a similar process towards the negative in Beckett's drama. *Waiting for Godot*, written at much the same time as *The Unnamable*, belongs to the stage reached in the trilogy though it does not take the Reduction as far as does *The Unnamable*. Vladimir and Estragon, though reliant on each other, experience the reality of solitude. Like earlier tramps they have minimal possessions – carrots, boots, hats, recalling Malone's inventory – are social rejects, physically decrepit, with only the vaguest sense of purpose in life. Estragon's failures of memory especially reiterate the argument of *Proust*, that without memory there is no enduring human presence, no identity. As the play proceeds, the pattern of disintegration becomes more pronounced. Pozzo, once something of a healthy bourgeois type, goes blind; Lucky, that inspired Beckettian orator, becomes dumb. In act two, all four characters collapse to the floor and remain so for some time. But the real *sine qua non* of the play is the situation of waiting. To wait is to do something so minimal that one may as well say that it is to do nothing. Waiting is action reduced to its absolute zero. The first words of *Waiting for Godot* are "Nothing to be done",[12] the last "Yes, let's go", with the stage direction, "*they do not move*" (p.94). Man, reduced to waiting, is reduced to negative action: he cannot act and yet he can *continue* not to act, he can even act less and less as he waits more and more. Thus the true *alogon* of *Waiting for Godot* is not that being-nothing, the tramp, but an irreducible of motion, the non-event which *takes place*. This is the impossible embodied in the situation of Vladimir and Estragon, that when action is shorn of all incidentals, something remains, the negative existence of a vigil: I wait therefore I am. We may, perhaps, discern a likeness between the absent Godot and Mr Knott. In that case Godot too is a kind of *sine qua non*, an absent presence recalling Knott's present absence. But fundamentally, the unnamable of *Waiting for Godot* is the nothing-happening, the fall of sand:

ESTRAGON: Let's go.
VLADIMIR: We can't.
ESTRAGON: Why not?
VLADIMIR: We're waiting for Godot. (p.71)

Caught in the tension of a spring which has been wound to a standstill the tramp murmurs: *e pur si muove.*

If *Waiting for Godot* is, among other things, about the tramps' inescapable presence, the impossible *fact* of being, *Endgame* (written in the mid-fifties) is, as the title suggests, about the inconceivable *end* of things, that is, about the legendary point – like Descartes' pineal gland – where two mutual contradictions merge. To exist, in *Waiting for Godot*, is miraculously to pass from the minus of nothing to the plus of being, the minimal positivity of waiting. To end, in *Endgame*, is to make the inconceivable transition the other way, from being to nothingness. The play is contracted to the room-skull milieu of the novels; Hamm, Nell and Nagg have lost control over their bodies and sit or crouch with little movement. Hamm is blind, Clov, the only one still on his feet, gazes through his telescope:

> CLOV: . . . Let's see. [*He looks, moving the telescope.*] Zero . . . [*he looks*] . . . zero . . . [*he looks*] . . . and zero.[13]

It is a game of chess with an unseeing Mr Endon and it is continually being lost as it continues to be played. Hamm's only action is to recall or invent a little; Clov is ready to leave in the final scene. The game is one of elimination and attrition, moving always closer to the unlikely goal: the end of things. Of course one cannot fix the point of the Irreducible: it always eludes one, it is an unnamable. So Hamm and Clov play the game, getting closer and closer *ad infinitum* to the end, just as in the trilogy the voice moves closer and closer to the silence. But because the gap between being and nothingness, positive and negative, is infinite, there is no getting closer, infinity subdivided remains infinity. Thus just as the more the Unnamable tells us about itself the *less* we know of it, so the nearer we are to the end in *Endgame* the further away we are. Like the renowned frog which is always able to jump half the distance to the bank, we shall never reach our goal. Certainly Beckett can and does stop the play after an hour or two, but that does not solve the mystery of endings. It merely shelves the problem. In fact there can be no solution and, at the end, something inevitably remains, the factual presence of the characters, the mind of Hamm that hovers on the brink of inexistence but, like the voice of the Unnamable or the murmur of *Texts for*

Nothing, continues to be. Clov does not quite leave and a child is discovered outside – which signifies, simply, that the game is not over since new life has appeared to upset the consistency of the void. Thus Clov's hope – "finished, it's finished, nearly finished, it must be nearly finished" (p.12) – is not realized and the silence of the Unnamable is out of reach. At the same time the mysterious actuality of the Irreducible is everywhere manifest. The impossible happens, not as the awaited end of things but as the fact of a happening – the advent of the child – which preserves the precarious balance of the *status quo*: "Grain upon grain, one by one, and one day, suddenly, there's a heap, a little heap, the impossible heap" (p.12).

Beckett's other stage plays observe the one phenomenon from different angles. *Krapp's Last Tape* (1958) shows the personality in disintegration by focussing on the failure of memory to link the man of the present effectively to his own past. It is Beckett's most concise comment on the Proustian solution. But while connections are lost the voice of the *cogito* drones on. Astonishingly, Beckett makes theatre out of a non-theatrical situation, that is, he creates drama involving not *two* actors but *one* – with the aid of the tape which, while underlining Krapp's breakdown of communication with his past, also transforms the single protagonist into an entire cast. The action, however, is held up, constipated. Krapp's eating and evacuation problems ("the sour cud and the iron stool")[14] are reflected in the blockage which prevents the transition from self to other, from present to past, from art to life. So Krapp is alone, dreaming bitterly of lost encounters, as remote as the dream of "unattainable laxation" (p.13). One might say this represents a nod not only to Proust's *madeleine* but also to Leopold Bloom's glorious morning crap in chapter four of *Ulysses*. Unfortunately human experience has here become infinitely divisible. Each of Krapp's instants of consciousness, whether in the stage-present or in the various past-presents imprisoned in the tape, is separated from every other, discrete. Not only is it incomprehensible to Krapp, it has no meaning *in itself* precisely because it is discrete. The tragedy (bitterness and all, *Krapp is* movingly tragic) is not a matter of psychology (e.g. Krapp's alienation from past events) but is built into the structure of human experience as envisaged in the play. Krapp too is van Velde (however *manqué*!), unable to assume responsibility for his inventions, in this case, the episodes in his life which, once reduced to tape, assume the nature of works of art. Time, in the form of an instant, has become its own jailer, its own impenetrable irreducible.

Happy Days (1961) shows a more advanced image of a collapse comparable to Krapp's in the figure of Winnie embedded in the sand – Clov's impossible heap – up to her waist in act one and, in act two, her neck. Like Vladimir and Estragon she has few possessions – her bag, her umbrella – and in the end loses the use of all of them. Winnie hears the fall of sand: "Sounds. (*Pause.*) Like little . . . sunderings, little falls . . . apart. (*Pause. Low.*) It's things, Willie."[15] It is a sound which affirms both the disintegration prophesied by Lucky, the Occasionalist fragmentation of life, and the positivity of an event, a being-nothing: "Yes, something seems to have occurred, something has seemed to occur, and nothing has occurred, nothing at all . . ." (p.30). If the Reduction has not gone so far in *Happy Days* as to really expose the void-that-exists, it does so in *Play* (1964). Here the characters are fixed in jars and unable to communicate. Each is a tormented voice affirming endlessly the reality of being-nothing. The *alogon* has lost his engaging intelligence and degenerated to a horrifying puppet.

Variations on the theme have continued to the present, and without any slackening of virtuosity and control. Sometimes, as in *Breath* (1969) – originally written for *Oh! Calcutta!* – Beckett's pruning of the inessential is drastic indeed, and the result is more in the nature of a Happening than a play. If the act of human breathing represents one kind of irreducible, other simple units will also serve the purpose: the movement of pacing feet, the sound of steps. In *Footfalls* (1975), a play which in more ways than one recalls the author's mother, May walks endlessly, revolving in her mind the question which torments her:

> V: Will you never have done? [*Pause.*] Will you never have done . . . revolving it all?
> M: [*Halting*] It?
> V: It all. [*Pause.*] In your poor mind. [*Pause.*] It all. [*Pause.*] It all.[16]

May's footfalls softly echo Arsene's slip of sand, her mind broods over "it", the unspoken, unable-to-be-spoken fact, that of *suffering*, that is to say of *being*. Of course, as with other Beckett situations, one may choose a variety of interpretations, and in this case biographical and psychological ones readily suggest themselves. Still, it is the philosophical which is relevant to the present argument, and in pursuing this line of analysis we inevitably encounter a return to the Irreducible. The brief *A Piece of Monologue* (1979) looks back to *Krapp*, but in it Krapp's flood of recorded words is reduced to the one that really matters, the word which designates the drawing of first breath. Alone, at nightfall, Krapp's avatar "waits for first word always the same. It gathers in his mouth. Parts lips and thrusts tongue forward. Birth."[17] From this we move to the obverse, the thought of death. "Trying to treat of other matters", we realize that "there are no other matters. Never two matters. Never but the one matter. The dead and gone. The dying and the going." (p.79). Diminishment is as always the substance of the tale. Even as the speaker on the stage describes his evening activities (in the *third* person, not the first), he stands fixed, thus distancing himself from his narrative and in a sense negating it. And yet, in the midst of "dying and . . . going", he is *there*, he remains.

Similar comments must be made of the female protagonist of *Rockaby* (1981). W sits, like Murphy, in a rocking-chair, listening to a voice, V. Voice narrates a story of decline telling how W decided to stop searching for company and remained at home, then how she searched for a mere sight of another from her window. The most she saw was a raised blind. Next she decided to withdraw to the rocker, to be *Other* to herself. At every point, when V utters the words "time she stopped", W joins in. Finally, the voice brings us to W's present state, which is her tortured cry for release:

stop her eyes
rock her off
rock her off[18]

Rockaby contains in its title all the layers of Beckett's play. It is a lullaby for nightfall, a dirge and a goodbye, a plea for final rest. As the play proceeds, the voice becomes softer, the light fades, until the movement of rocking ceases and the subject's eyes close, her head sinks. But there can be no end to this *diminuendo*. W's plea for oblivion has not been answered. There is no getting off, the chair will never "rock her off", she will find no more peace than Murphy. We realize now the irony of W's repeated instruction to the voice: "More". In my end is my beginning:

till in the end
the day came
in the end came
close of a long day
when she said
to herself
whom else
time she stopped
time she stopped (p.9)

Rockaby, like all of Beckett's recent work, has an importance which is incommensurate with its length. This is even more true of *Not I* (1973) and *That Time* (1974). Looking back on the long stage career which produced theatre of the calibre of *Godot, Endgame, Krapp* and *Happy Days*, one might be excused the temptation to seek for signs of artistic decline in the seventies and beyond. And yet the output of fine writing continues. Likewise the obsession does not wane.

That Time illustrates the contemporaneity of three distinct moments of consciousness. On stage is the face of an old man, the Listener, who has no lines to speak. Voices, labelled A, B and C come to him from three sides, each recalling a particular course of events in a pattern of precedence which alters as the play proceeds. The result is a discreet orchestration of motifs, each separate, each thematically and linguistically related to others. A describes a sentimental journey, a visit to a place associated with childhood, B a lovers' meeting, C the wandering of a tramp. The tone is one of reverie, worthy of the Nausicaa or Penelope episodes in *Ulysses* or of their counterparts in *Finnegans Wake*. In the broken tones of almost-suppressed pathos, voice B describes those despairing and evanescent vows, made in whispers, that is to say scarcely made, on a stone unfortunately reminiscent of a millstone, by a couple who neither touch nor gaze at each other. Like Krapp's memory of lovers floating on the stream of time, this sentimental memory is the memory *par excellence*: "one thing could ever bring tears till they dried up altogether that thought".[19] Of course tears, like romantic meetings, are in the protagonist's past. Indeed the protagonist has passed through several phases of his life since the interlude on the stone. To begin with he has ceased to believe in the reality of the meeting. Standing or sitting before a window, he has played the game most Beckett characters play, that of invention. Surely there never was any love, it was all a story created for the purpose of reassurance:

> . . . by the window in the dark harking to the owl not a thought in your head till hard to believe harder and harder to believe you ever told anyone you loved them or anyone you till just one of those things you kept making up to keep the void out (p.11)

Then came the time, when, like tears on a previous occasion, the stories dried up and emptiness took over. The experience, clearly feared for so long, is, as it turns out, something of a relief:

> that time in the end when you tried and couldn't . . . hour after hour hour after hour not a sound when you tried and tried and couldn't any more no words left to keep it out so gave it up gave up there by the window in the dark or moonlight gave up for good and let it in and nothing the worse a great shroud billowing in all over you on top of you and little or nothing the worse little or nothing (p.16)

This is the moment of conversion for so many Beckett characters from Murphy onwards. It ought to lead to the asylum or the open road. In this case, there is a particular complication, though, a second interlude which completes a cycle by returning us from silence to speech. The story of voice A is that of the traveller who comes by ferry (the Holyhead–Dun Laoghaire, perhaps?) to revisit a scene of childhood. In the event, he symbolically rejoins or rather reenacts the past he would like to forget. What this past involves is a child of ten, eleven or twelve who comes to an overgrown ruin to hide from – searching parents perhaps, to sit, like the lovers, on a stone, (another image of mortality) to read or, more significantly, to talk. Because the boy-protagonist invents reality, as does the lover, and for the same reason, for *company*: "talking to himself being together that way where none ever came" (p.14). In fact the picture of personality divided within itself in a process of multiplying identities is exactly the same as that of Listener and voices offered by the play as a whole. This inward disintegration has its counterpart in the ruins of the setting. Its progress demands an identification of visitor and child, and this occurs at the climax of voice A's narrative. What happens is that the visitor to his own past finds himself unable to get to the ruin. The tram, a number eleven which recalls the child's age, is gone, only old rails remain, like a memory. Since there is no train either, the visitor, like the lover faced with the inrush of the void, "gave it up gave up and sat down on the steps . . . a doorstep say someone's doorstep" (p.13), sitting on stone as did the lovers and the child. Gradually another metamorphosis is effected, one which involves negation of previous knowledge – "little by little not knowing where you were or when your were or what for" (p.14) – and then an uncontrollable flood of speech: "till there on the step in the pale sun you heard yourself at it again . . . drooling away out loud" (p.15). At this point the themes of verbal invention and identity are one, since, in his gabble, the visitor seems to create the entire story of which he is the supposed protagonist. The child and the ruin perhaps exist only in the visitor's imagination. More than that, the visitor himself now appears as a fiction perpetually recreating itself: "making it all up on the doorstep as you went along making yourself all up again for the millionth time" (p.15). And this is of course the situation of the child, prattling helplessly and endlessly like dozens of other Beckett characters, from Lucky to the Unnamable. By the end of the A narrative the visitor returns to the ferry without ever reaching his original goal. The past of mother and childhood which he abominates travels with him as before: the time of the visit was after all identical with that of childhood, and indeed with all other time, all time being "that time", the time of crisis, that is to say, of living.

The C narrative can be thought of as representing the final stage of the Beckettian tramp's progress; in any case it has the last word in the play. Its content is the simplest and the most moving of all. The protagonist is a down-and-out who haunts a wintry cityscape, finding his first refuge in a portrait gallery and sitting, inevitably, on a stone seat, the play's fourth and final image of the grave. Here he experiences the first of what he terms rather sarcastically his "turning points". As he gazes at an oil portrait he becomes aware of a face next to him, presumably his own. After this, the tramp is, as he puts it, "never the same" (p.11), and, one might add, in the fullest sense of the expression. The consciousness of self-identity has been shaken, in a fulfilment of the prophecy implicit in the child's game of otherness, but then had such a consciousness ever really existed? In fact there had never been any crisis point in the protagonist's life save one, the fact of birth (unsolicited, naturally), the fact of life itself. And *that* lacked credibility. We recall that the voices A, B and C who address themselves to a silent Listener throughout the play always do so in the second person, never in the first. The inexplicable tragicomedy of life happens, as always in Beckett, not to oneself but to oneself-as-other, to a stranger. Still the phenomenon has some status of reality and some relevance to oneself by virtue of its being painful, and, at this stage in the play, the protagonist still has two critical situations to face. The first of these eventuates in the post office, another place of shelter from the cold and rain. The tramp who, after his moment in the gallery, finds himself inhabiting an alien identity whose words are not his own, and who vainly tries, by the old formula of invention, to reintroduce himself into the third-person narrative of his own life, has now come to a stop. Like the lover's his words have "dried up" and like the lover and the visitor he has "given up", or rather "it gave up whoever it was" (p.13). Now it is Christmas, season of goodwill, as the tramp hesitantly takes a seat in the post office and sneaks a look at the rest of mankind, "at your fellow bastards thanking God for once bad and all as you were you were not as they" (p.15). The logic of the protagonist, though unstated, is clear. If you find it difficult to believe in your own identity, in your own existence, then you seek out the other's objectifying gaze, you find a witness in whose look you see proof of your own being. We recall Murphy's valiant attempts with the gloriously unseeing eyes of the lunatic Mr Endon and the long Kafkaesque series of perceivers and perceived in Beckett's work, all fulfilling the requirements of Berkeley's *esse est percipi*. As we might expect, the tramp in the post office is unsuccessful: "You might as well not have been there at all the eyes passing over you and through you like so much thin air" (p.15). Accordingly, he moves on to the public library where the final revelation awaits him. In fact we reach at this point the climax of all three narratives of the play. As voice A describes the visitor's flight from the place and memories of childhood, and voice B the ex-lover's once-and-for-all surrender to the void, the tramp of C's narrative reaches his last turning-point. Seated with old people at a library table, in a wasteland more absolute than any conceived by Eliot, he hears the ultimate sermon, What the Dust Said:

> not a sound only the old breath and the leaves turning and then suddenly this dust whole place suddenly full of dust when you opened your eyes from floor to ceiling nothing only dust and not a sound only what was it it said come and gone was that it something like that come and gone come and gone no one come and gone in no time gone in no time (p.16)

These are the last words of *That Time* and they look back to the title of an earlier play, *Come and Go*. Of course they constitute a restatement of the one truth *That Time* has pursued throughout, that of disintegration, mortality, loss. But if the situation of the Listener is one of breakdown, of ruin, the conclusion is not simply that of *Ecclesiastes*. Beyond the facile *vanitas vanitatum* lies a more tantalising truth: that the Listener, amid his ruins, *endures*. The message of the dust is, to be sure, *nothing*: "come and gone no one come and gone in no time gone in no time". Yet in the going there is of necessity a coming, in the no one an identity, in the no time temporality, in the nothing of the message a *something*, otherwise there would be no message. *That* time, then, which is time itself, any time so long as it is that of living, that is to say of dying, is, in the final reckoning, non-time, but a non-time which *is*. Time, like the identity of the Listener or the tramp, has the quality of a non-event which does, however, *take place*. Whether because they come into being or because they cease to be or, more importantly, because they continue in being in spite of endless diminishment, that is, they exist *as diminishment*, Beckett's units of reality, his presences on the page and on the stage, his events, changes, or turning-points, are all of them miracles. And the *fact* of their nothingness endlessly intrigues their creator. Beyond hope and despair Beckett is stirred by the ultimate philosophical curiosity at this tantalising irreducible: that when all that is conceivable is removed from life as contingent, as inessential, an inconceivable essential remains. *That Time* takes up the old search with time as its central theme. *Not I* does so with identity as its concern.

The stage arrangement of *Not I* is as simple as that of the other play. It allows the audience to make out, in partial darkness, the figure of the Auditor who, like the Listener of *That Time*, has no lines, and the outline of a mouth which functions in much the same ways as the voices in *That Time*. As Mouth speaks, Auditor listens and occasionally reacts by a lifting of arms. Mouth's utterance is garbled, quietly panic-stricken and feminine. In fact it is decidedly reminiscent of Winnie of *Happy Days*, particularly when it reflects, somewhat unconvincingly, on God's "tender mercies".[20] But the bourgeois frivolities and genuine charm of Winnie are gone, replaced by a personality akin to that of Molloy or Malone or, if it comes to that, the protagonist of *That Time*. Mouth tells yet another Beckett story, focussing on what could be termed, without too much reference to *Genesis*, a fall. Wandering over a field in spring, the female protagonist suddenly finds herself in darkness or near darkness in an indeterminate position, without the use of her senses or nearly so. The symptoms are those of the earlier Unnamable, more or less. There is a fitful ray of light, image of mind, and a buzzing in the ears like embryonic speech; for the rest, little or no feeling or activity of any kind except of course that of the unsilenceable brain. It is perhaps a death of sorts, a Beckettian death which brings not oblivion but continuation of life. Like Teresa in rapture or the subject of a catatonic trance, Beckett's protagonist experiences an *ex-stasis*, a withdrawal beyond the range of everyday sensations and faculties. Thus it seems she is weeping and therefore perhaps in pain since her eyes are moist. But the sufferer is not *herself.* One thing remains, however, and with a vengeance, or rather it begins gradually to assert itself: uncontrollable speech. The protagonist, it seems, once avoided words. At times an obscenely naked need to communicate had taken possession of her, but only briefly. Now the words return, in a rush and with the compulsion of a nervous fixation. At first it is possible not to recognize a voice so rarely heard, but, clearly, it is the protagonist's. The woman attempts to pretend she has nothing to do with it, until she feels her lips moving and not only her lips but her whole face:

> . . . lips . . . cheeks . . . jaws . . . tongue . . . never still a second . . . mouth on fire . . . stream of words . . . in her ear . . .

> practically in her ear . . . not catching the half . . . not the quarter . . . no idea what she's saying . . . imagine! no idea what she's saying! and can't stop . . . no stopping it . . . (p.17)

The protagonist's moment of crisis obviously parallels that of the visitor in *That Time*, although the portrayal of compulsive speech in *Not I* is more detailed and indeed more heartrending. What has occurred amounts in each case to a turning-point, in the words of *Watt*, a "change", a conversion away from everyday normality with its normal, everyday horrors to – what? The woman herself sees her situation as one of punishment, reiterating concepts which may be found in Beckett's work from the excruciating tale of Belacqua's boiling lobster to the theological speculations of Vladimir and Estragon. In fact the thought of divine vengeance is the first thought to occur to her after her collapse – until she realizes that, after all, she is not exactly suffering. With sublime irony and with the wonderful imaginative resources of the Beckettian she wonders if, perhaps, she is *meant* to be suffering. It's perfectly possible, given that in her life she frequently found herself in situations of *supposed* pleasure which were not pleasurable at all. Why not the reverse? In that case it might be as well to *act the part* of one suffering, just in case, to confuse the powers in control, by groaning, writhing or screaming, for example. However, the initiative for such complex deceit is lacking and the protagonist remains in her passivity. Still she continues to speculate. For a start, her punishment may well be a punishment not for sin but – a more satisfying concept – for its own sake: in Malone's words, "so long as it is what is called a living being you can't go wrong, you have the guilty one" (p.260). Seemingly, it is a torment like that of the Ancient Mariner: the protagonist is required, by an obscure authority, to say something, to tell a story, though *which* is not clear. Like the subject of *The Unnamable*, she is in a Dantean or rather Kafkaesque hell, speaking through Mouth to an Auditor who, in this context, suggests the scribe of other Beckett stories, stationed beside Mouth to receive and possibly to report on the correct story. Obviously the punishment is eternal, just as the correct story is always out of reach.

Viewed this way, *Not I* records a situtation in which consciousness exists as its own torment, a situation which begins with the protagonist's compulsion to speak and which has no end. But this is by no means the only or indeed the most significant element in the play. *Not I* differs from *That Time* in that its dramatic climax is disguised and comes not at the end but in the body of the play. Five times in the course of the narrative Mouth repeats the formula "what? . . . who? . . . no! . . . she!" Five times, in other words, it responds to a prompter who, we may assume, suggests that it speak of "she", the protagonist, in the first person. In each case and most forcefully on the last occasion, the answer is no: Mouth refuses stubbornly to speak of "I". That refusal is the key to the meaning of the play. Now Mouth is prompted by the voice of the female protagonist, repeating, often wrongly, the rush of words which originate in the protagonist. At the same time Mouth will not identify with the subject of its own story, who remains insistently not "I" but "she". So the voice which issues from Mouth is and is not that of the protagonist, it is a divided voice, speaking for the protagonist on the one hand and on the other for an unknown. This voice is required to tell something, perhaps "how it was . . . how she – . . . what? . . . had been . . . yes . . . something that would tell how it had been . . . how she had lived . . ." (p.19). But another story of a down-and-out is not what is called for:

> . . . what? . . . not that? . . . nothing to do with that? . . . nothing she could tell? . . . all right . . . nothing she could tell . . . try something else . . . think of something else . . . oh long after . . . sudden flash . . . not that either . . . all right . . . something else again . . . so on . . . hit on it in the end . . . think everything keep on long enough . . . then forgiven . . . back in the – . . . what? . . . not that either? . . . nothing to do with that either? . . . nothing she could think? . . . all right . . . nothing she could tell . . . nothing she could think . . . nothing she – . . . what? . . . who? . . . no! . . . she! (p.19)

What is called for is, it seems, unthinkable, unable to be told. At one level, the voice is asked to name itself, or rather to identify its true source, beyond the mind of the helpless protagonist. Because it cannot do this and consequently substitutes a story – that of the protagonist – it effectively reduces the entire play to a digression, an evasion of the truth, which has nothing to do with "she", the protagonist. At another level the voice is asked to say "I" rather than "she", to identify itself as none other than the woman in question. This it will not do, its true identity being an unknown. On the face of it we are left with a double frustration, the inability of Mouth to utter either the unutterable truth or the facile lie, the "I" which, one supposes, would satisfy the observing Auditor. But Beckett's play is not ultimately concerned with failure. While the unknown which is present within the voice or consciousness of the protagonist as her ultimate reality cannot be named, it can and is indirectly revealed. Every element of Beckett's drama, the woman, the voice, Mouth, is inexplicable taken by itself. Woman, voice and Mouth lack cohesion as well; their interconnection is mysterious, even negative, like the Occasionalist link which joins or rather fails to join mind and body in so many Beckett characters, beginning with Murphy. Yet there is *some* cohesive force, *something* of necessity in the contingency of the situation of the protagonist and her voice, otherwise there would not be speech, a certain *naming* and, above all, a *refusal* to name. The very disjunction of the elements in the play indicates the need for a presence beyond them to unify them, not the dubious "God" mentioned by the protagonist but an unknown, able to guarantee the protagonist and her voice a minimal status, that of a *fact*, tenuous in the extreme yet inexorably, eternally *there.* That Unnamable is, as in the trilogy, Beckett's fundamental concern. It is not simply a matter of depicting the agony of indestructible consciousness but of evoking, however obscurely, the ground as it were on the basis of which the action of the play becomes a possibility, the mystery which sustains consciousness and which distinguishes itself from it as "not I".

Beckett's work for radio, television and film play the old tune, but without repetition. The Reduction begins with *All that Fall* (1957), a study of decay, and *Embers* (1959), another dramatization of the inevitability and horror of solitude. Of course Beckett's embers will not go out any more than his endgame will end; they image both the Reduction and the indestructible residue. In *Cascando* (1963) we return to a voice obsessively seeking – in this case a tramp called Woburn, himself involved in an obscure search which, in the light of Beckett's work as a whole, is recognized as the old search for the negative source. *Eh Joe* (1966), a piece for television, shows us a man in a room and gradually brings him near until his face appears in an unbearable closeup. Something similar occurs in *Film* (1965). The key to it all is in Beckett's handling of the medium. Where the stage plays reduce man to an impossible presence, the radio plays reduce him to an impossible voice. If there were less than that, of course, there would be no play, just as in the context of the prose, there would be no novel or short story. But the voice says nothing, or very nearly so. Likewise, on the stage, the paradoxical minimum appropriate to the medium is doing nothing or as little as possible. In Beckett's television and film work the Irreducible appears as a mere image on the screen. Thus the overall pattern which emerges is that of a voice almost but not quite silent, an actor on the stage almost but not quite inactive, almost but not quite going away, a screen image almost but not quite vanishing.

It now remains to consider the treatment of the Reduction in Beckett's prose work after the peak of *The Unnamable*. Again we witness the phenomenon of variation on a theme. *How it is*, published in English in 1964, is really a prose poem like *Finnegans Wake*, so that the Reduction focusses on the use of language. There is a protagonist, sometimes known as Pim, who has the remains of a body and is capable of motion, crawling in the mud of a Dantean landscape, dragging a sack of provisions, edging towards another of his kind:

> take the cord from the sack there's another object tie the neck of the sack hang it from my neck knowing I'll need both hands or else instinct it's one or the other and away right leg right arm push pull ten yards fifteen yards halt[21]

When two creatures meet the relationship is hardly more fruitful than others depicted in earlier novels. Moreover, this relationship and indeed all that the voice narrates is at the end emphatically rejected as false. We are back to *The Unnamable*; there is no relation, no Pim, no sack, no movement, only a naked presence:

> if all that all that yes if all that is not how shall I say no answer if all that is not false yes
>
> all these calculations yes explanations yes the whole story from beginning to end yes completely false yes
>
> there was something yes but nothing of all that no all balls from start to finish yes this voice quaqua yes all balls yes only one

voice here yes mine yes when the panting stops yes (pp.157–8)

As in *The Unnamable* the voice itself is denounced as "scraps of an ancient voice in me not mine" (p.7). The novel's core, once again, is a reduction of reality ("how it is") to a mysterious substratum, the ghost in Beckett's machine.

Where are we to go from here? At times, after the trilogy, Beckett turns back. Thus *From an Abandoned Work* (1958) returns us to the wanderings in *Molloy* or the *Novellas*, and fragments like *Afar a Bird* and *I gave up before birth*, written in their original form around 1960, take us back to *The Unnamable*. But more often Beckett moves forward, regardless of the fact that forward movement has now become impossible. Beyond the negation–affirmation of the Unnamable there is nowhere to go. However, as in *How it is*, the Reduction is able to operate further and further in the sphere of language. So much so that it could be said that after the trilogy Beckett returns to his original inspiration, the poetry he wrote before he ever tackled prose. At any rate, in *How it is* and much of the work of the sixties and seventies, the prose has become indistinguishable from poetry. Of course this development echoes developments in the later work of Joyce.

Imagination Dead Imagine (1965), a bare seven pages of beautiful prose, describes a closed space, like the inside of an egg, containing two immobile and silent bodies not in contact with each other and barely conscious. It is the archetypal Beckett situation. Imagination is dead, there is nothing left, yet we continue: imagination dead imagine. This is Beckett's version of the celebrated: the king is dead; long live the king. Again and again, unable to proceeed, we proceed, and in that paradox of stillness and motion catch a glimpse of the elusive Irreducible, the almost-nothing without which there would be nothing. *All Strange Away* (1976) opens with the magical formula: imagination dead imagine. It then constructs a fantasy, a place, a subject. Certainly there is a proviso: "he's not here".[22] But we overlook this problem and remain with the subject, imagining his past life, which included a woman called Emma. Suddenly we reconsider: perhaps the subject is Emma herself, in which case the remembered partner was probably Emmo. With the subject's sex established, we return to her activities. In fact she has toppled over, in a restricted space, and her position is described in geometric terms.

Emma, totally immobile save for movement of the eyes, has something in her hand, which she squeezes gently, something like a rubber bulb which when crushed expels air, only to fill again when the pressure is relieved. This minimal act is tantamount to *breathing at one remove.* But no sooner are we led to this one terrifying positive – breath – than it is all demolished. "Nothing ever in that hand lightly closed on nothing" (p.64): the moment we focus on the Irreducible it disappears.

This is so in *Still* (written in 1973), one of the finest of the later pieces, somewhat less austere in style than the progeny of *How it is. Still* is concerned to delineate, with exquisite restraint, a moment of stillest anguish. Its subject sits, like Murphy, watching the close of day. Finally he makes an infinitesimal gesture of despair. Again, the title suggests unlikely continuity, the impossible encore at the end of time. A similar paradox is implied elsewhere, from *Ping* (1967) to *For to end yet again* (1975) and *Ill Seen Ill Said* (1981). *Ping* is close to *Imagination Dead Imagine*, with a cast reduced to one, "head haught eyes light blue almost white fixed front ping murmur ping silence".[23] Of course "ping" indicates the impossible happening, the nothing which is taking its course, the murmur which breaks the silence. *For to end yet again* may be described as Beckett's depiction of the last thought of all, last-yet-again, that is, while *Ill Seen Ill Said* suggests, in a context reminiscent of *Still*, a final memory, a last image – or invention. The entire futile round of endless dying life and living death is recapitulated in *The Lost Ones*, written in the late sixties and published in English in 1972. This text is not unlike *Imagination Dead Imagine*, which preceded it. It is also a Dantesque version of the Leibnizian *How it is*, focussing not on the mathematical perfection of an endless series of sadists and sufferers in the best of all possible worlds, but on what amounts to one of the levels of the *Inferno.* Again, however, when we have examined every detail of demonic existence in a restricted space, we leave the crowds to concentrate on one man at "the unthinkable end".[24] This creature makes his way to that equally unthinkable first, a woman, and inspects her eyes, observing her as Murphy did Mr Endon. Then he collapses, darkness falls and the temperature nears zero. But the Irreducible is perhaps most concisely expressed in the panting rhythms of *Lessness* (in English, 1970), where the poetic possibilities of spare prose are more evident than anywhere else in Beckett's later work, except, possibly, *How it is*. Here amid signs of advanced decay waits a "little body grey face features crack and little holes two pale blue".[25] The eyes are those of many Beckett characters, the vacant stare mirrors the indifference of the Geulincx Stoic: "blank planes sheer white eye calm long last all gone from mind" (p.8). No motion is possible, no change and yet "in the sand no hold one step more in the endlessness he will make it" (pp.9–10). It is the inconceivable step, the movement which is not movement, in a sand which gives no hold and which, in its granular structure, recalls the coexistence of incompatibles of a universe of monads. As long as the single step occurs the reduction to "lessness" continues and its irreducible goal – "true refuge long last towards which so many false time out of mind" (p.7) – remains just out of reach.

If *Not I* and *That Time* represent the best of Beckett's recent work for the stage, *Company* (1980) is probably the finest prose work of some scale since the trilogy and *How it is*. Like many of Beckett's writings since the fifties, it recapitulates and summarizes the entire search. Its opening – "A voice comes to one in the dark. Imagine"[26] – already invites us to disbelieve what follows. It may after all be yet another fantasy, something merely imagined. Still, "to one on his back in the dark a voice tells of a past" (p.8). The subject ("one") is not identified. Neither is the other protagonist of the story, the one who manipulates the voice: "In another dark or in the same another devising it all for company. Quick leave him". (p.8) This last cryptic command recurs whenever the Other is mentioned. We are not to enquire in that direction. Beckett now explains the protocol of the novel. Use of the second person indicates the voice (referring to the subject as "you"); use of the third the Other (referring to the subject as "he"); if the subject (of the voice's discourse) could speak, we would have a first person – "but he cannot. He shall not. You cannot. You shall not". (p.9) Clearly, as in the play, Beckett's protagonist will not, cannot say "I". He is not himself, the creature of whom the voice speaks. Who is he? To begin with the question receives no answer.

Rather we turn to the subject's situation, revealed not by anything the subject does or says but by second-person pronouncements made by the voice and third-person observations originating, or so it seems, from the Other. It is as if the subject were being spied upon, like the protagonist of *The Unnamable* on occasion, or like one of Murphy's inmates in his cell. With the proviso that all commentary proceeds from a source other than himself we may say that the subject ponders his situation. Is the voice speaking to him? If so, of whom is it speaking? Of himself or someone else? What is the import of its strange declaration, "You are on your back", etc. (p.7) or "You first saw the light at Easter" (p.19)? Does it require his identification with it? In that case he would be able to *be* himself through the voice, to say "I": "What an addition to company that would be! A voice in the first person singular" (pp.20–1). But we are far even from this rudimentary form of togetherness. Self-identity presupposes otherness, as otherness presupposes self-identity. Here there cannot be two because Beckett's arithmetic has yet to arrive at one.

At any rate the ingredients are all there. There is the voice, likened, in a moment of abandon, to parents bending over a child in a cradle, speaking in a flat tone, "no trace of love" (p.66). There is the place, perhaps a hemispherical dome of black basalt, housing the supine subject. There is light, that inescapable element in Beckett's fiction, even sound, though sound as elusive (and as suggestive) as the fall of sand in *Watt*: "Some soft thing softly stirring soon to stir no more" (p.24). Is there movement? We are not sure. There may be, eventually. Are there sensations? It is unlikely, though scarcely unimaginable. The subject imagines the possibility of sensations, in any case, just as he imagines that of speech. There is certainly an eye, opening, closing, "bared. Hooded again" (p.27). With all of this the subject is titillated, somewhat feebly to be sure, with the thought of further "improvements". Perhaps he could be envisaged as capable of reflection, or memory, "a trace of emotion. Signs of distress" (p.37). But we are now on "delicate ground" (p.37), in danger of rashness. More precipitate still is the thought of a possible rat, dead, of course ("What an addition to company that would be! A rat long dead", p.36) – or of a fly, to buzz over the protagonist's carcass, something he could brush off, a stimulus to activity: "But no. He would not brush away a fly" (p.38).

A large, perhaps the most moving, portion of *Company* is taken up with images, memories of, let us say the subject's, past, his birth, for example, when his father fled the house and walked the countryside; or the time he emerged from Connolly's Stores with his mother and enraged her with his comment about the distant sky; or the time at the bathing place when his father ordered him to jump; or, a related and more terrifying image (and one noted in Deirdre Bair's biography of Beckett), the time when, as a child, he repeatedly threw himself from a tree. There is also the visionary moment when, in "sunless cloudless light" (p.34), he saw the mountain, "palest blue against the pale sky" (p.33), or, again, the moment of misguided charity when he tried to save the hedgehog. These recollections are worthy of *The Prelude*; indeed they are subtler and more discreet in their implications than all but the finest episodes in Wordsworth. Moreover, with their childhood quality they combine a depth of sadness unknown to any other writer:

> Days if not weeks passed before you could bring yourself to return to the hutch. You have never forgotten what you found then . . . The mush. The stench. (p.41)

Elsewhere, they surpass the poetry of the memories in *That Time* or *Krapp's Last Tape*. This is yet another hopeless lovers' meeting:

> Eyes in each others' eyes you listen to the leaves. In their trembling shade. (p.67)

In the end, however, memories of childhood, parents and lovers are, as always, overwhelmed by those of solitude. We have now reached the stage represented by *Molloy* as the subject, like his father before him, walks the roads, an old man, perhaps a tramp. We see this same figure in the snow and, later, on a beach. At this point too we understand the nature of the transition from past to present. First the subject wandered with his father's ghost, then alone. Then he hesitated in midstep, slowed down and, finally, sat "huddled in the dark" (p.84). Unable to exit, he lay on his back. This is the present situation, at least in its beginnings.

As in the trilogy, the Reduction has led to a state of fixity and indeterminacy. All that remains is to explore once more the vexed question of identity. The subject tries on a name as one might try on a shirt. Perhaps he is H, a breath. He rejects that: "Let him be again as he was. The hearer. Unnamable. You" (p.43). Other names are attempted, M for the one who hears the voice, W for the one who devises it. But these two have to go, they are "creatures", figments of imagination, like the long line of Belacqua, Murphy, Watt, Molloy and the rest. At the same time *someone* must be responsible for the voice, not to mention the subject, who is listening, and himself as well. This X, who is doing it all "for company" (p.34), "devising figments to temper his nothingness" (p.64) is

> nowhere to be found. Nowhere to be sought. The unthinkable last of all. Unnamable. Last Person. I. (p.32)

"Quick leave him" (p.32), the voice adds in panic. At times the novel insists that the Other, the "deviser", does not exist; that hearer (the subject) and deviser are one and the same. It is all a game, "for company", something one invents in order to diminish the austerity of solitude. "Company" is tantamount to multiplicity. "Company" is the invention of oneself as a body (first mobile, then, as invention cools, fixed), with a place, a context, thoughts, emotions, memories and the like. Finally, "company" is the invention of an Other. It is all an attempt to bring into being a world of many (or, failing, that, of *two*) beings when in fact there is only *one*. The situation of the subject, then, if we take as definitive the last words of the novel, is that of one who invents a story now nearing its close,

> the fable of one with you in the dark. The fable of one fabling of one with you in the dark. And how better in the end labour lost and silence. And you as you always were.
>
> Alone. (p.89)

This seems to settle the matter, but in fact no settlement is possible. Even if there is no Other, no "company", the subject refuses to the end to identify himself as "I". On the contrary, he is, like the female of the play, *not* I. At best he remains "he" or, more intimately, from the point of view of the voice "you". In short, "company" remains, no matter how we struggle to banish otherness. Likewise the mystery of identity deepens when we remove the shadowy "deviser". If after all he is nothing more than a *deus ex machina*, like those tyrants imagined in *The Unnamable*, the question still remains: who *is* responsible for the situation? If we deny there *is* a situation, *who* is there to guarantee the status of our denial?

We have returned to the Cartesian position. Even in doubt, indeed, *because* of doubt, there must be certainty. Yet, as in *The Unnamable*, Beckett's evasive not-I refuses to wear the *commedia dell'arte* mask of the *cogito*. That farcical role belongs to the *voice*, and we disposed of *it* long ago. We cannot, then, cling to the Cartesian analogy to the very end. A brief survey of Beckett's output suffices to testify to the writer's extraordinary fidelity to a central question or mystery which I have termed the Irreducible and to a fundamental movement which is the reduction of reality to its zero point. This last stop is not, as many commentators believe, the *cogito* which in fact represents only the penultimate stage of the Reduction. It cannot be identified with the voice of consciousness, that is, with consciousness, but only with that obscure origin of things which is also the operative presence *beneath* the *cogito*. Nor is it the Leibnizian monad. As an absolute particular, the Irreducible cannot be conceived except as a negative, with the vital and paradoxical proviso that it must be said to *be*. We are brought back to van Velde's product, hitherto erroneously referred to as a painting. The extreme argument put forward in the dialogue with Georges Duthuit is actually put into practice again and again in Beckett's work. As Richard Coe argued as early as in 1964, Beckett wants to do the impossible; indeed he wants to *touch* the *void*, to be able to *point* to the intersection of silence and speech, nothingness and existence. It is as if he were obsessed by one thought: if only he could define this point, he would solve every problem. He would understand the mystery of transitions which so fascinated the Greeks, of beginnings and of ends, of rest and motion, of mind and body, of human communication, of life and death, of art, in short, of being itself. Above all else he would understand the meaning of pain. Beckett is a modern Faust and, like Faust, he cannot succeed. His is an art of failure and it is to Beckett's credit that he has clung to this triumphant failure more tenaciously than any desert hermit ever clung to the desert. There is perhaps a reward in spite of everything. We cannot *touch* the void but, in the end, we are made aware of its encompassing, god-like presence beneath the eternal fretting of consciousness on its wheel of fire – by the very fact of a surface disturbance. In Malone's words, "*Nothing is more real than nothing*" (p.193).

2 Beckett: The philosophical tradition

> Its Being-what-it-is (*essentia*) must, so far as we can speak of it at all, be conceived in terms of its Being (*existentia*).[1]
>
> HEIDEGGER

Beckett demands to be seriously treated as a philosophical writer and this fact is already generally recognized. There is no question of turning the writer into a philosopher pure and simple, of course, or into an imitator of the philosophers. Whatever Beckett shares with the philosophers, he has made it his own and he has made it art. With this proviso, however, the parallel is worth pursuing because it helps us to delineate more precisely the contours of Beckett's vision, that is, it helps us to see Beckett *as he is*.

So far critical discussion has tended to focus on the Cartesian and the Occasionalist element in the novels and plays, yet of necessity the relevance of seventeenth- and eighteenth-century systems to works of art produced in the twentieth century is limited. Beckett's Occasionalism is not exactly that of Geulincx or Malebranche; nor is his insistence on the *cogito* exactly Cartesian, nor his concern with the monad exactly Leibnizian. Beckett uses the philosophers as he uses Dante, without necessarily sharing their outlook. It is enough to point out that for Descartes, Geulincx, Malebranche and Leibniz a deity seemed a fundamental requirement of any philosophical system. Beckett borrows the structure but leaves out its soul, or rather replaces it with something of his own – the Unnamable. In so doing he is already, in a general sense, moving from the Cartesian scene to that of the modern world. This does not mean that the validity of the comparison with the above thinkers is to be questioned, only that a comparison with modern philosophy may begin where the other leaves off. One thinks immediately of likely candidates in the previous century: Schopenhauer, Kierkegaard, Nietzsche. Since so much modern thinking stems from these, it would be strange if one failed to find *some* parallels with the *Weltanschauung* of Beckett's work. At any rate it will be necessary to return to them, but in the context of the discussion of contemporary thought which is the central concern of this book. To some extent the need for a connection between Beckett and his philosophical contemporaries is assumed by most critics. But the appeal to Heidegger, Sartre or even Camus is inevitably made only in passing. We are told about the Void or the Absurd or Dread and always more or less in a context of vagueness and generality. As a result little of a concrete sort is settled either with respect to philosophy or to Beckett who takes on the anaemic appearance of a topical journalist, neither philosopher nor artist. But Beckett's work is far more than a statement of fashionable clichés, and consequently it is vital that we should be concerned not with superficial similarities but with fundamentals, properly analysed and brought to light. For this reason some trouble has been taken in the previous chapter to isolate the core of Beckett's obsession and further trouble will be taken to do full justice to the philosophers also.

If one can say that Beckett's novels often illustrate in miniature the novel's historical development from the picaresque to the psychological and beyond, one can with even more justification argue that Beckett's work as a whole represents nothing less than a literary recapitulation of an entire tradition in philosophy from Descartes and his contemporaries to the present day or, more specifically, from the rationalist stream of the seventeenth century to the Idealists and, finally, to the existential movement. What happens is that Beckett develops an essentially Cartesian Reduction along existential lines and, from time to time, with a backward glance at something approaching the Idealist solution. The truth of this statement needs to be demonstrated, of course, and it is the aim of the first section of this book to do it. Beckett's relation to the Occasionalists, to Descartes, to Leibniz and to Spinoza has already been touched on. That subject has been amply discussed by Hugh Kenner, Richard Coe, John Fletcher and others. It remains to link Beckett's approach to the existential and, to a very much lesser extent, the Idealist. This twofold comparison is important since it has some application to Ionesco and, in another context, to Genet. All of the writers studied in this book share, in different ways, elements of what we will term an existential vision while at the same time tending away from it, generally in the direction of Idealism, at least in one particular sense yet to be defined – and this is not surprising in view of the connection that exists between the two philosophies. However, only in Beckett's work do we find a perspective sufficiently broad to include the seventeenth-century origins of both Idealist and existential approaches. This chapter will introduce the discussion of Beckett's work in terms of philosophies of Existence with a brief survey of the existential tradition, particularly in so far as it relates to the other philosophies mentioned above.

Descartes' philosophical distinction between body and mind images the choice facing European thought after the Renaissance: on the one hand a stress on mind, on the other, on matter. The alternative may be expressed in various ways, as a choice between the mathematical and the experimental, or between the theory of innate ideas, upheld by Descartes and Leibniz, and that of the *tabula rasa*, upheld with variations by the British empiricists from Locke to Hume, or between a rationalist approach in general and one characterized by a distrust of reason and a respect for the inductive method. Of course it would be rash to suppose that such a neat division of philosophical trends after Descartes represents anything other than a convenient schematization of a complex truth. Nevertheless, there is some justification for emphasizing such a divergence between the rationalist and the empiricist lines since it helps to put the existential in perspective. Excessive stress on the primacy of mind has led historically to Idealism, to the assertion that Absolute Thought is prior to matter. Alternatively, an extreme emphasis on the priority of sense-impressions has defined the empiricist tradition from Locke to the present. On the one hand matter, enveloped by mind, begins to assume a nebulous quality, on the other, material processes invade the sphere of mind and reduce its activities to those of a mere mechanism. Existential philosophy has developed partly out of the systems of the German Idealists. To that extent it has retained the distinctive characteristics of a philosophy of mind: a vital awareness of the reality of the *cogito*, a sense of the creative power of thought. Yet at the same time it has emerged as a revolt against Idealism. Kierkegaard, one of the first and most seminal philosophers of Existence, attended Schelling's lectures in Berlin and understood the Hegelian synthesis as perhaps few have done. On the basis of this knowledge he delivered a most effective attack on Hegel, although one whose validity was not widely recognized at the time. Modern existential philosophy has preserved the ambivalence of these and similar origins. It has retained the Idealist bias in so far as it views the mind as creative, as active in perception rather than as simply subject to outside impressions, but has modified it in so far as it refuses to allow the *cogito* or the Idealist's pure Thought a reality philosophically prior to the material world of human existence. It is possible to maintain, therefore, that the existential represents a bridge between Idealism or, more generally, a rationalist approach, and the empirical tradition; that philosophers of Existence have in a real sense attempted to bring together again the two halves of human reality separated by Descartes – in very different ways, let us add.

Although the sources of the two most important, and divergent, contemporary existential thinkers, Heidegger and Sartre, may be traced back at least to the eighteenth and nineteenth centuries – to Kant, to Hegel and to Kierkegaard's celebrated critique – it is more usual to refer it to the immediate influence of Edmund Husserl. Husserl held the chair at Freiburg before Heidegger and gave the existential movement in the twentieth century an impetus as vital as that given by Kierkegaard, although it is necessary to add that Husserl's technical bias is as far removed as one can imagine from the spontaneous philosophizing of Kierkegaard and, moreover, owes nothing to it. It should be stated too that Husserl himself may scarcely be termed an existential philosopher and that his approach could only be adopted by Heidegger and Sartre in a modified form. In the *Ideas*, which appeared in 1913, Husserl, like Descartes before him, announces his discovery of a new basis for philosophy, comparable in its importance to the *cogito*. Writing with excited conviction, he calls it "the secret longing of the whole philosophy of modern times".[2] The parallel with Descartes is drawn deliberately, not only to point out the similarity of the two endeavours but also the difference between them. For Husserl:

> Philosophy can take root only in radical reflexion upon the meaning and possibility of its own scheme. Through such reflexion it must in the very first place and through its own

> activity take possession of the absolute ground of pure pre-conceptual experience, which is its own proper preserve; then, self-active again, it must create original concepts, adequately adjusted to this ground, and so generally utilize for its advance an absolutely transparent method. There can then be no unclear, problematical concepts, and no paradoxes.[3]

This reads like a Cartesian programme. There is the same concern for a systematic doubt, a movement back to a reliable ground, and, once that is found, for a process of rebuilding on a basis of what, for Descartes, were innate, clear and distinct ideas. Thus Husserl argues:

> . . . we would stress the point firmly, we have not been arguing academically from a philosophical standpoint fixed in advance, we have not made use of traditional . . . philosophical theories, but on lines which are in the strictest sense *fundamental* have *shown up* certain features, i.e., given true expression to distinctions which are directly given to us in *intuition*.[4]

In his *Cartesian Meditations*, an expansion of lectures given at the Sorbonne in 1929, Husserl makes the link with the French philosopher explicit. His approach, he states, "might almost" be termed "a neo-Cartesianism",[5] not in the sense that it borrows the content of the Cartesian philosophy but in the sense that it reaffirms the validity of its method. Husserl believes that what he has found avoids the weaknesses of the Cartesian, above all, that it is not a theory among others but a "concrete science"[6] – which he terms Phenomenology – a new and radical beginning:

> . . . we start out from that which *antedates* all standpoints: from the totality of the intuitively self-given which is prior to any theorizing reflexion, from all that one *can* immediately see and lay hold of . . .[7]

The new position which antedates all others is not exactly Cartesian. If it were it would lead to yet another philosophical rift between spirit and matter. Nor is it exactly Idealist, since Husserl does not begin with the privileged position of the Hegelian theorizer, the "thought without a thinker"[8] ridiculed by Kierkegaard in the *Concluding Unscientific Postscript*. In fact Husserl modifies nineteenth-century Idealism as Descartes modified the jaded Scholasticism of his day, although he does not move as far from Idealism as the other did from the philosophy of the schools. He begins with a doubt more systematic than Descartes'. Everything must go, even the *cogito ergo sum*. But one thing remains – not, as Descartes thought, the existing thinker – but a *phenomenon*. We cannot say whether this phenomenon, a thinker and the object of his thought, exists or not:

> But, no matter what the status of this phenomenon's claim to actuality and no matter whether, at some future time, I decide critically that the world exists or that it is an illusion, still this phenomenon itself, as mine, is not nothing . . .[9]

The whole sphere of what exists, then, "is not accepted as actuality, but only as an actuality-phenomenon".[10] And this because, even if in practice I must accept the ontological reality of things, a theoretical doubt is possible. It might be suggested that, in spite of appearances, a Cartesian demon is intent on fooling me, that everything which appears to be is in fact merely a dream or a hallucination. Husserl's conclusion is simple: he will accept reality as appearance, as a phenomenon, and no more. This does not mean that one doubts in fact, simply that for the sake of a possible doubt, one puts the existence of things as it were in a "bracket". Husserl asks us to suspend judgement on the existence of the phenomenon and to consider the phenomenon as phenomenon. It may be that there is no table but I do perceive a table and it is perfectly possible for me to discuss the phenomenon of the table even if I cannot be sure of the table's existence. In this way I sidestep the closed road of Idealism. To examine the phenomenon as such implies no outrageous metaphysics, only a descriptive, that is, a scientific approach to reality, an examination not of the Existence but of the Essence of things. Of course the phenomenon, as Husserl presents it, is an idea. Thus Phenomenology becomes a science of Essences, an eidetic science, and the celebrated "bracket" the Phenomenological Reduction, the *epoché*, "*a certain refraining from judgement which is compatible with the unshaken and unshakable because self-evidencing conviction of Truth*".[11]

But it is difficult not to feel that the phenomenological tightrope is ready at every moment to tumble us back into the Idealist net. If the truth of the table's existence is "unshaken and unshakable" the *epoché* would seem to be redundant. If the *epoché* is necessary then there is real doubt and the phenomenological odyssey has been less successful than the Cartesian because, while it escapes the mind–matter antithesis which follows from the *cogito*, it leaves us in a world of ideas. It is interesting to note that already in the *Cartesian Meditations* Husserl is placing less and less emphasis on existence and correspondingly more on the *epoché*. As long as the question of the ontological status of the phenomenon is left open, of course, Husserl avoids the tendency to give thought *priority* over concrete reality. At the same time his stress brings him close to the Idealist position.

The curious thing about Husserl's philosophy, however, is that it requires only one major alteration in order to serve as the basis for an existential approach. If we discard the *epoché* and call the phenomenon (or the transcendental Ego who contains ideally his entire world) Existence, then we leave Idealism behind and transform Phenomenology into a philosophical method for coming to terms not with ideas alone but with the whole of existing reality. This is precisely the shift which brings us to the position of Heidegger and Sartre. There is no point in "bracketing" the existence of a given phenomenon. In examining the phenomenon *as if* it existed one is in effect saying that it *does* exist. Consequently one may as well base one's philosophizing not on the phenomenon regarded as an idea but on the phenomenon regarded as existing, that is, on the *phenomenon of Existence*. "That which *antedates* all standpoints", the "intuitively self-given which is prior to any theorizing reflexion" now takes on a new meaning and one which is of central importance to the present argument.

Viewed retrospectively from the existential development of his position, Husserl appears to take his stand *behind* the *cogito* and the Idealist pure Thought because of his insistence that consciousness is "intentional", that it presupposes an object, that to be conscious is always to be conscious *of* something. The idea, as Husserl acknowledges, is Franz Brentano's, [12] but it is Husserl who makes good use of it: "In this manner . . . every conscious process is . . . consciousness *of* such and such, regardless of what the . . . actuality-status of this objective such and such may be . . ."[13] Of course the spectre of Idealism is present. The table of which I am conscious may simply be an idea, no more. But in the hands of later thinkers, that is to say once the "bracket" is ignored, Husserl's dictum is of major significance and its implications are many. Granted that we are speaking of existing reality and not simply of ideas, the statement that all consciousness is consciousness *of* something avoids the horns of the Idealist and the Realist dilemma by rejecting the independence in the act of perception of subject and object, that is, of mind and its world as object of knowledge. We do not, like the Idealists, reduce the world to mind or, like the Realists, speak as if knowing subject and known object were separate entities (or, like the empiricists, reduce the mind to matter). Rather we begin with a phenomenon that is *single*, the phenomenon of "consciousness-of", that is, with a phenomenological unity of mind and matter, subject and object, man and world. This is Husserl's ground of "transcendental subjectivity"[14] without its Idealist bias, not the subjectivity of the *cogito* or that of the Idealist Absolute, not the objectivity of the empiricist, but a *subjectivity* which links itself to the outside world and so *transcends* itself and turns into objectivity. From this standpoint the philosopher forfeits the privileged position of the Hegelian. There is no question of gazing detachedly at the world from the heights of an Absolute. On the contrary, the existential phenomenologist can only survey the world from the inside as it were, that is, as involved in the world about him, as mind intimately associated from beginning to end with what is other than mind. It follows that extreme epistemological scepticism is untenable. A consciousness which, unlike the *cogito* or the Absolute, is bound to exist as a consciousness *of* something outside itself cannot question the reality of the world any more than it can question its own reality. The primordial intuition of consciousness will be indistinguishable from the empirical consciousness of the world. Thus all philosophizing will follow, rather than precede, the spontaneous acknowledgement of the philosopher's connection with his environment. In this way a basis is discovered for a philosophy which can lay claim both to subjective and objective criteria, a philosophy which begins with mind but does not stop there, a concrete rather than abstract line of approach.

Husserl's difficulty is that he will not commit himself as regards the existential status of the phenomenon "consciousness-of". From the point of view of Heidegger and Sartre his approach suggests a way out of nineteenth-century metaphysics because it situates the thinking subject firmly in a world, Husserl's "*my world-about-me*".[15] At the same time, as long as we continue to question the existence of the phenomenon, that is, as long as we continue to apply the "bracket", we threaten the entire structure: what value is there in the idea of "intentional" consciousness if both consciousness and its intentional object remain in the shadowy realm of the *idea*? In order to safeguard what they see as the positive achievements of the phenomenological approach, Heidegger and Sartre therefore ignore Husserl's *epoché* and identify the unitary phenomenon, "consciousness-of", with Existence rather than with Essence.

In a late work, *The End of Philosophy and the Task of Thinking* (1964), Heidegger repeats the phenomenological motto – "to the things themselves" – which he voiced in *Being and Time* (1927), his first major work. The philosophical call "to the things themselves", that is to say, to the real, appears in Hegel, he argues, as a call to the idea. A hundred years later, he continues, it appears in Husserl as an attack against psychologism and historicism in philosophy. Unfortunately in both Hegel and Husserl, whose "methods are as different as they could be",[16] the call leads in the final analysis to "the subjectivity of consciousness".[17] Heidegger avoids what he sees as the Cartesian blind alley from the start. Instead of an Ego (however "transcendental"), his subject is *dasein*, man as being-*there* (*da*), mind not distinct from its world but *one* with it: being-in-the-world. This involves the proposition that man's

> "essence" . . . lies in its "to be". Its Being-what-it-is (*essentia*) must, so far as we can speak of it at all, be conceived in terms of its Being (*existentia*).[18]

Of course this quotation is from *Being and Time*. In fact, following its critique of Husserl, *The End of Philosophy and the Task of Thinking* does not go on to talk of *dasein* or being-in-the-world or, indeed, of Existence. Instead it focusses on the elusive notion of *Lichtung* ("lighting", "opening" or "clearing") with whose aid

Heidegger elucidates the nature of *alētheia*, "unconcealment". We shall return to these terms in due course. At this stage it is enough to stress that, in spite of appearances, the later Heidegger is in no way incompatible with the Heidegger of *Being and Time*. A deal has been said about the *Kehre*, Heidegger's "turning" from the existential philosophy of *dasein* to the later concern with *Sein* (Being). There is, however, only one Heidegger. In *Being and Time* he examines the existential context of man; in the later work, he moves beyond, to a sphere which cannot be termed existential. Nevertheless, the second phase is implicit in the first and in no way negates it. With these complicating factors in mind we may continue to speak of Heidegger's "existential" reformulation of Husserl's position, which involves the removal of the idea in favour of *the thing itself* – not the unattainable *noumenon* of Kant, nor Husserl's phenomenon as phenomenon, but the phenomenon as *existing*.

This simultaneous reliance upon and rejection of Husserl's approach emerges equally clearly in Sartre's description of the existential position in *Existentialism and Humanism* (*L'Existentialisme est un Humanisme*, 1945). Sartre is (rashly) speaking for Heidegger as well as for himself, and he sets out to illustrate the nature of the existential approach by contrasting it with the Cartesian. The existential thinker, he argues, does not begin with the *cogito*. Rather, the familiar dictum is reversed and "I am" precedes "I think". Existence is logically prior to the *cogito* and to the *res cogitans*, the subject of the *cogito*. This means that one *is* before one *thinks*, one *exists* before one is something in particular or, as Sartre puts it, Existence precedes Essence. In other terms again we can say that there is no such thing as an inbuilt Essence, that *what* a man is is precisely his manner of existing, or that a man *is* what he *does*. Thus Sartre does not talk about man as if he were the Cartesian thinking being. On the contrary, man is a being that exists and the implication of this is precisely the phenomenological approach as Sartre sees it. To begin with mind or thought is to separate subject from object, mind from matter, man from his world. To begin with man as *existing* is to base oneself on the phenomenological unity of consciousness and its object, to return to Husserl's dictum that consciousness is always consciousness *of* something. *Thinking* man has to make an effort to escape the Idealist conclusion – that mind is the fundamental principle of things – or the Occasionalist disjunction of mind and matter which is Descartes' legacy to Geulincx and Malebranche. *Existing* man needs to make no effort at all: one does not exist in a vacuum, one exists *somewhere* and so in relation to other existing things. If one is to *be* as a result of *doing* one needs a world as an area of operations. Thus Sartre does not speak of man as a substance, as something self-enclosed, separated from his world – even, as does Husserl, of man as an Ego – but of "human reality". We are returned to Heidegger's *dasein*, man as being-in-the-world. It is true that, as with Heidegger, we must add a proviso to all of this. *Existentialism and Humanism* represents Sartre in the role of popularizer, so that it cannot be allowed to carry too much weight. Still, it is, for all its simplification (and uncharacteristic sensationalism) in keeping with the tenets of *Being and Nothingness* (*L'Etre et le Néant*, 1943). There is a further caveat. Sartre's early philosophy, which is of interest to the present argument, is not clearly and in every respect compatible with the later developments represented by *Critique of Dialectical Reason* (*Critique de la Raison Dialectique*, 1960). If we insist that there is only one Heidegger, we cannot be quite so sure that there are not two Sartres. At any rate it is the first of these which is of interest here.

Having placed Sartre's early manifesto in proper context, we must also query its rather glib appeal to the authority of Heidegger, since Heidegger himself did so. Sartre argues, somewhat facilely, that existential thought presupposes atheism, then promptly enrols Heidegger as an ally against the theists, Gabriel Marcel and Jaspers. To his credit, Heidegger refused to take this bait. Rather he chose to reply to Sartre at a more serious level in the famous *Letter on Humanism* (1947). To begin with the *Letter* questions Sartre's reduction of human reality, the essence of man, to action pure and simple. In so doing it also rejects the Marxist notion of *praxis*, which is to figure so prominently in Sartre's later *Critique*. Not that Heidegger conceives of man as static. It is simply that Sartre's concept of *doing* is too limiting for him. Man *becomes* what he is by *doing*, but not quite in the way Sartre insists. This brings us to the issue of "humanism", which for Sartre means man-without-God, which is to say, man-without-essence (created by God), man-without-a-priori-values, in short, *man responsible for himself*, i.e. *free*. Such humanism has little place in Heidegger's thought. *Dasein*, though responsible, is responsible to – *Sein*, Being. Existing man is nothing by himself, his definition lies not in himself but in his relation to an Other: Being. Thus "in the determination of the humanity of man . . . what is essential is not man but Being".[19] Again, in the much-quoted phrase, "man is not the lord of beings. Man is the shepherd of Being".[20] These cryptic statements may be left for the present. What is important to note is that Sartre's notion of the existential is drastically different from Heidegger's.

And yet in speaking of Sartre and Heidegger as existential thinkers we are not led astray, provided we are aware of important differences, as well as the variations in emphasis (at the very least) between the early Sartre and Heidegger and the later Sartre and Heidegger. To the degree that Sartre defines man as *existing*, rather than as the realization of an idea, he is in general agreement with Heidegger. Moreover both stand in the same general relation to Husserl. We may then return to the original point. Husserl, in order to escape the Cartesian dichotomy, stresses the unity of consciousness and its world but at the price of focussing exclusively upon the sphere of Essence. The later philosophers retain Husserl's emphasis on unity, while, at the same time, grounding their arguments not in the notion of Essence but of Existence. Consciousness and its object remains a unitary phenomenon, a "consciousness-of" entity, but receives a new name: Existence. Phenomenology now ceases to be an eidetic science, a science of ideas, and becomes an existential approach, an ontology or study of the phenomenon *as* existing. In the early chapters of *Being and Time* (which he dedicates to Husserl) Heidegger proposes the Husserlian method and then adds: "With regard to its subject matter, phenomenology is the science of the Being of entities – ontology."[21] Sartre, writing sixteen years later in 1943, echoes this in the title of his major work: *Being and Nothingness, an Essay on Phenomenological Ontology* (*L'Etre et le Néant, essai d'ontologie phénoménologique*).

Thus in the hands of Heidegger and Sartre, Phenomenology becomes identified with the sphere of concrete being and the existential philosopher is rescued from the debilitating legacy of the *cogito*. Of course the partly Idealist origins of his stand are still evident. He is not an empiricist and continues to take his stand on mind. But because he insists on situating mind in a material environment, because he refuses to separate mind from its material context, he is able to construct a bridge which spans the extremes of Idealism and empiricism. A creature whose essence is *to exist* is necessarily, not simply accidentally, related to his world. In Heideggerian or Sartrean terms he is *ontologically* related to it, involved, in his very *being*, in a material and mental field of operation: the world. It could be said too, that in spite of its fundamental disagreement with Descartes, the existential or phenomenological approach preserves a Cartesian flavour and so clearly reveals its ultimate source. The *cogito ergo sum*, after all, may be taken in two ways. For all his stress on thought, for all his incipient Occasionalism, Descartes did not think of his dictum as an argument, he did not intend to give his *ergo* the force of a conclusion. Rather, he thought of the *cogito* and the *sum* as two closely related aspects of a single phenomenon. In this case *sum ergo cogito* might be thought an equally valid formulation of the idea – whose existential flavour is now apparent. To the extent that the Cartesian phrase may be reversed, according to the emphasis desired, it would not be misleading to say that in spite of the existential quarrel with Descartes and his legacy, the existential experiment is already implicit in the *cogito ergo sum*.

Enough has been said for something of the philosophical context of the existential to be apparent. The existential may be traced back through Idealism to Descartes. At the same time it represents a reaction against Descartes and the Idealists in the direction of the other great philosophical line, empiricism. Thus it may be viewed as a philosophy midway between two extremes, deliberately balanced between the mental and the material, between the ghost and the machine.

It now remains for the Beckett Reduction – which, as we have seen, is not quite Cartesian – to be examined in the light of the existential-phenomenological thought of Sartre and Heidegger. Is Beckett's subject, the tramp and, finally, the elusive Unnamable, more readily comprehensible in terms of the *sum* than of the *cogito*?

3 Beckett and Sartre: the Unnamable and the *pour soi*

Nothingness lies coiled in the heart of being – like a worm.[1]

SARTRE

I have termed the basic unit of Beckett's world the Irreducible and defined it as an impossible *sine qua non*, a residue that is left when all that is inessential is removed, a presence so minimal as to be nothing at all yet inescapably *there*, in philosophical terms, a being-nothing. This faint reality is attained after a painful reduction has taken us from the figure of the tramp to the voice of consciousness and, finally, to the silence of the Unnamable. The question immediately arises: if the Irreducible is a kind of nothing is it relateable to the Sartrean *néant*? Some critics have readily assumed that it is. In fact, the Sartrean and Beckettian worlds are very different from each other, radically dissimilar in perspective, orientation and tone. I intend to prove it by analysis, but it should be stressed that a proof of this kind merely confirms one's initial critical intuition, which requires no detailed knowledge of philosophy.

Sartre retains Husserl's idea that consciousness is always consciousness *of*, and on this basis constructs a unique philosophy. If it is not possible to be conscious without an object of consciousness, it follows that objects of consciousness are prior to the mind, that the perceiver presupposes the perceived. Using different but related terms, we are repeating the dictum that Existence is prior to Essence, that consciousness requires a concrete world. In *Being and Nothingness* this argument is central: "Consciousness is consciousness *of* something. This means that . . . consciousness is born *supported by* a being which is not itself."[2] Consciousness requires for its being something other than itself, it is by its very nature a moving outwards from the sphere of the ideal to that of Existence. Sartre in stating this is partly turning

Idealism upside down and partly introducing his own strange version of the Cartesian dualism of mind and matter. What is that something of which the mind is conscious? It is being, which is simply defined as anything of which one can say that it *is*. Being is positive, self-sufficient, requiring nothing beyond itself: it is therefore termed the in-itself, the *en soi*. Strictly speaking, being is self-identical, it is itself and only itself, "the inherence in itself without the least distance".[3] We can go on to say of it that it has always been, is beyond affirmation and negation or the opposition of activity and passivity. In short, we can say of it many of the things said by the theologians of God whom Aquinas defined in the terms of Moses' vision of the burning bush: I am I am. The *en soi* is *massif*, or "solid"[4] it enters into no relations with what is other than itself, it needs no explanation in terms other than itself. Transition, becoming, anything which permits us to envisage being as related to non-being – whatever changes from A to B must in some sense be conceived first as A-not-B and then as B-not-A, that is, as a not-yet or a no-longer – all that is forbidden on principle. Thus a chair simply *is*, absurdly, gratuitously, like God.

The mind in being conscious must of force be conscious of being, that is, of the *en soi*. But if it is conscious *of* being it cannot itself *be* being. Consciousness *of* implies a dualism, an ontological differentiation. But there is only one alternative to being and that is nothingness. Thus consciousness emerges as the contradiction of being – as nothing at all, a void. Sartre bases his system on a radical variation of the Cartesian severance of mind and body. Instead of these two alternatives he proposes a more existential division that cuts across the other: one between nothingness and being, between human consciousness, the void which Sartre terms *pour soi*, and anything which in opposition to it may be said to *be* – the *en soi*, subject of consciousness. The mind, *pour soi*, is *ce trou d'être*, a "hole of being".[5] To the question, "how does a hole exist?" the answer is simple: it exists by virtue of the edge around it, that is to say, the *pour soi* exists not "in itself" but in so far as it leans on the *en soi* which is self-sufficient. Sartre is repeating his original premise that consciousness is consciousness *of*. The mind, its own hole, exists by filling itself with what is other than itself, with *being*; that is, it exists by virtue of its objects of consciousness. I *am* In so so far as I am aware of things which *are*, my chair, for example. If there were no being there would be no mind; on the other hand, without the mind being would continue as before. Of course the hole which is consciousness cannot be "filled" until the moment of death, when *pour soi* is converted into *en soi*. No matter how conscious *of* things, the mind, by its very act of consciousness, maintains itself as *different from* things, as negative.

Since being does not act – it simply *is* – the onus of a relation between being and nothingness falls on nothingness. It is consciousness, which, by its action, relates itself to being and so maintains itself in precarious existence. As nothingness it can have only negative relations with being. A chair is being, *en soi*, so the mind cannot say "I am the chair". On the contrary, as conscious *of* the chair it dissociates itself from it. It must of force say "I am not the chair", thus constituting the chair as positive and itself as negative in the one act. The chair is *en soi*, the mind is *pour soi* and the ontological gulf cannot be bridged except by the motion of separation: my relation to being lies in my negation of a relation. It is in this way that consciousness constitutes its world. There is no question of an Idealist creation. The world, that is, being, is *prior* to mind. Nevertheless, being on its own is undifferentiated, it does not *know* itself. Only with the advent of mind or nothingness is being differentiated into a world of becoming, of transition, of variety. The mind separates being from being as Yahweh separated the waters of the firmament – and naturally it separates being from being by a film of nothingness, that is, by introducing *itself* into the very heart of the *en soi*: "Nothingness lies coiled in the heart of being – like a worm." The *pour soi* gazes at being and in so doing proclaims: the chair is *not* the table is *not* the window is *not* the wall and so forth. It is like an acid which creates holes wherever it appears or a lubricant which insinuates itself everywhere in order to open crevices and fissures in the *en soi*, retreating to allow these spaces to be filled, then returning once again to open them. In this rhythm of separation and reunion the world – the world as it is for man – comes into being.

It must be added that the *pour soi* which exists as non-being, negation of its objects of consciousness, exists equally as negation of *itself*. Nothingness is not itself; if it were self-identical it would be *en soi*. Rather, nothingness it separated from itself by itself, a hole torn apart by its own emptiness. The mind is, of course, self-conscious. But in being conscious *of* itself the mind is not viewing itself. It is focussing on itself as objectified, on itself as *being*. This objectified Self or Ego is not consciousness as such, it is one's personality, one's image of oneself, oneself as viewed from the outside only. In fact self-consciousness represents a *failure* on the part of the *pour soi* to coincide with itself, to *be* itself. The more consciousness tries to *be* itself by being conscious *of* itself, by as it were *filling* itself with itself, the more it proclaims its own non-coincidence, just as the more it tries to fill itself with being in general the more it constitutes itself as non-being, the more it *separates* itself from being.

It is clearly tempting to argue that the Beckett Irreducible secretes the same void as the *pour soi*, even, as some have done, to equate the two. Like Sartre, Beckett conceives of nothingness as something actual. We recall the words of Malone (and Democritus): "*Nothing is more real than nothing*" (p.193). In that case the Unnamable may be regarded as behaving like Sartrean consciousness, a hole separated from itself and all things by itself, and so neither itself nor anything else. It denies all positives steadily and for over a hundred pages, as we have seen, under the obligation "to begin again, to start again from nowhere, from no one and from nothing and to win to me again . . . unrecognizable at each fresh faring" (p.304), refusing to recognize itself in the "delegates", the tramps who represent it in the novels, those "mannikins" (p.308), "vice-exister[s]" (p.317) from Murphy to Malone, refusing to identify itself with its own situation ("sometimes it seems to me I am in a head . . . But thence to conclude the head is mine, no, never", (p.222)), refusing to acknowledge the voice as its own ("It issues from me, it fills me, it clamours against my walls, it is not mine." (p.309)) "Shall I come upon my true countenance at last, bathing in a smile?" the Unnamable speculates, only to conclude in the negative: "I could employ fifty wretches for this sinister operation and still be short of a fifty-first, to close the circuit . . ." (p.341). No number of "delegates", no amount of positivity, no image will ever suffice to reveal a void: "I knew it, there might be a hundred of us and still we'd lack the hundred and first, we'll always be short of me" (p.342).

Like the *pour soi*, the Beckett Irreducible is able to *be* only in so far as it is able to lean on a positive, on an image or reflection of itself: the tramp or the voice. Just as the *pour soi*, even as it relies on the *en soi*, must deny any connection with it, so the Irreducible, even as it seeks itself in the endless meandering of the voice or the tramp, is forced at last to collapse back on itself in the knowledge that it is neither tramp nor voice, that any connection with these is purely negative. In exactly this way Sartrean consciousness reflects itself in an image, an Ego or Self created in bad faith. The *pour soi* cannot *be* anything, it can only *pretend* to be. So Sartre's waiter plays at being a waiter. If he *were* a waiter he would not be conscious *of* being a waiter. Consciousness implies a role, an act of bad faith, because the self I perceive myself to be in the gaze of reflection is not myself, it is a *something*, an attempt on my part to *be* – to be *en soi*. Significantly, the Unnamable rejects any connection with an Ego, in spite of the pleas of its obscure tormentors:

> But my dear man, come, be reasonable, look, this is you, look at this photograph, and here's your file . . . come now, make an effort, at your age, to have no identity, it's a scandal . . . look at this photograph, what, you see nothing . . . no matter, here, look at this death's-head . . . (p.380)

But it is all denied. The Unnamable remains "something quite different, a wordless thing in an empty place" (p.390), repeating over and over "but it's not I, it's not I" (p.403). In like manner the female protagonist of *Not I* refuses the first person singular (". . . what? . . . who? . . . no! . . . she! . . . SHE!" (p.20)), the enquiring voice of *How it is* receives no answer ("what's my name no answer WHAT'S MY NAME", (p.159)), and the speaker of *Company* explains: "Could he speak to and of whom the voice speaks there would be a first [person]. But he cannot. He shall not". (p.9). Is the whole world of the tramps, indeed of Beckett's fiction, then, an act of self-deception, *mauvaise foi*, subsequently admitted by the Irreducible in "good faith"?

At this point there are important distinctions to be made, however. We need only recall the Unnamable's attitude to the voice: "Ah if only this voice could stop, this meaningless voice which prevents you from being nothing. . ." (p.374). The *pour soi*, though void, is nevertheless consciousness. But Beckett's Irreducible rejects the voice and in so doing places itself in a region situated *beneath* the level of consciousness. To this extent it is evident that the Irreducible can no more be likened to the *pour soi* than to the Cartesian *cogito*. Moreover, there is a further complication. Sartre, in his mock-sacrilegious way, speaks of the *en soi*, that is, of being, in the terms in which the Scholastics spoke of the deity. Thus the in-itself is self-sufficient, above change, above differentiation, above affirmation and negation and so on. It is difficult not to be reminded here of Beckett's *negative* Irreducible. The Irreducible, more negative than even the *pour soi*, bears at the same time a confusing similarity to that most *positive* of all things, the *en soi* which, as plenitude of being, must, in Sartre's system, be regarded as the *contradiction* of the *pour soi*.

We may observe the same problem from another angle. The *pour soi* as a void is not thereby passive. On the contrary it is pure dynamism, it cannot be pinned down and this is to be expected: if the *pour soi* were ontologically still for a moment it would turn into being. Something which is not itself and not anything else can only exist in a constant flurry of ontological motion, it must constantly alter its course so that it may be said, in the strictest sense, never to be anywhere. The *pour soi* escapes endlessly from itself and from all things; it *is* itself this very escape, this negation and this is made possible by the fact that the *pour soi* temporalizes itself, is a creature of time. Thus I live not in the present which is an infinitely small point – a void of consciousness – but in my past and future. The question cannot be elaborated here but it is central to modern existential philosophy in general and it accounts for what we may term the *pour soi*'s ontological objectives. Sartre argues that the *pour soi* is a self-contradiction, a creature which, by its very nature, cannot be, but which insists on linking itself with being even as it escapes it. The more it tries to join being – by being conscious *of* it – the more it negates it; the more it escapes being by negation, the more it relies on it for its precarious existence. In temporal terms this means that the more I seek to *be*, a waiter for example, the more I am forced to admit that my being a waiter relates to my *past* and so is no longer myself. Likewise the more I want to *stop* being a waiter, in order, say, to be a diplomat, the more I am convinced that I remain a waiter. If I succeed in becoming a diplomat, the problem will simply take another form. *En soi* and *pour soi* can never join. Human beings live a life which is both an escape and a search, projecting themselves towards a never-to-be-realized goal: the union of being and nothingness. The *pour soi* wants to be (that is, *en soi*, the past) and to be conscious (that is, *pour soi*, futurity) at the same time; it desires to combine the immanence of being and the transcendence of nothingness, in short, as Sartre puts it, to be God. Only God *is* and *knows* that he is in the one act, only God is above the dualism of time. But God is a logical impossibility in a system where *l'être* and *le néant* are mutually incompatible. The gap in the universe is unbridgeable, God is a futile ideal, the calvary of the mind is in vain: "man is a useless passion".[6]

At first glance much of this appears relevant to Beckett. If Sartre's world is in motion so is that of the Beckett Reduction. The Reduction may be represented either as a flight from or as a search for – an unknown. Murphy, escaping from himself, seeks the comforts of the darkness; Watt, seeking himself, is engulfed by the same darkness; the characters of the trilogy drift aimlessly, fleeing the world and seeking its source, Molloy's mother, Malone's small womb-like room; Vladimir and Estragon, like the characters of *Endgame* and the protagonist of *Rockaby*, groan in anticipation of the impossible end; Buster Keaton, in *Film*, seeks to evade his own eye in the moment of reflection. It seems that we are in the Sartrean world of futility since, ultimately, the tramps seek union with the Unnamable, and this union is inconceivable. From the trilogy to *Company*, voice and silence cannot be one, it is impossible to *express* the *absence* of Beckett's Irreducible. So even as the Unnamable identifies with its "delegates" it has to reaffirm its essential incompatibility with a positive, reject the tramps as fictions and swing back to itself: "it's not I , it's not I". Thus the movement from Unnamable to "delegate" and back again would resemble the abortive attempt of the *pour soi* to *be* – *en soi* – an attempt which continues even as it continues to fail, since in so far as Sartrean consciousness becomes being it ceases to be conscious and as soon as it is conscious it ceases to be being.

But we are returned to the fundamentally different assumptions made by Beckett and Sartre. It is true that the tramp's situation is not unlike that of the *pour soi*. On the other hand the tramp is not a negative. The Irreducible, which *is* negative, does not behave like the *pour soi*. Quite simply, in Sartre nothingness and consciousness are identical. In Beckett they clearly are not, since consciousness – that of the tramp or the voice – must be left behind if we are to reach the void of the Unnamable. Moreover, the Unnamable or Irreducible, that void beneath the level of consciousness recalls – and this is worth repeating – the positivity of the Sartrean *en soi*. Perhaps it is not misleading to suggest a parallel between the Irreducible and the *en soi–pour soi* synthesis which for Sartre defines God. The Irreducible's negativity does not exclude a certain positivity since, after all, the Irreducible *is* and so has been defined as a being-nothing. In that case we may say that God is possible in Beckett's universe, or rather that what is impossible for Sartre is impossibly *there* for Beckett. While no tramp can teach it, no voice utter its name, the Irreducible exists, for without its presence the whole Beckett system of things would collapse. Thus in returning to the inexplicable being of the Unnamable, the central and all-important fact of Beckett's world, we leave the Sartrean world of futility behind.

Put concisely, the difference between Sartre and Beckett is this: whereas the former bases his entire philosophy on the being-nothingness distinction, the latter, equally concerned with the reality of being and the void, is fundamentally oriented towards paradox, for the union of opposites which cannot eventuate in the philosopher is an undeniable, if embarrassing, fact in the writer. This conclusion should not take us by surprise. In spite of its frequent gloom, Beckett's is not a world of never-to-be-realized hopes, at least not fundamentally. The Reduction represents a positive movement, the uncovering of the hidden principle of things. That this principle of necessity remains a tormenting mystery is not a drawback. Where Sartre's is a closed system, Beckett's opens out to infinity: "all is possible, or almost" (p.297), says the voice of the Unnamable. Being-nothing *exists* and if we cannot quite put our fingers in its wound we may at least squirm closer and closer. It is this fascination for the darkness which keeps the Reduction going and differentiates Beckett sharply from Sartre. The Irreducible calls to Beckett. Sartre, after all, is a lover of the light. Mystery has no appeal for his secular mentality; his concern is with the human, and like a good Frenchman and in a most unlikely context, he will assert the value of logic, of *clarté*. No matter how complex and seemingly obscure, *Being and Nothingness* is a masterpiece of system and lucidity, of Classicism. Beckett's inspiration is essentially Romantic.

Once the notions of *en soi* and *pour soi* are seen to be inapplicable to Beckett's fiction all comparisons between the writer and the philosopher will founder on this rock since Sartre's entire structure rests on his initial distinction. One extended example – that of freedom – will suffice to show this. Sartre begins with the celebrated assertion that man is in every respect free. And he could hardly say otherwise. Consciousness is nothing and nothing cannot be determined. Therefore consciousness is free. The void which interposes itself between the *pour soi* and *itself* means that the *pour soi* cannot determine itself, it must by its nature act spontaneously; that is to say it has no "nature" fixed in advance – one *exists* before one is something in particular, one *is* what one *does* or, as Sartre puts it in *Existentialism and Humanism*, Existence precedes Essence. At the same time the void which slips between the *pour soi* and the *world* means that being cannot determine consciousness which has only negative relations with it. Above all, the same film interposed between consciousness and its *past* means that the past cannot determine the present. In my past I am *en soi*, my past is not myself. At every moment a new myself is born, a new void of freedom is opened and an old, now fixed, myself is discarded. For Sartre what I am is moulded by the future, not the past as the determinists would have it, and the future can influence but not force the present. Thus, freedom, futurity, nothingness and consciousness are synonymous terms. Freedom is not extrinsic to the *pour soi*, it *is* the *pour soi*, it *is* human consciousness, as Orestes sees in *The Flies*. To be consciousness is to be void, to be a void is to be a futural creature and to be a futural creature is to be a freedom. To exist is to constitute oneself in action, to live a perpetual choice.

This situation has its disadvantages. As Sartre puts it, *ma liberté ronge ma liberté*, "freedom eats away my freedom".[7] To begin with, freedom is a responsibility. I myself am answerable for myself, on nothing else can I lay the blame for my mistakes. It will be objected that I am not free to be born where I please or to be born at all or to be tall rather than short and so on. Sartre admits this but will not class such limitations as determinisms. One cannot be free in a vacuum. Freedom is existential in nature, it requires a situation within which to operate and it requires barriers, otherwise it cannot be freedom. Sartre calls this the facticity of freedom. Thus my *facticité* is my freedom to be free as a waiter, for example, and not as a diplomat. It is the *fact* of my being a void, the tenuous link I possess with being, the fact that I cannot choose *not* to exist, *not* to be conscious, *not* to be free, *not* to be in a particular existential situation. I am *forced* to exist and I am *forced* to be free. This is the second torment of freedom, that it escapes my control, that I myself escape myself, slipping through my own fingers: *ma liberté ronge ma liberté*. No wonder man prefers to live within a determinist system, whether that of the scientists or that of theological predestination.

Once again, Beckett's universe seems, at times, to obey Sartrean laws. Do not the tramps of the novels and plays, wandering from city to plain, from seashore to forest and finally into the confined space of the room, appear to have the boundless vacancy of freedom before them? Belacqua strolls through Dublin, Murphy, Watt, Molloy and Malone all forge into an emptiness filled with infinite possibilities, each as possible as the next. The voice meanders in the regions of the mind. In each case the very aimlessness of the journey suggests a parallel with Sartre. The tramps have nowhere to go or, conversely, they can go anywhere, do anything. It is true that Beckett's stories are filled with images of compulsion. Pozzo enslaves Lucky, Hamm dominates Clov. There is the goad in *Act Without Words II* which forces the two subjects to go through their little routine, the bell in *Happy Days* which controls Winnie's sleeping and waking, Croak, the tyrant of *Words and Music*, the Opener who controls the world of *Cascando*, the prompter of *Not I*, the Deviser of *Company*, and the inquisitorial light of *Play* at whose bidding the three characters vomit their sad tale. Frequently an image of divine manipulation is expressed in the form of an obscure tormentor, Godot or the mysterious Youdi of *Molloy* or Mr Knott of *Watt*, all absent Prosperos with sinister motives. But Beckett is obviously less than half serious when he speaks of such tyrants from the earliest work to *The Unnamable, How it is* and *Company*. Indeed they are rejected as fictions by the Unnamable and the narrators of *How it is* and *Company*. In the words of the narrator of *Company*: "the fable of one with you in the dark" (pp.88–9); and in those of the narrator of *How it is*: "yes all that all balls yes" (p.159). It is Beckett's answer to Molly Bloom's great affirmative and a final reply to the seventeenth and eighteenth centuries: the Occasionalist deity and the great ever-present Berkeleian eyes are denounced as frauds. If there is compulsion in the situation of the tramps, it is not something external but an interior goad, consciousness itself, the eternally-fretting *cogito* which worries itself to distraction. We are back to the burden of freedom and to Sartrean facticity. Beckett's tramps, like the *pour soi*, are a *fact*. They are not free *not* to be, nor are they free *not* to be free. Freedom, like consciousness, is something one suffers and to that extent all is determinism. For where is the freedom of freedom since one is not free to choose the only thing that matters, namely freedom itself? Given the *fact* of existence, what else is left, since that fact eludes our control and that fact alone is of supreme importance? Once Vladimir and Estragon *have* to be, what difference does it make whether they go or stay?

However, Beckett's attitude to freedom is not quite as simple as this suggests, nor is it so simply Sartrean. It should first of all be referred back to seventeenth- and eighteenth-century thought in which the freedom and determinism debate looms very large. Descartes saw consciousness as free but his legacy is confused, coloured as it is by the Stoic ethic of improving oneself rather than one's world. Thus Geulincx, for whom the body–mind chasm is unbridgeable, argues that man has no real power outside the realm of mind. The only solution left is Stoic detachment: *ubi nihil vales, ibi nihil velis*. This is the difficulty of Occasionalism, that one cannot envisage a world where all is kept in motion by God except as a world bereft of free will. Malebranche extricates himself from this dilemma with some anxiety. Leibniz, whose philosophy raises the spectre of Occasionalism, is faced with a similar problem. God has wound the gigantic clock that is the universe; what is left for man but to await its running down? If God made Adam as he is can Adam do anything but sin, granted that he is Adam or, as Sartre has it, that Adam's Essence precedes his Existence? Of course for some seventeenth- and eighteenth-century thinkers this problem does not arise: Hobbes opted for a mechanistic view, Spinoza for a form of Pantheism and in both cases strict determinism follows. In the case of the British empiricists culminating in Hume there is little alternative to determinism.

Beckett's depiction of freedom recapitulates a great deal of the above and is best summed up in the experience of Murphy. Murphy exists as an inexplicable conjunction – or disjunction – of mind and body. In so far as he is body he is subject to various determinisms, in so far as he is mind he is free. It is exactly the situation of the subject, described in the *Ethics* of Geulincx and referred to frequently in Beckett, who is a passenger free to walk east on the deck of a ship sailing west. The passenger is, of course, mind and the ship, body. But Murphy is unsatisfied with this situation and seeks a higher freedom, entering deeper into the area of mind, "a closed system . . . impermeable to the vicissitudes of the body" (p.77). As the body with its determinisms recedes, Murphy finds himself in the first and second zones of the mind and "in both these zones of his private world Murphy felt sovereign and free" (p.79). But there is a third zone where the subject loses himself in the depths of the mind within the mind till he reaches the shadowy outlines of the Irreducible. At this impossible point where being shades off into nothingness, Murphy *transcends* freedom: "Here he was not free, but a mote in the dark of absolute freedom" (p.79). It is the point where the human individual rejoins the Spinozan Absolute, where Murphy enjoys the freedom of God. This freedom, moreover, is indistinguishable from necessity. Sartre is right in maintaining that freedom requires obstacles to freedom. Absolute freedom, freedom which meets no obstacles, cannot be distinguished from absolute determinism. God wills and his act of will is, as the theologians maintained, creation. If Murphy's fiat could have this power there would be no point in terming it either free or necessary, since it would be both.

Murphy's threefold movement is, of course, a miniature of the Beckett Reduction. Thus we can say that Beckett's early characters enjoy the freedom of the passenger on the Geulincx vessel. As the vessel sails further and further west, as the body moves to its inevitable dissolution, the tramp exists more and more as mind. By the same token he becomes more and more free. Murphy is affected by the world about him. By the time we reach Watt this connection has been broken and causality disappears in a tangle of Occasionalism and Hume. Beckett is describing the succession of servants in the Mr Knott household:

> . . . and Dick's ten years on the first-floor are not *because of* Harry's ten years on the ground-floor . . . and Harry's ten years on the ground-floor are not *because of* Dick's ten years on the first-floor . . . (p.132)

By the time we reach the trilogy or *Waiting for Godot* the tramp is free of the body and of the world, at least to a great extent. It is at this point that we may legitimately speak of a Sartrean element in Beckett. Of course as in Sartre freedom is not felt as anything other than an inexplicable burden. The consciousness of the tramp has become its own exquisite torment and the whole of existence takes on the appearance of a new determinism, that of facticity: "free, yes, I don't know what that means, but it's the word I mean to use, free to do what, to do nothing" (*Molloy*, p.13). Nevertheless Beckett does not stop here, as Murphy's ascesis suggests. Sartre refuses to confound being and nothingness and, by the same token, determinism or necessity and freedom. Only God can be both *en soi* and *pour soi*, both necessary and free, and God cannot exist for Sartre. As we have seen, though, the Beckett Irreducible is precisely being-nothing. Not unexpectedly, it transcends the freedom–necessity dichotomy. While the tramp and the voice of the Unnamable suffer the fact of freedom, the Unnamable itself, which is something more mysterious than Sartrean or Cartesian consciousness, represents that point in Beckett's Reduction, as in Murphy's experience, where not only the body is left behind but also the freedom of the mind. In it freedom and determinism coalesce with the same facility as they do in the bosom of the Idealist Absolute or the Theologian's God. Beckett's treatment of the subject of freedom is little less than a philosophical encyclopaedia, spanning in its development a threefold philosophical development from the Cartesian and Occasionalist to the existential and, finally, to the Idealist.

Thus the parallel with Sartre breaks down and for reasons predicted earlier. Beckett, unlike Sartre, will not distinguish between being and nothingness. It follows that he will not distinguish between determinism and freedom but opts in the end for a paradox.

Repetition of this experiment would lead to comparable results if one were to consider Beckett's work in relation to other Sartrean notions. Beckett's creatures often exhibit a disgust for the flesh, for the materiality of things. One thinks of Murphy's "char Venus and her sausage and mash sex" (p.29). Reproduction is the one unforgivable sin: "Scoundrel! Why did you engender me?" (*Endgame*, p.35). A mother has become the most contemptible of all things: "her who brought me into the world, through the hole in her arse if my memory is correct. First taste of the shit". (*Molloy*, p.16). Thus Mahood tramples his family underfoot and the Unnamable's voice sighs: "Ah you can't deny it, some people are lucky, born of a wet dream and dead before morning" (p.383). In this context a Swiftian distaste, "horror of the body and its functions", appears as "the most fruitful of dispositions" (*Molloy*, p.118). It finds application in Murphy's escape from the opulent Miss Counihan, in all those descriptions of ludicrous copulations in rubbish dumps in the trilogy and, in the end, in the infernal love-making of *The Lost Ones*. But Beckett's disgust has nothing to do with *la nausée*. If his characters are liable to feel contingent – one thinks of Vladimir and Estragon, for example – this feeling corresponds only loosely with Sartre's Absurd. The reason for this is that nausea and the Absurd are inextricably bound with Sartrean facticity, the sense that, although I am a void, I nevertheless exist, as *pour soi* I lean on the *en soi*. Because the *pour soi* avoids utter non-existence by its connection with being. Such acquired positivity, properly speaking, cannot be said to belong to it, it is borrowed from the *en soi*. The *pour soi* exists as a negation of the *en soi*, as a parasite feeding avidly on what is other than itself. This is its facticity. The *pour soi*, though nothing, is a *fact*, it boasts one tenuous negative link with being. Facticity then is the fact that consciousness *has* to exist (once it *does* exist), that it cannot avoid having a particular birthplace, a particular body, a particular past. All of these are more or less fixed, *en soi*. Thus a man with a waiter's past cannot say that he is a diplomat. His being a waiter is his facticity. Now the *en soi* is gratuitous, it does not *have* to be (like a free human consciousness), it just *is*, absurdly. To the (negative) extent that I lean on the *en soi* I too feel *de trop*, gratuitous, nauseated by the ontological *fact* of existence, the weight of the flesh and of the past. My being-a-waiter oppresses me, it sickens me. This is the weight which bears down on Roquentin in *Nausea*, and the feeling described in *Being and Nothingness*: "a dull and inescapable nausea . . . reveals my body to my consciousness".[8] To feel a sense of nausea or the Absurd is, in Sartre, simply to suffer the only confirmation of being available to the *pour soi*. But in Beckett the fact of being – of being conceived, being born, enduring in life – while it represents a link with a positive, existence felt as torment, is above all a cry of despair at the *unattainability* of nothingness. This makes no sense at all in a Sartrean context. If Vladimir and Estagon feel *de trop* it is not because they exist as nothingness harnessed to being, but because they have no wish to *be*.

It is the same in the matter of relationships. From the standpoint of *Being and Nothingness*, the *pour soi* is ontologically constituted by its relations with other *pour soi*. After all, consciousness is Other even to itself, since it cannot be self-identical. The Other gives me being by objectifying me, by making me object of his perception. In this way I become *someone*. To myself, of course, I will always remain pure subjective consciousness, nothingness, *no one*. If I am to be Peter or John, it must be by virtue of there being other consciousnesses in the world besides myself. Thus I am a void until the Other constitutes me as object of his attention in a movement which Sartre terms *le regard*, the Look. I do not wish to anticipate a discussion of this aspect of *Being and Nothingness* since it belongs more properly in the chapters on Jean Genet to follow. However, a bare statement of the philosophy of the Look is necessary at this point. Nothingness can only relate by negation, its essential stance towards any object of its consciousness is: that is *not* me. Thus when two *pour soi* meet they must dissociate themselves from each other. For Sartre, Peter and John are ontologically distinct, because two voids can only repel each other. The basis of intercourse must be conflict, not agreement. When Peter and John meet each seeks to make the other the object of the Look. Both cannot succeed, however. Either Peter exists as object to John's gaze, that is, to John's subjectivity, or vice versa. It is not possible for Peter and John to meet intersubjectively, that is, to unite, since two *pour soi* negate each other. There can be no *mitsein*, as in the philosophy of Heidegger, for Hegel's master-slave pair has become the human norm. If Peter and John could unite, Peter, for example, would have to be subject and object at the same time, simultaneously *pour soi* and *en soi*. But in the moment of the Look, as at any time, being and nothingness are mutually exclusive. The ideal of love is therefore technically futile, as is that of God. It is true that on the face of it the later Sartre develops beyond this position. In *Critique of Dialectical Reason* he abandons entirely the standpoint of individual consciousness, the *pour soi*. Instead, with Marx as the inspiration, he sets out to build, from the foundations up, a structure which explains human relationships, conceived in terms of social groups and social action. However, while this represents a drastic change in emphasis, it does not necessarily represent disagreement with *Being and Nothingness*. At any rate that is a moot point. Certainly the *Critique* does not endorse the possibility of being-with, only of acting-with. That is to say it does not envisage human beings as united *except in action*. *Praxis*, the term which corresponds to "project" in the earlier work, binds human beings together in a common cause, it and it alone is the origin of reciprocity. At the same time human reciprocity continues to be exercised in a context of struggle, not, as in *Being and Nothingness*, because of the dynamics of the Look, but because Sartre now conceives of man's historical milieu as one of scarcity, *la rareté*. So while the *Critique* is able to explain philosophically every kind of shared human endeavour – from what Sartre calls the Collective, the sphere of the Practico-Inert, to the Group, to the Organization, to the Institution (the state, for example), to, in the end, History itself – it is required to do so on a shaky foundation indeed. Love has no more place in the *Critique* than it had in *Being and Nothingness*. Like the *pour soi*, it is a futile passion.

Observably, this is not the case in Beckett's work. Of course human relations are not exactly easy in the novels and plays. One thinks of the Proustian round of love frustrated in a thousand varied ways in the course of Beckett's fiction from the never-to-be kiss of Nell and Nagg in *Endgame*, to the sweet-sour memories of Krapp's tape, to that affection which, when requited in *Murphy*, makes for a short-circuit (p.7) and which mercifully remains unrequited in the unequal contest of Watt and the one-breasted Mrs Gorman, to the passion which horribly animates the idyll of Mac and Moll in *Malone Dies*, or which prompts Molloy to declare "a mug's game in my opinion and tiring on top of that" (p.56), to, in the end, the violent communion of *How it is*, the creatures "making unmakable love" (p.37) in *The Lost Ones*, and the mutual solitude of the couple of *Imagination Dead Imagine* or the lovers in *That Time*. Let us recall two of these examples, the love-interlude of Mac and Molly –

> And though both were completely impotent they finally succeeded, summoning to their aid all the resources of the skin, the mucus and the imagination, in striking from their dry and feeble clips a kind of sombre gratification. (p.261)

– and the communication, by signs, by the art of human intercourse in *How it is*:

> first lesson theme song I dig my nails into his armpit right hand right pit he cries I withdraw them thump with fist on skull his face sinks in the mud his cries cease end of first lesson. (p.69)

The landscape of *How it is* is composed of an endless line of creatures edging forward in the slime, alternately tormentor and tormented, first master, then slave, an infinite series "and always two strangers uniting in the interests of torment" (p.131). And yet, if this terrifyingly concise statement defines the *reality* of life with the Other in Beckett's work, it does not negate its *possibility*. The story of Mac and Moll, however grotesque, is told with compassion: it *is* a love of sorts. Even the horrors of *How it is* may be interpreted in this way:

> if Pim loved me a little yes or no if I loved him a little in the dark the mud in spite of all a little affection find someone at least someone find you at last live together glued together love each other a little. (p.82)

At Murphy's Magdalen Mental Mercyseat a kick in the seat is a small mercy, it indicates a meeting of monads; in the trilogy Molloy is able to reach his ageing parent by tapping her on the skull. If, as in *No Exit* (*Huis Clos*), *l'enfer c'est les autres* – hell is other people – there are compensations. Murphy has genuine feeling for the lunatics of the Mercyseat, Watt's experience with Mrs Gorman has its soothing moments, Vladimir and Estragon make something of their relationship ("we don't manage too badly, eh Didi, between the two of us?" (p.69)). At the end of *Happy Days* Willie, hitherto largely out of sight, emerges to crawl to Winnie's face above the sand. Winnie reacts with joy and a tragicomic rendition of the song from *The Merry Widow*: love, that inconceivable, indeed, irreducible, touch of fingers, is, in the end a reality – as the lyrics of the waltz assure us. Of course love may achieve nothing, like the child's act of kindness to the female beggar in *Company*, or it may do harm, like the same child's care for the hedgehog which dies. It is not, however, impossible. We must conclude that, no matter how cramped, Beckett's world is open to possibilities in a way Sartre's is not, precisely because it is based not on a principle of exclusion but on a paradox. There is a limit to what can happen in the light of Sartrean reason; in Beckett's darkness rules and systems do not apply.

This fundamental divergence of approach applies also in the case of Camus. Camus is not significant as a philosopher but as a writer he has had a considerable impact on the postwar world and is often mentioned in Beckett criticism. For good or ill the label "theatre of the Absurd" is here to stay and it points more or less specifically to Camus. While one need not quarrel unduly with Martin Esslin's use of the phrase within the very general limits proposed by his book, the fact remains that when we attempt to relate in any detail the work of Beckett and Camus we come up against major difficulties.

The Absurd is defined in *The Myth of Sisyphus* (*Le Mythe de Sisyphe*) as a confrontation of man and his world, "this divorce between man and his life".[9] As a feeling it occurs when one's normal habits are suddenly or unexpectedly interrupted: without one's routine one feels uncomfortable, useless, absurd. Or it occurs when one realizes that one is ageing or perhaps about to die; man wants to be young, he wants to live, yet he must die: this is absurd. Or when one realizes one is alone in spite of one's need for human support. Even inanimate nature may be a source of the Absurd. This pen with which I write, this paper on which I write, the desk at which I sit, all these are totally *indifferent* to me: matter, the environment in which I live, does not *care* about me, it feels *nothing*, only I, a human being, alone of all things in a vast universe, am capable of feeling. This too is absurd. Above all, it is absurd that man is brought into the world with an immense desire to understand, a desire which must be frustrated to a greater or lesser degree. The mind seeks lucidity and order, categories into which much that exists cannot be introduced: "But what is absurd is the confrontation of the irrational and the wild longing for clarity whose call echoes in the human heart."[10] All of this is simply summed up: man and his world do not fit, they are not made for one another, creation is a mistake and man must make the best of it. There are echoes of Sartre here although in terms of philosophy the Camus Absurd rests on a vague and unspecified foundation. Sartre's nausea is the malady of being, the malady of consciousness – of one's flesh, of one's life, of one's milieu, of all of these as utterly contingent, utterly unnecessary and yet massively *there.* Camus' Absurd is likewise an awareness of the inexplicable nature of the human condition, of the world as an obstacle to man's understanding, and, like nausea, it focusses attention on the realities of physical existence, although, unlike nausea, it also represents a sigh of regret. Sartre does not linger on the pleasures of the flesh, on the excitement of youth. For Camus, on the other hand, these are the most difficult things to give up.

If at first glance the Camus Absurd seems relevant to Beckett, there are important differences, as there are between Camus and Sartre. Beckett's tramps are pathetically alone, alienated from their world, unable to make sense of their situation, plagued by the shortcomings of their condition. But Camus is a humanist and makes his position clear throughout *The Myth of Sisyphus*. Camus loves the life of sensation and seeks after order and proportion. One does not imagine Murphy or Malone playing *au football* or sunbaking on an Algerian beach. Camus will not acquiesce in the sufferings of life because he regards pleasure as a supreme value. In like manner he cannot be reconciled to the irrationality of things because reason too is a value. Hence *le pari de l'absurde*, "the wager of the Absurd",[11] the resisting of any *acceptance* of suffering and the irrational such as Camus imagines is the case in Christianity. This resistance is also at the core of *The Rebel* (*L'Homme Révolté*) and indeed defines Camus' notion of revolt. The absurd man gives up all otherwordly attempts to explain away the disparity between man's aspirations and life as it is. Rather he rebels against the state of things, faces their absurdity and gets down to the business of enjoying life within the given limitations. Thus *The Myth of Sisyphus* rejects suicide as a solution and *The Rebel*, murder. Life is sacred and moreover may be better enjoyed by *l'homme absurde* than by others since the former is aware of life's limits and so also aware of the value of every transient moment: "Being aware of one's life, one's revolt, one's freedom, and to the maximum, is living, and to the maximum."[12] It is necessarily an ethic of *carpe diem*, even an ethic of quantity rather than of quality, and the types of absurd man are Don Juan, the actor and the adventurer, men whose aim it is to live entirely for this world by cramming as much sensation, as much experience into the moment as possible. We have gone from Beckett's universe of despairing hope and hopeful despair to a hedonism reminiscent of the *fin de siècle* aesthetes. It is the triumph of the flesh, with renunciation as the one sin. *Il faut imaginer Sisyphe heureux*: Sisyphus, rolling his boulder to the top of the hill only to see it roll down again, is happy.[13] Man labours all his life to live, only to die at the end of it; yet this life is worth the anguish of the Absurd. In *The Rebel* Camus concludes with a plea for moderation, a defence of the Mediterranean love of life and of nature against what he terms German ideology and the enthronement of history in opposition to nature. It is an argument for a Latin *via media* against northern excess, for a life in the sun. From beginning to end, then, the ideal is a humanist and hedonist one and is coupled with a hatred for the otherwordly and for all that lessens the pleasures, whether physical or emotional or intellectual, of human existence.

But Beckett is in love only with a negative, mercilessly satirizing the rest with the zeal of a desert father. If Camus is a moralist and *philosophe* in the French Enlightenment tradition, Beckett is as far removed from this as is St Jerome in his cave from Voltaire. Beckett makes mention of physical fulfilment only to evoke a sad smile of sarcasm, and of intellectual desire for clarity only to guffaw as he does in *Watt*. A life of rich experiences, a respect for moderation – this is precisely what Beckett has reduced to zero. In the Reduction, he seeks to *further*, not to lessen, any divorce between man and existence, driving inwards, seeking not human values but the abyss, like the most otherwordly ascetic. This is not to deny Beckett's own peculiar humanism and his very considerable intellectuality: positive values are implicit in Beckett's work, but they are nothing like Camus'. The Camus Absurd reflects the humanist's regret at the transience of the flesh and the Stoic's acceptance of it. By and large Beckett regrets, and accepts with Stoicism, the fact that the Reduction does not *sufficiently* remove one from the human farce: "Who shall deliver me from the body of this death?" Of course it would be rash to conclude that Beckett is the greater pessimist and indeed the truth may be quite the opposite. But the point to stress here is that if the Beckett tramp is ever in an absurd situation it must be in a framework which is not Camus' any more than it is Sartre's.

The argument of this chapter is easily summarized. Those critics who have suggested similarities between Beckett and

Sartre have on the whole fostered a misconception. In fact a thorough comparison reveals differences. Sartrean consciousness is negative, *pour soi*; the voice of consciousness in Beckett is a positive. Moreover, the Irreducible, the basic unit of Beckett's imagination, acts as a being-nothing, both positive and negative. Sartre's thought is based on the distinction of *en soi* and *pour soi*, the mutual contradiction of being and nothingness; in Beckett we are removed gradually from the sphere of mind to one *beneath* the level of consciousness, a point at which opposites merge in the reality of the Unnamable. This question may be examined from another angle. Sartrean man projects himself towards the union of being and consciousness, of being and nothingness, a union Sartre calls "God". Because this union is by definition unrealizable, man's existence is futile, his deepest desire is a chimera: "there is here a passage which is not completed, a short circuit".[14] But Beckettian man is precisely oriented to the Unnamable, a creature who, impossibly, *exists*. The implications of Beckett's willingness to blur Sartrean opposites are very great: the world of the Unnamable is not one of futility: "God", the metaphysical, is not ruled out, and the Beckett ascesis to the Irreducible, far from being a Sartrean short-circuit, represents a positive movement of discovery.

Sartre's work, then, is based on a distinction, Beckett's on a paradox and we may logically expect this difference to extend to areas of detail. For example the Sartrean distinction between being and nothingness becomes also one between determinism (or necessity) and freedom. What emerges from Beckett's work is more complicated, and we are in fact able to distinguish three phases in the writer's treatment of freedom: an Occasionalist, a Sartrean and, finally, an Idealist phase. This last comes as no surprise: just as the Unnamable combines the extremes of being and nothingness, so also it manages to exist as both necessary and free. Inevitably, the Sartrean distinction is transcended. Similar results are obtained if one analyses Beckett's work in terms of Sartrean nausea and the Absurd or if one interprets human relations in Beckett in terms of the Sartrean opposition of subject and object: a single fundamental divergence in approach is necessarily responsible for differences in detail. Again we must stress, though, that while it is illuminating to define this divergence philosophically, analytical procedure merely confirms one's initial *critical* judgement – and this assertion holds for the chapters to follow. Beckett is a Romantic, fascinated by the darkness, Sartre is a Classicist and a logician. Similar conclusions apply in the case of Beckett and Camus, although here philosophical analysis may be dispensed with very quickly: the Camus Absurd is based on premises and values totally foreign to Beckett. Both Camus and Sartre are creatures of daylight, each in his own way representative of a central tradition of French thought. Beckett, like Minerva's owl, sees best by night.

4 Beckett and Heidegger: being-in-the-world and the concept of *Angst*

> Everyday familiarity collapses. Dasein has been individualized, but individualized *as* being-in-the-world. Being-in enters into the existential "mode" of the "not-at-home".[1]
>
> HEIDEGGER

> For Watt now found himself in the midst of things which, if they consented to be named, did so as it were with reluctance.
>
> (*Watt*, p.78)

Can a comparision of Beckett's work with Heidegger's fare any better than the comparison with Sartre's? It is true that, since, for all its originality, *Being and Nothingness* owes a great deal to the German philosopher, notions which, in a Sartrean context, appear to bear little relation to Beckett may seem rather more relevant in a Heideggerian one. But on the face of it Beckett and Heidegger seem not to have much in common. Beckett is a comic writer, capable of evoking a smile in the most tortured situations. Indeed the anguish of the Unnamable, the useless antics of the tramp are – whatever else they may be – *amusing*. If at times humour is not possible, there remains *wit*. And this quality takes us to the heart of Beckett's genius: Beckett is essentially a writer of *sensibility* (in the eighteenth-century as well as the modern sense), open to fine shades of meaning, sensitive to the hint of irony, fastidiously conscious of his aesthetic effects, in short, a writer keenly and critically selfregarding, *aware* (painfully and excitingly so) of the precise immediacy of experience. Now Heidegger has immense erudition, profound insights – but hardly wit. He is not as ponderous as impatient readers are liable to feel, but he is ponderous. Speaking of his processes of thought, however stimulating they may be, one is tempted to recall the remark made by Brahms of Bruckner's symphonies: that they are like boa constrictors. To English-speaking readers in particular his earnest seriousness must appear humourless, even, in spite of the astonishing novelty of what he has to say, pedantic. It may be that some of these comments are harsh. At any rate they serve to underline the point: in tone the work of Beckett is very different from that of Heidegger. And yet in one crucial respect there is a resemblance. One cannot read Beckett without a sense of his obsessiveness. This reveals itself even on the most superficial examination as a return to identical themes, situations and so on. It reveals itself more significantly still in Beckett's tenacious need to come to terms with his Irreducible. Heidegger too is obsessed by one idea, one reality. Obsession *defines the nature of his talent*, as it does Beckett's. Because of this, the comparison which will be developed in this chapter and the next is not without relevance to the world of the tramps and the Unnamable. Indeed it illuminates it, since it focusses attention on its structural essentials, those elements without which Beckett's work would not be what it is.

Heidegger's philosophy does not begin with man but with Existence, that is, with a unity of man and his world, with man involved in his world and not suspended in the speculative regions of the *cogito* or the Idealist Mind. It is not a question of saying that man exists but rather that he *is* an Existence, that his being is not enclosed but, in its very nature and not by a mere coincidence, a *relationship*. This position follows – as does Sartre's with somewhat different results – from Husserl's description of consciousness as inevitably consciousness of something other than itself. In *Being and Time* Heidegger introduces it by means of the central concept of *dasein*. *Dasein* is man, but man so viewed as to necessitate a new name for him and one which will not set him apart from his milieu but place him in it; thus it may be translated as being-there or *da-sein*. "There", of course, is the world. *Dasein* is not distinct from its surroundings. It is not such as to first *be* and then be *somewhere*, its being is a placing: it *is* "there", in the world, and it cannot, even theoretically, be separated from its "there" without which it would perhaps subsist but not *exist*. This means that *dasein* is not something in its own right, its "thereness" is not as it were *added on*. It is not an essence, a substance or *res* – *which also happens to exist*, like the Scholastic soul or even like the *cogito*. It is nothing but its Existence or, as Sartre would put it, its Existence is prior to its Essence. Heidegger sums up all of this by saying that *dasein* is a being-in-the-world.

Obviously being-in-the-world cannot be broken down into its constituent parts of "being" and "world"; it must be taken as a whole. Consequently the word "in" is to be understood in a more than spatial sense. *Dasein* is not "in" the world as, for example, a match is in a matchbox. Since *dasein* and the world imply each other, the world penetrates to *desein*'s very being, the relation is not external or measurable. Rather it is an internal relation of the kind we refer to when we speak of organic form in literature. In saying that a poem is an organic whole we mean that to change a part is to change the whole, that is, that a part of the poem in a real sense *contains* the whole, is as large as the whole. Heidegger is not putting forward the idea that without the human mind to observe it the material earth would no longer be. Without man *something* would be, but it would not be a *world*. It would be an inconceivable, undifferentiated material presence, much like the Sartrean *en soi* before the advent of the *pour soi*. But this is not what we refer to as the "world" – that comes into being with man. *Dasein*, then, is not in the world as a stranger. It exists in it in the sense of being "familiar" with it as one is with one's home as distinct from another's house. All this is not to deny that *dasein* is also a spatial being. But its spatial relations follow from and do not precede its ontological being-in-the-world. The Heideggerian notion, which goes beyond Husserl's stand, is at the heart of the comparable Sartrean concept of *situation*. To be in a situation, for Sartre, is to be inwardly penetrated by it, to be "there" in a sense of involvement. Of course in this case involvement is based, as we have seen, on negation: the *pour soi* can only *be outside itself* because it is not self-identical. In Heidegger's work I and my "there" represent a single phenomenon of a positive, not negative kind.

Like the *pour soi*, however, *dasein* is "ecstatic" in that it temporalizes itself, it spreads itself out, it lives *futurally* (and therefore free), as a being of schemes and plans. Thus I open a door in the *present* because I plan to be in the next room in the immediate *future*, because opening a door is a necessary part of my futural project to enter the next room. Clearly I am not bound by this, since I can always opt *not* to enter the room. What the future does is to determine not the performance but the *meaning* of present actions. We are now in a position to grasp more fully what Heidegger means by being-in-the-world. The "world" is not the brute presence of matter which could as easily be without man. It is man's own sphere of action, that framework of significance with which man surrounds himself. Again it may be defined as the meaning which the future confers upon the present. And this must be understood concretely. *Dasein* is involved with things, it confers meaning on them by utilizing them. It proclaims a door by opening it in order to get into another room. Thus a door becomes a means, a tool, something ready-to-hand: *zuhanden*. For *dasein*, existence is a vast ensemble of such means towards particular ends. To be "there" indicates just that. This fact is not without its implications in the sphere of social relations. Heidegger also calls *dasein mitsein*, being-with, since its human relations, like its relations with things, are not simply a matter of spatial proximity. The "with" suggests involvement, *dasein* is "with" in its very being, it is ontologically legion – which is as much as to say that it would not be *dasein* if it were alone, that the Other is built into its own makeup. (The same, of course, is true of the *pour soi*, but in a negative context, that is, not as *mitsein* but as ontological conflict.) For Heidegger, then, to say that man *exists* is to point to his nature as a thereness and a withness, that is, as a *relation*.

We may note at once that as Heidegger's philosophy, though existential in the same general sense as Sartre's, is not based on a contradiction, it approximates more closely to the world of Samuel Beckett. Yet Beckett's world is scarcely harmonious; the garrulous voice of consciousness is radically alienated from its context, the tramp is neither "at home" in his environment nor one with his fellows:

ESTRAGON: [*feebly*] Help me!
VLADIMIR: It hurts?
ESTRAGON: Hurts! He wants to know if it hurts!
VLADIMIR: [*angrily*] No one ever suffers but you . . . I'd like to hear what you'd say if you had what I have.
ESTRAGON: It hurts?
VLADIMIR: Hurts! He wants to know if it hurts! (p.10)

Likewise a concern with futural projects is conspicuously absent in the novels and plays. By the same token the degree of significance attached to the present is minimal. The point does not need to be laboured. From Belacqua to the weary narrator of *Company*, Beckett's subject lives in a "world" that has shrunk to a minimum. Moreover, since there is only one end in view, all things are invested with a single purpose, all reduced to a single function and, since the end is obscure, unable to be named, everything else is reduced to the status of an obstacle. Thus objects such as the glorious bicycle of the early work vanish from the austere standard equipment of the later tramps and even coats, hats, boots, turnips and the rest disappear by the time we have reached the end of the trilogy. It must be the same with human relationships. Murphy's affair with the devoted prostitute Celia is not viewed entirely with scepticism. By the time we reach the trilogy, love, though scarcely futile in the Sartrean sense, is rendered somewhat difficult. Molloy watches a couple in the window who "cleave so fast together that they seem a single body"; but it is all in vain for "when they totter it is clear that they are twain, and in vain they clasp with the energy of despair, it is clear we have here two distinct and separate bodies, each enclosed within its own frontiers" (p.238). Of course, even in the later work the Beckett subject may expect to be watched at every moment of its existence, in accordance with the Berkeleian dictum that to be is to be perceived. But the spectator is rejected as a fiction, from *The Unnamable* to *How it is* to *Company*. At this point being-with has been banished as effectively from Beckett's work as was being-in-the-world. More precisely, if the Beckett character inhabits a world of projects and companions, he does so in a strange way: his world collapses around him, objects lose their usefulness (Estragon's belt breaks, Malone misplaces his stick), then disappear (not even a fly can penetrate the chamber of *Company*'s narrator); people are distanced, then removed. Everything, in short, is in a state of disintegration. This fact has already been briefly analysed as an Occasionalist phenomenon, but it requires other perspectives as well.

Of course there are characters in Beckett who are not at odds with life. There is Moran (in *Molloy*) who owns a house, goes to church, has a job and is, all in all, as solid a citizen as one may hope to find in the trilogy; there is Pozzo. These characters may be thought of as representing what Heidegger terms "inauthentic" *dasein*, man "fallen" into everydayness, absorbed in inanities, unaware of himself or his situation. Their world, like that of their less conformist colleagues, falls quickly apart: Moran turns into his alter ego, the tramp Molloy; Pozzo goes blind. In the end, no matter where he began, the Beckett character is left with nothing. To see a relation between this phenomenon of disintegration and Heidegger's philosophy we must combine the idea of being-in-the-world with its obverse, that of *angst*.

In Kierkegaardian terms *angst* (or dread or anguish) is largely associated with the situation of sin, though it may also be regarded as *educative*, in the experience of faith. It is this second context which is more relevant here (both are discussed in *The Concept of Dread*). At the same time the specifically Christian colouring of Kierkegaard's notion may scarcely be expected in Heidegger's version and indeed may scarcely be expected to provide parallels with Beckett. Even so Kierkegaard introduces those critical elements of the concept which reappear in Heidegger: the idea that *angst* is connected with nothingness, with possibility – which is to say futurity and freedom – with a kind of vertigo, the individual's awareness of "I *can*".

Heideggerian *angst*, like that defined by Kierkegaard, represents an experience of reality. In this mood of terror *dasein* is said to face itself and its situation in a way it does not normally do when it is absorbed in everyday things. Under the influence of *angst* normality collapses. Inauthentic schemes and plans lose their credibility. Objects assume an alien form and the safety of social existence disappears. Everything previously familiar to *dasein*, its very world, is now steeped in strangeness, in a feeling of otherness which Heidegger terms the Uncanny. It is as if *dasein* were no longer a being-in-the-world, but had acquired a new identity, alone, set apart from all things and from itself. In fact it remains all that it was, but in a new way:

> Everyday familiarity collapses. Dasein has been individualized, but individualized *as* Being-in-the-world. Being-in enters into the existential "mode" of the "*not-at-home*".[1]

In his 1929 lecture "What is Metaphysics?", Heidegger explains this feeling as an awareness of the reality of nothingness. As the everyday recedes into meaninglessness, *dasein* feels that its world has lost its solidity and hovers over a vast emptiness. It becomes aware that it itself is a void, a mere phantom, not the substantial Self it supposed itself to be but a freedom or a possibility. To be free, as *dasein* normally is, to build a house or buy a car is one thing, to be faced with the fact of freedom in its entirety is another. *Dasein* becomes dizzy on the edge of the void which is inescapable since it is itself that void. At the same time its every action seems permeated by nullity, it becomes a kind of nothing, since, after all, it is free, it may be carried through or not depending on *dasein*'s choice. "Why do this?" *dasein* finds itself asking of everything it does. Why not? However, the experience of nothingness is also an experience of being. Even as it reveals the immaterial transparency of things, *angst* underlines their substantiality. As nothingness pours into the world, *dasein*'s existence also obtrudes in all its monolithic facticity, that is, as an inescapable *fact*. Thus *dasein* is simultaneously exposed to the void and stifled by being, everything recedes only to crowd, the world retreats as "uncanny" only to advance as an inexorable presence. *Angst*, then, may be simply defined as a revelation of man's situation. Man is free and so, as in Sartrean philosophy, a kind of nothing. He is also *dasein*, being-*there*. Thus what is most vivid in the experience of *angst* is the sense of being thrust into an unbearable disclosure, as if existence were precisely "thereness", a being-out-in-the-open, a standing out or *ex-sistere*. At the same time *angst* highlights existence by situating it over the void of the unfamiliar, indicating clearly to man that he is free, a being shot through with holes. No more ingenious torture could be devised for one whose greatest impulse is to avoid responsibility and the facts of his position. *Angst* is, above all, heightened consciousness, the truth of existence seen not blindfold as it were but in the glare of a horrifyingly simple insight: Heidegger's "Moment of Vision".

It is not difficult to relate much of this to the Sartrean concepts of Nausea and the Absurd, as well as to Camus' Absurd. In spite of radical differences, *dasein* and the *pour soi* are plagued by the burden of existence, by freedom and facticity. Without doubt, Sartre had *Being and Time* in mind when he wrote a great deal of *Being and Nothingness*. Camus himself, in his description of the Absurd as a break with habit, as an alienation, probably owes something to the same source, though his immediate mentor is Kierkegaard. But his treatment of the great Kierkegaardian theme is, by comparison with Sartre's and Heidegger's, imprecise and journalistic.

As early as *Proust* Beckett shows an interest in the breakup of habit ("the ballast that chains the dog to his vomit", (p.19)) and the moment of discomfort and insight which results. It means an entry into "perilous zones . . . dangerous, precarious, painful, mysterious and fertile, when for a moment the boredom of living is replaced by the suffering of being . . . that is, the free play of every faculty" (pp.19–20). We can see in this a partial description of *angst*, that intense consciousness of being unrelieved by the opiates of doing. Once we turn to Beckett's own work it is soon evident that the tramps, alienated from the everyday world of the sane, exist in a no-man's-land which is precisely this perilous zone of contact with reality and which is for them a natural and enduring state.

However, an analysis of Beckett in terms of Heideggerian *angst* must begin with *Watt* and particularly with the fascinating incident of the piano-tuners. The Galls, father and son, arrive at Mr Knott's to tune the piano and Watt observes them as they go about their job. When they have finished the two leave and, for Watt, the torment begins:

> . . . the scene in the music-room, with the two Galls, ceased very soon to signify for Watt a piano tuned . . . an exchange of judgements more or less intelligible, and so on . . . and became a mere example of light commenting bodies, and stillness motion, and silence sound, and comment comment. (pp.69–70)

The more Watt tries to plumb the significance of this obscure visit the more it evades him until he finds himself confused about his very acts of perception. The event seems to dissolve into nothingness and yet it cannot be overlooked. In a sense it is a nothing that continues to happen as he broods over it in its

> . . . complex connexions of . . . lights and shadows, the passing from silence to sound and from sound to silence, the stillness before the movement and the stillness after, the quickenings

> and retardings, the approaches and the separations, all the shifting detail of its march and ordinance, according to the irrevocable caprice of its taking place. (p.69)

To settle the question by insisting that there is nothing out of the ordinary here, simply a pair of workmen, a piano, an arrival, a few words and a departure, would suit Watt very well. But the event acquires an impenetrable density to Watt's mind. How to comprehend, to rationalize a brute fact, if the visit was that?

> What distressed Watt in this incident . . . was not so much that he did not know what had happened . . . as that nothing had happened, that a thing that was nothing had happened, with the utmost formal distinctness, and that it continued to happen, in his mind, he supposed . . . inexorably to unroll its phases, beginning with the first (the knock that was not a knock) and ending with the last (the door closing that was not a door closing) . . . (p.73)

The Galls' visit is, of course, an irreducible, a non-event which takes place. Watt needs a hypothesis to explain it unless he is to admit utter bankruptcy in his attempt to give human meaning to reality. As it happens, he fails and the disintegration of experience involved in the incident of the Galls gradually extends to all his life: "for Watt now found himself in the midst of things which, if they consented to be named, did so as it were with reluctance" (p.78).

Watt is faced with a unique experience, the falling away of normality and everyday significance characteristic of Heideggerian *angst*. In spite of all his efforts his world takes on an alien colouring, a strangeness akin to the Uncanny. As he gazes at a pot in the kitchen

> . . . it was in vain that Watt said, Pot, pot . . . For it was not a pot, the more he looked, the more he reflected, the more he felt sure of that, that it was not a pot at all. It resembled a pot, it was almost a pot, but it was not a pot of which one could say, Pot, pot, and be comforted. It was in vain that it answered, with unexceptionable adequacy, all the purposes, and performed all the offices, of a pot, it was not a pot. And it was just this

> hairbreadth departure from the nature of a true pot that so excruciated Watt. (p.78)

No finer tragicomic parallel to the Heideggerian experience could be found in modern literature. As Watt's sense of the familiarity of things is undermined by a kind of vaporous nothingness, his being-in-the-world, as Heidegger would say, takes on the aspect of the not-at-home. Bereft of purpose, everything sinks into the night of the Uncanny as Watt makes "the distressing discovery that of himself too he could no longer affirm anything that did not seem as false as if he had affirmed it of a stone" (p.79). Panic-stricken he attempts to assign names arbitrarily. But the "pseudo-pot" (p.80) is no more responsive when labelled a shield or a raven. As for himself:

> . . . he continued to think of himself as a man, as his mother has taught him, when she said, There's a good little man, or, There's a bonny little man, or, There's a clever little man. But for all the relief that this afforded him, he might just as well have thought of himself as a box, or an urn. (p.80)

The "pillow of old words, for his head" (p.115) is gone. Watt is alone. Between him and other human beings, as between him and his world in general, is a film of strangeness. In Heideggerian terms being-in-the-world has been challenged by the void. Yet, as in the experience of *angst*, nothingness *crowds*. Even as Watt is separated from normal reality the impenetrable *fact* of things, or rather nothings, is thrust upon him. The simple event which may be termed the Galls baffles but it is there, a fact without content, a happening without meaning and so a non-event, a being-nothing. Everything recedes and sinks into an abyss only to torment Watt with its inexplicable presence. As he founders, Watt is forced to question even sense perception. Perhaps there is a brute *sine qua non*, and all the rest is fantasy, human construction: "were there neither Galls nor piano then, but only an unintelligible succession of changes from which Watt finally extracted the Galls and the piano, in self-defence?" (p.76). Heideggerian *angst* and the empirical scepticism of Hume are here combined. Watt has plumbed a certain depth of being, away from the facile explanations of the sane, and has gazed at a void emanating from himself and engulfing the whole of life about him.

We may say the same of Vladimir and Estragon who experience a breakdown similar to Watt's although Beckett's emphasis in *Waiting for Godot* differs from that in the novel. Unlike Watt, the tramps have something to anticipate; thus the present becomes partially meaningful, there is something to *do*. But since Godot cannot be reached except negatively, through waiting, doing is reduced to a minimum: "this is becoming really insignificant" (p.68). Vladimir's and Estragon's power to act is simply a licence to wait, to madden themselves with what is, in effect, *negative* action. Thus, after all, there is "nothing to be done" (p.9) and the vision of *angst* is inescapable. The two exist in a world that is strange to them, alienated from all sense of purpose except for the imperative of waiting. Under these conditions normal living is reduced to very little, to minimal human relations, to minimal utilization of material objects. An emptiness of futurity; which is an emptiness of freedom, invades the present:

VLADIMIR: . . . What do we do now?

ESTRAGON: Wait.

VLADIMIR: Yes, but while waiting. (p.17)

It is the very magnitude of their possibilities that cripples the tramps. The world is theirs to fill with significance, but where are they to begin? The vision of freedom with its naked austerity can only be expressed as *angst*; one gazes, fascinated and appalled, and one continues to gaze, indefinitely. At the same time it would be quite inadequate to consider *Waiting for Godot* simply as a play illustrative of the existential breakdown of being-in-the-world, of meaning, of relations. Over and above all of this it requires to be considered in terms of Heideggerian facticity. Even as they are assailed from all sides by freedom, by nothingness, the tramps are obsessed with the *fact* of being, with the inescapability of existence, in a way Watt is not. Of course they feel their being-*there* because they are waiting, but even if there were no Godot, if this were merely a waiting for the end of existence, it would make no difference. Godot, after all, is that one necessary reference point, that one brute fact which explains all other brute facts, and is not that existence itself? Waiting is not incidental to Vladimir and Estragon, it is their very being, an image of their facticity, and so the two are necessarily, abnormally aware of being *there*, without reprieve. This is not simply the facticity of the Sartrean *pour-soi*, any more than their freedom is that of Sartrean consciousness. It resembles it, of course, as Heidegger's system resembles that of Sartre, but it does not presuppose any of the radical antinomies of *Being and Nothingness*. The tramps know that they *are* and cannot help it, that they *have* to be free. To their eyes this is no freedom at all. They may choose to go or stay, but what difference does it make, since whether here or there they are forced to exist? With this monstrous proviso anything they choose to do is the same as anything else, any place they choose to occupy is the same as any other, it is all a being-in-the-world:

> ESTRAGON: . . . Look at this muckheap! I've never stirred from it! (p.61)

One can argue along comparable lines for most of Beckett's characters. There is Winnie of *Happy Days* who is in some respects more clear-sighted than Vladimir and Estragon. Of course she exhibits what Beckett has termed "our pernicious and incurable optimism" (*Proust*, p.15), but her presentation is not antipathetic. In any case, she is no naive optimist. Her little games, her song, her memories, all this exists on the brink of the void and Winnie knows it. Like Vladimir and Estragon she tries to fill her empty day with trivia, unable to escape the awareness of her precarious hold on things. In the final analysis she faces her despair and makes the best of it, living in the Heideggerian Uncanny: "Strange? (*Pause.*) No, here all is strange" (p.33). Winnie is alone, knowing how little she may rely on Willie. There are little comforts of course – the bag and its contents, sad relic of *dasein*'s triumphant projects into the world of doing, her prayers and her thoughts of the past – but there is no question of shutting out the terror of being: "sorrow keeps breaking in" (p.27). She opens with an act of calculated self-control: "Begin your day, Winnie". (p.10). It is the motto of the voice of the Unnamable: "On, Winnie". (p.12). If Winnie is a little person, a conventional lady with conventional illusions, there is nothing conventional about her courage: "Brush and comb the hair . . . these things tide one over". (p.20) Significantly, as in *Waiting for Godot*, the full force of *angst* is concentrated on the awareness of one's Existence as a naked *fact*. The tramps have no wish to move: being in one place is no different from being in another if one has no option about being-in-the-world. In Winnie's case this is underlined by the image of immobility. The sandpile which gradually swallows her up (but of course never *completely*) is a mirror of her existential predicament, an image of the facticity of Existence which prevents her from embracing the only real alternative: non-being. No wonder Winnie moves closer and closer to panic as the play proceeds. It is a panic which underlies many of Beckett's plots. The dialogue of *Embers* is punctuated with it in the form of Henry's anguished pleas ("Ada! (*Pause.*) Father! (*Pause.*) Christ!")[2] or the frenzied cries of the suffering child, Addie, or the imploring feminine "don't! Don't" (p.31) of a sexual encounter. The mood of terror is captured for the play as a whole in the begging of Bolton to Holloway: "Please! (*Pause.*) Please! (*Pause.*) Please, Holloway!" (p.38) What Bolton probably wants is merciful release, but his "please!" may also be taken in the sense of an insistent human demand for pity. *Embers* illustrates a situation of disintegration in which Henry, the protagonist, vainly seeks to keep the void of total solitude at bay. The need for amusement which drives Vladimir and Estragon to their games is here reduced to a terrifying struggle. In desperation Henry invokes the voice of memory, that of Ada, his wife ("Keep on, Keep on! (*Imploringly.*) Keep it going, Ada, every syllable is a second gained," (p.36)). But everything fades except the protagonist's voice. This is a radio play, moreover. Any silence whatsoever here means *oblivion*. The sense of *angst*, a simple, total facing of the reality of the human abyss, is nowhere more clearly evident in Beckett's work. Still, one thinks, for example, of the frenzy of the protagonist of *Film*, shrinking from the observing eye. In this case we may say that Buster Keaton, in flight from the gaze of his own *cogito*, is equally in flight from the awareness of Existence. And here the link between the entire Cartesian tradition with its stress on mind and the concept of *angst* is evident. To suffer *angst* is to suffer one's own consciousness, enclosed within the boundaries of Existence, which is to say, of oneself. Of course the Beckett character from Belacqua onwards is condemned to such self-knowledge.

On the whole it is the privilege and curse of the characters of the trilogy and the later work to see the truth most clearly and with least evasion. It is true that they tend to live in a state of torpor, but this is only in respect of everyday things. When it comes to the one thing necessary the tramp's mind is horrifyingly active: "a fine rain was falling and I took off my hat to give my skull the benefit of it, my skull all cracked and furrowed and on fire, on fire" (*Molloy*, p.61). Molloy, like Watt, has lost all contact with normality: "and even my sense of identity was wrapped in a namelessness . . . there could be no things but nameless things, no names but thingless names" (p.31). Malone is in the same situation, living "in strangeness" (p.183), absorbed in the wisdom which puts all else in the perspective of existence: "dish and pot . . . these are the poles" (p.185). The tramp has left behind inauthentic relations, he does not act, he is alone, able to do everything and nothing (it is now the same thing), aware only of the fact of being, a growing claustrophobia and immobility imaged in the little room, the bed, or, worse, the area of the skull. Even more clearly than in *Film* we see the family relationship between the Cartesian tradition and the idea of *angst*. To be in the state of *angst* is to be conscious, to *be* – obsessively. It is a situation none can escape: "so long as it is what is called a living being you can't go wrong, you have the guilty one" (p.260). All of this is taken to its ultimate point in *The Unnamable*. Of course we cannot speak of the Unnamable itself as suffering the awareness of existence. This plight is reserved for the voice of the Unnamable, the voice of consciousness which, as we have seen, is not to be confused with the true Irreducible. Here, more than ever, to be conscious is to groan in *angst*, to live out one's time in a Heideggerian Moment of Vision. The Voice has cut all links with normality, it is supremely individualized in its utter solitude, it is supremely free, without interest in any particular project, unconcerned with everyday significance, above all, painfully existing as *there*, in situation. Thus its immobility goes beyond anything envisaged by the tramps. Its space is that of the *cogito*, of course, the dimensions of a skull, but it is equally that of Heideggerian "finitude", the space of a moment of agonizing lucidity. Like the tramps, the Voice has no choice: it gazes at itself, drawn by the power of the terrible vision. Such torment coupled with clear-sightedness is the mark of most later Beckett characters (though it should be added that the old razor-edge of panic is less sharp in some of the very recent work – like *That Time* or *Company* – where the tone is more elegiac than anguished). One thinks of the repressed agony which breaks out at the end of *Rockaby* ("rock her off/rock her off", p.20), or of the terrible "white nights" casually referred to in *Ohio Impromptu* ("the fearful symptoms described at length page forty paragraph four")[3], or of the exquisite fineness of torment depicted in *Still*, or of the confused, panic-stricken outpourings of *Not I*.

Without unduly blurring the distinction between art and philosophy it is possible to read a great deal of Heidegger into the situation of the Beckett character. If at first sight the world of the tramps and the voice seems unlike that of *dasein* it is because it is viewed through the eyes of subjects for whom something very like Heideggerian *angst* is a natural condition. The Beckett tramp recalls *dasein*, but *dasein* scarred by self-knowledge. Moreover, in so far as his situation resembles that in Heidegger it will also resemble that of Sartre's *pour soi* and of Camus' *l'homme absurde*. The latter similarity, though, must be regarded as somewhat incidental: Beckett's world is based neither on a Sartrean dichotomy nor on the humanism of Camus but, as we shall see, on assumptions very like Heidegger's. At this point it is evident that Beckett's Reduction, that pruning down to essentials, is once more in philosophical focus. The Reduction, which approximates to the disintegrating vision of the Occasionalists, may be viewed in modern terms as analogous to the levelling gaze of Heideggerian *angst*. Thus in Beckett's hands the *cogito* transforms itself into a startling awareness of existence, the previously underestimated implications of the seemingly innocuous *ergo sum*. One might well say, with a little poetic licence, that a student of the history of philosophy from the seventeenth century to the present could learn more from *Watt* or *Waiting for Godot* or *The Unnamable* than from a great many conventional histories.

5 Beckett and Heidegger: Existence, nothingness and Being

> The being that exists is man. Man alone exists. Rocks are, but they do not exist. Trees are, but they do not exist. . . God is, but he does not exist.[1]
>
> HEIDEGGER

> It would be premature to . . . adopt the facile explanation that Nothing is merely the nugatory, equating it with the non-existent . . . we should rather equip ourselves . . . to experience in Nothing the vastness of that which gives every being the warrant to be. That is Being itself.[2]
>
> HEIDEGGER

> . . . a being so light and free that it is as the being of nothing.
>
> (*Watt*, p. 38)

So far, little has been said about the Irreducible, that core of Beckett's inspiration. *Angst*, which threatens existence with the presence of the void, nevertheless *affirms* existential realities. Beckett, on the other hand, takes trouble to depict the existential predicament of the tramp or the voice of consciousness only as a means to an end: the uncovering of the vital mystery of the Irreducible, which resides *beneath* the level of consciousness. It follows that the Irreducible stands aloof from the torments of *angst*, indeed from existence itself as understood by Heidegger. As a being-nothing it represents that impossible point, infinitely close and infinitely distant, just *beyond* the area of the existential. There is, however, a comparable development in Heidegger's philosophy. To illustrate this point we must return to comments made in chapter two: in spite of its prominence in Heidegger's first work, *Being and Time*, *dasein* is not the central protagonist of the Heideggerian stage. As early as *Being and Time* Heidegger states that the analysis of *dasein*, that is, of the existential, is of secondary importance and that the real search is for *Sein*, that is, for Being as distinct from being-there:

> Do we in our time have an answer to the question of what we really mean by the word "being"? Not at all. So it is fitting that we should raise anew the *question of the meaning of Being*. But are we nowadays even perplexed at our inability to understand the expression "Being"?[3]

The trouble is that we are not. Being, says Heidegger, has been "forgotten" and this term has technical connotations in *Being and Time* which link it to inauthenticity. Lost in the confusion of the mundane, *dasein* is so alienated from *Being* that it has no idea of it and even no idea that there is something there to be understood. And to the reader's surprised "is not man, being-there, a particular example of Being?" Heidegger's disconcerting answer is "no". *Dasein*, being-there, existence – the terms are synonymous – is not merely identical with Being. As Heidegger puts it in his introduction to "What is Metaphysics?":

> The being that exists is man. Man alone exists. Rocks are, but they do not exist. Trees are, but they do not exist . . . God is, but he does not exist. (p.214)

Thus *Being and Time* will begin with *dasein* or existence and, by an analysis of this, attempt to approach Being itself. At this point the empirical philosopher throws up his hands in exasperation, but Heidegger is undeterred and insists on a distinction between Being and existence or between Being and human consciousness. Of course Sartre preserves this distinction: the *en soi*, after all, is defined as being and the *pour soi* as existence. Existence, in other words, is a term applicable only to humans. But in Heidegger the consequences of this approach are quite different. The German thinker does not see Being as Sartre sees the *en soi*. Nor does he see it as a Universal. On the whole when we think of being we are likely to say "it is that which all existing things have in common"; in other words, we are likely to think of all existing things as *particular* cases of being. In this way of looking at things, being is not something in its own right but a class within which all that exists must fall, the most universal of all concepts. Heidegger flatly rejects this way of thinking: Being is not a *genus*, it is not a category, a mere abstraction. On the contrary it is more real than particular existing things. Far from being the lowest common denominator of everything, arrived at by a process of abstraction from the Particular, Being is what is *originally* manifested. Everything *presupposes* it, it is the *condition* of things. Being enters the world through man, that is, it is situated or "placed" as being-there. Without *dasein* or man Being would "be" but it would be concealed, it would not be "there", it would not "ex-sist" or stand out in the light. Thus man, who is Existence, may be said to *exist Being*. Of course he does not create it, he is merely the agent of the revelation: Being cannot be "the product of man".[4] If we persist in thinking in terms of concrete and abstract, of Particulars and Universals, Heidegger's stand will remain incomprehensible. But perhaps the student of literature will more readily accept the imaginative leap that is necessary for the reader of Heidegger than will some professional philosophers. Heidegger's case is argued again and again, in *Being and Time* (1927), in the lecture "What is Metaphysics?" (1929), in "On the Essence of Truth" (1943), the *Letter on Humanism* (1947), *An Introduction to Metaphysics* (1953), *The Question of Being* (1956), *Discourse on Thinking* (1959), "The End of Philosophy and the Task of Thinking" (1964) and elsewhere. Being is prior to speculation, it is the *ground* of things, an *urgrund*, revealed in *dasein*'s instinctive recognition of it. Moreover it is not something obvious but a forgotten mystery requiring constant rediscovery. We may say concisely that Being is not synonymous with "beings". The distinguishing feature of man is that his relationship as being-there to Being is unique.

The issue is nowhere more strongly stated than in the two lectures (given in 1957) which constitute *Identity and Difference*. In the first of these, "The Principle of Identity", Heidegger asks simple questions about and gives complex answers to the nature of "sameness". A = A or, better still, A is A implies not mere unity but (using an Idealist term) *mediation*, in short, sameness implies difference. The key to it all is in the "is" of A is A, since that "is" tells us as much about being as sameness. Thus the principle of identity, that a thing is itself, leads us to the question of being, or rather of that fundamental sameness-in-difference, the relation of beings with Being, the Being of beings. Heidegger, with his usual appeal to the pre-Socratics, expounds all of this on the basis of the Parmenidean text: "being and thinking are the same". Of course "thinking" here is readily understood as *dasein* or consciousness, so that the text may be read in the following way: "Being and beings (or *dasein*) are the same." It may be objected that this is a very complicated way of saying that something (man, for example) *is*, that his being is his identity, his sameness with himself. But for Heidegger these notions are not self-explanatory or transparent. To exist is to "belong together"[5] with Being, with the emphasis not on the second but the first word. This is because Being and beings are not *first* posited, *then* related. On the contrary, we first posit their *sameness*, then their being *themselves*. All this brings us to the notion of "appropriation". Man *is* his relation with Being. Open to Being, he "lets Being arrive as presence".[6] Rather than saying that self-identity is a characteristic of being, we must say that "being belongs with thinking [i.e. man] to an identity whose active essence stems from . . . the appropriation",[7] that is, from the primordial act in which the two, Being and man, are as it were delivered over to each other, "appropriated" one for the other. If we may talk of the relation in terms of sameness, we may equally do so in terms of difference, especially since this difference is always glossed over by philosophers who make no distinction between Being and beings. In his second *Identity and Difference* lecture, "The Onto-Theo-Logical Constitution of Metaphysics", Heidegger follows such a procedure. Just as previously he argued that the notion of sameness is not *added on* to the being of things, so now he stresses that the notion of difference is prior also. Just as sameness *was* (prior to) the relation of Being and beings, so too difference *is* that relation, is presupposed *in* the relation. To quote an example from Hegel (adapted for rather different ends by Gilbert Ryle in *The Concept of Mind*), one can buy apples, pears, etc., but one cannot buy "fruit". Being is that which says "I'm here already",[8] whether we speak of likeness or unlikeness. The heart of Heidegger's argument is that Being as it were *transits* over to beings, but not in such a way as to suggest the one without the other. It is an *überkommnis*, a coming-over or over-whelming, an unconcealing which leaves man, its point of entry, obscure about the nature of the event, yet totally dependent on it. Man's role is to *bear* this "arrival" (*ankunft*) which is its own self. The role of Being is to over-whelm man, in whom it is revealed as "*unconcealing keeping in concealment*".[9] But these concepts may be left for the present, since their bearing on the discussion will be more apparent in the context of later chapters.

In order to see the relevance of all of this to the concept of *angst* we must elaborate another aspect of Heidegger's philosophy. In his *An Introduction to Metaphysics* Heidegger discusses the fundamental question first raised by Leibniz: "Why beings (instead of nothing)?" Actually, it is the question which is of interest rather than the answer, since its asking is a "privileged happening", a Kierkegaardian "leap"[10] beyond security. And this because the question recoils threateningly on itself and turns into "why the why?"[11] One cannot ask "why do things exist?" without questioning onself and taking the ground as it were from under one's feet. Heidegger thinks of the Question as the origin of metaphysics, that is, as a *meta-physis*, a going beyond all things. To question is to transcend or, again, to go beneath all things, to the ground of all things. Now what is beneath, what supports all "beings", is Being. Thus the effect of the Metaphysical Question is to rediscover forgotten Being in a movement which belongs to the very nature of man since the function of *dasein* is precisely to reveal *Sein*. We may state the issue concisely by saying that the Question takes us to the Being of beings. Only in freedom can this discovery be made. That is to say, no amount of intellectuality will suffice. Man *chooses* to see Being, it is a case of *crede ut intelligas*. The link between the Question and *angst* should now be clear: they are two sides of the same coin. One cannot ask, "why beings?" except in fear and trembling, that is, in *angst*. *Angst*, like the Metaphysical Question, is a questioning of all things which disintegrates everyday, inauthentic reality. Of course in questioning and so placing everything over the void one also affirms its actuality, one highlights one's own thereness and the concrete fact of one's world even as one holds it all at arm's length. Thus *angst* reveals man as existing, as being-there and in the same breath, it reveals Being itself, the substratum on which existence rests. It shows me that I exist but it also questions my existence and so points to something *beneath* it. Existence, then, is not obliterated but seen in true perspective, as contingent, as originating in something beyond itself.

Heidegger does not always need to use the term *angst* to refer to the complex of ideas outlined above. In *Identity and Difference*, he speaks simply of a "leap" from man to Being which defines the nature of "appropriation":

> This spring is the abruptness of the unbridged entry into that belonging which alone can grant a towards-each-other of man and Being . . . The spring is the abrupt entry into the realm from which man and Being have already reached each other in their active nature, since both are mutually appropriated, extended as a gift, one to the other. Only the entry into the realm of this mutual appropriation determines and defines the experience of thinking.[12]

It is, as Heidegger adds, a very curious leap, since it takes us to the place we inhabited from the beginning, that is, it returns us to ourselves. Of special interest, however, is the reference to "thinking". At the end of "On the Essence of Truth" Heidegger speaks of a "way of thinking which, instead of furnishing representations and concepts, experiences and tries itself as a transformation of its relatedness to Being".[13] A similar point is elaborated in the *Letter on Humanism*, in that case as a reply to Sartre. Thinking, Heidegger stresses, is not simply an activity in the Sartrean sense, "*l'engagement dans l'action* for and by beings"; it is "*l'engagement* by and for the truth of Being".[14] Again: "said plainly, thinking is the thinking of Being".[15] This does not mean that all human thought is the thought of Being, understood in the sense of a Hegelian Absolute. It means that thought cannot be regarded as passive, a mere "furnishing" of "concepts": it must be seen as a way of being, something that expresses (or rather *actualizes*) reality. Thus "to 'philosophize' about being shattered" is a very different thing from "a thinking that is shattered".[16] We are again in the sphere of *angst*. Thinking, as Heidegger conceives it, is yet another – or rather the one – way to uncover the ground of existence, namely Being. Man, "belonging to Being, because thrown by Being into the preservation of its truth and claimed for such preservation . . . thinks Being".[17] Thought of this kind represents a more important, though essentially humbler, form of activity than Sartrean (or Marxist) *praxis*. The same truth emerges in the 1951–2 lectures gathered under the title "What is Called Thinking?". Of course it all boils down to something drastically simple: in redefining thought in this way Heidegger is merely asking for a kind of thinking which really *is* thinking. It is here that the connection between concepts as diverse as those of the Question, Thinking, the leap and *angst* becomes evident. In order to act in a way that is properly human, man, the *dasein* of the earlier work, must shake his own foundations. In so doing he will *affirm* their reality and also *query* it, he will *be* a being-there and also a creature whose home is not in himself but in Being, the Other which is *dasein*.

The parallel with Beckett is immediately obvious. The whole of Beckett's work is a voice which questions and so undermines all reality, seeking to reduce it to its ultimate unit: the Irreducible. It is the voice of Cartesian doubt translated into the modern predicament of existential *angst*, questioning which questions itself. In the opening words of *The Unnamable*:

> Where now? Who now? When now? Unquestioning. I, say I Unbelieving. (p.293)

Just as the Reduction initiated by these precarious statements leads us beyond the area of consciousness that is, of the existential, to that of the Unnamable, that hidden presence on which all else depends, so Heideggerian *angst* or, in the strictest sense, "thinking", leads beyond the sphere of *dasein* to that of the ground phenomenon of Being. The same distinction made in Heidegger's work between existence and Being or between *dasein* and *Sein* appears in Beckett as the distinction between the anguished situation of the tramps or the voice of consciousness on the one hand and the utterly different reality of the Unnamable on the other.

What happens in Beckett is this. The voice opens in *angst*, instantly dispelling the world of normality, tumbling it into the void, negating everything including itself ("I, say I. Unbelieving"). In doing so it paradoxically *affirms* as well, both itself and its world, it proclaims tormentedly its *thereness* in a stifling universe. So the end result is both denial and affirmation, a denial which turns into an affirmation and so requires to be followed by another denial which itself stands as a new affirmation. The pattern then becomes one of deny-affirm-deny, of question-establish-question, the "eternal tautology" of "yes or no" (*Murphy*, p.32), the "screaming silence of no's knife in yes's wound" (*Texts*, p.135), the "old road . . . up yes and down no" (*Texts*, p.123), the struggle of "choke, go down, come up, choke, suppose, deny, affirm, drown" (*Molloy*, p.210). The finest examples of this pattern are found in the *Texts* and *The Unnamable*. Thus the fourth Text opens with a question which is at once followed by an astonished: "who is asking this?" It is a stranger who seeks the subject, the source of all questioning, the one who is and is not there:

> I'm not in his head, nowhere in his old body, and yet I'm there . . . That should have been enough for him, to have found me absent, but it's not, he wants me there, with a form and a world, like him . . . me who am everything, like him who is nothing. (p.87)

Clearly "he" will not be satisfied until he has reduced the Other to himself, let us say to a "head" or a "body", that is to say to a voice or a tramp or, failing that, to an absence – but an absence comparable to his own:

> And when he feels me void of existence it's of his he would have me void, and vice versa . . . The truth is he's looking for me to kill me, to have me dead like him, like the living. He knows all that, but . . . I don't know it, I know nothing. (p.87)

In this last statement it may be said that the Irreducible has assumed its primal identity as the impassive "I" behind the tormented "he". But this is not possible, since we began with the question. "who is asking this?" Beckett's Irreducible can no more be "I" than "he". The one who asks is the Unnamable (who else *could* ask?), yet the Unnamable *cannot* ask, it must be someone else. It is the same at the conclusion of the trilogy, where the narrator speaks of "he who lived, or saw some who had, he speaks of me, as if I were he, as if I were not he, both . . .". The one who lived is the sufferer, the Other is removed from all that. Yet in uttering this statement the narrator, that is, the Other, is required to attribute it to the sufferer: "he is the afflicted, I am far, do you hear him, he says I'm far, as if I were he, no, as if I were not he . . .". As in the *Texts*, the result of this tortured dialectic is an endless coming and going, an advancing and a receding in the face of the impossible *fact*, that something which is nothing is taking place, that someone is speaking of no one – and vice versa:

> . . . it's he who speaks, he says it's I, then he says it's not . . . he calls me, he wants me to come out, he thinks I can come out, he wants me to be he . . . he thinks he's caught me, he feels me in him, then he says I, as if I were he . . . it's always he who speaks . . . I never spoke, I seem to speak, that's because he says I, I nearly believed him, do you hear him, as if he were I, I who am far . . . (p.407)

At critical points of this constant negation, it is as if the (infinite) distance between the two were about to be bridged. Just then the Unnamable swings away from the "delegate" and affirms its separateness – precisely by *vanishing*, by attributing *the negation itself* to someone other than itself: "do you hear him . . .". In other words we begin with the voice saying "it's me", which is followed by the Unnamable saying "it's not me", which is followed in turn by the Unnamable saying "the one who says it's me *and* the one who says its not me is the voice". At this point the identity behind the voice disappears, nothing is left *but* the voice, and moreover, we are assured nothing was *ever* there except the voice. But then where does the voice come from, *whose* voice is it? It must be the Unnamable's. So we begin again, only to end as before, to begin again as before. This is Beckett's creative rhythm – the expansion and contraction of excretion, the spasm of birth and death, the logical pattern of *pro* and *contra*. But it is not a rhythm of frustration, like that of the Sartrean *pour soi*. On the contrary, it is Beckett's way of pointing to the Irreducible and comparable to the Heideggerian uncovering of Being. The voice whose task it is to name the Unnamable begins by denying itself since the Unnamable is other than itself. As it denies, it also affirms – as Descartes saw, my doubting proves that I exist. But to affirm consciousness is to deny the Unnamable beneath it, so the voice again denies itself. The pattern continues indefinitely and of course the Unnamable is never reached. But this does not matter. Indirectly, the Unnamable *is* revealed – as the reality *beneath* the wrestling of Yes and No, as the ground which makes affirmation and denial possible. In like manner the experience of Heideggerian *angst*, able to speak *directly* only of existence, that is, of itself, manages to speak *indirectly* of Being, that mystery at the heart of existence.

But the Irreducible is also a negative, or rather a paradoxical being-nothing. Again the comparison with Heideggerian Being can be sustained, in this case by reference to "What is Metaphysics?", the lecture Heidegger delivered to the University of Freiburg when he took up the chair of philosophy vacated by Husserl. Heidegger proposes to discuss nothingness, which, he argues, is not simply an abstraction, as most logicians have assumed, but something which "is" in a distinctive way and consequently deserves serious consideration. He refers his audience to the phenomenon of *angst*. Nothingness is actually *experienced* in the uncanniness of *angst* and so *angst* is the starting-point for the analysis of nothingness:

> All things, and we with them, sink into a sort of indifference. But not in the sense that everything simply disappears; rather, in the very act of drawing away from us everything turns towards us. This withdrawal of what-is-in-totality, which then crowds round us in dread [*angst*], this is what oppresses us. There is nothing to hold on to. The only thing that remains and overwhelms us whilst what-is slips away, is this "nothing".[18]

In *angst*, man experiences a sense of the whole of existence and of nothingness simultaneously, the whole of things being *questioned*, that is, undermined by the void, and accentuated by this same void, at once invalidated and reaffirmed. But what is this nothing that is revealed in *angst*? Heidegger replies that it is something which enters the world through man. Nothingness is active, it does not obliterate things but reveals them in their strangeness, as if hanging in mid-air. In questioning the reality of things, nothingness affirms them, it reveals them as positive in contrast to itself, it serves as it were a *creative* function. This is a surprising conclusion but it follows from the entire philosophy of *angst*. All things emerge *ex nihilo*, nothingness is the origin of things. It follows that nothingness is responsible for man also and indeed this idea is implicit in Heidegger's earliest work. *Dasein* is free:

this means that it is "permeated with nullity through and through".[19] To be free is to be shot through with nothingness, much as is the *pour soi*. To be free and to exist are one and the same. Thus *angst* shows man that he is a void, in short, it shows him his existence. At the same time it shows man that he exists in a "world" whose own differentiation is possible only through man. Man projects his freedom into his world, he fills the world with his own nothingness and so, as in Sartre's philosophy, he *constitutes* the world, he reveals it. Without nothingness as it appears in man, then, there would be no existence, there would be no man and no "world", only an unknown undifferentiated *something*. It is clear that nothing, as Heidegger conceives it, is not simply opposed to being, as in Sartre. Rather it is a prerequisite for the revelation of all things positive, it stands behind or supports them. We arrive at the centre of Heidegger's argument: *nothingness is identical with Being*. It is not identical with existence, of course. Nothingness props existence up, it makes it possible as does Being. Thus the void is not something to be glossed over but the central concern of philosophy:

> It would be premature to stop thinking at this point and adopt the facile explanation that Nothing is merely the nugatory, equating it with the non-existent . . . Instead of giving way to such precipitate and empty ingenuity and abandoning Nothing in all its mysterious multiplicity of meanings, we should rather equip ourselves and make ready for one thing only: to experience in Nothing the vastness of that which gives every being the warrant to be. That is Being itself.[2]

Life as we know it exists in that act of consciousness by which Being *or nothingness* pours into the world. That act of creative or at least revelatory consciousness, moreover, is indistinguishable from the vision of *angst*.

Beckett's Irreducible is now fully in focus. It behaves like Heideggerian Being to the very end. It is a negative but one which, unlike the *pour soi*, may be related to a positive, a being-nothing in the Heideggerian sense in which Being and nothing ultimately coalesce. On the one hand we have the world of the tramps and of consciousness, the world of the voice of the Unnamable, and, on the other and supporting it as its ontological ground, we have the

Unnamable itself, a creature in whom positive and negative are confounded. The Unnamable, itself a void, is the origin of the entire Beckett creation, a source of all things. Just as Heideggerian *angst* finally takes us to the Being of things which is also nothingness, an obscure transcendental expressing itself through man, so the Beckett Reduction takes us to the irreducible being of things, an unnamable emptiness expressing itself vicariously through the voice of consciousness, through the "delegate" tramps from Murphy to Malone. Just as *dasein* is a *platzhalter* or stand-in for Being, so Beckettian consciousness is a representative of the Other, the Irreducible. Beckett's entire literary output, which may be regarded as an extraordinary search for the origin of things and one continued obsessively for some fifty years of writing and always with the one seemingly hopeless goal, is entirely comparable to Heidegger's lifelong philosophic quest for Being.

It may be added that in his work Heidegger is not unwilling to evoke theological echoes. Of course Sartre does the same but he does it facetiously, in order to dispel the ghost of theism, whereas Heidegger's attitude is quite different. *Angst*, after all, may be thought of as an experience analogous to a religious conversion:

> Readiness for dread [*angst*] is to say "Yes!" to the inwardness of things, to fulfil the highest demand which alone touches man to the quick. Man alone of all beings, when addressed by the voice of Being, experiences the marvel of all marvels: that what-is *is*.[20]

One might say the same for what Heidegger terms "thinking". It is a call to which man responds, and the call comes from Being. We are asked to listen to it at the conclusion of the *What is Called Thinking?* lectures, and, at the close of the "Conversation on a Country Path about Thinking" (in *Discourse on Thinking*), Heidegger's protagonists, the scientist, the scholar and the teacher, prepare for it as they walk into the night. Clearly the reponse to Being must be free and it must involve the whole man. Thus *dasein* "expends itself in Being for the truth of Being".[21] It is a "freedom of sacrifice"[22] which prompts *dasein* to "preserve the truth of Being no matter what may happen to man" in answer to the "grace wherewith Being", deity-like, "has endowed the nature of man, in order that he may take over in his relationship to Being the guardianship of Being".[23] Authentic *dasein* has become a saint of the existential, a means chosen by Being so that it may enter the world. This is that celebrated role of guardian or shepherd of Being outlined in the *Letter on Humanism*. Genuine humanism, Heidegger argues *contra* Sartre, lies not in man's declaration of his independence, which fails to rate his humanity adequately. Rather it is in the service of Being that humanism, the essence of man, is realized:

> Man is . . . "thrown" from Being itself into the truth of Being so that ek-sisting [ex-sisting] in this fashion he might guard the truth of Being, in order that beings might appear in the light of Being as the beings they are . . . Man is the shepherd of Being.[24]

Equally: "Man is the neighbour of Being."[25] But Being, "nearer than the nearest" and "farther than the farthest"[26] is not easily reached. Modern man is "homeless", expelled, for a purpose no doubt, from his own origins and therefore from himself. The return is a dread-ridden project, a learning "to exist in the nameless".[27] It is difficult not to see the Heideggerian search as a patient movement towards a First Cause, although with overtones not of Aristotelian Scholasticism but of something approaching Platonic mysticism, the *via negativa* of Dionysius the Areopagite. Of course Heidegger is critical of both Platonism and Christian theology. Yet his Being is well on the way to having the characteristics of the totally Other, the Immanent-Transcendent of the theologians, the *nada* of John of the Cross, even, the "I am" which Aquinas found in the story of the burning bush and made the basis of his system.

Beckett's work is equally characterized by an oblique (sometimes not so oblique) appeal to mysticism. Of course there is no question of anything like conventional theism. But it would be more misleading to speak of atheism or, for that matter, agnosticism. Like Heidegger Beckett is essentially concerned with the sphere of the numinous. There is, however, no similarity of tone whatsoever. Heidegger listens patiently for the least whisper that will reveal the presence of Being. To prepare himself for the task he will wait humbly in silence or, if he must speak, he will do so thoughtfully, with care, out of reverence for his subject. But this kind of piety is totally foreign to Beckett, whose relation with his irreducible is in the nature of a life-and-death struggle. Beckett is Jonah, *prophète malgré lui*, Habbakuk lifted bodily by the hair, begging the angel to release him. We shall return to this point in a later chapter.

Beckett begins with Belacqua, in the *Dream of Fair to Middling Women*, withdrawing from Parisian life to enter the dark tunnel of his own mind, where alone a measure of peace is to be found. This movement is, of course, potentially there in the depiction of the idle Florentine of the *Purgatorio*. All that is necessary is that Beckett, inverting Dante, should regard sloth not as sin but as a sign of the contemplative. Add a little Descartes (the Descartes who liked his bed), the passive ethic of Geulincx, the *accidia* of the *fin de siècle*, the denial of activity which stems from Schopenhauer and the East, as well as from Joyce's ne'er-do-well artist who, like his predecessor Flaubert, foregoes *kinesis* – and you are well on the way to at least a version of the ascent prescribed by *The Cloud of Unknowing*. The ascent is initiated half-seriously, or in deadly earnest, depending on the viewpoint, with that mystic of our times, Murphy, sitting naked in his rocking-chair, awaiting the revelation of the darkness and the silence, "silence not of vacuum but of plenum" (p.103). Murphy has something like a success:

> . . . the positive peace that comes when the somethings give way . . . to the Nothing, than which in the guffaw of the Abderite naught is more real. Time did not cease, that would be asking too much, but the wheel of rounds and pauses did, as Murphy . . . continued to suck in, through all the posterns of his withered soul, the accidentless One-and-Only, conveniently call Nothing. (p.168)

Murphy's trance combines neo-Platonic mysticism and the "nothing is more real than nothing" of Democritus of Abdera with the quest for the Irreducible. Watt's experience represents an escape from, rather than a search for, the hound of heaven. Nevertheless Watt discovers in Mr Knott that same nothing than which naught is more real as he struggles up his ascent of the sacred mountain, an unwilling ascetic:

> *Of nought. To the source. To the teacher. To the temple. To him I brought. This emptied heart. These emptied hands. This mind ignoring. This body homeless. To love him my little reviled. My little rejected to have him. My little to learn him forgot. Abandoned my little to find him.* (p.164)

Although Knott sadly fails to respond to this comic and moving sacrifice, one is forcefully reminded of the John of the Cross lines echoed in "East Coker":

> In order to arrive at being everything,
> Desire to be nothing.
> In order to arrive at knowing everything,
> Desire to know nothing.[28]

The Johannine ascent is expressed concisely in the diagram of the mount of perfection: "*nada, nada, nada, nada, nada, Y en el Monte nada*".[29] Watt too, goes by the way of fivefold nothing and at the top discovers that same nothing:

> What had he learnt? Nothing.
> What did he know of Mr Knott? Nothing.
> Of his anxiety to improve, of his anxiety to understand . . . what remained? Nothing.
> But was not that something? (p.147)

One cannot expect too much from Knott, the *deus absconditus* whom Watt desires to see "face to face", or, if that proves impossible, at least "from behind" (p.145), as Moses saw Yahweh. In fact the difficulties are enormous and Watt must be content with the Pauline formula, with glimpses "not clearly caught, but as it were in a glass" (p.146). As the wise Arsene tells him: ". . . what we know partakes in no small measure of the nature of what has so happily been called the unutterable or ineffable, so that any attempt to utter or eff it is doomed to fail . . ." (p.61) We are on the ground of negative theology as Beckett well knows:

> For the only way one can speak of nothing is to speak of it as though it were something, just as the only way one can speak of

> God is to speak of him as though he were a man . . . and as the only way one can speak of man, even our anthropologists have realized that, is to speak of him as though he were a termite. (p.74)

A concern with what can neither be uttered nor effed takes us quickly to the search in the trilogy which ends with the Unnamable, that mysterious being so reminiscent of divinity. The Irreducible does not *exist*, in Heideggerian terms, it *is*, outside space and time, outside relations and mutability. As argued earlier, it combines the opposites of nothingness and being, freedom and necessity. Not surprisingly, then, affirmative theology makes no inroads into it: one must speak of it as if it were a human being, then deny all that one has said. Thus the voice is in an impossible position. Whatever it utters comes from the Unnamable but loses its connection with it even as it is expressed, that is, named. The only answer is a continuing Reduction, a negative way: "mutilate, mutilate, and perhaps some day, fifteen generations hence, you'll succeed in beginning to look like yourself . . ." (p.317) Thus the voice edges its way around the borders of the void: ". . . our concern is with someone . . . with something, now we're getting it, someone or something that is not there, or that is not anywhere, or that is there, here, why not . . ." (p.408) The oscillation between first and third person is, as we have seen, remarkable:

> . . . there I am the absentee again . . . he who neither speaks nor listens, who has neither body nor soul, it's something else he has, he must have something, he must be somewhere, he is made of silence . . . he's the one to be sought . . . the one to be spoken of, the one to speak . . . then I could stop, I'd be he, I'd be the silence . . . we'd be reunited, his story the story to be told, but he has no story . . . he's in his own story, unimaginable, unspeakable, that doesn't matter, the attempt must be made, in the old stories imcomprehensibly mine, to find his . . . the story of the silence that he never left . . . (p.417)

It may, of course, be objected that the *via negativa* is the butt of a Beckett joke. No question of it, Beckett smiles (painfully) as he invites us up the slopes of the holy mountain. Mr Knott and

Godot do not cut a fine figure as divinities; Youdi of *Molloy* is even less seriously presented; the tyrants and manipulators who are initially supposed to control the Beckett universe, all absent answers to the riddle of existence, are rejected in *The Unnamable*, *How it is* and *Company* as mere inventions. Moreover the Unnamable is always out of reach. But the mystery remains even as Beckett works the last relics of the anthropomorphic illusion out of his system. If the search for the Unnamable is depicted as a farce it is also something very serious. Beckett may satirize conventional religious attitudes but he does not do so from the standpoint of the true sceptic. Watt *does* discover something-in-nothing, the later tramps lead us gradually to the reality of the Unnamable. Certainly the writer has rejected the Cartesian and modern *deus ex machina*, but only to replace it with a deity more appropriate to the times, a God who is not there and yet who, in the final analysis, belongs to a long tradition of religious thought. The image of Beckett which emerged from the comparison with Sartre and Camus is reinforced by this perspective. Beckett is otherworldly not only in a negative, but in a positive sense also.

Of course in so far as the Irreducible resembles the deity it also recalls, in general terms, the Idealist's Absolute. The same may be said of Heideggerian Being. Being is not arrived at by a process of abstraction, naturally, nor is it conceived as an *idea*, any more than is Beckett's Irreducible. Still, as in the Hegelian System, substituting Being for the Idea, "the happening of history occurs essentially as the destiny of the truth of Being and from it".[30] But to draw this parallel is perhaps to do no more than to assert a remote debt and one present not only in Heidegger's work but in that of any existential thinker. The fact remains that Heidegger, unlike Sartre, develops his existential analysis to a point where the existential itself seems to be surpassed. The Question which transcends the everyday points also to a reality which, while not remote from existence – Being is, we recall, that which is nearest to and farthest from our experience – cannot be identified with it. At least in one way, Being shows traces of Idealist origins. In Beckett's case there is, if anything, less ambiguity. The Irreducible is, in its way, an Absolute. It is removed from the limits of time, free of all relations with any finite, namable thing, alone, bodiless, transcending every existential quality. Its freedom is without bounds and identical with necessity. It does not suffer from the pressure of Sartrean or Heideggerian facticity or *angst*. It is neither a being-there nor a being-with. Thereness, withness, a painful awareness of one's inescapable situation, all these belong to the tramp and the voice which speaks for the Unnamable. But the Unnamable itself is totally removed from them. It is a creature in whom opposites merge for the simple reason that at the level of ultimates all is one: nothing at all, yet the source of everything, a still point at the centre of the moving wheel, like Mr Endon in *Murphy* or the unborn Worm in *The Unnamable*,

> the all-impotent, all-nescient . . . who, having nothing human, has nothing else, has nothing, is nothing. Come into the world unborn, abiding there unliving, with no hope of death, epicentre of joys, of griefs, of calm. Who seems the truest possession, because the most unchanging. The one outside of life we always were in the end, all our long vain life long. . . The one ignorant of himself and silent, ignorant of his silence and silent . . . Who crouches in their midst who see themselves in him and in their eyes stares his unchanging stare. (p.349)

Where are we to find a philosophic model for this catatonic divinity? In the Berkeleian or Spinozan deity? It is worth recalling that Berkeley's *esse est percipi* is, more properly, *esse est aut percipi aut percipere*. That which is perceived, namely nature, points to the ultimate perceiver, the one who remains to sustain the room in being when everyone else has left it, "*omnipresent, eternal Mind*".[31] But Beckett's Irreducible is all-nescient, all-impotent, ignorant, silent – in the terms applied to Worm. If its eye mirrors all others who in turn mirror its "unchanging stare", the Unnamable is nevertheless a very tenuous *percipere*. If we may put the matter anthropomorphically, it has *no wish* to perceive, no wish to be the source of Beckett's creation. One thinks of the self-sufficient, indeed creation-exhausting God of Spinoza's *Ethics*, beyond pleasure or pain, one, infinite, eternal, free – but not from its own necessity, out of which come "an infinite number of things in infinite ways", such that "individual things are nothing but modifications of the attributes of God". Urged out of itself into nature, this God remains itself, in whatever form it takes. Its activity is purposeless: "nature has no particular goal in view . . . final causes are mere human figments".[32] It may well be that

Beckett borrows something of this for his portrait of the solitary, world-generating Unnamable. At any rate, as we have seen, he is acquainted with Spinoza's ascent beyond the passions to the intellectual love of God, which is parodied in *Murphy*. Since Murphy's own progress reflects the Spinozan movement, the parody implies respect for the original. In the end, though, the workings of the Irreducible are more dynamic than those of either Berkeley's or Spinoza's God.

What Beckett offers is, in a manner of speaking, a theology or, better still, a theophany. We have only to see the Reduction and its end product not from the viewpoint of the tramp or the voice, that is as a search, a movement towards the Irreducible, but from the other side as it were, from the viewpoint of the Irreducible: as a never-ending, never-beginning drama taking place in the cranium of the pseudo-divine. Such a perspective brings us to an Idealism more recent than Berkeley's. In Fichte's system the pure or transcendental Ego, which is supra-individual, a form of ceaseless activity, *imagines* the world of non-ego and of individual consciousness. In so doing it finds itself, it expresses its moral will in and through human freedom. The later Fichte replaces this Ego with Absolute Being, with God who externalizes himself in his creation. Schelling's Absolute Ego exists as a timeless act of self-knowledge in the fusion of Nature and Spirit, Object and Subject. It transits over to the objective, returns in Nature's self-awareness, which is Spirit, then synthesizes to rest in its own identity of opposites, the fusion of the two. At one level the activity takes place in the sphere of art. Ultimately it is what Schelling termed an *Iliad* and an *Odyssey*, motion outwards, followed by the circuitous return. The Absolute Idea freely alienates itself, it produces a Fall into the world, then returns by the route of human consciousness. The act is eternal, it takes place within the Absolute. Thus the entire universe represents the inner life of the Absolute, a dialogue with self rather like that which the theologians envisaged as taking place within the bosom of the Trinity. In Hegel's thought the oneness of the Absolute and the world is taken as far as might be thought possible. For the Absolute is now seen entirely as process, as identical with process in the world, that is, in history. The Idea, which is absolute freedom and absolute necessity, above all, which is the whole of things, the Totality, objectifies itself in the world, becomes alienated from itself only to return as Spirit, *geist*. This return is nothing other than the thought which thinks the absolute, in short, Hegel's System. No wonder Kierkegaard was appalled. Schopenhauer called it charlatanism, the work of "that intellectual Caliban",[33] Marx brought it down to the factory floor. For Hegel reality is nothing other than the Absolute thinking *itself*, via its creation, and doing so dialectically, as a creative and generating tension of oppositions and reconciliations within its own eternal mind.

In the inward dynamics of Beckett's Absolute what happens is reminiscent of the pattern Fichte, Schelling and Hegel, for all their disagreements, have in common. The Irreducible thinks the world (of the tramps) into being, or, if we prefer, thinks the world as it thinks itself, seeking to know itself in its world. Creation, with its tramps, is an invention of the Unnamable which projects itself out from its unknown and then returns to itself, witness to its own motion but through the eyes of its creatures, the voice in particular. It is as if the whole Beckett creation were an attempt on the part of the Unnamable to name itself. It cannot do so, since it is a negative, and its attempt results in the naming of *something else*, that is, its creation. Once creation is a fact, the Unnamable must deny any connection with it: "All these Murphys, Molloys and Malones do not fool me. They have made me waste my time . . . speak of them when . . . I should have spoken of me and of me alone" (p.305). But in the very act of denying its *creatures* the Unnamable reasserts *itself*. Encouraged, it sets out again to name itself and promptly names its creation instead. The oscillation of Yes and No continues for ever and in the process the Absolute brings into being a world, by *mistake*, and preserves it, also by mistake. So: "it is I invented . . . so many others, and the places where they passed, the places where they stayed, in order to speak, since I had to speak. Without speaking of me, I couldn't speak of me . . ." (p.399). Two small works, the radio piece *Cascando* and the prose *For to end yet again*, may be taken as concise statements of the entire process. Of course as the title indicates *Cascando* illustrates a fall; its characters, like the earlier character of "The Expelled" (who is introduced to us in flight, thrown out of a house), and the later heroine of *Not I*, enact the primal expulsion, the falling off. Yet this decline is also a return, a search. The play has two protagonists, the Opener and the Voice. Opener gives the order and Voice, with the help of Music, begins to narrate its unceasing quest for the tramp Woburn, following him on his journey as he stumbles to a boat and heads out to sea. Opener acts as a First Cause, in short, as the Irreducible, prompting the Voice to undertake the search. In Heideggerian terms Opener may be thought of as Being, responsible, through Voice, for existence. It may also be regarded as a Beckettian Absolute, expressing the rhythm of alienation, the going out into the tramp, and, in the tramp's and the voice's search, the re-entry into self. Just as the voice seeks Woburn – himself searching – so Opener, we can say, seeks himself vicariously in his puppets in the very act of abandoning his world for theirs. Behind the tramp is consciousness, behind that the Unnamable: Woburn, Voice and Opener. Woburn will never reach his goal, Voice will never quite reach Woburn, Opener will never reach himself through his creatures, any more than the Unnamable will succeed in identifying himself with his "delegates". Beckett has here reproduced in miniature the movement out from the Irreducible and the constant dynamism of the impossible return. Everything happens in the mind of the Opener. "It is the month of May", he tells us, "the reawakening",[34] genesis. *For to end yet again* completes the picture by viewing the process from the other end; it is Beckett's Apocalypse. A skull appears to loom over a blasted landscape, surveying as it were its own thought, in darkness and emptiness. Glimmering for the last time it lights up the prospect of sandy grey waste, in the middle of which is an erect human, or rather its remnant, "the expelled". This creature in turn observes two dwarfs carrying a litter (of dung). If the dwarfs (body and mind? the passions of love and fear, attraction and repulsion?) suggest the past of the expelled, his memories, the meanderings of a meaningless life, the expelled himself appears to be no more than an extension of or a projection of the brooding skull. When the expelled collapses amid his ruins, the dwarfs stop, darkness descends. But the skull will surely rouse itself once more to reveal yet further disintegration, another expelled, more dwarfs, "through it who knows yet another end . . ."[35]

Can anything ever be achieved by this sad intercourse of Beckett's Absolute with itself? Something *is* achieved. In this dialectic, the narrator of *How it is* postulates a deity responsible for its infernal creation (p.151); it then denies it (pp.158–9). The narrator of *Company* postulates a "deviser", then tells us it is alone, no "deviser" has ever existed. At the end of *How it is* we are left with one who, it seems, had nothing to do with the story and its torments ("never crawled . . . never stirred . . . never made to suffer . . . never suffered", p.160). Yet *someone* never crawled, never suffered. If it is not the already rejected deity, it must nonetheless be acknowledged. Likewise *who* is it that is alone at the end of *Company*, *whose* solitude is it we are speaking of? The Irreducible who cannot be revealed is nonetheless revealed. Creation, a self-alienation of divinity, implies a creator, however absent he may be, the Word implies eternal lips. Thus even God, the greatest sceptic of all, is assured of his own reality. The Irreducible is a fact.

But is this pattern of Beckett's imagination which we have outlined anything other than an astonishing *parody* (let us say, unintentional) of the systems of the German Idealists? Undeniably. Beckett's Absolute is utterly confused, frustrated – if it may be said to be anything. It wants to have nothing to do with its Iliad *or* its Odyssey, only to re-enter into its own "unthinkable unspeakable, where I have not ceased to be, where they will not let me be" (*The Unnamable*, p.337). If we find we cannot attribute this anguish to the Unnamable itself, but only to that voice through whose distortions it needs must speak, we must still insist that Beckett's Absolute is, at the very least, an *uncomfortable* Absolute. It appears – through the antics of its voice, *bien entendu* – not to behave with the cosmic rightness of Fichte's Ego or Being or Schelling's God or Hegel's Idea. Clearly what we are witnessing is an Absolute without confidence in itself, a post-Idealist phenomenon.

In an earlier chapter we have already pointed to a general kinship between Idealism and the existential approach. The same might be said for Romanticism and the existential, since there are obvious links between the philosophies of the German Idealists and the work of their Romantic contemporaries. Existential *angst*, which comes to Heidegger via Kierkegaard, has close affinities with the Romantic *Weltschmerz*, its historical antecedent. In Romantic literature *Weltschmerz* expresses itself as a search for an Absolute. It is as if the Romantic were filled with a sense of endless possibilities, of metaphysical *space*, of freedom, as if the world offered no final obstacles to limitless development. Euphoric confidence has a short life span, and the sense of the

Absolute scarcely survives beyond 1830, but while it lasts it produces that heady excitement which characterizes the work of so many Romantics. In Idealist philosophy – itself weakened after 1830 in spite of its continuing vogue – the desire for Absolutes is translated into the standpoint of the Absolute. Where the Romantic conceives of personal, and collective, fufilment in terms of the vast, the heroic, the Idealist thinker sees the act of philosophizing as the adoption of a God-like view of things. Of course this is most marked in Hegel, but it is true of Fichte and Schelling to the extent that they too take their stand on a privileged position. Inevitably the Idealist who seeks to know the Absolute affirms *some* identity with it. To this (in Hegel's case, outrageous) conceptual flight corresponds the Romantic's extravagant longing for complete fulfilment, for the attainment of all desire – one thinks of "joy" as envisaged by Schiller, Beethoven, and Coleridge. Post-Romanticism, post-Idealism abandons this ambitious programme. Perhaps Kierkegaard's critique of Hegel, particularly in the *Concluding Unscientific Postscript*, best sums up the shift in metaphysics. Kierkegaard ridicules the professor who thinks himself out of the world and into the shoes of the Absolute. We are beings in a particular situation – in later terminology, beings-in-the-world – and there is no getting out. The Absolute is a fiction. We can only philosophize from one standpoint, and that is not a transcendent but an immanent, an existential one. Thus the sense of privileged position, of unbounded freedom is replaced by that of freedom within limits. Man's world, his existence, closes in around him, and the Romantic craving for what is now seen as unattainable turns into the existential ethic of patient effort in the shadow of the grave. This shift defines the difference between *Weltschmerz* and *angst.* Whereas the one represents an awareness of oneself in a world which opens out towards infinity, the other represents a realization that oneself and one's world are limiting factors. How would one express it in Idealist terms except as a crisis within the Absolute itself, a cosmic *shrinkage* as it were? That is precisely the position in Beckett's work. The Absolute is *there*, but its wings are gone, it gazes out feebly from the narrow confines of its existential cage.

It would be perfectly possible to interpret this creature and its terminal state in terms of post-Hegelian thought in the nineteenth century. Beckett, we may assume, is as well acquainted with Schopenhauer as with the Cartesians and post-Cartesians. He mentions him approvingly as early as the *Dream of Fair to Middling Women*. Schopenhauer does away with the grandiose systems of his immediate predecessors, though *The World as Will and Representation* is scarcely an unambitious work. At any rate the Absolute is absent and in its place we find the will-to-live. Reality is entirely composed of Will which objectifies itself as Idea or Representation. This objectification is the world. It follows that this world is Maya, illusion. Moreover the Will is a constant striving, without goal, without any possibility of satisfaction. This means that "there is no measure or end of suffering".[36] We conclude that "*all life is suffering*".[37] Far from saying with Leibniz that this is the best of all possible worlds, "we may even oppose seriously and honestly the proof that it is the *worst* of all possible worlds".[38] The life of the Will expresses itself as a round of futility, an "unquenchable thirst". What is lacked is desired and desire involves pain; what is possessed is no longer desired. In this way want which turns into satisfaction results in tedium. All living is a pendulum swinging "between pain and boredom."[39] Birth into this world, then, is the true original sin. In Calderón's words, "*el delito mayor del hombre es haber nacido*".[40] Only one thing remains, to make an exit as quickly as possible, though not by means of suicide (which logically *affirms* the will-to-live): "existence is certainly to be regarded as an error or mistake, to return from which is salvation".[41] Clearly Beckett has absorbed this relentless critique and found it congenial. Birth is the one thing Vladimir and Estragon must repent (p.11) and in *Malone Dies* the tramp thinks of punishment, reasoning that "living was not a sufficient atonement . . . or that this atonement was in itself a sin, calling for more atonement . . ."(p.240). We are in the sphere of what Schopenhauer terms eternal justice, retribution which is contained in the very nature of sin. The point need not be laboured. We have only to think of human relations in Beckett to see how much might have been borrowed from Schopenhauer's depiction of the round of desire and satisfaction, pain and ennui. It may well be, then, that the Irreducible itself owes something to the model of Schopenhauer's Will, that Will which is *one* behind all its objective manifestations, "unmoved in the midst of . . . change".[42] If that is so, then we must say that in Beckett's work the world realized by this Will is collapsing into an

Occasionalist scrap heap, while the Will itself perseveres, painfully, impossibly, with its cosmic error.

However, Schopenhauer's prison is equipped with an escape tunnel. Man as a creature of Will is tied to Ixion's wheel, carrying water in a Danaid sieve, thirsting like Tantalus. But if he suspends the operation of willing, if he turns the Will against itself, that is, wills not living but *denial* of living, then "we celebrate the Sabbath of the penal servitude of willing; the wheel of Ixion stands still".[43] Such suspension is possible in the aesthetic act, and here Schopenhauer's doctrine resembles the theory of *stasis* put forward by Stephen Dedalus and the will-lessness advocated in the Duthuit dialogues. It seems likely that Beckett's emphasis on passivity – the idleness of Belacqua in the *Purgatorio* – represents a post-Cartesian notion coloured by the pessimism of Schopenhauer. At the same time Schopenhauer locates the final escape not in art but in sanctity. In a passage whose chess reference looks forward to Beckett's one-and-only endgame he offers a portrait of the man who has ceased to will:

> He now looks back calmly and with a smile on the phantasmagoria of this world which was once able to move and agonize even his mind, but now stands before him as indifferently as chess-men at the end of a game, or as fancy dress cast off in the morning, the form and figure of which taunted and disquieted us on the carnival night.[44]

The transition from willing to denial-of-willing in a world *composed* of Will is, despite Schopenhauer's explanation, hard to comprehend. Nevertheless it is the point to which the whole philosophy of Will tends. *The World as Will and Representation* ends with a panegyric of the great mystics and ascetics of the Western and Eastern traditions, Francis of Assisi, the followers of Buddha, Madame de Guyon, Eckhart, Tauler and others. What exactly is it these negators of Will have chosen? It must be *nothing*, since all that exists, exists as Will: "what remains after the complete abolition of the will is, for all who are still full of the will, assuredly nothing. But also conversely, to those in whom the will has turned and denied itself, this very real world of ours with all its suns and galaxies, is – nothing".[45] It is possible to read Schopenhauer's doctrine as nihilism pure and simple and to gloss over his eulogy of the saints. But to do this is to disregard a great deal that is in *The World as Will and Representation*. Schopenhauer underlines the point in his second volume: if something is nothing we know, then it is for us nothing; on the other hand, "it still does not follow from this that it is nothing absolutely . . . only that we are restricted to a wholly negative knowledge of it".[46] Follow references to Plotinus, Böhme, Madame de Guyon, Angelus Silesius, Eckhart and the Sufis, in short to the tradition which, in Christianity, has come to be known as the *via negativa*. But Beckett's link with this tradition, which has been outlined, is much more tenuous and parodic. Even if we allow that the depiction of the Unnamable constitutes a negative theology of sorts, we must add that in Beckett's hands this theology has become ironic; ironic, that is, not in the sense of "sceptical" but in the sense of "problematical". Beckett, like Schopenhauer, leads us to the void and yet, astonishingly, Beckett's void is deeper, less amenable to manipulation – even for the purposes of ascesis. Where Schopenhauer's saint attains to the void as fulfilment, Beckett's character can never reach this haven of quiet. The result is that whereas the former views nothingness as passive, as non-being, the latter sees it as a dynamic paradox, a being-nothing. In the futile world of Schopenhauer one searches for rest and one finds it, howbeit in the void. In Beckett's, one searches for much more than rest, one hunts for an explanation of the old mystery – and one finds *nothing*, and in that, a clue to the nature of *everything*. Beckett's world is both more negative and more positive than Schopenhauer's. Put concisely: it is more paradoxical, it exhibits the characteristics not of willing and cessation of will but of miracle, doing that is nothingness and nothingness that is doing.

We will not find a parallel for this in the work of Nietzsche, where the will-to-live metamorphoses into the will-to-power. The Eternal Recurrence may suggest Beckett's whirligig of struggle and pain, but only superficially, for the simple reason that Nietzsche's is a philosophy of Yes where Beckett's is one of No. Nietzsche identifies (however ambiguously) with the strong, the ones who can will their own pain for all time and so overcome the world in the direction of the *übermensch*. Beckett, however, identifies entirely with the weak, his hero is the all-nescient, all-impotent. Beckett refuses to will suffering. By the same token he refuses to say yes to life, to accept it. To that extent his stand is closer to Schopenhauer. If there is a parallel in the post-Idealist nineteenth century it is with the work of Kierkegaard. Of course we have already examined this to a degree, since we have interpreted Beckett in the light of the concept of *angst*. That concept makes more sense in a Beckettian context without its Christian elements, that is, by way of Heidegger's reinterpretation of Kierkegaard. But the real parallel is not with respect to context: it is a matter of *tone*. Beckett's Irreducible recalls Kierkegaard in its appeal to miracle, to paradox, in its being *precariously* as it were, in ontological fear-and-trembling. If the leap, the notion of freedom, of faith (all forms of nothingness) are at the heart of Kierkegaard's work, then we can say that in spite of its seeming bleakness Beckett's creation is closer to Kierkegaard than Schopenhauer.

It is not the aim of the present argument to go into these nineteenth-century parallels in any detail, only to sketch possible avenues for comparison in the context of a discussion of Beckett's work in the light of modern existential thought, in particular that of Heidegger. I have concentrated on the notions of *angst*, existence, being and nothingness. Heidegger begins with *dasein*, a creature at home in its world, then goes on to endow his protagonist with *angst*, the faculty of vision. In *angst*, *dasein* sees its little world collapse into the strangeness of the Uncanny, invaded by waves of nothingness and yet at the same time unmistakably and oppressively *there*. In short, it knows itself as a void which exists, which is a being-there. Such is the fate of Beckettian consciousness. The tramp or, in some works, the voice, knows itself as suspended in mid-air and yet as enclosed in a stifling facticity. Watt's experience seems to focus on the void, the disintegration of normality, that of Vladimir and Estragon on the inescapable fact of existence. Thus we may argue that the Beckett Reduction functions in a way resembling the phenomenon of Heideggerian *angst*: it annihilates the inessential and reduces man to fundamentals, to bare existence. *Angst*, however, is also said to involve a "metaphysical" questioning of things and so an uncovering of the ground of the existential, Being. In the same way the Reduction takes us to the heart of the Beckett world, the Irreducible. Moreover as Heidegger's Being appears in the end as identical with nothingness, so the Irreducible or Unnamable exhibits the dual nature of a being-nothing. Neither Cartesian and Occasionalist, nor Sartrean philosophy, nor the Camus Absurd serve to bring us as close to the centre of Beckett's imaginative inspiration as Heidegger's concept of Being. Both Beckett and Heidegger are above all absorbed in a search for the ground of things, both persevere in this one search with an obsessiveness which is rare in the history of philosophy and art. Both tend, finally, away from the sphere of the existential, towards a *primum mobile* reminiscent of the hidden deity of negative theology and also of the Idealist Absolute. In Beckett this shift is particularly marked. It may in part be referred to Beckett's interest in Spinoza and Berkeley. On the whole, though, the theophany of the Unnamable suggests the dynamics of the Absolute as conceived by the German Idealists, but with a post-Idealist colouring. It is here that we must recall the historical relationship of the existential to the Idealist and the comments made in chapter two. Just as modern existential thought looks back, through figures like Kierkegaard, to its Idealist origins, so in Beckett's work the existential element has its roots in the quasi-Idealism of the Irreducible. At the same time Beckett's Absolute exhibits all the fragility of a post-Hegelian conception. In so far as Beckett leads us to an Absolute, it is through the mediation of Schopenhauer and Kierkegaard. We are not, however, speaking of "influences". Beckett knows the Cartesians, he knows Schopenhauer; he may or may not know the Idealists and Kierkegaard.

In the end, then, Beckett's work illustrates nothing less than the three-stage development of a major philosophical tradition in which the Cartesian *cogito* is transformed into Idealist Mind and, finally, existential consciousness. Or rather, in the order in which this occurs in Beckett, the *cogito* is translated into existential consciousness, then into the Absolute or at least the pseudo or quasi-Absolute, cooped up in its unthinkable cell. In an invisible room resides the one to whom I say "not I" or more accurately, the one who first says "not I" to me. This *ur*-identity is not to be trivialized by a name or, what amounts to the same thing, by facile association with myself. Nevertheless, in so far as I exist I do so by virtue of a minimal negative connection with it, that is, I exist by virtue of its saying "not I" to me, by virtue of its *denial* of me. Beckett retraces the path from the no-man's-land of his characters to an aboriginal ground of being over and over again. Nothing could be more natural or simpler than such a search. Nothing is more liable to end in failure. But Beckett finds only the impossible worthy of an attempt, anything less would not be worth the trouble. That is the essence of his Romanticism, his desire-in-chains for the Absolute. This Romanticism, whose connections with the nineteenth century are so evident in the light of a philosophical analysis, is by no means a mere looking back. It is something quite new, a modern Romanticism pledged to defeat, a search for the unattainable precisely *because* it is unattainable. That seems to be the only Romanticism the twentieth century can afford.

II Ionesco and the experience of wonder

6 Ionesco: claustrophobia and euphoria

All my plays have their origin in two fundamental states of consciousness . . . These basic states of consciousness are an awareness of evanescence and of solidity, of emptiness and of too much presence . . .[1]

IONESCO

Wonder is my basic emotional reaction to the world.
(*Notes and Counter-Notes*, p.223)

In Ionesco's work (as in Genet's or Pinter's) we do not find that breadth of reference which allows us to consider Beckett in relation to an entire philosophical tradition. Consequently the following chapters are bound to concern themselves merely with aspects of existential thought. Moreover Ionesco is not philosophic in the same sense as Beckett: strictly speaking, he is a visionary moralist, more absorbed in the Good than in the True. There can, once again, be no question of arguing for the "influence" of modern existential thought, except in the most general sense. Ionesco does not pretend ignorance of the philosophers, as Beckett is wont to do, but he dissociates himself firmly from any school. If Heidegger has made any impact on him, he tells the critic Claude Bonnefoy, it is because he has thrown fresh light on Ionesco's own experience: "The philosophers which I have been able to read . . . have perhaps . . . illuminated what was still for me a rudimentary intuition".[2] With respect to Sartre and Camus Ionesco explains:

We have certainly undergone . . . the influence of certain things we have read . . . We are always influenced by what we live through, by what we see, by what we read . . .

What of it? Those whom we read have in their turn absorbed

ideas and attitudes from their reading: "... and the authors we read have themselves been influenced by their age, by what they have read, seen and lived through" (*Entretiens*, p.142). This stand is hardly surprising and does not preclude the kind of argument proposed by the present study. Ionesco is no more an imitator of others than is Beckett.

A glance at his first full-length play, *Amédée or How to get rid of it: a Comedy* (*Amédée ou comment s'en débarrasser*, written in 1953), is enough to reveal the basic pattern of all of Ionesco's work. Act one depicts an enclosed, claustrophobic situation, with the protagonists in their small flat, cut off from outside contact. The very image of the situation is the growing corpse, but there are other elements, Amédée's dejection, his sense of heaviness, weariness: "I feel so tired, so tired ... worn out, heavy. I've got indigestion ... I feel sleepy all the time."[3] Amédée is a failure as a writer. All about him dampness is suggested by the plague of mushrooms and in this close atmosphere relations are strained, conjugal incompatibilities heightened. Above all, the corpse in the next room grows disturbingly in size until it seems to squeeze the couple out of the flat. Act three is in direct contrast to all this. The night is lit by a great moon; stars, comets mingle with the display of fireworks as Amédée becomes lighter and lighter, rising in the sky out of reach of the excited crowd below. Every possible stage resource is needed to give the effect of brilliant clarity, noise and excitement, a dazzling apotheosis comically and futilely disavowed by Amédée himself. Whatever the precise significance of all this, it is clear that the success of the play depends on the successful orchestration of its contrasts. It is worth noting too, that these are presented simultaneously in act two, in the interval between the early action and the coming of night. As the protagonists wait, images of the past arise, embodying in the feelings of Madeleine and Amédée the basic contrast of the play. Amédée's is a world of light and joy, of curtains parted on the dawn of spring: "Madeleine, wake up, let's pull the curtains, the spring is dawning ... the room is flooded with sunshine ... a glorious light ... a gentle warmth!" (II, p.197) Madeleine sees the opposite, darkness, rain and mud. To the man's vision of green valleys covered with flowers, his awakened perception ("In a blaze of joy ... The light's gone mad ... Love's gone mad ... Mad with happiness", II, p.198), the sense of weightlessness ("wings on our feet . . . gravity abolished . . . no more weariness," (II, p.200)) and the glory of a universe of air and freedom ("An insubstantial universe . . . Freedom . . . Balance . . . airy abundance," (II, p.200)), Madeleine juxtaposes mushrooms, the sense of stifling in darkness and dampness. As her vision begins to dominate, hopelessness grows, density invades the scene. An important, and much commented upon, aspect of Ionesco is made apparent. It is a proliferation of matter, of words, whose weight deadens the spirit and which recalls the proliferation of mushrooms in the flat and the growing tissue of the corpse, multiplying itself in all directions.

The basic antinomies evidenced in *Amédée*, which may be termed the poles of the claustrophobic and the euphoric, are found in all of the plays to a greater or lesser extent. We may note the way in which they dominate Ionesco's second full-length play, *The Killer* (*Tueur sans Gages*, 1957). *The Killer* presents us with an image which epitomizes the feeling of joy and release, the "radiant city" (III, p.11). As the play begins, an effect of autumnal or wintry grey, produced entirely by lighting, is suddenly metamorphosed into brightness. Light, whiteness and blueness, emptiness, strangeness are powerful motifs in what follows. Bérenger, the protagonist, congratulates the architect on the radiant city, on its sunny avenues, streaming with light, in contrast to Bérenger's own city of dust, mud, rain and cold where everything, even fire, is damp and cheerless. Now it is spring for Bérenger, he has found the city of light which, it seems, recalls an experience of his earlier life. Once Bérenger possessed within himself a luminous source:

> . . . once upon a time there was a blazing fire inside me. The cold could do nothing against it . . . a spring no autumn could touch; a source of light, glowing wells of joy that seemed inexhaustible. (III,p.20)

Some half a dozen times in his life he has been filled with an unknown joy, in silence, at midday, in spring or in summer. His description of the experience must be quoted at length since it represents Ionesco's most fundamental concerns:

> . . . I was walking along a narrow street . . . with low houses on

> either side, all white . . . I was all alone in the street . . . it was fine, not too hot, with the sun above, high above my head in the blue of the sky . . . I was deeply aware of the unique joy of being alive. I'd forgotten everything, all I could think of was those houses, that deep sky and that sun, which seemed to be coming nearer . . . Suddenly the joy became more intense, breaking all bounds! And then, oh what indescribable bliss took hold of me! The light grew more and more brilliant, and still lost none of its softness, it was so dense you could almost breathe it, it had become the air itself, you could drink it like clear water . . . It's as if there were four suns in the sky . . . The houses . . . were like immaterial shades ready to melt away in that mightier light, which governed all . . . Not a man in the street . . . not a sound . . . And yet I didn't suffer from being alone . . . I was filling the universe with a kind of ethereal energy. Not an empty corner, everything was a mingling of airiness and plenitude, perfectly balanced . . . Oh, I'm sure I could have flown away, I'd lost so much weight . . . (III, pp.22–4)

In this description we find in more elaborate form the elements of Amédée's joy and of his unwilling Ascension. The world is filled with light as Bérenger walks down a little street of white houses; Bérenger is overcome by an unexpected euphoria, everything material sinks into evanescent luminousness; drunk with the sense of lightness and plenitude, the protagonist is ready to float into the sky, to fly away.

But, as he tells the architect, this experience is a thing of the past. His normal setting is that degraded city of dampness and cold whose presence in this play undermines that of the radiant city. If the radiant city, like the euphoric experience it recalls, represents a world transfigured by wonder (III, p.17), a world seen as if for the first time in all its newness and innocence, the other city represents the world of everyday banality, always the same, its snow dirty, its wind biting, its people neither happy nor unhappy but, what is worse, ugly because neither the one thing nor the other (III, p.19). At the end of act one the stress moves from the radiant city to the other and throughout act two the image of greyness is elaborated in all its ugliness of noise, aggressiveness and litigation. Clearly the nightmarish quality of Bérenger's home and its inhabitants points to the claustrophobia and disharmony in Amédée's flat. Act three of *The Killer* focusses gradually on this final situation. Anxiety mounts as Bérenger seeks to thwart the mysterious assassin whose existence turns the city of light into a trap. Traffic banks up, recalling the sense of proliferation of matter and enclosure in the other play, and, at last, Bérenger is left alone, darkness closes in and with it the murderer. The narrow road in which the protagonist is cornered functions as an ironic counterpoint to the sunny road of white houses, the setting for the vision of the euphoric.

It should be emphasized, though, that Bérenger's two experiences have something in common. In each case the world is observed with a sense of surprise. "Everything was virgin, purified, discovered anew, I had a feeling of inexpressible surprise, yet at the same time it was all quite familiar to me" (III, p.23), says the protagonist of the experience of euphoria. In this case the world is observed with both wonder and recognition: it is the world of ordinary living transfigured by joy. In the experience of claustrophobia the familiar is also seen with new eyes but with different results: Bérenger observes the inhabitants of the rainy city in all their hopelessness and drabness, something which they themselves are unable to do. The same point could be made of Amédée's dual experience of reality: on the one hand an amazing vision of normal conjugal living as stifling and depressing, on the other an extravagant sense of liberation in a world transformed into light. But this common ground of wonder in the two experiences will become more evident as we proceed.

Much of what has so far been discussed in *Amédée* and *The Killer* emerges in what Ionesco has said about himself and his work:

> All my plans have their origin in two fundamental states of consciousness: now the one, now the other is predominant and sometimes they are combined. These basic states of consciousness are an awareness of evanescence and of solidity, of emptiness and of too much presence, of the unreal transparency of the world and its opacity, of light and of thick darkness. (*Notes and Counter-Notes*, p.169)

Ionesco himself describes his own life in terms of such antitheses. There is, for example, the vision of euphoria, associated in

Fragments of a Journal (*Journal en Miettes*, 1967–8) and elsewhere with the writer's childhood at La Chapelle Anthenaise. The description of this experience in Ionesco's life, as given in the interview with Bonnefoy, differs remarkably little from Bérenger's in *The Killer*. Ionesco explains that he was seventeen or eighteen at the time of its occurrence, walking down a road in June, at midday:

> Suddenly I had the impression that everything simultaneously receded and approached me . . . that I was in another world, more my own than the last, infinitely more luminous . . . it seemed to me . . . that the light was almost tangible, that the houses had a radiance never previously witnessed, an unusual radiance, really freed from habit . . . I felt enormous joy . . .
> (p.36)

As in the play, light invades the scene, the world is transfigured in brilliance, the habitual assumes an air of wonder and joy. In the *Journal* the narration of this same event is still more personally revealing. Again, it is midday and June and this time, as in the play, little white houses along the road figure prominently; again, Ionesco emphasizes the interplay of familiarity and surprise:

> The whole town was suddenly transformed. Everything became at once profoundly real and profoundly unreal . . . There was something quite new and unsullied about the light, this was an unfamiliar world which I seemed to have known from all eternity . . . An overflowing joy . . .

The dazzling light is portrayed as the agent of the transformation, as the force of dissolution and renewal. Thus the new world is one which "the light dissolved and yet reconstituted".[4] This point is stressed also in the second volume of the *Journal* where the experience is again recounted. Here the walls of the houses shine with such brightness

> that they seemed to want to disappear, to melt together in the intensity of a burning, pervasive, total light that was trying to escape from the forms that contained it . . .

"In the presence of such light", the passage continues, "the world seemed about to efface itself, to fade from sight". Finally,

> . . . I felt as if I had received a blow right in the heart, in the centre of my being. A stupefaction surged into being, exploded, burst its boundaries, dissolving the limits of things . . .
>
> (II, p.154)

At the height of this heart-piercing Ionesco approximates, like Bernini's Teresa and like his own Amédée, to the sensation of flight. It is a moment of supreme naiveté in the wonder of a universe which has been annihilated and renewed, and the author has never tired of extolling it, most recently in essays collected under the headings *Antidotes* (*Antidotes*, 1977) and *Un Homme en Question* (*A Man in Question*, 1979).

It is understandable that Ionesco's stress should be on the euphoric. On the other hand the vision of the mundane, of claustrophobic proliferation of things, also recurs. Ionesco frequently describes nightmares of claustrophobia in the *Journal*. In the Bonnefoy interview he associates these with Paris, a city hideous to him as a child after the serenity of the village of La Chapelle Anthenaise. Thus the duality of evanescence and enclosure is in part translated as that of country and city, childhood and adulthood. In *Découvertes* (*Discoveries*, 1969), for example, this results in a distinctly Wordsworthian tone: childhood has eyes for the glory about it, adulthood simply entails the loss of vision.

In the critical writings, collected in *Notes and Counter-Notes*, Ionesco indicates a little more clearly the relationship between the two feelings. First of all there is the euphoric in which ordinary existence collapses into light and air and in which one senses ". . . that the substance of the world is dream-like, that the walls are no longer solid . . . a spaceless universe made up of pure light and colour" (p.169). Euphoria is not without ambivalence, however. For example it may turn into a kind of vertigo, an unpleasant feeling of emptiness: ". . . the sensation of evanescence gives you a feeling of anguish, a form of giddiness" (p.169). From this state it requires very little to plunge us into the claustrophobic where lightness becomes weight and the universe bears down on us, filling all with the dead presence of matter:

> . . . what is light grows heavy, the transparent becomes dense, the world oppresses, the universe is crushing me . . . matter fills every corner, takes up all the space, and its weight annihilates all freedom . . . the world becomes a stifling dungeon. (p.170)

The possibility of a rapid transition from one state to the other is explicable in terms of what euphoria and claustrophobia have in common. In "Why do I write?" ("*Pourquoi est-ce que j'écris?*" first published in *Antidotes*) Ionesco speaks of an original wonder before the consciousness of existence, seen as joy and light, and of another which follows, the sense of evil which stifles joy. Both apprehensions are coloured by astonishment. The point is already made in the *Notes*. "Wonder is my basic emotional reaction to the world" (p.223), Ionesco argues, and he may be taken at his word. Wonder is the key to his universe and the link between its opposites. A brief look at *The Bald Prima Donna*, the first of the plays, and at what the author has said about it illustrates this fact very well.

The interesting thing about *The Bald Prima Donna*: *an Anti-Play* (*La Cantatrice Chauve*: *anti-pièce*, 1950) is that it offers us a vision of disintegrating reality analogous to that involved in the euphoric experience. In this case, however, the sense of wonder has turned into a brooding awareness of strangeness, a depressing amazement at the banality of life. "Goodness! Nine o'clock", exclaims Mrs Smith in her famous opening as the clock strikes three,

> This evening for supper we had soup, fish, cold ham and mashed potatoes and a good English salad, and we had English beer to drink. The children drank English water. We had a very good meal this evening. And that's because we are English, because we live in a suburb of London and because our name is Smith. (I, p.86)

As this play, in which the most ordinary things take on a monstrous shape, proceeds, the proliferation of things – of Bobby Watsons, for example – signals the growing sense of panic and enclosure. Frenzied dialogue proclaims not only the wonder of everyday language but also its nightmare disintegration:

MR SMITH: The Pope's eloped! The Pope's no soap! Soap is dope!
MRS MARTIN: Bazaar, Baseball, Bassoon!
MR MARTIN: Business, Bosnia, Buster!
MR SMITH: Aeiou aeiou aeiou! (I, p.118)

The Bald Prima Donna, in short, provides an example of the sense of wonder in the service not of euphoria but of claustrophobia. The effect is the same – to translate the commonplace into the unusual – but the mood is radically opposed. As Ionesco complains, the critics saw everything in the play: its parody of theatre, its satire of the bourgeois, of the modern puppet, unable to communicate with himself or others, everything, in fact, but the essential. "What did this play mean to me?" he asks in the Bonnefoy interview and replies to his own question:

> It expressed the unusual, existence seen as something totally unusual. There is a degree of communication between people. They talk to each other. They understand each other. That's what is astonishing . . . The unusual is everywhere: in language, in the act of lifting a glass, drinking from it . . . in short in the fact of existing, of being. (pp.69–70)

The aim of the play is less to parody normality than to expose it to the gaze of wonder in the light of which the most normal things – the fact that people *do* communicate, for example, that one uses words, that one lifts up glasses in order to drink – become amazing, unbelievable, strange. In the very act of burying himself in the banality of the Smiths' existence Ionesco reveals its immense *otherness*: "nothing surprises me more than banality; the 'surreal' is there, within our reach" (*Notes*, p.172). This sense of wonder, we are told, was in this case the particular result of Ionesco's reading an English manual for beginners. As he began to learn his English phrases, Ionesco made a startling discovery. He learned, as he puts it, not English but other surprising truths: for example, that there are seven days in the week and that the floor is below, the ceiling above. All this was not new, but it was something never before apprehended in all its unbelievable truth (*Notes*, pp.181–3). It was to convey to others his surprise at this discovery that Ionesco claims he wrote his play. The essential comedy of the explanation should not mislead. Clearly, in its way, the vision of *The Bald Prima Donna* is comparable to Bérenger's in *The Killer*, with the difference that in the the former wonder allies itself with horror rather than joy. Ionesco himself was put out by the audience's reaction to the first play: it was a tragedy and everyone laughed (*Notes*, p.86). Of course comedy and the tragic are always linked in Ionesco – like the poles of euphoria and claustrophobia – but it is undeniable that *The Bald Prima Donna* is overwhelmingly nightmarish. "Overcome by a proliferation of corpse-like words, stunned by the automatism of conversation, I almost gave way to disgust, unspeakable misery, nervous depression and positive asphyxiation" (*Notes*, p.86), is Ionesco's comment on the writing of the play. If there is a little of the tongue-in-cheek in this melodramatic avowal, the statement remains a valid description of the feelings engendered by *The Bald Prima Donna.* Actually Ionesco returned to the strangeness of speech in his *Exercices de conversation et de diction françaises pour étudiants américains* (*French Conversation and Diction Exercises for American Students*, 1974) – in this case, however, without the overriding sense of threat.

It is clear from the examples so far given that the two feelings which dominate Ionesco's writing should not be thought of as totally opposed. For one thing transition is possible from the one to the other, as Ionesco argues and as *Amédée* and *The Killer* illustrate. In the former play we move from the sense of enclosure to that of euphoria, in the latter the motion is reversed. In addition, and this is a related fact, the euphoric may be experienced as ambivalent and as tending towards its opposite. Examples of this in the plays will come later in this chapter. Most important of all, both the euphoric and the claustrophobic are the product of something more fundamental in the Ionesco vision and may be regarded as modalities of the experience of wonder. Wonder destroys in order to recreate, sometimes, as in *The Bald Prima Donna*, in a mood of stifling horror, sometimes, as in the first act of *The Killer*, in one of delight.

A number of plays are dominated by the sense of amazement in conjunction with a proliferation of matter which hems in and stifles. *The Lesson: a Comic Drama* (*La Leçon: drame comique*), *Jacques or Obedience: a Naturalistic Comedy* (*Jacques ou La Soumission: comédie naturaliste*), *The Future is in Eggs or It takes all sorts to make a world* (*L'Avenir est dans les Oeufs ou il faut de tout pour faire un monde*) closely resemble *The Bald Prima Donna* in this respect. The teacher of *The Lesson* (1950) overwhelms his pupil with a mass of words before he murders her. Murder itself proliferates: there are forty victims a day. The tangle of the arithmetic lesson – numbers are always ominous in Ionesco – and of the lesson in philology recalls the verbal avalanche of the final scene of *The Bald Prima Donna*. *Jacques* (1950), facetiously subtitled "naturalistic comedy", heightens the banal and lends it an air of surreal horror. Ionesco's lighting comments unambiguously on the mood: "a dull, grey-looking set" (I,p.121). Later the light is brighter, a watery green in the crucial love scene, and, finally, the stage is darkened. We are obviously in an early version of Amédée's flat or Bérenger's rainy city. As large numbers of relatives, all Bobby Watsons with more or less identical names, close in around him Jacques capitulates to normality in a marshy wasteland prefiguring Madeleine's in *Amédée*. The dream of the guinea pig in the bath, the story of the miller who drowns his child, all emphasize Jacques' predicament and at the climax of the scene watery immanence images his claustrophobia. The social institutions of marriage and the family are dissolved in an unreal vision of strangeness. Roberte II, Jacques' bride, forced on him by the parents, is herself the marsh in which the protagonist is trapped: ("I'm all moist . . . I've a necklace of ooze, my breasts are melting, my pelvis is soft, I've water in my crevices", (I, p.148)). In scenes reminiscent of the tortured Picasso of the war years everything has only one name – "cat" – and from Roberte's three noses we go to her hand with nine fingers and to a reptilian greyness. *The Future is in Eggs* (1951) carries this action to its conclusion and, as the two lovers begin to reproduce, the scene is overwhelmed with impossible quantities of eggs. At the same time, proliferation of objects has its correlative in a frenzied speeding up of action. As more and more eggs are produced the pace increases in the same way as it does in the climax of *The Bald Prima Donna*.

This world made strange, disjointed and reassembled in an atmosphere of claustrophobia, is the theme of *The New Tenant* (*Le Nouveau Locataire*, 1953), where the stage is filled to overflowing with furniture. As the protagonist turns off the lights not only the house but the entire city, the underground, the Seine, indeed, the whole country, are filled with his objects. The situation in *Rhinoceros* (*Rhinocéros*, 1958) is comparable to this. Bérenger (Ionesco's Everyman who appears in *The Killer*) suffers from the same ailment as Amédée, a nagging weariness; at the same time his friend Jean ludicrously waves his arms as if to fly: ". . . I feel light, light as a feather!" (IV, p.18). But the play is dominated by the negative state of leaden weight and hopelessness. The world, falling apart before Bérenger's amazed eyes, reveals itself in a proliferation of monsters. And yet to some the plague is nothing unusual. Dudard, in accepting the normality of rhinoceritis, is simply facing facts, according to his own defence of himself: "I'm trying to be realistic" (IV, p.83). Bérenger, surrounded by human beings who have been metamorphosed into rhinoceroses, is confused and hemmed in. Normality and the abnormal are impossibly entangled, everything is strange and threatening: "the 'surreal' is there, within our reach".

Although many of the plays depict only the negative pole of the Ionesco experience there are some which, like *Amédée* and *The Killer*, give both sides of the picture. *Victims of Duty: a Pseudo-Drama* (*Victimes du Devoir: pseudo-drame*, 1952) is Ionesco's first ambitious attempt here. In it the protagonist Choubert undergoes an immersion comparable to Jacques' into mysterious inner depths of darkness and mud, encouraged by his wife (another Madeleine) and by a detective. In the mud up to his chin, then his mouth, Choubert finally vanishes in the dark bottom of the ocean, miming his journey for the audience. Later the situation is reversed. He emerges from the depths and begins to climb imaginary mountains, in the sunshine, until, at the top, he is ready to fly, like Amédée. His feelings also anticipate Bérenger's in *The Killer*: "It's a morning in June. The air I breathe is lighter than air . . . The sun's melting into light that's mightier than the sun" (II, p.300). However, the sense of claustrophobia returns, this time in the proliferation of cups of coffee which Madeleine brings into the room and, above all, in Choubert's being stuffed with bread – grotesque anticipation of the furniture blockage in *The New Tenant*. Choubert's choking continues at the end to a chorus reminiscent of the climax of acceleration and proliferation of matter in earlier plays. It is not difficult to go from the contrasts of *Victims of Duty* to those of later plays. In *Exit the King* (*Le Roi se Meurt*, 1962) Bérenger, now of royal blood, watches his kingdom sink into the earth as he struggles to recapture the moment of euphoria. Again Ionesco focusses on a sense of wonder in the light of which things disintegrate and fall away from the little king. The opposition of release and claustrophobia is even more fully expressed in *A Stroll in the Air* (*Le Piéton de l'Air*, 1962) and *Hunger and Thirst: Three Episodes* (*La Soif et la Faim: trois épisodes*, 1964). Possibly the most extravagant of Ionesco's plays, *A Stroll* involves light effects and a prolonged flight above the stage. We are in the England of *The Bald Prima Donna*, this time transfigured by April sunlight. The sky is pure and blue and visible in the background are the sunny white houses of Ionesco's euphoric experience. Yet another Bérenger basks in the wonder of things. The sense of evanescence is underlined by the periodic appearance and disappearance of the mysterious traveller from the "anti-world" who moves through invisible barriers. The scenery, with its little red train in the distance, recalls the Mediterranean colours of the Fauves, perhaps the fantasies of Dufy, although Ionesco specifies an atmosphere of Rousseau, Utrillo and Chagall. There is a turreted palace, a picture of the Eiffel tower, a red balloon, a blue lake, even a rocket. Bérenger feels lighter and lighter, more and more happy and, above all, amazed: "When I look around me, it's as though I was seeing everything for the first time. As though I'd just been born" (VI, p.36). At last, excusing himself like Amédée, he rises in the air, performs on a flying bicycle and is eventually lost from view. However, the claustrophobic is also present. It appears with the background characters, reminiscent of the grotesque creatures of *The Bald Prima Donna*, who speak of walls hemming them in, of weight, of the dirty London snow; it reappears in Bérenger's wife's nightmare. Most important of all, the euphoric flight itself turns sour and becomes a vertigo of the kind described in *Notes and Counter-Notes*, in short, transforms itself into its opposite. Excess of space becomes a kind of claustrophobia. Bérenger, high above the world, sees blood and mud, confusion and fear. Looking back from here we can interpret the slight alarm felt by Amédée as he rises in the air and the sense of artificiality and foreboding present in the very heart of the radiant city in *The Killer* as a foretaste of the ambivalent vision of *A Stroll*. In *Hunger and Thirst* a similar transition occurs between the two Ionesco feelings. Jean, the protagonist, suffers from the sense of enclosure in the first act.

The house is sinking into the mud and darkness and he dreams of release in images of houses without walls and roofs, houses open to the light. But in act two the scene is very different. Jean has left his wife and daughter and the doomed house and finds himself on a high, empty plateau. On the face of it the image is one of release. However, the ambivalence of the flight in *A Stroll* mars the experience. Space oppresses, it becomes a torment, it shades off into claustrophobia. "Rather an empty . . . brilliance" (VII, p.37), someone comments. In the third act matter once again weighs heavily and we are left with the contrast between the vision of a luminous garden with its silver ladder to the sky – much like the silver bridge of *A Stroll* – and the nightmare enclosure of the monastery-prison where Jean is trapped. Jean serves the brothers more and more quickly but their hunger and thirst is infinite and the service, it seems, must continue indefinitely, endlessly postponing the protagonist's reunion with his family in the garden of light. Disintegration and the sense of oppression go together. Dishes multiply and as matter swamps the stage, Jean's inner emptiness grows. As in other plays, evanescence and excess of matter, the euphoric and the claustrophobic, are confused. The more Jean eats in the monastery the more he is hungry, the more he attempts to fill himself the emptier he becomes, just as in act two the more he tries to liberate himself, to seek the openness of the high plateau, the more stifled he becomes. Thus, while the sense of release turns into a new kind of prison, the old prison of the family appears as a place of sunshine and joy. In fact Ionesco later added a fourth act, *The Foot of the Wall* (*Le pied du mur*, 1966), which is some respects returns us to the claustrophobic vacuity of act two – and this is also the mood of a more recent work, *The Man with the Luggage*, (*L'Homme aux valises*, 1975). But on the whole it is the sense of oppression which is most evident in the plays of the seventies. In one of the most moving scenes of *Here Comes a Chopper* (*Jeux de Massacre*, first performed 1970) an old man explains how, to begin with, he was stupefied by the wonder of his life; then, gradually, he saw only the strangeness of menace, until, in the end, only the sense of threat remained: "Life is no longer a miracle, it's a nightmare" (VIII, p.80). This last is the tone of *Here Comes a Chopper*, with its accumulating burden of bodies, and also of *Macbett* (1972). *Oh what a bloody circus* (*Ce Formidable Bordel*, 1973) and Ionesco's novel on which the play is based – *The Hermit*

(*Le Solitaire*, 1973) – both emphasize the negative pole of the Ionesco experience, proliferation, the sense of stifling, combined, however, with emptiness. The solitary protagonist in each case lives in a vacuum – yet hemmed in by other people, by matter, by human confusion. In one scene of the play a restaurant is for a time bathed in light, transfigured, and at the end, too, there is a sign of joy: light, evanescent walls, a burgeoning tree. In the novel walls vibrate, then fall away into air, like transparent curtains or images in water, finally disappearing. The protagonist's room remains suspended in blinding light, while he himself sees a parade of symbols comparable to those of *A Stroll* or *Hunger and Thirst*: trees, a brightly lit path, blue and white flowers, a perfect garden, a silver ladder to the sky. All this disappears, but the protagonist takes it as a pledge.[5]

In one play – *The Chairs: a Tragic Farce* (*Les Chaises: farce tragique*, 1951) – Ionesco concentrates entirely on an effect of paradox. An old couple receive large numbers of visitors and seat them in dozens of chairs ranged about the stage. But the visitors are invisible and so the more they arrive, the greater the multiplication of chairs, the greater the emptiness. Absence presses densely from all sides, crushing the hosts, the only actors whom we are able to see. Ionesco has gone to some trouble to express his views on this play which has been interpreted as variously as *The Bald Prima Donna*. The point is not, he explains in *Notes and Counter-Notes*, to focus on the illusions of an old couple but to depict the void, to create a sense of positive absence (pp.196–7). This means that the visible characters are not to be regarded as being any more real than those we cannot see. *The Chairs* is an image of euphoric evanescence turned sour, as in *Hunger and Thirst*, of space viewed as stifling and expressed partly in terms of its opposite in an accumulation of objects. Ionesco puts it simply:

> To express the void by means of language, gesture, acting and props.
>
> To express absence . . .
>
> The unreality of the real . . .
>
> The voices at the end, the noises of the world . . . the world in

> ruins, the world going up in smoke, in sounds and colours that fade away, the last foundations collapse or rather break up. Or melt into a sort of night. Or into a dazzling, blinding light. (*Notes*, p.199)

All the elements of the Ionesco vision are mingled, perhaps even confusingly, in this picture. By every means possible Ionesco will convey to the audience the identity of opposites, in this case in a mood of claustrophobic terror, of amazed despair. He will show normal reality as unreal, the world itself as falling apart in a chaos of vague noises, as disintegrating into darkness. Or perhaps, he adds in a revealing afterthought, into a blinding light. Emptiness and density, evanescence and enclosure are closely allied, as indeed are the fundamental experiences of joy and claustrophobia. Each of the two experiences involves a sense of wonder and in each case, whether in darkness or in light or in a mixture of both, the world is broken down and reconstituted, shaped anew, witnessed as if for the first time. The element of wonder is essential. Ionesco cannot accept the normality of things and neither can his characters. Again and again, from *The Bald Prima Donna* to *Hunger and Thirst* and beyond, they gaze in stupefaction, sometimes enraptured, at other times uneasy or, finally, horrified. What they see is a world either collapsing under its own weight or dissolving into air, but never a world at rest.

7 Ionesco and Heidegger: authenticity and the collective

> I have the impression of being with extremely polite people . . . Suddenly something breaks down, gives way and the monstrous character of men appears . . .
> (*Entretiens avec Eugène Ionesco*, p.167)

Clearly if a comparison of Ionesco's vision with modern thought is to be attempted the notion of *angst* must be the starting point. Like Beckett's world, Ionesco's falls apart, it tumbles into the existential void. "For me", Ionesco explains,

> it is as if at every moment the actual world has completely lost its actuality. As though there were nothing there; as though there were no foundations for anything . . . Only one thing, however, is vividly present: the constant tearing of the veil of appearances . . . Nothing holds together, everything falls apart. But I am merely repeating the words of King Solomon: all is vanity . . . (*Notes*, p.141)

The reality of things is doubtful, the everyday turns out to be nothing at all, founded on nothing. A single truth remains, that of the disintegration, as all things give way. The entire world stands revealed as monstrous vanity. Ionesco appeals to *Ecclesiastes* but the language is that of Martin Heidegger:

> I have never quite succeeded in getting used to existence, whether it be the existence of the world or of other people, or above all of myself. Sometimes it seems to me that the forms of life are suddenly emptied of their contents, reality is unreal, words are nothing but sounds bereft of sense, these houses and this sky are no longer anything but facades concealing nothing, people appear to be moving about automatically and without

> reason; everything seems to melt into thin air, everything is threatened – myself included – by a silent and imminent collapse into I know not what abyss, where there is no more night or day. (*Notes*, p.163)

What one normally takes for granted becomes uncertain: the world, other people, oneself. Everyday structures appear pointless, words, as in *The Bald Prima Donna*, become mere noises, the houses and the sky of the euphoric vision perch on the edge of the void, human beings and their normal activities seem incomprehensible, robot-like. Above all, everything, including oneself, seems menaced by a dissolution into amorphousness. At this point, though, Ionesco differs greatly in emphasis from Samuel Beckett. Where the latter finds in the experience of *angst* grim and irrefutable evidence of one's being-there, the former concentrates rather more on what Heidegger terms the Uncanny. *Angst* reveals the everyday as strange by situating it over an abyss of nothingness. In the work of Ionesco the picture is unchanged: for the Uncanny we substitute the sense of wonder which the author himself refers to as his fundamental response to the world. One of the most revealing descriptions of the Ionesco vision from this point of view occurs in the *Journal*:

> Walls collapsed, definitions were dislocated. There was no longer any direction. The names of things drew apart from things . . . our reality broke up into thousands of pieces . . . Everything that I had thought to be solidly built was only castles of cards that had tumbled down. (II, pp.171–2)

The passage continues:

> I was a stranger and alone, infinitely a stranger to myself. I was waking up or being born in a new universe . . . The stupefaction was so great that it cancelled out all fear and . . . was only an echo of plenitude, and what was strange immediately was transformed into what was familiar.
> (II, pp.171–2)

Disintegration of what appeared to be solid, dislocation of everyday meanings, loss of direction or purpose, all recall the Beckett experience of *angst*. There is even an echo in the above passage of Watt's difficulty with names and their relations to objects. But the stress is on the strangeness of it all. Ionesco is strange to himself, reborn in a new world which is, however, also familiar because it is simply a transfiguration of the old as the substance of things dissolves into the essential. Elsewhere this is concisely summarized. Just as Heideggerian *angst* reveals the true status of things so Ionesco's experience has the effect of suddenly opening one's eyes to the alien quality of normal life:

> I have the impression of being with extremely polite people . . . Suddenly something breaks down, gives way and the monstrous character of men appears or rather the scene becomes strangely unknown and men and the scene thus perhaps reveal their true nature. (*Entretiens*, p.167)

This could be a description of *The Bald Prima Donna* or, indeed, of any Ionesco play. Of course there are two sides to the experience of wonder and the passage relates particularly to the claustrophobic whereas the one quoted before it relates to the euphoric. This fact must be translated into the terminology of Heidegger's philosophy if the parallel with the idea of *angst* is to be sustained.

Angst, as Heidegger sees it, simply reveals the make-up of man, that is, existence, *dasein*. It reveals both the freedom and the facticity of existence: man as a project into the future; man as *there*, as situated, whether he likes it or not. These two aspects of the experience are immediately recognizable in the Ionesco polarity of euphoria and claustrophobia. If the sense of wonder in the plays parallels the disintegrating vision of the Uncanny, then the two modalities of wonder parallel the major revelations of the Heideggerian trauma. But we must examine the matter in greater detail.

To begin with, the euphoric itself suggests both aspects of *angst*:

> . . . when . . . I wake to myself and the world, and suddenly gain . . . an awareness that I *am*, that I exist, that I am surrounded by something, all sorts of objects, a sort of world, and everything seems strange and incomprehensible to me and I am

> overwhelmed by the wonder of being alive . . . Then the universe seems to me infinitely strange and foreign.
>
> (*Notes*, p.141)

In this passage to exist and to be aware of oneself as existing is to be a being surrounded by one's world or, in philosophic terms, a being-in-the-world. Ionesco's euphoria represents a realization that all is strange and alien but it is this very realization that confronts one with the *fact* of existence. Of course Ionesco insists on the strangeness of the experience rather than on its facticity but to some extent the two concepts merge in the euphoric. Moreover the Ionesco experience equally asserts the reality of freedom. In Heidegger the emptiness which invades the everyday and threatens it is the void of freedom. Indeed, freedom and existence are synonymous terms. A similar conjunction is evidenced in Ionesco's work. Amédée, flying above the stage, experiences a release, lightness and liberty, "an insubstantial universe . . . Freedom" (II, p.200). Choubert, also "surprised to be, surprised to be" (II, p.301) as he climbs high mountains of the imagination and prepares to ascend into the air, experiences existence as a liberation. Freedom, emptiness, a sense of the void in a mood of joy, light and air, the power to fly, all these go together. Bérenger of *The Killer* or *A Stroll in the Air* is aware above all of his possibilities. To feel joy in the radiant city, in the experience of the luminous houses and in the toy landscape of *A Stroll* is to feel that one can achieve anything or, in more existential terms, it is to confront an open future, the nothingness, filled with possibilities for action and fulfilment, of freedom itself. Once we recognize the very close parallel between the Ionesco euphoria and Heidegger's vision of existence as freedom we are also in a position to explain along philosophic lines the ambivalence of the euphoric. *Angst* itself is ambivalent. In so far as it is an experience of one's freedom it may be felt as exhilarating. But existential freedom also presents itself as a responsibility, as something one cannot escape, and so as a threat, a torment even, as we have seen with reference to Beckett's work. Likewise in Ionesco a character may comment wrily "rather an empty . . . brilliance" (VII, p.37). Jean of *Hunger and Thirst* leaves his home and finds freedom on the high plateau, in the emptiness and the light. But then freedom is felt as a frightening void which thrusts itself on one. Bérenger of *A Stroll* has a similar transition from joy to anxiety in his flight above the world and in *The Chairs* emptiness is very definitely felt as frightening and claustrophobic, that is, as *crowding* one. Thus the experience of Existence as *freedom* throws one back on that of Existence as an inescapable *fact*. I am free but I *have* to be free, I cannot escape responsibility. The sense of possibilities and the void comes at every turn upon that of one's concrete, particular *thereness*. The Ionesco flight is suddenly transformed into an imprisonment because freedom is inconceivable without the world, without a restricted, limited space as its area of operations. Euphoria now turns into its opposite but the common ground remains: it is Ionesco's wonder which, like Heideggerian *angst*, focusses in turn (if not all at once) on every aspect of the human situation. Once we are in the power of the claustrophobic we are aware only of the monolithic *thereness* or facticity of life. Amédée is tired, weighed down by the body, hemmed in on all sides by the existential situation, unable to escape until the final act. Matter, the brute weight of Existence, swamps the whole scene in plays like *The Bald Prima Donna, The Lesson, Jacques, The Future is in Eggs* and *Rhinoceros*. In each case the overwhelming sense is comparable to that found in Beckett: to exist is to suffocate, to be enclosed in a room or stifled by objects or words or people. At the same time, as in the euphoric, all is strange and Ionesco writes *The Bald Prima Donna*, as he writes plays depicting freedom, in order to underline the astounding fact, that of existing, of being, "*le fait d'exister, d'être*" (*Entretiens*, p.70)

If euphoria suggests Heideggerian categories of freedom and facticity (freedom viewed as release and facticity as plenitude) or, at times, effects a transition to feelings of vertigo (freedom experienced as menace) or even to its obverse, claustrophobia (facticity experienced as restricting), then claustrophobia too has more than one face. Now Heideggerian existence has not a twofold but a threefold structure: man exists as facticity, freedom and as "falling". In order to grasp this last category we must return to the analysis of *dasein* in *Being and Time*. When Heidegger poses the question of the original identity of *dasein* the answer is given as *das man*, meaning "they", as one says *on* in French. Heidegger's first subject is not "I" but an indefinite plural. Absorbed in "everydayness", *dasein* does what anyone does, what "other people" do, it *is* anyone: "we take pleasure . . . as *they* take pleasure; we read, see and judge . . . as *they* see and judge".[1] This is a descriptive, an ontological, not a moral observation. For the most part *dasein* has no real personal identity: it *is* "they" in the sense that it participates in a general ethos which proceeds from no one in particular but is "in the air" as it were. Some things "are done", others are "not done", one does things as they "ought to be done". While the origin of such imperatives remains obscure, their power is immense. As a "they" *dasein* lives in the public eye, its activities are always on show and therefore characterized by superficiality or, more specifically, by what Heidegger calls Idle Talk, Curiosity and Ambiguity. *Dasein* is said to "fall" from an "authentic" mode of existence into "everydayness", into "inauthenticity" or the role of the "they". The dubious "supposition of the 'they' that one is leading . . . a full and genuine 'life', brings Dasein a *tranquillity*, for which everything is 'in the best of order' ",[2] and in this comforting illusion it busies itself distractedly with its schemes, "alienated" from its authentic possibilities, "entangled" in a mass of short-sighted objectives. But *dasein* is not merely confused, it *is* this confusion, this falling into incoherency, itself its own trajectory, its own plunge. In what follows we shall see that claustrophobia in Ionesco's work relates especially to the pressure of the collective, of everyday social norms, and euphoria to the experience of authenticity. Of course it is the function of *angst* to shake the foundation of normality, to distance man from the "they". It could be said that in *angst dasein* acquires an authentic identity: no longer legion, it is now individualized, what Heidegger refers to as "being-one's-self" – in short, it is *alone*, ontologically so. *Angst* points up *dasein*'s vague, all-pervasive "guilt", its unwillingness to assume responsibility. It therefore acts as a "voice of conscience". In a world of Idle Talk, Curiosity and Ambiguity the call of Conscience is silent, single-minded and categorical. Like *angst*, Conscience says "nothing" at all, it simply nullifies all else, repeating itself with the insistence of fact, undermining the everyday, bringing before *dasein* its own image, alone, free, "forsaken", "abandoned", without alibi. If *dasein* acknowledges the call it is said to bear its guilt, to be "resolute", answerable for itself. Resolute *dasein* and authenticity are one and the same. Heidegger sums up his entire argument by saying that the voice one hears in *angst* calls one to oneself as existing and by terming this the voice of Care. Care, *sorge*, is *dasein*'s being as a creature of constant project, of worry and anxiety over the emptiness of a free future. Angst simply reveals man to himself as a being shot through and through with Care. It also offers him an opportunity to face his own nature authentically and to live without disguise. It happens that this choice is scarcely the issue in Beckett's work. Authenticity is a luxury the tramps cannot afford – and that precisely *is* their authenticity. But Ionesco, unlike Beckett, is concerned with the sphere of the ethical, so that in considering the plays in the context of Heideggerian *angst* we are bound to focus on the phenomenon of the "they" and on its counterpart: the Resolute, authentic hero, one who is in some special sense identified with the euphoric vision and set against the stifling world of "falling", inauthentic beings.

A strikingly Heideggerian image of the "they" is offered in a slight, but interesting, play entitled *The Leader* (*Le Maître*, 1953). A public figure, perhaps a political leader, executes a series of magnificent gestures before an enthusiastic crowd but out of sight of the audience: he has his trousers ironed, smiles, walks about, tastes flowers, fruits and roots, suffers children to come to him, shows confidence in all, institutes a police force, salutes justice, honours the great conquerors and conquered of the past, recites a few lines. Everyone cheers wildly. At the end, the great man appears on stage. But he is headless. Suddenly each character is breathlessly enquiring of his neighbour: "What's your name?" (IV, p.117) The play reads like a Heidegger parable. The great man is *nobody* at all, he has no head and his followers are no better: everyone is, as it were, someone else, everyone is "they", an indefinite plural, a projection into another who has himself no personality.

This is the world of Ionesco's first play, *The Bald Prima Donna*. Early criticism of *The Bald Prima Donna* was quick to see it as a satire of the bourgeoisie (Ionesco made it evident that it was not to be regarded as a satire of English manners). But for the author the bourgeois is not limited to a particular social class: "the petit-bourgeois is for me a man of fixed ideas, one who turns up at every period in every society: a conformist . . ." (*Notes*, p.135) The early Ionesco character is one who is interchangeable with another. Thus at the end of *The Bald Prima Donna* the action recommences with the Martins in place of the Smiths. The horror of the play is the claustrophobia of a world of stereotypes:

> As far as the characters of my first play are concerned . . . they are robbed of any psychology. They are quite simply mechanical things . . . They are remote from themselves. They are in the world of the impersonal . . . of the collective.
>
> (*Entretiens*, pp.132–3)

In Heideggerian terms such characters are not themselves but "they", *das man*. Puppets whose reactions are stilted and impersonal, whose language consists entirely of common platitudes, the Smiths and Martins are "nobody", like "the leader". Ionesco's equivalent for Idle Talk is, obviously enough, the proliferation of words which chokes the action as the play proceeds. Again, the characters are "curious", in Heidegger's technical sense, in that they lack a centre of personality. Their attention moves constantly outwards to new irrelevancies. Above all, their language is not used to express truths, to establish relationships, but to disguise reality, to render everything ambiguous. Clearly, in the Heideggerian system, the primary aim of inauthentic behaviour, that is, the Idle Talk, Curiosity and Ambiguity, is to keep the condemning vision of *angst* at arm's length. Two facets of inauthentic, collective behaviour stand out in Ionesco's portrayal: aggressiveness and irrationality. Emotion is always present as a repressed undercurrent in *The Bald Prima Donna*, constantly liable to break out and transform seemingly innocuous words into deadly threats. Logic is simply the servant of such emotion, which builds up in a series of tense situations, moving to a climax near the end. The "they" hides its hate behind a mask of reason. In Punch and Judy fashion, by starts and jerks and yet with frightening consistency, the characters advance to a confrontation. Of course we laugh. Nevertheless the dialogue moves us gradually from comedy to threat. In the maid's poem everything catches fire and from then on Smiths and Martins are more and more at each others' throats. They begin to shout commonplaces and absurdities as the mass of sounds more and more images the emptiness within. There is no point of reference here, since everyone is equally inauthentic. If the play communicates a sense of wonder or *angst*, if the climax is experienced as a disintegration of normality, it is because Ionesco has the *audience* supply its own point of authentic reference. The characters erupt and then subside, normality has been revealed for a while as situated over the void. But it is the spectator, not the protagonist, who is stifled by a nothingness which crowds, who, in a mood of Ionesco wonder, feels the evanescence of everyday reality and its density, sees the Smiths and Martins hanging in a void and yet enclosed by the pressure of their being-*there.* Ionesco himself has described the writing of the play in terms reminiscent of the experience of Heidegger's Uncanny:

> An extraordinary phenomenon took place, I know not how: before my very eyes the text underwent a subtle transformation . . . those inspired yet simple sentences which I had so painstakingly copied . . . changed places all by themselves, became garbled and corrupted. (*Notes*, p.184)

As straightforward, lucid statements from the English manual for beginners begin to alter, to deteriorate, the affirmation that there are seven days in the week is monstrously distorted to argue that there are three: Tuesday, Thursday and Tuesday. Comically and tragically,

> . . . what had happened was a kind of collapse of reality. The words had turned into sounding shells devoid of meaning; the characters . . . had been emptied of psychology and the world appeared to me in an unearthly . . . light . . . (*Notes*, p.185)

Even as he writes, the author is overcome by *angst*, by the vision of humans emptied of all everyday motivation or significance, of a language reduced to its outer shell, what in the later *Découvertes* Ionesco terms language from which thought has withdrawn as from a dead body, "*cadavre, corps sans âme*".[3] *The Bald Prima Donna* depicts man as immersed in the world in the form of the collective, that is, as an inauthentic or "falling" being-with, a creature whose identity is legion, one of innumerable Bobby Watsons. We are in the world of *guignol*, following the antics of *père* Ubu. But in other plays the element of *guignol* is slowly modified, and a movement towards the human is discernible. This is synonymous with the gradual emergence of an authentic hero. What happens is that the crowd of *The Bald Prima Donna* differentiates, in later plays, into victim and aggressors, so that the stage is set for one of Ionesco's central concerns, the struggle of the authentic individual against the collective.

Already in *The Lesson* one of the characters is victim and the other aggressor. More obviously than in *The Bald Prima Donna*, normality turns into a nightmare. The teacher, a respectable figure of authority, imposes his will on the young girl; education is revealed as disguised sexual sadism. Gradually the pupil ceases to resist and at the end, before the murder, has been rendered totally passive, swallowed up by a fury of irrational platitudes. In *Jacques* and *The Future is in Eggs* the victim is a youth and the family is the aggressor. As always normality is supported by reason and reason serves to disguise underlying violence. Jacques is asked to submit to tradition and the family: he must marry and reproduce. As well he must utter a ludicrous formula of submission: "I love potatoes in their jackets" (I, p.128). In this case the situation of claustrophobia indicates not only the pressure of the family but, more specifically, the force towards conformity inherent in the sexual relationship. Roberte, young Jacques' chosen mate, is the prime agent in his surrender to society. She is all moisture, inviting the experience of sinking into darkness and mud so familiar in the plays. When everything becomes "cat", "it's . . . absence of language, it's . . . abdication of the rational, of freedom in the face of the organic" (*Entretiens*, p.159). This victory of the "they" receives confirmation in *The Future*, where the reference is to a wider social world. Submission to conformity leads to frenzied reproduction. Grandfather has died and the family must replace him, must, in its mechanical way, produce another replica. At the end the proliferation of eggs in which the entire set is swallowed up is, in fact, the proliferation of the Ionesco puppet, the "they". The parallel is with industrial mass production and the overtones are those of right-wing politics. The situation is only a little altered in *The Chairs*. Here the protagonist has lived a lifetime of experience and yet has only a garbled, incoherent message to deliver. Like the old couple, the crowd which arrives is simply an *emptiness* which clutters the stage, an accumulation of chairs. And yet there are hints that the old man has been victimized and is comparable to young Jacques. In all of these plays the vision of *angst* belongs properly not to any one character but to the audience, as in *The Bald Prima Donna*. In each case we are faced with violence, confusion and banality, with disintegration coloured by the sense of the strange. Marriage and reproduction, education, personal relations appear grotesque, as if set on the backdrop of the void. As all everyday meaning falls away we are left only with a massive presence, the "thereness" of the everyday, a stifling pressure of inauthentic being. If the "they" crowds, though, it does so only to proclaim its nothingness, as in *The Chairs*.

The word "duty", significantly mentioned in *The Future*, becomes the theme of *Victims of Duty* where the individual once again suffers at the hands of others. Choubert, the protagonist, is no rebel but a little man who readily bends before prevailing norms. At the same time his dream journey to the heights of the Alps illustrates what he himself is unable to express, his desire for authenticity, that is, for the euphoric experience of freedom. At first Choubert is simply the little bourgeois who is eager to believe in authority, if also slightly apprehensive. The threat to freedom comes from a number of sources. The detective who forces Choubert on his dream journey and who tyrannizes him represents authority and is in addition a father figure. Madeleine, who helps the detective, is a threat as wife and, later, as mother. As the play proceeds the detective takes on the appearance of an inquisitor and of a psychoanalyst. Choubert descends into his own depths, only to discover there the claustrophobia of the "they" – since he is at this stage a kind of nobody. But the quest for an identity goes on with the detective and Madeleine anxious lest Choubert should stumble on the experience of freedom. Time is reversed. The detective and Madeleine become Choubert's parents for a while. Clearly we are back in the setting of *Jacques*. Thus Choubert's humiliating journey into the depths involves an immersion in sensuality, a descent to the infantile and, above all, a submission to "duty", society's sanction for the guilt with which it burdens the hapless individual. It is impossible to miss autobiographical echoes at this point. Ionesco's parents are clearly reflected in the detective and Madeleine, particularly in the quarrel scene. Ionesco's father, closely associated in the mind of the playwright with Romanian Nazism, is easily linked with the figure of authority. As Choubert turns into a child he witnesses what Ionesco witnessed and describes in his *Journal* (II, p.20–21), his mother's attempted suicide. In the play, though not in the *Journal*, the father forces poison on the wife. For a little while Choubert escapes this stifling family milieu when his dream journey takes him to joy and liberation. "I'm alone" (II, p.299), he laughs on the heights of the Alps. To bring him back the others recall him to his "duty", to the advantages of normal social existence: "The country that bore you has need of you . . . You've got your life, your career ahead of you! You'll be rich, happy and stupid . . ." (II, p.300). Above all, their argument is for the collective: "It's not good to be alone . . Remember the solidarity of the human race . . ." (II, p.299). But solitude *is* good, Choubert sees. Dimly aware of a transfigured world, the first of Ionesco's characters to tentatively approach the apprehension of *angst*, he is in the process of discovering his true identity, his being distinct from the crowd or, in Heidegger's terms, his being-one's-self. Certainly Choubert is defeated: his tendency to airiness is counterbalanced by his being stuffed with bread. Moreover, no one is responsible for this outrage. Everyone is a "victim of duty", the aggressor is everyone and no one, it is the all-embracing and elusive "they". But if Choubert is overwhelmed he nonetheless achieves much more than his predecessors: for the first time in Ionesco there is a character in a play to act as mediator to the audience. Where in the case of *The Bald Prima Donna* an authentic point of reference does not exist in the play, Choubert is a standard of sorts. However fearful, he emerges from the ocean of the collective, he is more human, more individualized, than, for example, Jacques.

Amédée represents a further development in this direction. Again we begin with the repressive situation, in this case the pressure of normality in the impossibly crowded flat and, of course, the pressure of the growing corpse. This last may be variously interpreted. Here it suffices to suggest that it images Amédée's own past which lives on to stifle him. As in *Victims* and *Jacques*, woman is associated with the repressive. There seems little doubt that Madeleine (also the name of Choubert's wife) weighs heavily on Amédée and indeed that, in some sense, it is she who represents the power of the inauthentic in the deadening pull of female immanence, the claustrophobia of the conjugal situation. It is therefore not fanciful to identify the corpse with Amédée's wife, though this is clearly not the whole story, and to suppose that the subtitle of the play – *How to get rid of it* – refers to Madeleine. Amédée is Jacques fifteen years later: "We've been living shut up here for fifteen years" (II, p.161). In addition he is a playwright, so that his conflict with his wife may be taken as a picture of the artist's relation to society. While Madeleine works at the telephone, in contact with the busy sphere of the "they", Amédée attempts to write, hopelessly and without inspiration, crushed by the presence of the corpse whose silent multiplication can only remind us of the proliferation of matter and the pressure of inauthenticity in earlier plays. Ineffectually, Amédée protests, adding that one must have joy in order to create (II, p.158). It is Coleridge's problem and the situation is unchanged. Amédée is unheroic. If he differs from Choubert it is only that he is more fully realized as a human being with a capacity for suffering and hope. At any rate his sense of vaguely apprehended *angst*, an all-pervasive unease, coupled with a confused and timid longing for release, introduces a new element into the Ionesco play though one implicit even in *The Bald Prima Donna*. Reality, for the couple in *Amédée*, is dense and heavy and yet it is falling apart, full of holes, a void which presses in upon one as in the Heideggerian experience (II, p.200). On the whole, however, it is the woman who is most tormented by the claustrophobic facticity of things, by the weight of the past while the man longs for the euphoric. Inevitably, it is he who breaks out. Husband and wife slowly pull the giant corpse out of the window in the second act and in Ionesco's directions this must suggest that the very entrails of the house and of the characters are being hauled out (II, pp.211–2). It is, of course, a birth. Where Choubert mimes his sense of release in a dream state, Amédée actually experiences the joy of flight in act three. Symbolically, he rises above the mass of onlookers. Like Choubert's Madeleine, his wife attempts to stop him, but unsuccessfully. It is true that he is an unwilling individualist, excusing himself profusely as he rises in the air ("I'm all for progress, I like to be of use to my fellow men . . . I believe in social realism", (II, p.225). But neither Social Realism nor the desire to serve the collective can prevent the assertion of Amédée's deepest instinct for freedom. He continues comically, assuring us that he is opposed to transcendence, until he disappears in the brilliant night sky.

The authentic character is fully developed in *Rhinoceros* which recapitulates all the earlier Ionesco themes but moves out of the conjugal sphere and into that of the socio-political. Bérenger (another of that name) is at once contrasted with the other characters in the play. Whereas his friend Jean is well-dressed and tidy in his opinions and ideas, Bérenger is a doubtful case, like Choubert and Amédée. Again *le devoir* is a key issue. Unlike Jean, Bérenger has no willpower and consequently little sense of duty. "The superior man is he who fulfils his duty" (IV, p.7), the former argues. It is the argument for control, for power, the Nietzschean position as interpreted by the Nazis and it highlights the first characteristic of the inauthentic collective: aggressiveness. As we have seen, irrationality disguised as logic is the other characteristic of the "they". And indeed, as Bérenger argues with his friend, a logician at the next table is putting forward views paralleling Jean's. From the start Bérenger feels ill at ease, weighed down, like Amédée, feeling "a sort of anguish difficult to describe . . . out of place in life, among people". The *angst* of earlier characters is now out in the open: "I can't seem to get used to myself. I don't even know if I *am* me" (IV, pp.17–18). Bérenger is a stranger to himself, a misfit in society, even out of step with existence. The world of the logician and of Jean is precisely that world of certitudes that is slipping from him. As it does so Bérenger is possessed by a feeling of something wrong, not quite the feeling of wonder but a distant apprehension of the Uncanny. This is the usual plight of the Ionesco rebel but it is conscious in Bérenger, whereas Choubert and Amédée are misfits in spite of themselves. It does not follow that the protagonist of *Rhinoceros* emerges as a powerful figure, quite the contrary: he too is an unwilling hero, full of doubts and contradictions, but his approach is fundamentally authentic since he questions the platitudes of the "they". For this reason Bérenger is more than a passive victim. As the characters continue their conversations, more and more people are turned into rhinoceroses. In act two Jean is transformed and by the third Bérenger, who cannot resign himself to rhinoceritis, is left almost alone. The disease is a madness, but one which is contagious and dangerously attractive. As Jean gives way to his bestial nature, his ideas appear progressively simpler and more lucid. At the same time his sense of purpose is undergoing a similar simplification, a concentration of the will – and this is the meaning of the rhinoceros image. Jean and the others will charge straight ahead, enslaved by a mass of prejudices which take on the appearance of a terrible, warped lucidity. As more metamorphoses occur, normality and rhinoceritis coincide. Eventually even Daisy leaves him and Bérenger is alone, assailed by doubt. But he does not give in, nor is the ending of the play morally ambiguous, as some have suggested. Certainly there is an element of the ridiculous in Bérenger's resistance but this in no way makes it "absurd". On the contrary, Ionesco affirms the value and dignity of Bérenger's solitude. Initial criticism insisted on misunderstanding the playwright on this score from *The Bald Prima Donna* on, but he has made his stand clear: "for me it was neither a matter of incommunicability, nor of solitude. On the contrary, I'm in favour of solitude" (*Entretiens*, p.69). Bérenger at the end of *Rhinoceros* has reached a point of truth sought after confusedly by Jacques, by the old man of *The Chairs*, by Choubert and Amédée. Of course the "they" has won and this is imaged in the proliferation of animals and the sense of claustrophobia, but the protagonist triumphs also and that despite the open possibility of his capitulation. Bérenger's strength is his naiveté, his embryonic sense of wonder, the sense of *angst*. Precisely because of it he sees what no one else does, the strangeness of the metamorphosis from man to beast. From the start and more clearly than Amédée, he sees the world of the "they" as falling apart, as insane and dangerous. Indeed it is the void of this world, its nothingness which hems him in at the end. Although initially hardly qualified to play the hero, he is in Heidegger's terms individualized or set apart by the experience of *angst*, no longer a Ionesco puppet, a rebel rather than a mere scapegoat; in short, he possesses a real identity as an authentic hero. Bérenger is committed to the truth – "I feel involved. I just can't be indifferent" (IV, p.78) – and "resolute" in the Heideggerian sense. Moreover his commitment is indistinguishable from his sense of wonder: "I'm frankly surprised, I'm very, very surprised. I can't get over it" (IV, p.79). Because of this the sense of *angst* is not thrust directly upon the audience, as it is in *The Bald Prima Donna*. Rather, disintegration and claustrophobia are experienced from Bérenger's point of view. Ionesco has found a spokesman for the underdog, the man of good will.

Like all else in Ionesco's work the parable of *Rhinoceros* is surprisingly autobiographical. Rhinoceritis recalls the rise of

Nazism, minutely described in Ionesco's *Journal* as personally experienced by the playwright in pre-war Roumania. When Ionesco tells Bonnefoy about his homeland the latter exclaims "but it's the story of Bérenger . . . you're telling me" (*Entretiens*, p.26). Ionesco's sense of hopelessness in Bucharest is exactly Bérenger's situation and it mirrors, as Ionesco points out, the difficulty of standing firm even in one's own mind against the collective and its dominant ideologies. The enemy in *Rhinoceros*, however, is not simply Fascism. Botard, for example, tends to the left and is notwithstanding metamorphosed. The true enemy is the conformist, a fact which explains Ionesco's intense dislike of Sartre's politics, as he understands them, and his disagreement with Kenneth Tynan, as well as his fear of Nazism. Whether in a revolutionary or in a reactionary society,

> . . . for me the *petit bourgeois* is just a man of slogans, who . . . repeats the truths that others have imposed upon him, ready-made and therefore lifeless. In short . . . a manipulated man.
> (*Notes*, p.67)

The political emphasis of *Rhinoceros* should not, however, obscure the other dimension of repression: the sphere of marriage and the family.

I have already pointed out the identity of Nazism and the father figure in Ionesco's mind, a fact immediately explicable in autobiographical terms. Like D.H. Lawrence, however, who initially sided with the mother in the family situation, only to take the man's part in later life and in his writings, Ionesco clearly moves from a fear of the paternal to a revulsion against the maternal. Ionesco's parents quarrelled violently and the boy grew up in his mother's care. We cannot fail to see that in Ionesco's work the woman – mother or wife, it is all one – generally stifles the man. This is the case in *The Chairs*, though not to a marked degree, and evident in *Jacques*, *Victims* and *Amédée*. Bérenger of *Rhinoceros* is abandoned by Daisy and the pattern is repeated in later plays. Thus while it is tempting to identify the claustrophobic with the father figure, the fear of authority and the totalitarian, and the euphoric with Ionesco's pleasant childhood with his mother, it is equally important to relate the claustrophobic to the feminine. Ionesco has offered a Jungian interpretation of the two feelings, but, in view of his prolonged confession, particularly in the *Journal*, it is not easy to avoid a Freudian conclusion as well. One might tentatively suggest the following picture: a claustrophobic feminine, not unlike the Freudian Id, struggling against the Superego, the euphoric, evanescent, masculine transcendence identified with an absent father. Nevertheless the bias of the present thesis is philosophical, not psychological, and it is suffices to note here a number of links between the claustrophobic and the euphoric at the conjugal and at the political level. In Heideggerian terms we must say that as he grows in authenticity the Ionesco protagonist must free himself of all stifling social and personal ties. The world of the "they" exerts its influence first in the home, then over the entire globe. If the point is not sufficiently clear in some of the earlier plays it becomes evident later. In *Frenzy for Two . . . and the same to you* (*Délire à Deux . . .A tant qu'on veut*, 1962), conjugal discord takes place in the midst of revolution. In the film sequence *Anger: a Film Scenario* (*La Colère: scénario de film*, 1961) there is a steady progression from minor conjugal conflicts to a world conflagration and the explosion of a nuclear bomb.

The aggressiveness of the "they" is evident on a political or at any rate mass scale in the work of the seventies. *Macbeth*, in Ionesco's hands, turns into terrifying farce: *Macbett. Here Comes a Chopper* details grotesquely the spirit of egotism which prevails during an epidemic. One could say that in both these plays Ionesco has returned to the tormented puppetry of *The Bald Prima Donna*, though this is less true of *Here Come a Chopper* than *Macbett* for reasons to be explored in the next chapter. At any rate, there are no authentic characters in these works, only violent automatons. In *The Hermit* and *Oh what a bloody circus*, however, this is not the case.

Ionesco's first novel and its accompanying piece actually look back to the achievement of *Rhinoceros*, while at the same time introducing an entirely new element in the depiction of the authentic protagonist: inwardness. At least this is so with *The Hermit*, Ionesco's first attempt at first-person narration and so his first portrayal of solitude *from the inside*. The protagonist is, indeed, Bérenger of *Rhinoceros*, though he remains nameless, another *naïf*, someone who questions, unable to accept the normality of things, "an obsessional neurotic", a sufferer from "metaphysical anxiety" (p.88). Towards the end of the novel he is as alone, as surrounded by violence and unreason as Bérenger. Everywhere revolution rages, the city is being destroyed, the population is dying. It is, in fact, another kind of rhinoceritis. In the play, while the situation is broadly identical, we cannot, for obvious reasons, share the protagonist's thought. Instead, Ionesco has The Character maintain his integrity through silence. Everyone talks around him – it is the triumph of Heideggerian Idle Talk – but the protagonist has almost nothing to say, and the dramatic effect is convincing, more so perhaps than the technique of the novel. The Character gives the impression of well-meaning, confused vulnerability. He is a more shell-shocked Bérenger, part victim, part observer of the human comedy. Once again, both in *The Hermit* and *Oh what a bloody circus*, we are in a universe infected with the disease of disintegration, *angst*. For the first time, however, Ionesco introduces a variation on the theme which is surely a very personal one: the protagonist of the novel seeks to *induce* the feeling of strangeness. Deliberately, he distances himself, eyeing reality as if he had never encountered it before, listening to conversations whose meaning he labours to abolish. By an act of concentration he stares at a wine stain on the tablecloth ("it was all a question of looking . . . until you no longer remember what it was," (pp.50–51)) or, again, he rapidly repeats a word – table, for example – until it is emptied of sense. Later he encourages a feeling of alienation in the street ("that vision of the strangeness, the unusual aspect of the world", (p.76)), all the while wishing to be closer to his fellow human beings. Movements become disordered, words merely sound; as he watches holes opening in human faces to receive the contents of glasses, the houses all around lose their solidity, the protagonist's own moving fingers give cause for laughter. In the middle of it all, he exists: "I was . . . *there*, in the heart of things" (p.77). An even closer parallel to the Heideggerian experience is found in another episode (p.93). Like Watt, the protagonist is in the midst of things which are no longer themselves, in particular a large container for clothes and linen with a double door which refuses the name of "closet". At the same time he himself is void of identity. In fact everything, himself included, has become fragile, as if it were all collapsing into nothingness. "The nausea of nothingness" and "the nausea of surfeit" (p.95) combine. As in Heidegger, strangeness focusses the sense of existence only to question it, it overwhelms only to disintegrate. Something similar happens in the play where, following the speech of the Russian lodger (scene VII) in which the world is seen as flux, as subject to seismic tremors of metaphysical proportions, the protagonist anxiously checks walls and floors for signs of weakness. And then of course both novel and play end with scenes of disintegration, though in a context of revelation. Clearly the "they" rule the streets, but a victory of sorts is reserved for the authentic individual, one hardly envisaged for the earlier Bérenger. In *Entre la Vie et le Rêve* (*Between Life and Dream*, 1966–7), a new, expanded version of the original interview with Claude Bonnefoy, Ionesco discusses the Kafkaesque inanities of the crowd in *The Hermit* and *Oh what a bloody circus* and the moment of truth for the protagonist at the end of the play in particular. In order to comment on this, however, we need to place the struggle of the Ionesco individual in a wider context than that so far examined.

8 Ionesco and Heidegger: authenticity, death and the search for being

> We are all going to die? Tell me the truth!
>
> (*Entretiens*, p.12)

> How blind I had been . . . I was saved now . . . because I knew now . . . I am, I myself am, everything is. The miracle of being, the miracle of being, the miracle of being.
>
> (*Journal*, II, p.156)

So far this argument has stressed the progressive emergence of an authentic hero in Ionesco's work, a character distinguished from the collective, first as its victim, then as a full-fledged rebel, inspired by the vision of *angst*, the awareness, denied to the earlier puppets, of existence as alternately euphoric and claustrophobic. But the struggle against female immanence, against the inertia of matter and the past, against the family and the state is only the beginning. There is another, more formidable, adversary.

The Killer, a work written a little before *Rhinoceros*, provides an important perspective in this regard. Here another Bérenger sees clearly enough the dreariness of the everyday, the futility of life in the rainy city whose inhabitants are ugly because neither ugly nor beautiful, "creatures that are dismally neutral", suffering existence unconsciously. Not through intelligence but through simplicity Bérenger is "not so wise, not so resigned, not so patient" (III, p.20, p.21), he cannot accept the everyday precisely because in his naiveté it appears to him as strange. In act one he experiences everything in terms of freedom and the euphoric as he tours the radiant city. Here wonder conjures up the lightness, brilliance and evanesence of Ionesco's personal encounter. It is *angst*, a vision of nothingness, but with a positive emphasis, a sense of an open future, of boundless possibility in a world suddenly made fragile and intoxicating. Not unexpectedly, there is an undercurrent of uneasiness. While Bérenger pours out his heart, enthusiasm is questioned by the behaviour of the architect and the girl Dany and above all by the pool full of corpses set in the heart of the city of light. Obviously euphoric freedom is not the whole story. Existence has another facet, a fact which elsewhere explains the element of ambiguity in Choubert's temporary elation and in Amédée's flight. Freedom is not possible without limits, that is, without facticity; to be free is equally to be *there*, to be situated. This means that even as it projects us into an open future freedom recalls us to the past, to our being "thrown" into a world of finitude. More importantly, the experience of freedom in *angst* makes us aware of that other limit coexistent with our birth, our futural limit, death. *Angst* reveals man to himself, it shows him that he exists, in other words, it faces him with his ontological bounds, it disconcertingly outlines the limits of the box into which he has been thrust. *Dasein* or being-there means being hemmed in on the one hand by birth, on the other, by death. Of course these are not phenomena *external* to man, incidentals as it were. They *define* man, because man is precisely *da-sein*.

The question of death does not properly arise in the context of Beckett's work but in Ionesco it is of crucial importance. Moreover the parallel with Heidegger is very close. For Heidegger *angst* and authenticity are organically linked with the fact of death. Death, in this context, is not an event in one's life or, as Sartre thinks, simply cessation of life, transformation of *pour soi* into *en soi*, but one of the limits of existence. It is a part of life, *the* possibility or project towards which *dasein* travels as it plunges into the void of its freedom, that is, its future. It is a project which modifies all lesser projects, a possibility that belongs to *dasein* as individual since it cannot be shared or, in Heidegger's language, "that *possibility which is one's ownmost, which is non-relational, and which is not to be outstripped*".[1] Of course, death is revealed by *angst*, since *angst* is said to individualize man or set him apart from the crowd of the "they". For Heidegger authenticity requires that death be "anticipated", that it permeate one's present. Man is a being-towards-death, finite not in the sense that he "will die" some day but in the sense that he is *made for dying*, whether he likes it or not. Inauthentic man escapes the recognition of death as he escapes *angst*. Authenticity means, among other things, an inward acknowledgement that one is being "thrown" into existence and consequently "falling" into the arms of death.

In *The Killer* the collective avoids this difficult conclusion, partly by burying itself in everyday trivia, partly by concentrating on what Ionesco regards as less important spheres such as the political. Act three for a while takes us to a rally headed by mother Pipe and her geese. In a tangle of leftist propaganda and echoes of Facism reason is shown as subservient to prejudice and hate. It is the world of earlier plays and also of *Rhinoceros*, the sphere of the "they". Amid this violence and hubbub someone exclaims: "we are all going to die. That's the only alienation that counts!" (III, p.83) Political alientaion pales into insignificance beside the fact of death. This is one of the themes of *The Killer* and Ionesco stresses it elsewhere as well: ". . . no political system can deliever us from the pain of living, from our fear of death . . ." (*Notes*, p.95) Again, there is the story, attributed to Malraux, of Stalin's deathbed admission that in the end death is the only victor (*Un Homme en Question*). Inevitably, and in contradiction to the Marxists, Ionesco reaffirms the primacy of metaphysics. Significantly, Bérenger refuses to follow mother Pipe and the geese. As a true Ionesco rebel, however, he must go beyond a mere rejection of the "they", he must come face to face with the human condition itself.

Early in the play, the theme is already emerging. Bérenger's experience of joy is related to a feeling of youthfulness, "a spring no autumn could touch" (III, p.20), and at its height the sense of existence merges into a certainty of immortality: "I *was*, I realized I had always *been*, that I was no longer going to die" (III, p.23). I shall return to this unexistential assertion in due course. Here it must be stressed that Bérenger is deceiving himself in wishing to gloss over the fact of mortality. The radiant city is not eternal, far from it; indeed it is inhabited by a *tueur sans gages*, a merciless killer, death itself. Once acknowledged, this truth alters Bérenger's life. Like Heidegger's authentic *dasein*, the protagonist henceforth lives in "anticipation" of his meeting with the killer. Naively, but full of good intentions, he imagines that the killer may be eliminated and his surprise when he discovers that everyone else knew about the murderer all along is not expressive of a desire for escapism. On the contrary, it is the most authentic response possible for Bérenger until he grows in understanding. His "anticipation" is a kind of Heideggerian Resolve. On the other hand the architect's resigned attitude is quite inauthentic and represents the everyday desire to forget the truth, the unwillingness of the "they" to see death as a part of life. "If we thought about all the misfortunes of mankind," argues the architect – a figure of authority and so a representative of the collective – "we could never go on living". The argument is familiar. Every day there are catastrophes, "houses collapsing on the tenants . . . mountains crumbling away . ." (III, p.36). The vision of disintegration, image of the true human condition, is here robbed of its wonder and becomes simply normal. But Bérenger's world is altered by the truth and he cannot go on as if nothing were happening. "Control yourself. We've all got to die" (III, p.42), he is advised. This is the logician's argument in *Rhinoceros*, and Bérenger rightly refuses to accept it. At this point the *angst* of euphoria more and more gives way to the claustrophobic, a sense of enclosure which is partly a sense of the pressure of the "they", as in other plays, but above all agonizing awareness of human limits and the reality of death. From the enclosed space of his room Bérenger goes to the stifling press of the political rally and to the traffic jam. As action accelerates, anxiety grows, obstacles proliferate. At the end the protagonist is alone in gathering darkness, walking down a long, narrow street. Suddenly time stops and the killer appears. In a long and dramatic monologue Bérenger defends himself with every conceivable platitude. Naturally it is all to no avail. He is "guilty" in the Heideggerian sense in which Vladimir and Estragon are guilty, "thrown" face to face with death and the more he argues the more he pleads against himself. There is a pathetic surrender, but this should not confuse us. Bérenger is something more than the little bourgeois of earlier plays and in effect what we witness is not his defeat but that of the "they". Platitudes fail and precisely for this reason death is honestly faced as inescapable, as a fact of life, strange and terrifying. At the end Bérenger is as authentic as his counterpart in *Rhinoceros*. He is hardly a hero. His strength lies in his sense of the real, of the immediacy of things, which, for all his fears and weaknesses, makes it impossible for him to overlook the truth.

Actually, Bérenger's feelings are remarkably accurate as a portrait of Ionesco's. As a child, the playwright tells Claude Bonnefoy, he lived in a timeless world. One day, however, he asked his mother: ". . . we are all going to die? Tell me the truth!" He was four or five and became frightened at her reply. The story is repeated in *Découvertes*: "At the age of four I became aware of death. I screamed with despair. After that I was afraid for my mother, knowing that I was going to lose her . . ." (p.58). Childhood experiences of this sort are also stressed in the *Journal*, where the fear of death reappears. In *Notes and Counter-Notes* Ionesco writes: "I have always been obsessed by death. Since the age of four . . . this anguish has never left me" (p.235). As in Heidegger death is seen as a power which sets the individual apart and, significantly, a parallel is drawn with another experience in solitude, the euphoric. Of course the common factor is wonder or *angst*. Other passages echo these. We are made to be immortal, or to wish to be, and yet we die. I see Camus, says Ionesco, and then he is gone: "how can I trust in a world that has no stability . . .?" (*Notes*, p.114). In *Antidotes* the *memento mori* is always present. In particular "Why do I write?" reiterates the venerable literary motif, familiar to English readers from Shakespeare to Keats, that art offers a means to immortality: "one writes . . . to conquer death" (XI, p.134). Ionesco is, as always, speaking for himself.

At this point a reassessment of plays already discussed is rendered necessary. Claustrophobia and release are not simply identifiable with the poles of the collective and the authentic individual but also relate to the awareness of death. Ionesco's vision of wonder reveals the natural as well as the social or human limits of man's lot. The complexity of Ionesco's images arises from the fact that death, which stifles the individual and so relates to the claustrophobic, also enables the authentic hero to stand alone, most secure in the moment of greatest anguish, and so relates to the experience of freedom and evanescence – if it does not quite spill over into the ultimate experience of liberation, the euphoric. The pattern emerges in the earliest plays, even in plays concerned directly not with mortality but with the "they". Already in the proliferation of words at the climax of *The Bald Prima Donna* we are offered an image of burial. In *Jacques* fear of burial underlies the imagery of water and mud; love, after all, has frequently been depicted in literature as a dying but in this case there is a complex fusing of associations: feminine immanence, the sexual act, the maternal bosom, the weight of society, tradition and the past, the cold embrace of the wet earth. The protagonist of *The New Tenant* is buried alive by furniture, grasping a bunch of flowers: criticism, commenting on this last scene of the play, has rightly interpreted the whole as a subtle evocation of a funeral. And Choubert's odyssey too is nothing less than a journey to the underworld as the victim suffers metaphoric burial. A similar pattern underlies *Amédée*, whose growing corpse, Bonnefoy is told, represents time (*Entretiens*, p.97). It has "the incurable disease of the dead", that is, "geometrical progression" (II, p.178) and as it expands, the hands of the clock advance (I, p.193). In that case the magnificently suggestive sequence of uprooting and evicting the corpse as well as the protagonist's euphoric flight may well image a victory over death. For the most part, however, it is death which conquers in Ionesco. A short story called "The Slough" ("*La Vase*"), published in 1955 and later turned into a film with Ionesco as the actor, provides a good example of this. We are with a prosperous traveller, bursting with energy, in a setting partly Kafkaesque and partly Beckettian. To begin with he tells us of his euphoric days, when he breathed deeply and enthusiastically, drunk with enjoyment of the landscape, immaculate seas, shining meadows. Later, the picture changes, the traveller grows tired, more and more weighed down the more he rests. He is forced to stop at an inn, unable to rise from his bed until one day he drags himself outside and collapses in the rain. Dreaming of sunshine and mountain heights, he is swallowed by the mud. The story enacts a death and burial and presents the opposition of euphoria and claustrophobia as the contrast between youth and age.

Two other plays, *Exit the King* (*Le Roi se Meurt*, 1962) and *Here Comes a Chopper* (*Jeux de Massacre*, 1970), have death as their most specific theme. The first of these was written at a time of illness. "I had just been ill", the playwright explains,

> and I had been very frightened. Then, after . . . ten days, I relapsed and was again ill for a fortnight. After that fortnight, I began again to write. (*Entretiens*, p.90)

Thus the play was written in two phases, once between two bouts of illness and once after the second bout was over. According to Ionesco, it reflects this fact in a pause or break in the middle. *Exit the King* is a story of yet another Bérenger, another Everyman who has to learn to face the end. Bérenger is now a king whose kingdom is in ruins, a sign of the destruction wrought by time and also, as elsewhere, of a world collapsing into the void of *angst*. Here *angst* relates specifically to the awareness of mortality, of course. Bérenger has two queens, Marguerite and Marie, whose task it is to plead for death and life respectively and who obviously polarize two aspects of the Ionesco woman previously contained in a single figure: the conjugal and the maternal. Marguerite, a figure of authority, prepares the king to face death as his kingdom disintegrates about him: "His palace is crumbling. His fields lie fallow. His mountains are sinking. The sea has broken the dykes and flooded the country" (V, p.16). In spite of such imagery, the play is as much comedy as tragedy, highlighting the impossible arrogance of the little king who refuses to die and his outrageous cowardice. Bérenger grows weaker and weaker yet still imagines the end to be far away. Marguerite puts the matter bluntly: he will die at the end of the play, within an hour and a half, an hour and twenty-five minutes, and so on. Once finitude is admitted, of course, the longest life is reduced to an instant and Bérenger, "anticipating" the future, curses his birth. Why be born if not to live for ever? "I came into the world five minutes ago . . ." (V, p.44). But it has been two hundred and eighty-three years. For the king,

> if every universe is going to explode, explode it will. It's all the same whether it's tomorrow or in countless centuries to come. What's got to finish one day is finished now. (V, p.49)

It is an existential conclusion. Man projects himself into futurity, into the ultimate wall of his finitude. Once revealed by the consciousness of *angst*, the end is already reached and death becomes one's lifelong companion. If Marguerite appears as spokesman for Heideggerian "anticipation", Marie, the younger queen, emerges as champion for the present. Once again it is the old opposition of the euphoric and claustrophobic. Marie wishes to live in a euphoric present characterized by the sense of boundlessness, infinity. She urges Bérenger to immerse himself in wonder, *l'étonnement*:

> Dive into an endless maze of wonder and surprise, then you too will have no end, and can exist for ever. Everything is strange . . . Let it dazzle and confound you! Tear your prison bars aside . . . Open the floodgates of joy and light . . .
>
> (V, p.50–51)

But Bérenger is stifling as he suffers the death agony of all mankind: "millions of the dead . . . My death is manifold. So many worlds will flicker out in me" (V, p.55). The king is not simply an escapist. As he prepares to die he sees for the first time the wonder of life. For the most part, however, he wishes to avoid the issue. But Marguerite is inexorable: "We're poised over a gaping chasm. Nothing but a growing void all around us" (V, p.76). Bérenger himself is this structure of holes: "I'm full all right", he says, "but full of holes. I'm a honeycomb of cavities that are widening, deepening into bottomless pits" (V, p.66). The language recalls Sartre but the void is Heideggerian, revealed in *angst* as the king's trajectory to the limits of this future. In so far as Bérenger succeeds in facing this truth, he grows in stature, progressing from the position of the frightened child to that of the "resolute" monarch. Like the second act of *Amédée*, the end of *Exit the King* depicts a birth with Marguerite acting as midwife. There is a difference, though, between the king and, for example, the earlier Bérenger of *The Killer*. Where the latter, like other Ionesco characters, is ultimately swallowed up by death, the former undergoes a positive ascesis, although without any supernatural point of reference or a specific belief in immortality. *Exit the King* is dominated by the image not of burial but of disintegration. In other words it combines the theme of death less with the claustrophobic, as we might expect, than with evanescence. All of this suggests, therefore, not only the horror of dying but a search for a positive ethic, an authentic acceptance of *angst* and a preparation for death. Like earlier Bérengers the king is a little man yet ready at the end to stand before the truth, if somewhat shakily. The authentic man in Ionesco, always a weak individual but endowed with the strength of naiveté, has emerged from the undifferentiated ranks of the "they", has survived the repressive situation of the family and the pressures of political conformity to face the ultimate claustrophobia, death, the ultimate proliferation of matter, burial. *Here Comes a Chopper* depicts the final

Brueghelian triumph of this sinister reality. In fact the inspiration is Defoe's *Journal of the Plague Year*, as the author explains in *Between Life and Dream* (*Entre la Vie et le Rêve*, 1966 and 1977). During the plague, Ionesco argues, people turned their backs on the danger, losing themselves in politics, unaware of identity, the sense of existence: "they illustrated what Heidegger says, that we live in the midst of Care". Whatever the merit of bringing in at this point a reference to Heideggerian *Sorge*, Ionesco's stress on the link between authentic existence and the *memento mori* is completely relevant: "the meaning of our existence is that we are 'there' in wonder and that we are made for death."[2] In eighteen loosely-knit scenes the author has his – largely interchangeable – characters die mysteriously as they go about their business. For the collective death is utterly negative in its effects. For the authentic man, however, it offers an opportuntity of finding oneself. In *The Hermit* the protagonist is haunted by mortality, frightened enough to turn on all the lights and to run from room to room of his flat (p.58); all around him the citizens sublimate their horror by means of violence. *Oh what a bloody circus* too is obsessed with passing time (which, at one point, accelerates dizzily), just as is *The Man with the Luggage* with its sad images of the dead and gone persisting in the minds of the living. In the end, though, the plays can offer no encouragement. Beyond the recognition of death, Ionesco remains powerless.

Yet the dynamic rhythm of his work is hardly one of resignation and failure, in spite of an element of profound pessimism. There is a positive movement, even if this movement is frequently frustrated, and to examine it it is necessary to turn to the most important aspect of the Heideggerian experience of *angst* which emerged in the discussion of Beckett. For Heidegger the real function of *angst* is to point beyond existence, to the ultimate ground of the existential, Being. Now Ionesco's description of the euphoric usually stresses the discovery of oneself as existing, as we have seen. Is it legitimate to suppose that the writer is concerned with something more? "When . . . I . . . suddenly gain . . . an awareness that I *am*, that I exist . . . and I am overwhelmed by the wonder of being alive . . ." (*Notes*, p.141), he begins in a passage quoted earlier. Examples of this kind of statement abound. Full of joy, Ionesco finds himself "at the centre of pure, ineffable existence", aware of "the one essential reality, when . . .

I was overcome by . . . the stupefaction of being, the certainty of being" (*Journal*, II, p.150–1). Awakening from a sleep peopled by the phantoms of everyday existence, he knows he is "saved" in the unshakeable certitude *que je suis*:

> I was saved now . . . because I knew now . . . that I am, I myself am, everything is. The miracle of being, the miracle of being, the miracle of being. (*Journal*, II, p.156)

At this point it is inadequate to suppose that being, *l'être*, simply signifies the *je suis*, Ionesco's personal awareness of consciousness, although the two are obviously linked. The euphoric experience involves a sense of "pure" existence, as Ionesco has it, an awareness of the "ineffable", of "essential reality". It is analogous to a religious conversion and in its suggestiveness transcends the *je suis*, moving outwards to the whole universe, the *tout est* (everything is). *Le miracle d'être* is not just the miracle of consciousness, then, it is the miracle of that mysterious presence which sustains all things. Of course Heidegger terms this Being. But I do not wish to insist on a too precise identification between the philosophy of Heidegger and Ionesco's art on this issue. It is enough to say that Ionesco's experience bears a striking resemblance to the Heideggerian discovery of Being, that in both cases what is involved is first a sense of the strangeness of things coupled with a heightened awareness of them, then a luminous insight into the very heart of the existential even as it vanishes into nothingness. In each case the quality of the insight inevitably suggests a numinous object, and it is this above all else which differentiates it from anything envisaged by Sartre. If, as in Sartre, it were simply a question of discovering *oneself* as free, the euphoric Ionesco protagonist would be little concerned with the experience of freedom and joy, he would set out to work upon the raw material of the world, to *act* upon his environment. What in fact he does is to gaze in wonder and fascination at the revelation itself. It comes as no surprise, then, that the Ionesco void, the evanescence of the euphoric experience, is experienced as plenitude, like Heideggerian *Sein* and, of course, like the divinity of the theologians. Amédée calls it "airy abundance" (II, p.200). In Bérenger's vision as described in *The Killer* the universe is filled with "ethereal energy", nothing is left empty even as the world vanishes into light and air: "everything was a mingling of airiness and plenitude" (III, p.23). Strictly speaking, freedom is a negative, an emptiness filled with possibilities. For Ionesco as for Heidegger, however, it ultimately rests in the darkness of something which stands behind or beneath the human, a positive, god-like power. This explains why the negative experience of the void turns into an experience of fulfilment and joy. We can go so far as to say that Ionesco is less interested in the world ("I am not interested in the mechanism") than in the Unknown: "what lies behind, the Unknown, He or It, is alone worthy of our interest" (*Journal*, I, p.33). This Unknown is mysterious, its primary symbol being a question mark, its experience that of wonder: "I cannot be astonished enough . . . I cannot ask enough: 'How is this possible, how in the world is this possible?' " (*Journal*, (II, p.162). More concisely: "why this Being?" (*Journal*, I, p.68). We are on the same ground as that of the Heideggerian Question, and Ionesco knows it: "these fundamental questionings, we know them well: for example: why is there something rather than nothing. It's Heidegger's celebrated formulation . . . which puts you in a state of vertigo . . ."[3] This statement comes from the collection of essays significantly entitled *A Man in Question*, and it echoes earlier comments to Bonnefoy concerning the "fundamental intuition" "that we are 'there', that something exists and that this something prompts the question" (*Entretiens*, p.144). Bonnefoy asks if this is a reference to Heidegger and the reply is properly ambiguous. The point, Ionesco argues, is that theatre, like philosophy, must pose the most basic question of all. Given such perspectives we may well say that the euphoric flight functions like the Heideggerian leap beyond the existential, the flight of *meta-physis*. Again and again, Ionesco returns to "this monolithic, inexplicable presence of the world and of existence" (*Entretiens*, p.144), his one obsessive concern and comparable in its intensity to Beckett's fascination for the Irreducible. Where Beckett pruned his world of all that is contingent, Ionesco, stunned by the sense of wonder, questioning everything, attempts to distil the quintessence of things, to refine his world until, for a moment – the most theatrical of all – it is pure light, pure being. Just as in Heidegger Being has been forgotten, so, in Ionesco, the original radiance of things has been lost: "it's the fall . . . the loss of the faculty of wonder; forgetfulness; the sclerosis of habit"

(*Entretiens*, p.35). What else should the whole of Ionesco's writing represent, then, except a search for light, that is to say, for the essential reality of, if not exactly Heideggerian Being, at least being as Ionesco apprehends it?

Before turning to this search, though, it is as well to amplify the earlier reference to Sartre. Some critics have seen the Ionesco character as a kind of *pour soi* or hole in being, and in any case one might be tempted to try to fit the Ionesco polarity into Sartrean categories. It is already clear, however, that euphoric freedom scarcely recalls the Sartrean void – it *combines* Sartre's opposites of emptiness and plenitude, *pour soi* and *en soi*, in Sartrean terms it evokes the by-definition-impossible divinity. In fact Ionesco's goal is visionary and ecstatic, and while this goal, as we shall see, is often unattainable in the plays, the result is not a short-circuit. The mood of the work is awed reverence before the wonder of man's depths and heights, a mixture of naiveté and piety quite alien to the spirit of Sartre. What we find in the souls of Ionesco's creatures is not nothingness understood as consciousness, a purely secular reality, but a *lack*, an anguished desire for fulfilment. I shall return to this point in due course. Here it suffices to stress the metaphysical dimension of Ionesco's writing, even, at times, the appeal to mysticism (*Entretiens*, pp.47–8). Ionesco writes, as he explains in "Why do I write?", because he cannot accept everyday reality, its suffering which no philosopher or theologian has ever been able to justify, because he sees no answer to ultimate questions, "what are we, where have we come from, and where are we going?" (XI, p.130): the echo is of Gauguin's famous painting). There is of course the claustrophobic which at first sight might be regarded as a variation of Roquentin's experience of nausea which, after all, involves a sense of one's inescapable link with the material. But nausea is a feeling of disgust, of contingency, whereas the Ionesco hero, overwhelmed by matter, feels horror and astonishment. Claustrophobia, as we have seen, relates to the menace of the collective, the fear of irrational politics, Ionesco's refusal to accept mortality. These concerns suggest little or no meeting-point with Sartre, who is in any case repeatedly attacked in Ionesco's essays and interviews.

In spite of Ionesco's sympathy for Camus, it is worth noting in passing that this parallel is not much more profitable. It is true that Ionesco is closer to Camus than is Beckett, for example. Ionesco is a humanist, as is Camus. Both are lovers of the world (if in diverse ways), both deplore the existence of suffering, both stand for tolerance, moderation, an end to violence, both are essentially moralists. On occasion Ionesco is capable of a reference to the Absurd (*Entretiens*, p.143; XI, p.125) and, if we do not examine our terms too closely, we may perceive a similarity between the Camus experience and that of wonder. The Absurd alienates man from his normal life, it highlights the limits of social ties, it conjures up the spectre of death, it frustrates the mind's desire for clarity. Some of these categories are applicable to Ionesco. Yet the Ionesco hero is *in search of* solitude (understood in a context of authenticity), and hungers less for order and clarity than for the experience of something obscure, mysterious and wonderful, less for human reason (which is associated with violent *un*reason) than for its ravishment and abolition in the moment of vision. In short the parallel breaks down at the point where Ionesco's humanism shades off into the metaphysical and the religious. For Camus the difficulty is the divorce between man and his world. For Ionesco it is that between creature and demiurge, man seen as fallen angel and the diabolical authority in control over him (*A Man in Question*, which argues belief in the devil). Camus lives by daylight, Ionesco – if not by darkness, like Beckett – by his dreams. If there is a similarity, it is misleading and largely explicable in terms of Camus' dependence on the idea of *angst* for his theory of the Absurd. Perhaps the last word should be left to the playwright himself. If he has admired Camus, as he admits in *Notes and Counter-Notes* (p.246), Ionesco is careful to dissociate himself from Absurdist interpretations of his work:

> I have been called a writer of the absurd; this is one of those terms that go the rounds periodically, it is a term that is in fashion at the moment . . . vague enough . . . to mean nothing any more and to be an easy definition of everything . . . in reality, the existence of the world seems to me not absurd but unbelievable. (*Notes*, pp.224–5)

Again: "I prefer to the expression 'absurd' that of strange or sense of the strange". (*Entretiens*, p.144) Wonder is not the same as the Absurd. There seems no need to press the matter further.

We are now in a position to examine in some detail what is in effect the essential dynamism of Ionesco's work, the positive movement alluded to earlier in this chapter: not an exploration of Absurdity but a search for the miracle of one's being, *le miracle d'être*. Once this search is recognized as Ionesco's abiding concern new perspectives are possible on the early plays and qualities obscured by overemphasis on the Absurd stand out distinctly. In fact the search begins even before the emergence of the authentic hero. The old couple of *The Chairs* dream of a lost city of light (I, p.43) and the aim of their *soirée* is to share this long-vanished reality with others. As the guests arrive and excitement grows, the release of pent-up feelings in the hosts is movingly suggested. The two are possessed by an unnamed and hardly acknowledged yet profound longing for fulfilment. In retrospect, we are not surprised that the evening is a failure: the vision of being, as it is elaborated in later plays, requires solitude and the collective is a hindrance rather than a help. That the old man has no message to give through the Orator other than garbled noises does not mean that we must look to the Absurd for an explanation, far from it. Ionesco's characters certainly do have something to say, although at this early stage they are insufficiently emancipated from the inauthentic to be able to say it. Of course the old couple (particularly the old man) want to tell the world of their yearning for freedom, light and joy. Doubtless at this stage Ionesco is uncertain about his direction, so that the search remains partly disguised. In *Victims of Duty* the nature of the quest is still obscure but the fact of it is out in the open. On the face of it Choubert is looking for a mysterious person known as Mallot, for the mystery of his own identity, perhaps. He finds only depths and heights, emptiness and fullness and to some this has suggested Sartre. Esslin, for example, sees the play as a search for a Self which does not exist, that is, a search in Sartrean bad faith.[4] There is undoubtedly some truth in this, but it is not the most important point. Certainly the goal of the search, from the detective's point of view and perhaps Madeleine's, is for a neat definition which cannot exist. At the same time Choubert's search and Ionesco's must be distinguished from the detective's, except in so far as Choubert himself partly confuses his quest with the sterile search for definitions, the solving of the puzzle, as if being could be reduced to a mere detective's riddle. The play proves that when the question is posed in inauthentic terms, no answer is possible. It also illustrates in embryo the true quest for Ionesco's Unknown. In *Amédée* the obscure search continues and, unlike Choubert, the protagonist is not unsuccessful when, like Saul on the Damascus road, he is lifted up by an alien force. It may be argued too that Amédée has been actively, if somewhat vaguely, preparing himself for his apotheosis. Like the old man of *The Chairs* and like Choubert, he has powerful desires from the start and the search for being in Ionesco inevitably begins with these. Amédée's goal, the "house of glass . . . of light" (I, p.201), becomes Bérenger's city of light. In Bérenger's case, of course, and for the first time in the plays, search and goal are explicit. "For a long time . . . I tried," the seeker explains, "consciously or unconsciously to find the way" (III,p.16). Moreover at this point the euphoric is clearly linked to the experience of being: "I . . . cried: I *am*, I *am*, *everything* is, everything *is*!" (III, p.24).

By the time we reach *A Stroll in the Air* and *Hunger and Thirst*, the fact that the movement towards authenticity and the search for the experience of being are one and the same is evident. In an atmosphere of happiness and in brilliant sunshine Bérenger of *A Stroll* flies off into the sky. In this work Ionesco has allowed his imagination free play and has depicted soaring liberation without timidity. Bérenger is an artist who, like Amédée, cannot write and who, like Bérenger of *Rhinoceros*, refuses to conform. Paralyzed by the knowledge of death and at the same time seeking a way out of his situation with his less resolute wife and on the background of the English characters – inauthentic, mechanical puppets recalling those of *The Bald Prima Donna* – he awakens to the revelation of freedom and light. While the others evoke images of claustrophobia and hopelessness and fail to respond to the beauty of the sunny landscape, he rises in the air. Only his daughter is able to share his qualities which are those of earlier authentic heroes: naiveté, spontaneity, faith, the capacity for wonder. Bérenger's apotheosis recalls Amédée's but with a difference. Bérenger is not loth to fly but, on the contrary, wishes to do so, fully conscious (as Amédée and the earlier heroes are not) of the truth of things, that is, aware of the claustrophobic predicament of man, of social pressures to conformity and of death, and eager to experience release. In short, Bérenger's *angst* is quite out in the open, as if the lessons taught all previous Bérengers were known to him. As he vanishes from sight, the claustrophobic dominates in his absence. Josephine, his wife, suffers like other Ionesco women from her own fears of the past, of death, of the collective. In fact she experiences that half of the experience of *angst* which complements Bérenger's. But, as it happens, Bérenger's vision turns into a nightmare also. Freedom becomes vertigo and the flight ends by revealing the hopelessness of the human lot, depravity, slaughter, mud. It is the vision of the apocalypse, of the atom bomb, the world of the "they" falling apart in violence and confusion. The important thing to note, however, is that this vision is seen through the eyes of an authentic character, the solitary Ionesco hero. Bérenger, even more than his predecessors, questions the everyday in the Heideggerian sense and so recognizes the truth. In the end he faces not only the limits of existence but also what is beyond, the void: "nothing. After that, there's nothing, nothing but abysmal space" (VI, p.77). In *A Stroll* the nothingness beyond the human offers no consolation. Nevertheless the longing of the Ionesco hero and the search for plenitude are not stifled. Thus in *Hunger and Thirst* the search begins all over again, though only to be again frustrated. Jean is like earlier Ionesco protagonists but his yearning is even more acute and he is, from the start, possessed by *angst*, crushed by the sense of the Uncanny. Once again the woman represents the forces of immanence. Jean hates the house which is sinking in the mud, the conjugal situation, the dead weight of the past: it is as if he were being buried alive. For him the entire world is a stifling enclosure. For Marie-Madeleine normality is acceptable: "most people live like this" (VII, p.11), she argues. Jean, however, is tormented by hunger and thirst for fulfilment, for space and light. The husband and wife pair are curiously unlike Amédée and his Madeleine. Whereas in the earlier play the woman is on the whole a negative force, Marie-Madeleine of *Hunger and Thirst* possesses a certain wisdom, an ability to see beauty in the limited conjugal situation where Jean sees only ugliness. The suggestion is that for once the transcendent male is making a mistake and will seek fulfilment precisely where it is not to be found. This does not mean that Jean is inauthentic. On the contrary, his longing is genuine and expresses most fully and unambiguously the more or less secret aspirations of every Ionesco hero from *The Chairs* onwards. As he puts it: "it's not peace I want . . . It's boundless joy and ecstasy for me" (VII, p.14). As in other plays, however, joy is not easily attained. Jean is seeking in the wrong place and in act two the woman he hopes to meet – an idealized version of the Marie-Madeleine he has left behind – does not arrive. He remains on a high plateau, alone and bathed in a cold light: the claustrophobia of normality has given way to the void of desire unrequited. Later, Jean can only continue to search, as he explains his predicament: "I wanted to escape old age, keep out of the rut. It's life I'm looking for! Joy I'm after! I've longed for fulfilment and all I find is torment" (VII, p.46). To this extent his experience completes the pessimism of *A Stroll.* At the same time his poetic outburst in act three summarizes the anguish of every authentic character in Ionesco and expresses it with the insistence of despair. Once he was happy, he tells us like Bérenger of *The Killer*, filled with ecstasy and astonishment, unaware of hunger and thirst. Why, suddenly, was there a change, a sense of absence and loss, an emptiness constantly enlarging itself? Was he right or not to set off in search of Joy?

> It seems to me that I haven't always been swept by this consuming fire. Once upon a time . . . I'd stop in the heart of the countryside . . . lost in unspeakable wonder and delight . . . Everything was complete, sufficient unto itself. I wasn't hungry. I wasn't thirsty . . . Why this sudden change? This sudden deprivation? . . . This dissatisfaction and the anguish . . . this hollow feeling inside me, that's grown bigger and deeper ever since? . . . Why were there no more luminous days . . . Was I or was I not meant to roam those twilit autumn roads in search of light . . . or mirages? (VII, p.98)

No answer is given by the play. Jean finds his way to a monastery whose walls recall a prison or a barracks. In search of freedom he has returned to the collective, since the monastery represents the "they" at its most menacing and claustrophobic. At the end, as in *The Chairs*, emptiness increases as matter proliferates. Eating the food of the place, Jean grows ever more hungry. He witnesses an indoctrination during which two prisoners are taught that truth is defined by the authority of the collective. We are in the world of *Jacques*, of mother Pipe and her geese and of *Rhinoceros*. Jean sees his vision of light, an image of his wife and daughter (reminiscent of the family in *A Stroll*), of a spring garden and a ladder to the sky. But he cannot leave the monastery. The Ionesco hero who asks Heidegger's Metaphysical Question, abandons the everyday, and, driven by *angst*, sets off in search of being and the experience of euphoric wonder finds a prison much worse than the one he left behind. It seems that the movement towards authenticity is for ever hindered and the final, liberating experience of plenitude always beyond reach. In *The Foot of the Wall*, the act Ionesco added to the play, we are returned to the search and, in particular, to an image of frustration, that of the wall, suggestive of the old motif of finitude and death but also looking forward to ideas elaborated in works to come.

After *Hunger and Thirst* Ionesco once more depicts a search, this time in a minor key, however, with the emphasis on confusion and loss rather than on desire. The unnamed traveller of *The Man with the Luggage* finds himself beside a gloomy river, a kind of deathly waterway with its own suggestive boatman. In the distance there are fires, hints of violence which recur throughout. People whom the traveller knows or has known make appearances, then vanish, like the elusive past, while, in the background, a house perpetually burns. Later the traveller, who has failed the test of the Sphinx, lives out a series of archetypal anxiety dreams: he fails to catch a train, he worries about his writings which are lost along with a third case – while his two cases become heavier and heavier – he reaches a strangely familiar city whose surreal power closes in on him as he finds himself interrogated by police, unable to find papers and luggage, desperately anxious to use a phone to reach a consulate. No sooner does he get papers than the consulate is abolished. Now the sense of stifling grows. In a hospital for the aged specializing in euthanasia, in a courtroom where his guilt is proved and his cases are shown to contain vegetables and cement, the traveller panics. Hints of beauty in a place reminiscent of Ionesco's childhood home in the country are replaced by images of grime and threat. In the end there is a traffic jam on stage, a ghostly chaos of wheelchairs, suitcases and people. The traveller has failed to reach his obscure goal, indeed, he has scarcely set out on his search. Ionesco has said that what he wanted to depict in all of this was the "fundamental anguish" of his dreams (*Antidotes*, p.266), dreams which are recounted in the *Journal* and which relate to the past, Ionesco's experiences of Roumania, his fears of totalitarian regimes, his family conflicts, above all, his ambivalent political status. Thus the traveller, he tells Bonnefoy in *Entre la Vie et le Rêve*, is a stranger to the country while belonging to it, anxious to escape, yet, it seems, newly-arrived (pp.172–3).

Within a loose oneiric structure held together by the presence of the traveller, that is to say, the dreamer, we witness a search for the identity of Ionesco's family, and for Ionesco's own (*Entre la Vie et le Rêve*, p.169). It is the old metaphysical search, this time given a concretely autobiographical focus, that of earlier work like *Victims of Duty*, and, more decisively than ever, it ends in failure. Can Ionesco ever provide a solution to the riddle of his Sphinx?

He does so, after a fashion, in his novel and its accompanying play. *Oh What a bloody circus*, like other works, presents us with a character confusedly engaged in the search for joy – we recall its images of light – and the flight away from the collective. The desire of Jean of *Hunger and Thirst* is there – in the words of the Russian lodger, "we're all hungry, thirsty and unsatisfied" (X, p.41) – but it is stifled in the protagonist's silence, which is that of despair. At the end, *le personnage* remains alone as light invades the scene, a tree grows miraculously, shedding leaves and flowers. Finally the astonished protagonist understands. Laughing, he chides the creator (God, or Ionesco's inept demiurge): it was all a farce, a joke, *blague, bordel.* What exactly are we to make of this? Is Ionesco's laughter simply that of somewhat theatrical despair? It seems not, though one would not know it from the play alone. The author has voiced his belief in "a clumsy demon who created this universe" (*Un Homme en Question*, p.114), a belief echoed by the Russian lodger of the play. In *Entre la Vie et le Rêve* Ionesco talks of history as a cruel game indulged in by God (p.163); again, he tells the story (pp.113–14) of his quasi-experience of death, during an illness, in which he had the overwhelming sense of the futility of all he had done in life. It is, perhaps, a gloss on the void encountered by the flier of *A Stroll*. In "Why do I write?" too, there is mention of the divine farce, yet, on one occasion (XI, p.127), Ionesco recounts how an old Zen monk who had all his life searched for an answer to the riddle, finally saw the truth – and laughed. So the laughter of *le personnage* is presumably as much that of vision as of despair – it occurs, after all, in a visionary context. This is even more obviously true of the conclusion of *The Hermit*. Once more the protagonist sees a tree in bloom, after which everything dissolves in light, in the midst of which appears a garden, complete with the silvery ladder to the sky of earlier plays. Eventually the vision fades, but, in the final words of the novel, Ionesco's solitary takes it for a sign, let us say, a *pledge*. The end of the search, then, need not be seen as failure, though the tone of the play in this regard remains less reassuring than that of the novel. All we can say is that Ionesco's search is never complete. Sometimes it ends in frustration, sometimes in ambiguous laughter, sometimes in that radiance of being which was, from the beginning, Ionesco's goal.

One last comment needs to be made on all of this. Much more than Beckett's, Ionesco's *angst* bears the stamp of its Romantic antecedent, *Weltschmerz*. Like the Romantic, the existential hero suffers life, but in a way that is more austere and inward because more resigned. Romantic *angst* therefore appears as more passionate and frenzied than its modern counterpart. The difference here between Ionesco and most of his contemporaries is striking. The Ionesco hero speaks of nostalgia, a crushing sadness, unknown desire, unbounded regrets:

> . . . my . . . mind . . . was . . . pervaded by that profound, intolerable nostalgia, an overwhelming sadness, a nameless longing, boundless regrets and remorse, an indefinable pity . . .[5]

Of course this man in particular is about to die. But why "nameless" ("*sans nom*"), why the mystery, why the stress on the illimitable: "boundless" ("*sans bornes*")? This is not simply an existential complaint before the inevitability of death. It is also a metaphysical protest and characteristically Romantic in its intensity of feeling, above all, in its lofty vagueness. There is a felt presence of infinity here, a sense of longing and suffering which is not explicable in existential terms alone. Ionesco writes in a similar vein in *Notes and Counter-Notes*. "I . . . see myself invaded", he explains,

> by inconceivable distress, by nameless regrets and inexplicable remorse, by a kind of love, by a kind of hate, by a semblance of joy, by a strange pity (for what? for whom?) . . . (p.163)

Whatever the exact meaning of this, the Romantic colour is inescapable. Ionesco's passion rarely has that specifically concrete quality which is the mark of the existential. Rather it is a passion directed beyond the narrow confines of existence, towards the infinite, an object that is not an object, the soul of man conceived as absolute.

Moreover, Ionesco's unbounded feeling focusses on the past in a way that recalls not merely the existential awareness of man's situation but a Romantic nostalgia, a longing for paradise lost, for a plenitude man has never possessed and yet forever recognizes as his own, "memory of a lost world" (*Découvertes*, p.108), "things I have lost for ever, which I have never had, never seen; I have never even known what they were" (*The Colonel's Photograph*, p.131). Of course Ionesco is a timid Romantic and the nineteenth-century vigour is restrained, but it is there nonetheless. The existential hero suffers the present, the concrete burden of the past, the void of futurity. He does not suffer the exquisite pains of the unknown. Nor is he concerned with the myth of Eden. Ionesco's heroes suffer undefined regrets about the past, yearnings for something lost, for the innocence of childhood – innocence, one may add, in the sense in which Blake uses the term. There is the couple of *The Chairs* with their memories of joy, Choubert with his despairing "the enchanted garden has folded into night" (II, p.280), his vision of loss: "where has beauty gone? And goodness?" (II, p.292). There is Bérenger of *The Killer* recalling the vision of the past and seeking to heal a tragic and intolerable separation. There are those luminous gardens so tantalizing to one Ionesco hero after another. There is the author himself with his memory of La Chapelle Anthenaise. Of course only the vision of the child is able to pierce through this world of Platonic shadows and regain, if only momentarily, man's true home. Thus every authentic character in the plays is marked by naiveté and the capacity for amazement. At the same time the fascination for the past is coupled with a desire for a future that will restore freedom and undo the effects of the Fall: "What I am really looking for is a world that is virgin again, the paradisiacal light of childhood, the glory of the first day" ("Why do I write?" XI, p.121). No truly existential character would dare hope for liberation of this kind. Like many Romantics Ionesco seeks the apotheosis of man in the spirit of Blake's "damn braces, bless relaxes". But while waiting for this, the experience of transfigured nature, a revelation, in solitude, of the mystery of life, is his reward and a fresh spur to his desires. If, in the end, he is crushed, it is because society or death or a capricious demon has betrayed him. For the most part, however, he continues his search, impelled by the eternal "I want . . . I want" (*Victims*, II, p.280). The Romantic tone of this quest is especially evident in Ionesco's later plays where, significantly, the echo of Strindberg is most pronounced. Now the influence of Strindberg's expressionist work on Ionesco has been noted, although it has been insufficiently stressed, and Ionesco has replied both in *Notes and Counter-Notes* and in his interviews with Claude Bonnefoy:

> It was proved to me that I was very much influenced by Strindberg. This forced me to read the Scandinavian dramatist: and I realized it was in fact true. (*Notes*, p.89)

This comical admission should not mislead us. It does not matter that Ionesco read Strindberg after he wrote his plays. The point is that Ionesco's manner is very close to the late Romanticism of the other. In every respect the similarities are astonishing. Both dramatists are deeply concerned with the male–female struggle, both project themselves into their work and so reveal their lives and their dreams. When Ionesco says in *Improvisation* (*L'Impromptu de l'Alma*), "you see, this time I'm going to put myself in the play!" the critic rightly counters "that's all you ever do" (III, p.113). Anyone who is acquainted with Ionesco's journal or even simply *Notes and Counter-Notes* cannot fail to realize to what extent the plays are autobiographical. Both Ionesco and Strindberg are concerned with a metaphysical Fall, with guilt and remorse. Both depict a quest for salvation. The protagonist of *The Road to Damascus* with his endless wanderings, his search for the ideal feminine and for a religious truth, closely resembles Jean of *Hunger and Thirst*. Like Jean, Strindberg's Stranger ends in a monastery, though not one that is a prison. Similar are the Daughter of *A Dream Play* or the Student of *The Ghost Sonata*, all impelled by obscure yearnings for fulfilment and peace. But the greatest resemblance between Ionesco and Strindberg lies in their common dramatic use of the dream for confessional purposes. The dream is not congenial to the strictly existential writer but it flourishes in the area which we may term expressionist and which marks the transition from the Romantic to the existential. Ionesco's plays, like many of Strindberg's, appear as dream projections, sometimes as nightmarish, and indeed Ionesco has made no secret of this and has related most of the plays to specific dreams, some of which – the flying dream, the dream of a wall, dreams of alienation and of euphoria – are narrated in detail in the *Journal* and in the Bonnefoy interview. But this aspect of Ionesco may be left for the present. The point to be emphasized here is the parallel with the Romantic, a quality of Ionesco's work – understandably – missed by early criticism, with its emphasis on *guignol* and the Absurd. In fact, his 'Pataphysics notwithstanding, Ionesco differs from Jarry and the Absurd of Punch and Judy in the direction of *feeling*: his Romantic spirit is ampler. Of course the element of *guignol* is there, from *The Bald Prima Donna* to *Macbett*, but it represents only one aspect of the whole, by no means the essential. Ionesco has always been a man of feeling and he has publicized the fact, a little timidly in his early work but with increasing conviction after *Victims, Amédée* and *The Killer*. Read in order of composition the plays on the whole reveal a development of the Ionesco character from puppet to human being; read the other way they reveal something of the human element, the element of Romantic feeling, present from the start. Thus Jean, Bérenger of *A Stroll* and the protagonists of *The Hermit* and *Oh what a bloody circus* help to bring into the open earlier Romantic characters, the Bérengers of *Exit the King*, *Rhinoceros* and *The Killer*, and these in turn express more fully the Romanticism present in the still earlier Amédée and Choubert. Once the line of development is recognized it is possible to see the germ of the Romantic in Jacques, in the old couple of *The Chairs*, even in the situations of *The Lesson* and *The Bald Prima Donna*. What must be stressed, then, is that even the early puppets are not really absurd. On the contrary, they are unhappy people, bursting with repressed violence and ultimately longing for the experience of the euphoric. This longing is first brought into focus in *The Chairs* and after that more and more openly revealed in subsequent plays in a way reminiscent of a personal psychoanalysis. *Victims* and *Amédée* represent the process of this birth, *The Killer* and *Rhinoceros* confirm the trend. First in *A Stroll* and *Hunger and Thirst*, then in *The Hermit*, its accompanying play, and *The Man with the*

Luggage the movement from puppet to human being, from a disguised to an exuberant Romanticism, reaches it climax.

All this raises the possibility of an interpretation of the search for plenitude along Idealist lines. And it is true that the euphoric experience with its mood of joy appears to take us beyond the existential. As we have seen, the euphoric is not only a revelation of man's concrete existence but also an experience of something approaching Heidegger's Being, and Heidegger's Being – and this has been brought out in the analysis of Beckett – itself perhaps escapes existential categories. What is true of Beckett's work and Heidegger's philosophy is even more true of Ionesco's plays. A phrase descriptive of the obsessive search for joy undertaken by all of Ionesco's protagonists is significant here: "our thirst for the absolute" (*Notes*, p.95). Again, there are those repeated references in "Why do I write?" to "absolute" light. If Ionesco can speak in this way the question of Romantic Idealism becomes pressing: is the Ionesco search to be viewed in the final analysis as a flight from the limits of the existential, as a movement towards a privileged metaphysical position, in short, towards the infinite, the eternal, the Absolute? We have already noted an otherworldly, even mystical tone in Ionesco's work, as if those passionate, if uncertain, seekers were made not for this world but another ("have we not the impression that the real is unreal . . . That this world is not our true world?" *Notes*, p.114). In this context the movement from the claustrophobic to the euphoric in the plays would seem to represent an escape not merely from the inauthentic collective but something more radical, a flight from the existential situation, a transition from Existence to Essence, from the direct experience of one's human finitude in *angst* to a more extravagant revelation of Being understood as an ideal state outside the limits of space and time. It is here that we must recall that the Ionesco hero regards euphoria as a possible safeguard against the onslaught of time and death. Of course the existential hero accepts his finitude as inescapable. In Ionesco, however, if claustrophobia relates to the fear of burial, euphoria acts as an antidote to this fear: "I said to myself . . . that since this experience had happened . . . I could never be unhappy again, for I had learnt that man does not die" (*Journal*, I, p.68). Choubert, like Ionesco, thinks of joy as a source of life eternal: "the wells of life, of immortality" (II, p.281). If Amédée's corpse represents, as the writer argues, the burden of time, the ending of the play surely suggests a victory over death, a resurrection. Bérenger of *The Killer* is convinced that the experience of light means a transcending of death: "I *was*, I realized I had always *been*, that I was no longer going to die" (III, p.23). In *Exit the King* the younger queen pleads for life against the other whose role it is to prepare the king for the end. She asks Bérenger to rise above his fears and to immerse himself in joy and wonder. "Then you too will have no end, and can exist forever" (V, p.50), she tells him. It is significant in this context to recall that Ionesco has, especially in his discussions with Bonnefoy, clearly linked the euphoric to his own childhood at La Chapelle Anthenaise, to the period of his life when he did not know about death and had not yet discovered time. In the later work these concerns take a different, but related form. When a sick man approaches the king in *Macbett* with the complaint that he is in a prison, unable to live or die, afraid of light and darkness, of others and of solitude, unable to weep or to know joy, Duncan replies "forget that you exist. Remember that you *are*" (IX, p.78). The choice of terms is significant. Existence is a wall (*The Foot of the Wall*), or a box (*Oh what a bloody circus*, X, p.42), closing in, barring the way. Ionesco's characters cannot accept this, yet, like the Russian lodger of *Oh what a bloody circus* or the protagonist of *The Hermit*, neither can they conceive of infinity, except as, in the former case, boxes-within-boxes or, in the latter, worlds-within-worlds. In each case the concept comes up against a wall, "the nausea of . . . finitude . . . the nausea of the infinite" (*The Hermit*, p.42). The same point is reiterated in "Why do I write?" (XI,p.124). We are in a situation in which "existence" is a jail and "being" is inconceivable, unattainable. Hopelessly yet stubbornly, Ionesco refuses to accept limitations. There remains the promise of light, when "I know with certainty that I was born for eternity, that death does not exist and that everything is miracle." In this state, Ionesco adds, one knows that once participating in the divine one will do so eternally ("Why do I write?" XI, p.122). This, presumably, is the pledge received at the end of *The Hermit*, and it is one which challenges the reality of the existential cage.

We must conclude that, even more than Beckett, Ionesco is a Romantic Idealist in an existential world. Historically, the Romantic world and the world of the Idealist is an open world in which anything is possible. By the time we reach Strindberg the position has altered and man is losing the sense of the Absolute, the confidence of a privileged position. In Ionesco, as in Strindberg, something of the Romantic remains, but it is affected by a new sense of limitations. The existential hero knows that he is a being-there, a creature involved in a finite world, ontologically immersed in the concreteness of the situation, able to be only within the bounds of the situation. The major tension in Ionesco, the constant struggle between claustrophobia and euphoria amounts in the end to a conflict between the triumphant existential and a surviving but disillusioned Romanticism. On the basis of a fundamentally existential vision, Ionesco, like Beckett, hungers after spiritual space. Where Beckett creates a new, tortured Romanticism, Ionesco, with greater emotional abandon, looks back to the Romantic sources of modernity – and, by implication, to the Idealist sources of the existential. Of course Romanticism contains the germ of the existential as its notion of the organic unity of things contains an implicit grasp of the notion of situation. The Romantic hero becomes existential when the situation closes in on him, when he begins to measure freedom and fulfilment in terms not of absolutes but relatives. And this development is to be expected: if man and his world represent an organic, let us say Coleridgean whole, it follows that man exists not as a privileged Ego but in a situation, that the Absolute is no longer conceivable. Ionesco's work offers a unique perspective on this transition from one *Weltanschauung* to another.

III Genet's solitude

9 Genet: solitude and the Sartrean Look

> Solitude, as I mean it, signifies not a miserable state but rather a secret royalty, profound incommunicability but a more or less obscure knowledge of unassailable singularity.[1]
>
> GENET

Giacometti's portrait of Genet represents a head shrinking back from the observer and from itself, straining back and upwards into the space of the picture so that the effect is both concentrated presence and flight. It is a portrait of a skull emerging into focus even as the flesh recedes, as if the representation were turning itself inside out, the whole in constant state of movement and yet locked tight in an unbearable tension. Comparable to it and to other paintings by Giacometti are the well-known sculptures with their small, elongated heads. The artist has explained that during the war years his figures became minute in size even to the point of disappearing at the last stroke of the knife. Clearly, as in the case of the skull-like portraits, the guiding principle is one of merciless reduction:

> So one dreams nostalgically of a universe in which man, instead of acting with such fury upon visible appearance, would have striven to be freed from it, not only in refusing all action upon it, but in stripping himself sufficiently to discover that secret place, within ourselves, on the basis of which a totally different human adventure might have been possible. (*L'Atelier d'Alberto Giacometti*, p.9)

This is Genet himself commenting on Giacometti's work and offering at the same time a valuable comment on his own. Just as the dialogue with Georges Duthuit is of primary importance to an understanding of Beckett and *Notes and Counter-Notes* a necessary adjunct to Ionesco's plays, so *L'Atelier d'Alberto Giacometti* (*The*

Workshop of Alberto Giacometti, 1958) provides one with a direct entry into the world of Jean Genet. Genet dreams of a universe where man, instead of concentrating on the surfaces of things, will lay bare that secret place within himself and reveal possibilities of an altogether different life. Giacometti's work speaks of just such a revelation. His statues seem to have passed through a terrible fire which has devoured all but the core, "*elles sortent d'un four, residus d'une cuisson terrible*" (p.30). The Platonic echo is emphatic: "to lay bare what will remain of man when the layers of make-believe have been removed" (p.10). As Genet sees it, Giacometti wishes to remove the inessential, to reach the heart of things. If he could, he would do it to himself, he would reduce himself to elemental dust (p.52).

Concisely stated, the aim is as follows:

> Beauty has no other origin than that wound, singular, different for each one . . . which every man guards within himself, which he preserves and into which he withdraws when he wants to leave the world for a temporary but profound solitude . . . The art of Giacometti seems to me to want to uncover this secret wound . . . (pp.10–11)

The important words are "wound" and "solitude". At the heart of man is the true source of beauty, a point of utter solitude. Giacometti's art seizes this presence, "*la solitude de chaque être et de chaque chose*", "the solitude of each being and each thing", which is man's glory, "*notre gloire la plus sûre*" (p.19) and in uncovering it opens up to us the timeless world of the dead (p.13). Genet elaborates. When I examine the beauty of a face I isolate it from its surroundings and see it in its particularity. In a work of art this process is initiated by the artist who in effect depicts the discontinuous:

> So it's the solitude of the person or the object represented which is given back to us, and we, who observe, in order to perceive it . . . must experience the space not of its continuity but discontinuity. (p.20)

It is difficult not to be reminded of Beckett's object "perceived as particular and unique and not merely the member of a family".

We have reached a point where man is returned to what is irreducible within himself, "that precious point . . . his solitude . . ." (pp.23–4). Solitude is singularity, the autonomy or separateness of a given thing or, let us say, its integrity in a sense not unlike the Scholastic *integritas* spoken of by Stephen Dedalus. At the same time it encompasses something more, approaching Stephen's *claritas* or essence, the radiance of a thing which manifests what it is or rather, as Genet suggests, the fact that in being itself a thing totally excludes all that is not itself:

> Solitude, as I mean it, signifies not a miserable state but rather a secret royalty, profound incommunicability but a more or less obscure knowledge of unassailable singularity.[1]

Solitude, conceived in this way, has nothing of the wretched about it. It is a hidden stamp of nobility. With this definition in mind we can understand Giacometti's statement to Genet. One day, he says, he saw a napkin resting on a chair and suddenly felt that had the chair been removed the napkin would have remained suspended:

> One day . . . I was looking at a napkin resting on a chair. Then I really had the impression that, not only was each object alone, but it had a weight – or rather an absence of weight – which prevented it from pressing down on the other. The napkin was alone, so alone I felt I could remove the chair without the napkin changing its position. It had its own place, its own weight, almost its own silence. (pp.30–1)

The napkin is itself and only itself; thus it is alone. The point is the Giacometti reveals this inalienable solitude in all his work, taking off layers of appearance until the object is left in all the rigour of its simplicity, its mere presence. Furthermore, such nakedness manifests the glory of the object, however mean or insignificant. With Giacometti at a cafe Genet meets a half-blind idiotic Arab. The creature has no wife; he masturbates. And yet Genet knows that Giacometti believes the Arab to retain a quality which

> makes him the same as anyone else and more precious than the

> rest of the world: what remains when he draws back into himself. . . as when the sea withdraws and abandons the shore. (p.50)

Giacometti's statues, Genet adds, are like this. They have left the shore and withdrawn to the secret place in which each man is more valuable than all else, "*à cet endroit secret*" (p.50).

Solitude is certainly not to be identified with personality, since, like Beckett's and Ionesco's, Genet's interests are metaphysical rather than psychological. It is a numinous identity hidden beneath the surface of the personal in a way comparable to the "individuality" which D.H. Lawrence distinguishes from "personality" in *Psychoanalysis and the Unconscious*. The question arises: how does one attain solitude? Obviously one must undergo the same purifying fire which has consumed the statues of Giacometti. This process is described minutely in *Le Funambule* (*The Tightrope Walker*), published in the same year as the reflections on Giacometti. The tightrope walker is his own work of art, escaping himself and seeking himself like the Genet of the portrait, "and always within this mortal and bleached solitude" (p.194). Indeed he is nothing other than solitude (p.182) and, as in *L'Atelier*, to become solitude is to become one's secret wound:

> It's within this wound – which cannot heal because it is himself – and within this solitude that he must hurl himself; it's there he will be able to discover the strength, audacity and skill necessary to his art. (p.182)

One does not reach oneself except through a rigorous process of ascesis, even a mutilation. Thus the tightrope walker lives not for himself but for his wire, for the moment when an admiring audience will say: What an astonishing wire! (p.177) Or, again, he lives in order to incarnate an image of himself, of his deepest being, that is, of solitude. This is not egotism. Rather it is death (pp.179–80). The artist is a dead man, dead to self, emptied of frivolity. It is not he but the image or perhaps the wire which dances (p.180): "The one dancing will be dead . . . It's then your precision will attain perfection" (pp.180–1). Only in a perfect medium, one dead to self, can beauty be manifest. Giacometti's art is great because the artist obliterates himself. So also the artist on the wire, himself his own work of beauty, must become abject – that is the practical meaning of his dying – in order to be possessed by art alone. He must be a transparency, offering no resistance to the light which shines through him. The principle is that of the prophet-saint, unworthy medium of divinity, and, the more unworthy, the better the medium, the greater God's glory. To be an artist is to die in order to attain a higher level of being, a life-in-the-Other. It requires other-worldliness, a rejection of all comfort, indeed, a veritable contempt for society. One must smell so foully as to frighten off the world:

> To acquire this absolute solitude . . . he pushes aside every curious bystander, every friend, every overture which might seek to incline his work in the direction of the world . . . around him he releases a smell so nauseating, so dismal that in the midst of it he finds himself . . . half asphyxiated by it. Everyone avoids him. He is alone. (p.187)

Genet will go so far as to advise the artist to limp, to cover himself in rags and lice, to stink, since the greater his abjection, the brighter shines the image of solitude, an image inhabited by a corpse:

> His character should become less and less so as to allow to shine forth . . . this image . . . inhabited by a dead man. He should in the end exist only in his appearance. (p.184)

At the heart of Genet's ideal is a perpetual tension. The artist on the wire dies not once but many times or rather maintains himself at every moment in an excruciating, and so beautiful, equilibrium of living and dying, like Bernini's St Teresa, pierced by the seraph's dart. Genet addresses him excitedly as a creature on fire:

> . . . you who burn, who last a few minutes. You burn. On your wire you are lightning . . . a solitary dancer. Set on fire by whatever it is which lights you, consumes you, it's a terrible wretchedness which makes you dance. (p.195)

Genet concludes: "Get your prick and theirs up" ("*Bande, et fais bander*", p.196). Rigidity, tautness is the essence of the tightrope walker's art, of his glory, its symbol being the wire itself or the erect penis, a sign of austere nobility and poise. Thus: "Your body will have the arrogant vigour of a bursting, irritated member" (pp.191–2).

To summarize. Giacometti has uncovered the place of solitude where every given thing is itself, singular, god-like, and has revealed it in the meanest of objects. The tightrope walker, a secular ascetic, sets out to incarnate solitude, to become alone and god-like by a systematic obliteration of his everyday self. In abjection, a spiritual death, he shines or rather offers no impediment to the light which shines through him. This is what it means to be a work of beauty, to exercise that perfect control transcending mere human effort which for Genet is best exemplified by the rigidity of the penis, combining as it does power and the ardour of sexual desire.

We may ask why Genet chooses such a term as "wound" to describe the uniqueness of the individual. The fact is that the arduous search for solitude does not begin as a search or an ascesis. It begins as a flight. To reach into one's own depths is glorious in the rich sense of the French *gloire* because it means the attainment of divine beauty. Yet the artist is first *driven* to solitude, wounded by his fellow men, as Genet clearly suggests. Solitude is a place of sorrow, a reality due to the pressure of the Other. Only subsequently does it become a place of safety and a refuge from the Other:

> I wonder where resides . . . the secret wound in which every man seeks refuge when his pride is threatened, when he is wounded. It's this wound . . . which is going to swell, magnify. Every man knows how to enter it, to the point of becoming the wound itself, a kind of secret and suffering heart.
>
> (*Le Funambule*, p.181)

The paradox implicit in this passage summarizes the pattern of Genet's vision. Genet's constant aim in all his work is to represent a search and an escape or, better, an escape which by its nature becomes a search. The Other wounds me and I escape to the refuge of solitude. But, as it happens, solitude is found to be also something objectively desirable, a positive. Thus escape becomes ascesis, a willed progress to a predetermined goal. I begin to *desire* the wound which leads to solitude, I *wrench* myself from my everyday self which is my life with others so that my wound, original cause of my escape, becomes the goal of my pilgrimage, a sign of separateness from other men and so of my deepest self. At this point solitude, the wound, one's uniqueness are all one and the same, the wound is selfinflicted, not simply through masochism – although, as we shall see, masochism plays an important part in the Genet ascesis – but through openness to divine election, willingness to be consumed in glory. Thus solitude is a curse which turns into a blessing. Genet's wounds are holy, like those in the poems of John of the Cross, and, like those of Crashaw's Teresa, they metamorphose into precious stones:

> All thy sorrows here shall shine,
> All thy SVFFRINGS be diuine.
> TEARES shall take comfort, & turn gemms
> and WRONGS repent to Diademms.

A Teresian ecstatic, raised far above the ground and, in this case, far above the crowd, the tightrope walker escapes the Other to discover his singularity in beauty, power and death.

If we look more closely at the nature of the wound which is inflicted in Genet's world we can see why the ascesis of solitude begins as an escape from society. In the Barrio Chino district of Barcelona Genet is invited to a table of French officers. A middle-aged lady is with the group and, smiling, she addresses a question to him:

> "Do you like men?"
> "Yes, madame, I do."
> "And . . . when did it start?"[2]

Genet instantly represses his sense of humiliation, since there is nothing he can do. A comparable experience occurs when he attempts a bold entry in woman's dress. Acutely sensitive to possible slight, he wears his trousers under the skirt. A moment later the material is torn by a clumsy young man who apologizes and, amid the laughter of observers, Genet can only whisper a mild "excuse me" (p.55). In that is compressed enough anger and shame for a tragic stage. Nothing happens, though. As in the other incident, emotion is turned inwards and contained. Genet leaves and, as he puts it, drowns the dress in the sea nearby. His revenge would be comic if it were not so brutal. The fact that these examples relate to Genet himself is beside the point, of course. We are concerned not with biography but with the world of Genet's fiction and it happens that much of Genet's work is to a certain extent autobiographical. Examples from the novels and plays, some relating to fictional creations, substantiate the above pattern. The Genet character is wounded by other men, subjected to humiliation and suffering. As stiff in his sense of honour as a character of Corneille, he is open to continual affronts upon his dignity. Inevitably, emotion is disguised, intensified by being driven inwards. This represents an escape before a foe one is too weak to face directly. At the same time, however, the inward movement reveals new riches and opens new possibilities for fulfilment: we are now in the world of the tightrope walker. Following chapters will trace this pattern more closely as it is suggested in the novels and plays, but we may already state that the basis of the desire for solitude in Genet's work is society's treatment of the individual. A more positive ascesis to solitude and self-respect comes after. The full truth of these statements will emerge as we proceed, however.

Some, though not all, of the most important points to be elaborated in these chapters are not new. From a biographical point of view they have been treated in Sartre's study, *Saint Genet, Actor and Martyr (Saint Genet, cómedien et martyr*, 1952). One may disagree with aspects of this work, even reject completely its philosophic assumptions, the assumptions of *Being and Nothingness*. It remains notwithstanding superior to anything else in the field and obviously relevant to the present argument. Sartre has interpreted Genet's development as man and artist in terms of the philosophy of the *pour soi*. My aim is to concentrate on Genet's *work*, on the whole regardless of biography, in terms of Sartrean thought. In so doing I shall not be unduly concerned to stress the relevance of *Saint Genet* to a study of Genet's work, but shall try to relate Genet's novels and plays to Sartre's thought in general, or rather to the early Sartre, since the *Critique of Dialectical Reason*, with its determined focus on group action, sheds no new light on the problems of the Genet solitary. It must be evident even at the start that one cannot expect Heidegger to appear in these chapters. Genet's approach resembles Sartre's rather than that of any other existential philosopher, although, as we shall see, there is a significant point where the comparison breaks down. Sartre's study, published in 1952, does not cover Genet's most important plays, an examination of which will take up the greater part of my discussion. At the same time one of its most central arguments must be made the basis of the present thesis, although, as I have said, I am not primarily concerned with the *man* Genet. Sartre's point is as simple as it is perceptive: Genet has been a victim of *le regard*, the Look.

In Sartre's philosophy man, as consciousness, is *pour soi*, a void, utterly unlike anything that is, the *en soi*. To be nothing at all is to be free, a subject or centre of outward-going activity, above all, a power of negating. We recall that the *pour soi* observes a table and in that act of consciousness constitutes the table as an object, as something that *is*, in short, being, *en soi*. By the same token it constitutes itself as nothingness, *pour soi*: I am conscious *of* the table, so I am *not* the table, I negate it. The table stands as passive object to my free subjectivity. No other activity than this is possible for consciousness, since nothingness cannot do anything positive; it can only say: I am *not* this, *not* that, and so forth. This activity is also at the basis of human relations, of course. I, John, am conscious of Peter. Consequently I constitute myself as negative, *pour soi*, and Peter as positive, *en soi*. I, as subject, have objectified Peter. At this moment, in so far as he is gazed at, Peter is an object. If Peter has the initiative and gazes first at me, I am aware of my being objectified by my feeling of helplessness. It seems as if my world has a "drain hole in the middle of its being and that it is perpetually flowing off through this hole".[3] My freedom seems to escape me on all sides. The Other appears to me for the first time as the one responsible for my being objectified, for the loss of my freedom which I feel as "an internal flow of the universe, an internal haemorrhage", as "the subject who is revealed to me in that flight of myself towards objectification".[4] Sartre's classical example is the ontology of Shame. I am peeping through a keyhole, pure activity, subjectivity, consciousness, that is, *pour soi*, nothingness. Suddenly I am discovered and instantly I am acutely *self*-aware, a *something*, an object to myself and to the Other who watches me, in short, I feel *shame.* To be a victim of the objectifying Look is to be enslaved, to be placed in a situation of danger in which one's subjective consciousness slips away and comes under the control of another. As object in the Look of the Other I am vulnerable because, *en soi*, I acquire an outside, something which gives the world a hold on me. For example, I become predicatable, I become John who does such and such or has such and such a character. Of course as subject I am always free to change, and, strictly speaking, have no character. As object, that is, in the eyes of Peter, I am more or less fixed as, for example, timid or bold, intelligent or stupid. But I can never be bold or timid or anything else to myself since to myself I am nothing, pure outward-going consciousness *of* – something other than myself. Thus in so far as I am forced to accept a nature or label or character I am forced to see myself as *Peter* sees me. I am forced to be *other* to myself. Sartre calls this an *alienation, ma chute originelle*, "my original fall".[5] Of course its effect is felt at all times, even when I am alone, since the Other's gaze, once experienced, stamps me for ever. It follows that under these circumstances human relationships can only exist as conflict. Either I objectify the Other or he objectifies me. There can be no *mitsein*. Either I am subject or object, no middle way is possible since to unite John and Peter in what Heidegger calls being-with implies a union of subject and object and for Sartre these are as incompatible as *pour soi* and *en soi*. We are left with the master–slave relationship as the one possibility.

In *Saint Genet* the author convincingly analyses the psychology of Jean Genet in the above terms, although these are at no time overtly stated. Genet is haunted by a childhood incident which made him a hoodlum and throughout his life returns to it as if it were the basis of a sacramental rite: "The argument of this liturgical drama is as follows: a child dies of shame; a hoodlum rises up in his place; the hoodlum will be haunted by the child".[6] Shame, in this context, recalls the situation of "being looked at". To die, of course, is to be fixed as an object. Genet's drama is therefore that of one who has died of shame, who is made object by the Look and struggles to react. The subject in this case is the Other in the widest sense, society. Sartre's analysis is fascinating enough to warrant retelling. It begins with an examination of Genet's childhood. Genet is an orphan, ward of the state, on *loan* to a family of peasants. He is from the first aware that his origins are suspect, that, without his knowledge, society has already fixed him with its gaze. As he explains in *The Thief's Journal* (*Journal du Voleur*, 1949) at the age of twenty-one he obtained his birth certificate, dicovered his mother's name, his father's anonymity and the address of his place of birth, 22 rue d'Assas. It was simply a maternity hospital (p.34). Sartre comments. As Genet moves to uncover his origins he comes up against a sign of refusal:

> Whenever the child tries to reach . . . to his true origins, he finds that his birth coincides with a gesture of rejection . . . Later, it is all of society that will cast him out, but this social rejection is latent in the maternal rejection . . . he is not that woman's son but her excrement.[7]

Thus from the first Genet has no sense of freedom, of subjectivity. Rather he is aware of himself as powerless before the Other. He plays at pilfering to make up for his spiritual and material poverty. Of course he is not "stealing", but he is "*caught in the act*",[8] *pris la main dans le sac*, and from that moment his identity is inescapably objective: he is a thief. The Other catches him stealing, fixes him in that act by the Look and gives him a positive being for ever: "Genet learns what he *is objectively*. It is this *transition* that is going to determine his entire life".[9] The Other's logic is unassailable. He who steals *is* a thief. Nothing can prevent the transition from *pour soi* to *en soi*. Sartre stresses that Genet's undoing is that he is still a child. Had he been older he might have managed to counter the Other's view of him. As it is he has complete trust in the adult world. If they say he is a thief then he believes it and if they say that theft is evil then he believes that he is evil. This is the extent of his alienation from himself. Not only does the Other objectify him and steal his freedom but he continues to do so, forcing Genet into a future of further theft. The Look is installed within Genet's own mind so that he becomes his own accuser, an Other to himself. Thus on the one hand Genet becomes a criminal because the power of the Other, who insists that he is as it were *eternally* a criminal, is too much to resist. On the other, he *accepts* the law he breaks, he loves his accusers and is the first to take their part and to condemn his own acts. Quite simply, his trouble is that he has been *named*, reduced to a passive object: "the result has been a radical metamorphosis of his person . . ."[10] The Look *transforms*. As Sartre sees it, whatever Genet does from this point can only lead him, as in fact it does, to the reformatory and, finally, to prison. Freedom and futurity are synonymous in existential philosophy and Genet has lost both.

Sartre's analysis resembles *pirandellismo* and the fact is worth mentioning because it is true that in so far as Genet's work is amenable to Sartrean interpretation it is also broadly comparable to Pirandello's. The unknown girl of *Come tu mi vuoi* (*As you desire me*), Mrs Ponza of *So it is* (*if you think so*) (*Cosí è* (*se vi pare*)), both victims of a Look which makes them what they are, are willing to assume identities perhaps not their own. In varying contexts, a great many of Pirandello's characters find themselves in this situation. As in Sartre, to be *someone* (as in *When you are Someone*, *Quando si è qualcuno*) is to be fixed, to die in the sense in which a work of art is dead. One has only to think of *Six Characters in Search of an Author* (*Sei personaggi in cerca d'autore*) or a lesser play like *Diana and Tuda* (*Diana e la Tuda*) and to substitute for the *pour soi–en soi* dualism the Pirandellian antithesis of Life and the Mask.

Sartre's conclusions in *Saint Genet* are, as I have said, not simply literary ones. I want to make use of them in an exclusively literary context, since what I have termed Genet's desire to escape the Other and to find refuge and fulfilment in solitude may be discussed entirely in terms of Genet's work.

The theme of objectification is especially evident in *The Maids* (*Les Bonnes*, 1947) and in the plays following it. Genet, however, goes beyond a mere presentation of human relationships in terms of the Look and seeks to probe the *reason* for social objectification. His answer is a variation of Blake's "without Contraries is no progression". To "prisons are built with stones of Law, Brothels with bricks of Religion" Genet adds "so maids and mistresses, blacks and their white masters, criminals and law-abiding men depend upon each other for existence". The phenomenon is analysed by Sartre in *Saint Genet* in terms of "projection" and it follows from the assumptions of *Being and Nothingness*. No man is good or evil (or anything else) since man is nothing. In order to *be*, to be good for example, I must first invent an evil man. For this purpose I will project all that I fear or dislike upon another. This enables me to objectify or reify evil, to localize it in another who is the object of my Look. By a process of negation I am now able to regard myself as good. The other man is evil; I am *not* that man; it follows that I am good. Of course the conclusion is in bad faith, because it overlooks my freedom just as the rest of the process overlooks the freedom of the other man. It is a case of one illusion propping up another. Nevertheless it is effective and it enables me to regard myself as honest because there are thieves, white because there are blacks and so forth. Clearly society, viewed in this way, cannot do without its underworld, whether this be the world of servants or criminals or supposed racial inferiors. In *The Maids* the relationship is sketched from the start. On the one hand is the darkness, the world of the servant about which respectable folk know little, "our darkness, ours",[11] as Solange puts it, degradation and despair. On the other is Madame, with her vulgar and ostentatious nobility. Speaking for Madame, Claire expresses concisely the respectable man's attitude to his own dark side:

> I loathe servants. A vile and odious breed, I loathe them. They're not of the human race . . . They're a foul effluvium drifting through our rooms . . . seeping into us, entering our mouths, corrupting us. I vomit you! (p.34)

The servant – and we are here speaking of the underdog in general, even of the criminal – stands for all that the righteous wish to forget. Once vomited out of the respectable man's mouth, he becomes a mirror in which his master may see not *himself*, but himself as he is *not*. Thus Madame is not filth *because* the maids are that, "our distorting mirrors, our loathsome vent, our shame, our dregs" (p.35).

But the exact nature of this relationship is presented most successfully in a later play and one not yet written at the time of Sartre's study, *The Balcony* (*Le Balcon*, 1956). The first few scenes illustrate some of the sexual fantasies practised in madame Irma's brothel. A bishop and a judge, among others, are shown in relation to their social complements, the sinner and the thief. Let us for the present ignore the fact that all the roles are imaginary, that the dignitaries are clients and the victims madame Irma's girls. Everything depends on the Look without which social differences would be impossible. Society divides into two parts, the master and the slave. Just as in objectifying the maids Madame constitutes herself as mistress, so bishop and judge constitute themselves in opposition to the sinner and the thief. As scene two opens the thief is "caught in the act", like Sartre's Genet. The proof is on her: she has stolen. Consequently, she *is* a thief. The judge's sense of security is the other side of the picture. If the girl is a thief, it follows that, as he condemns her, he becomes a judge. Thus, referring also to the executioner, he tells the thief: "we are bound together, you, he and I".[12] Everything depends on the existence of a complementary opposite. The world is an apple, as the judge argues, which he cuts in two, the good and the bad. This is his "sublime function" in the service of justice and it is made possible by the thief's willingness to be evil:

> THE JUDGE: And you agree, thank you, you agree to be the bad! (p.17)

The danger is that the thief my not cooperate:

> You need only refuse – but you'd better not! – need only refuse to be who you are – what you are . . . for me to cease to be . . . to vanish, evaporated . . . But you won't refuse, will you? You won't refuse to be a thief? That would be wicked. It would be criminal. You'd deprive me of being! (p.19)

So at the end of the scene the judge crawls before the thief, licking her feet, imploring her to be a thief: he *needs* her. So also with the bishop who is bishop *because* he is not the penitent kneeling before him. Good springs into being only at the appearance of evil. The bishop is justified in the act of absolution he performs since this act, even as it forgives sin, confirms the sinner as evil – at least for that moment, otherwise there would be no need for absolution. It is interesting to note in this context that Genet as a confirmed thief could not bring himself to steal in Nazi Germany, or so he claims in the *Journal*. It was a country of thieves, hence theft was impossible. In Genet's words, "I'm stealing in the void" (p.102). One cannot steal except under the gaze of the just man, which has the power – no theft alone can do it – to *make* one a thief.

However, it must be stressed that the relationships depicted in Genet's work and involving an interdependence of complements are entirely one-sided. It is true that judges *need* their thieves but this does not mean that the two sides have achieved parity. I shall modify some of these conclusions a little with respect to *The Balcony* in a later chapter but at this point a sharp distinction must be drawn between the two halves of Genet's world. One is object, the other subject. In spite of their tendency to label themselves in bad faith, judges and bishops escape being *named* in the sense in which thieves and sinners are named. They remain subjects, they retain the initiative, the power, in short, the Look. In Sartrean terms they are *pour soi*, free – free to *act* – for that is precisely what it means to be a subject, to exercise the sovereignty of the Look. On the other hand, as objects, thieves and sinners can only undergo passively: their place is to be condemned or to be forgiven. And this is especially true in the context of mistress and maids in *The Maids*. Sartre calls an active–passive social relation of this kind the relation of the Us-object and the We-subject (*le nous-objet, le nous-sujet*).[13] The We is that part of society which has the initiative. Certainly it cannot exist without its complement. Nevertheless the Us always retains an inferior status in the relation. The Us has no sense of solidarity, it exists only as passive, as acted upon: its only cohesion is the bond of the oppressed, dependent at every instant upon the continuance of oppression. Genet's notion of the underdog, expressly stated in the *Journal* (p.81) and made clear in the plays, is similar to Sartre's. Claire and Solange, the servants of *The Maids*, are anonymous from a philosophical point of view. The object is simply there to provide a context in which the subject may *act* and so be himself. Thieves are that only so that judges may exercise their sublime function of condemnation; sinners are that only in order to provide bishops with an opportunity for using their power of forgiveness; Claire and Solange are there so that their bad smell may differentiate Madame from them.

It is here that the full impact of the Look becomes obvious. The object exists to serve another's subjectivity. To be object is to be something one is *not* except in the eyes of the Other, it is to be *Other to oneself*, to be alienated from oneself. In the especially relevant case of *The Maids* the unequal subject–object relation of mistress and servant means that Madame is emotionally self-sufficient, in Sartrean terms *free* of her servants even though without them she could not be. Claire and Solange, on the other hand, are mere objects, not free human beings. Their existence is felt as that of a parasite or fungus. They depend entirely on Madame's Look whereas she exists as a kind of *primum mobile.* This means that while Madame is indifferent to her maids, they themselves are emotionally involved in the relationship. Of course they cannot hate Madame. They *accept* their status as objects; consequently they see themselves through *Madame's* eyes, not their own, and so hate themselves. For Madame they feel love, or rather a confused love which turns into hate and a hate which turns into love. It is the child Genet's reaction to society, as Sartre sees it. Thus Madame (speaking through Claire) complains of Solange's attentions. But Solange is not being purely ironic in her reply as she insists "I wish Madame to be lovely" (p.8) or, more simply, "I love you" (p.9). Of course she loves her "as one loves a mistress" (p.9), that is, with intense hatred. Claire's soliloquy, which exists only in the French version, expresses this perfectly:

> Car Madame est bonne! Madame est belle! Madame est douce! Mais nous ne sommes pas des ingrates, et tous les soirs dans notre mansarde . . . nous prions pour elle . . . Ainsi Madame nous tue avec sa douceur! Avec sa bonté, Madame nous empoisonne. Car Madame est bonne! Madame est belle! Madame est douce![14]
>
> For Madame is good! Madame is beautiful! Madame is nice! But we're not ungrateful, and every evening in our garret . . . we pray for her . . . In this way Madame kills us with her kindness! With her goodness, Madame poisons us. Because Madame is good! Madame is beautiful! Madame is nice!

All this is true. Madame destroys the maids with her goodness in which they truly believe. She allows them a weekly wash in her bath; with her discarded clothes she will dress them like princesses (p.26). In fact she loves them – as she loves her other things:

> CLAIRE: *She* does, *she* loves us. She's kind. Madame is kind! Madame adores us.
>
> SOLANGE: She loves us the way she loves her armchair. Not even *that* much! Like her bidet, rather. Like her pink enamel lavatory seat. (p.16)

It follows that the maids detest each other since each reminds the other of her own degradation:

> SOLANGE: . . . And we, we can't love one another. Filth . . .
> CLAIRE: Ah!
> SOLANGE: . . . doesn't love filth. (p.16)

Again:

> SOLANGE: I want to help you . . . but I know I disgust you. I'm repulsive to you. And I know it because you disgust me. When slaves love one another, it's not love.
> CLAIRE: I'm sick of seeing my image thrown back at me by a mirror, like a bad smell. You're my bad smell. (p.21)

The last phrase expresses perfectly the only human bond that is possible in Genet's world of the alienated. It is the bond of the Sartrean Us, a shared ignominy. Madame has viewed both maids with the Sartrean Look and *that* is what Claire and Solange have in common.

It is now possible to return to the question of solitude as an ideal in the works of Genet with new perspectives. The theme of solitude, so far examined in *L'Atelier* and *Le Funambule*, is inexplicable except in terms of that other major theme of Genet's, the theme of personal alienation and the Look. In other words the search for a metaphysical goal which is to be charted in this argument must be seen on the backdrop of a struggle against the Other. Genet's characters are wounded by society and forced into themselves. Just as Genet in the Barrio Chino internalizes his despair, so they withdraw to a point which they hope will prove impregnable. But the movement is not merely escapism. It is a negative which naturally transforms itself into a positive. The ensuing discussion will trace this progress, as it is found in Genet's work. In so doing it will establish the importance of the idea of solitude in the novels and plays – an importance which has been noted by, for example, Richard Coe,[15] but which has not been investigated in the terms I propose – and also the relevance of Sartre's thought, as expressed in *Saint Genet* and, more importantly, in *Being and Nothingness*, to an understanding of the Genet ascesis. It must be added that, in spite of a great indebtedness to *Saint Genet*, these chapters will not restate Sartre's thesis but will pursue an altogether different line.

10 Genet and Sartre: the murderer and the saint

1 The murderer: fake sadism

I want to sing murder, for I love murderers.[1]

GENET

Genet's literary ascesis has four phases, that is to say, Genet depicts four distinct character types in his work, each of which represents a particular solution to the problem of the Other. Where the Beckett subject progresses gradually from the situation of the tramps to that of the Unnamable and the Ionesco subject moves from inauthentic to authentic existence, Genet's hero seeks a gradual emancipation from other men and the fulfilment of solitude. Of course it is obvious from what has already been said that solitude is not here synonymous with merely being alone; nor is it synonymous with self-sufficiency, understood psychologically, nor even with self-respect. Solitude is a metaphysical reality, a being-oneself that transcends the narrow bounds of the personal. Thus the four types are something more than mere solitaries in the usual sense. All are outcasts, though in different ways, all react to the effects of the Sartrean Look and all achieve a particular kind of glory in solitude.

Genet's first literary attempt to realize his ideal is the least convincing yet, at first glance, the most obvious from a Sartrean viewpoint. If the Other has me pinned down by the Look the simplest thing for me to do is to transcend his gaze, to return the Look. Two Sartrean Looks cannot meet for that would mean a subject–object synthesis which is a contradiction in terms. If the Other looks at me he is subject and I am object. If I look back the situation is reversed, but either way neither he nor I can be subject and object at the same time. Let us assume that I have regained the initiative. There are various ways in which this may be expressed and they are outlined in *Being and Nothingness*, but in Genet's case one of Sartre's categories is here applicable above all others and that is aggressive hate or sadism. For Sartre, hatred is a resolute decision to treat the Other only as object, to abolish him as a free subject in his own right, to wipe him out as *pour soi*. This amounts to murder and the reason for this is clear if we recall that to objectify is to fix, to reduce a dynamic human freedom to the passivity of a corpse. Death in the Sartrean system after all represents the final hardening of the personality, the definitive conversion of nothingness into being, of *pour soi* into *en soi*. Genet's first move, then, is a direct assault on the Other and, not surprisingly, its representative is the murderer.

We are now in a position to take seriously that incredible statement – "I want to sing murder, for I love murderers" – and to understand Genet's fascination for the man who has killed. The murderer is an outcast, enemy of society and a victim of its Look, one who has been labelled a criminal or *named*. Yet he responds to the outrage with cold hatred and in a symbolic act takes his revenge, killing a representative of society and in so doing reducing society itself to a helpless object. Before the body of the particular victim, he is free of the Other, gloriously alone, a superhuman being, in the words of Genet's idol, the criminal Weidmann, "already beyond that" (*Our Lady*, p.59). Of course for Sartre this is a meaningless claim. The Other is ontologically part of me, I cannot exorcize his presence, I cannot exist without him. Genet, however, is as yet undeterred. Thus he dedicates his first novel to Pilorge, a soldier who murdered his lover, and in the same work commemorates other killers: Angel Sun and Weidmann, describing how he cuts out their photographs and pastes them on the wall of his own cell.

In *Miracle of the Rose* (*Miracle de la Rose*, written in 1943) he sings the praises of Harcamone, a murderer confined in the same prison as himself and awaiting the guillotine. Harcamone is a Christ-like figure of somewhat effete beauty, a sacrificial offering whose chains metamorphose into garlands of roses before Genet's eyes. His struggle with the Other is minutely described in symbolic terms at the end of the novel, through the medium of a series of dream visions. In the last and most powerful of these we see Harcamone awakened by four men in black, the judge, lawyer, executioner and chaplain. But as he awakens he begins to swell in size, breaking through the walls of the cell, then those of the prison, until he seems to fill the universe. Compared to him the four accusers are now the size of fleas. Notwithstanding this, they climb into his body through the mouth and ear. Inside they find another and more mysterious world. Terrified, they stumble into forests, over stones, through fields of flowers, asking "the heart – have you found the heart?"[2] Eventually they are in a luminous corridor lined with mirrors and reach a door, itself a mirror, on which is scratched a heart pierced by an arrow. The four enter. It is a bare, white room, empty save for an adolescent beating a drum. The men continue through another door. They are now at the deepest centre of Harcamone and this centre, guarded by the boy with the drum, is a giant rose, a Dantean rose of paradise. In this holy place the tiny representatives of society rush about excitedly, lifting the petals of the flower as if they were petticoats. But the grandeur of the rose overpowers them and, as they stare into its depths, they become dizzy and fall. The dream vision ends here. Clearly it images the actual execution of Harcamone, in short, his victory over society even as it destroys him. Other elements of the vision suggest the larger Genet pattern: the essential violation of the criminal through the medium of the Look. Thus society enters into the very soul of the killer and as its four representatives approach the heart they are shown reflections of themselves: it is they who have made the heart as it is. Moreover, the door of entry carries the emblem of love, a wounded heart. The symbolism is movingly transparent: Harcamone, like the tightrope walker, bears in his deepest self a wound inflicted by the Look of the Other. But it is a wound of love, suggesting the original alienation of the victim of the Look. Furthermore, the killer is a child, an innocent, perhaps frightened child watching over the drumbeats of the heart. We are reminded not only of Harcamone's first crime at the age of sixteen but, more importantly, as Bettina Knapp suggests in her analysis,[3] of the sixteen-year-old Genet who was branded a criminal and sent to Mettray reformatory. Still, Harcamone is not conquered. Even as he dies he affirms the ultimate inviolability of the heart, that is, of solitude, and the ultimate glory of the murderer.

Of course under these circumstances our definition of murder must be rigorous. A soldier, for example, or a madman, or one who kills for material gain or even for personal reasons will not do.

Murder must represent a real transcending of the Other in an obscurely religious act, it must echo the ascesis of the tightrope walker. This question is raised most explicitly in Genet's first play, *Deathwatch* (*Haute Surveillance*, 1947), a short, tightly-knit work, set in a single cell and involving for the most part only three men. Green Eyes is about to die for his crime, like Harcamone. Maurice and Lefranc admire his power and attempt to discover the secret of one who is "already beyond that", beyond the law, beyond life itself: "I'm no longer alive! I'm all alone now!"[4] For in a sense Green Eyes, in his solitude, is already dead. Moreover his death is a death to self and a living in a god-like life outside the self whose origins may be traced back to the day of the murder. And this because, strictly speaking, the killer does not commit his crime for any human motive but for the sake of a higher power, just as the tightrope walker dances not for personal glory but in order to exalt the wire. Put a little differently, he does not kill at all but is *led* to murder in a brutal but finely revealing transposition of the Pauline "not I but Christ lives in me". Green Eyes describes the state. Like St Teresa in ecstasy he is falling, carried away so gently that he cannot resist, "so sweetly, the thing that's making me fall is so nice that out of politeness, I don't dare rebel" (p.22). He is in the arms of Providence or Fate. On the day of his crime a passer-by raises his hat to him. Everything is ordained and it is as if the whole world knows it. Green Eyes is not abandoned for a moment, things move on their own initiative – "there was nothing more to be done" (pp.22–3) – he has only to resign himself, like Peter in the last chapter of John's gospel, going through the motions of living while another acts for him:

> It was destiny that took the form of my hands . . . And for me everything became simpler. The girl was already under me. All I had to do was put one hand delicately on her mouth and the other delicately on her neck. It was over. (p.24)

Green Eyes' hands, not Green Eyes, kill the girl; his part is simply to have the courage of solitude, the courage "to be all alone. In broad daylight" (p.31). This point is underlined when Lefranc attempts to emulate Green Eyes by killing Maurice:

> GREEN EYES: . . . And you thought you could become . . .

> without the help of heaven, as great as me! I didn't want anything . . . I didn't want what happened to me to happen. It was all given to me. (p.39)

Green eyes did not choose his Fate, it chose him: "It fell on my shoulders and clung to me" (p.40). But Lefranc's crime is his own, only he is responsible. There has been, then, no dying to self and therefore no murder. Or again, as Sartre puts it in *Saint Genet*: "One kills in order to *be* a criminal but it would be vain merely to try to become a criminal if one *were* not a criminal in advance."[5] We are in the realm of the theology of Grace. In order to become one of the elect I must be one from the start: "You have not chosen me, but I have chosen you" (John 15:16).

Comparable things may be said about all of Genet's heroic murderers. In each case to kill is to turn the objectifying Look upon the Other, but in a context of spiritual sublimity. Through murder one raises oneself to the heights of Fate, of inevitability, to a region where the killing of the victim becomes no more than a *sign* of the *real* death that is taking place: the oblation of the murderer himself. Murder remains a revenge upon society, but in the very act of revenge the subject transcends the issue of the Other and transforms his situation into a lonely apotheosis, an *ex-stasis* or going beyond oneself and the bounds of the human. In *Our Lady of the Flowers* (*Notre-Dame des Fleurs*, written in 1942) the youth Our Lady strangles an old man with his own tie. As with Green Eyes the killer is not responsible – it is the *tie* which, knotted just a little tightly about the old man's neck, *demands* to be made tighter still. And the killer's triumph is complete when he confronts society at his trial: it is as if the crowd were Bernadette and the accused the Virgin, his namesake, uttering the famous words of Lourdes: "I am the Immaculate Conception" (p.250). In the same novel the negro Village, who has murdered his mistress, determines to elevate the act to the level of the inevitable, the numinous. Poised on a fine point of tension he allows himself to be possessed by a spirit which saves him from collapse:

> By powerful effort of will, he escaped banality – maintaining his mind in a superhuman region, where he was a god, creating at one stroke a private universe where his acts escaped moral control. He sublimated himself. (p.166)

Village transcends the moral considerations of society and transforms his act of violence into a religious ritual. By an immense effort he remains calm and walls up the body of his victim.

But in all these episodes we are faced with an insurmountable obstacle. In spite of all that has been said, the eulogy of the murderer does not ring true and this not for any reason extrinsic to the novels and plays. On the contrary, Genet himself has second thoughts. Let us take the example of Green Eyes after he has killed the girl:

> I saw the danger . . . of finding myself in someone else's boots. And I was scared. I wanted to back up . . . No go! I tried every form and shape so as not to be a murderer. (p.23)

The subject struggles against Fate, seeking to be anything at all, a dog, a cat, a horse, a tiger, a table, a stone, anything but what Fate now imposes on him, a new skin, the identity of the murderer. Like Querelle in *Querelle of Brest* (*Querelle de Brest*, 1947) Green Eyes has committed an act of absolute finality, in which is contained a whole chain of inescapable consequences: capture by the police, imprisonment, the death sentence. More important still, in that moment when the world seems to bear down on him, he has once and for all assumed a persona, he has allowed himself to be *named* by society. The problem of the Look is now acute. Who has been objectified, the victim, that is, society, or the killer? It is difficult to avoid the conclusion that the act of murder has the effect of objectifying the criminal, of reducing him to the status of a passive creature, meekly advancing to the guillotine. Certainly it is Fate which takes him by the hand and leads him forward. The fact is that Fate at this stage is suspiciously indistinguishable from the police, from those same social forces which the killer is attempting to conquer. The suggestion, therefore, is that murder is no solution to the problem of the Look. Far from liberating the criminal who is initially the object of society's gaze, murder simply confirms the status quo by more than ever reducing the outcast to an object, by killing the murderer *metaphorically* during his crime and *actually* after it. The whole presentation of the killer as a victorious hero then begins to take the appearance of an argument which, on the whole, fails to convince Genet himself. For we must remember that submission to what Genet calls Fate implies the loss of Sartrean freedom. To be a subject is to be free, to initiate, to be master of the Look. But the killer's crime condemns him to pure passivity. It is as if he were now *en soi*, a *something*, labelled for life. Our Lady's first thought after the crime is "murderer" (p.114). The omnipresent Other gazes at him and fixes him in his persona for ever, and this explains why the killer is so anxious to escape the inevitable unfolding of his Destiny. Rather than a murderer Green Eyes will be a stone, Village a priest of evil, Our Lady his namesake. Still, we cannot escape the element of *mauvaise foi*. Like the child Genet, the criminal is pinned down by the Look. Of course he may argue that society, even as it destroys him, is merely an *agent* for a higher power, the will of Fate itself. The only answer to this objection is that Genet seems only half to believe it.

At any rate, there are strong hints of this, particularly in *Deathwatch*, a play which becomes more ambivalent the more closely it is examined. It is true that, in so far as Green Eyes is idealized, the conscious, willed action of Lefranc in killing Maurice is viewed with contempt. Yet the moral of the play as a whole is scarcely so clear-cut. Green Eyes, the chosen killer, is a simple illiterate with the natural dignity of this type. Lefranc, on the other hand, is a self-conscious man, a man divided within himself, lacking in spontaneity, simply because he is something of an intellectual. Whereas Green Eyes is a man, Lefranc, plagued by Sartrean consciousness, acts the part of a man (p.29). Indeed the Sartrean pattern is straightforward. Lefranc exemplifies the free man, the *pour soi*, the initiating subject forced to play a role precisely because he is free, because he has no fixed identity, because he has not been *named*. Green Eyes, by contrast, exemplifies the passive object, frozen in his identity, unable to shake off the effects of society's Look. Now if Genet has any doubts about the glory of the unthinking murderer, they emerge in this contrast. For while, on the face of it, Green Eyes is the idol of the cell, Lefranc is successfully working to undermine his status, swallowing him up, "gulping [him] down" (p.25). The final scene, a confrontation of the two after Lefranc has killed Maurice, restates all the ambiguities of the play. Where Green Eyes killed because Fate willed it, the other killed freely, consciously and, it follows, clumsily. Who then is the true murderer, the man who has attained to true solitude? Seemingly Green Eyes – yet the suggestion is inescapable that, magical hocus-pocus aside, a willed and so utterly *human* act requires greater courage. If this is so, Lefranc's last words – "I really am all alone!" (p.40) – may be taken to clinch the argument.

Genet is perhaps not altogether willing to make up his mind, but it seems that, in the final analysis, the murderer's claim to the glory of solitude is doubtful. The killer's achievement is a fake because his revolt against society is no revolt at all. In Sartrean terms one may overcome the Other's Look and so seize the initiative: sadism or Sartrean "hate" represents such a move. But Genet's killer does not return the Look, and far from undermining the power of society he strengthens it. Indeed, his crime may simply be seen as a confirmation of society's will, a death – of the killer – which leads to his final death on the scaffold and which follows logically from the *original* death of the social outcast when he suffered the gaze of the Other for the first time. *That* gaze made him a murderer, chose him for murder long before the event and for prison and the death cell. Thus Genet's first attempt at depicting a type of solitude is a failure. What appears as an act of sadism and aggression is in reality passive, masochistic, and what appears as an ascesis oriented towards the supernatural is in reality a further submission to the Look. Compared to the true assassin the intellectual Lefranc is far more active and Lefranc, although he has killed, is not and can never be a murderer. He is not the type, which is to say he is not *chosen* because he chooses for himself, because, in Sartrean terms, he is free, *pour soi*, nothingness. Thus Lefranc suggests a second Genet type and it is on this type that Genet's interest is in fact focussed. A simple question points to the direction in which the author is moving: how do I know that the murderer achieves a unique glory? The answer is that all our knowledge of the murderer comes to us through the medium of an altogether different character type. It is through Divine's eyes that Our Lady and Village are seen as triumphant in *Our Lady of the Flowers*; in *Miracle of the Rose* Harcamone's glory is described for us by Genet, a character in his own novel. Now Divine and the Genet of the *Miracle* are the antithesis of the murderer type. Rather, they resemble Lefranc. We are therefore not surprised to see that, alongside his experiment with the murderer, Genet is already transferring his hopes to a different solution to the problem.

II The saint: fake masochism

> Jean Genet, the weakest of all and the strongest.[6]
>
> GENET

Once again, we begin with the social outcast, but from this point all similarity with the murderer ceases. The new approach consists not in attempting to return the wound inflicted on oneself by the Other, but in *accepting* this wound and entering deeper into it. In other words, the victim refuses to fight; rather he sides with the enemy against himself, he acknowledges that he deserves to be an outcast, he strives to be ever more an abject creature. Thus a new ascesis is postulated, one of shame and misery. Instead of the murderer, a heroic – if disappointing – type, Genet depicts the lowest of the low, the outcast among criminals.

In Sartre's system this represents another possible approach to the Look, that of masochism. Of course masochism is implicit in the situation of the Look. As object of the Look I am alienated from myself and, as already shown, this means that I am liable to love, as much as hate, my oppressor and to hate, as much as love, myself. Still, from a Sartrean standpoint, masochism, like sadism, must be interpreted as a move to overcome the Look. The difference is that where sadism seeks to transcend the Look, to regain the initiative and freedom by objectifying the Other, masochism submits to the Look and wishes to retain for itself the status of an object. The Other objectifies me, turns me into a *thing*. Very well, then I will *be* just that, like a beautiful woman I will *cultivate* my passivity before the Other's advances. This attitude is not to be understood merely as a surrender, however. On the contrary, masochism is more ambitious than sadism, for Sartre's woman will not be satified to objectify her partner as he objectifies her – she will possess the Other, *as subject*, that is, by his free choice. In order to ensnare the dominant male she accepts alienation, she *wills* to be what she is not – a thing, an object, *en soi* – hoping, like the Christian martyr, to conquer in defeat. Something comparable to this happens in some Genet situations, as Sartre has seen in *Saint Genet*. However, unlike Sartre's unliberated female (or perhaps after all like her) the Genet masochist is less interested in the Other than in himself, aiming in his relation less to win the Other over than to make a fool of him. Masochism then takes the form of disguised aggression, a subtle kind of one-upmanship born of frustration and despair: the Other dominates me with the Look and I have no means of defence; in order to turn the tables in this hopeless situation I determine to accept the Look freely, to *will* my inferior status. In this way I am able to remain one move ahead. The Other *makes* me a slave – then I *will* to be a slave; the Other drives me to new depths of abjection – then I *will* new depths of abjection. It is a way of snatching a minimal dignity out of my abjection or a possible victory out of defeat, since whatever the Other imposes, I determine to assent to it. Of course I have no choice, the Look is all-powerful, I *must* submit. But in the very act of *willing* my submission do I not recover a little of my autonomy? The Other is master but if I *will* to be his slave, even though I have no choice, does not my slavery become self-imposed? In this case I am no longer a slave, I regain my freedom and, conceivably, make an idiot of my master. Thus the mechanism of escape, if it succeeds, achieves two aims. On the one hand the masochist hopes that if he *will*s to be the object he is *forced* to be, he is in fact exercising his freedom, that is, by a sleight of hand, he is no longer being an object but a free subject. On the other, he hopes to hoodwink his oppressor, to *use* him as a means of self-assertion. Thus the *more* the Other dominates me, the lower I sink, the *more* I will my utter poverty, the *more* I assert my spiritual triumph, the *more* I am indebted to the Other for his unknowing cooperation. It is the martyr's indebtedness to his tormentors.

If the masochist, Genet's second character type, adopts a new form of asceticism, the goal remains the same: to regain the initiative over the Other and, more importantly, in so doing to find one's true self in the glory of solitude. At this stage, though, solitude must be envisaged as the solitude not of the heroic criminal but the abject "saint". Genet chooses the term deliberately and I shall use it from now on without quotation marks on the understanding that I refer to Genet's own definition of sanctity. The saint in Genet is one whose seeming passivity disguises real initiative. This is the opposite to the murderer who masquerades as active subject when in fact he is passive object. The saint loves his enemy – society – in order to transcend it. Like Margaret Mary Alacoque, he accepts all the humiliations placed in his way by Providence – in this case, by society. The result is a dying to self and a spiritual resurrection. It is a making use of suffering for higher ends: "Saintliness means turning pain to good account" (*Journal*, p.170). Thus the sole basis of sanctity is renunciation (*Journal*, p.174). Instead of submitting to Providence or to the Other, as does the killer, however, the saint cooperates and so in a way rises above the constraint of the situation: he *wills* his Fate, as Sartre suggests in *Saint Genet*. Thus we have an embracing of total abasement, even of failure, the ethic of the passive homosexual, the petty criminal and the squealer or traitor, a eulogy of suffering unsurpassed by any conventional ascetic: Genet will give all his wordly goods for "the reality of supreme happiness in despair" (*Journal*, p.173). Even the example of "My God, my God, why have you forsaken me?" which comes to mind is insufficient to illustrate the ideal. Genet himself uses that of Hitler at the moment of defeat (*Journal*, p.173) and this because he considers that the conventional ascesis of the religious figure does not go far enough. Christ, after all, is not a sinner: how, then, can his humiliation be complete? Genet's saint must be the lowest of the low (and so perhaps the highest, according to Christian saying), lowest in every sense, a saint who is a sinner of the worst kind, a Magdalen without tears. Of course there is a reward and it is implicit in the ascesis. The way of abject sanctity leads to solitude because, like beauty, sanctity implies uniqueness: "Like beauty . . . saintliness is individual. Its expression is original" (*Journal*, p.174).

Genet's finest example of the saint is his first, Divine of *Our Lady of the Flowers*. Divine is graceful, fragile and beautiful, a butterfly, a flower. She is also Louis Culafroy. a despairing and tormented homosexual living among brutal men in a dingy quarter of Paris. Her life emerges as a sensitively realized combination of fantasy and squalor, degradation and spiritual splendour, a rococo flourish in the gutter. We may take the example of her arrest, lovingly described, like all the episodes of this novel, with multi-layered irony and also genuine lyricism. Divine is drunk, singing the *Veni Creator* "in a shrill voice" (p.99). Her march to the station in the company of two constables is a nuptial procession, followed eargerly by excited crowds of fairies. Back the next day, she recounts her marvellous adventures. She was on the verge of swooning and the police had to fan her with their check handkerchiefs, wiping her face like so many attentive Veronicas:

> My God, Beauties, I almost passed out. The policemen held me up. They were all standing around me fanning me with their checked handkerchiefs. They were the Holy Women wiping my face. My Divine Face . . . (p.100)

Like Chirst, Divine is a religious martyr, but with the difference that she goes by the way of sin and not of virtue. Still, hers is an ascetic way to total self-transcendence and so the novel is structured as a record not of her life, but, as befits a hagiography, of her journey to death. In the author's words: "Slowly but surely I want to strip her of every vestige of happiness so as to make a saint of her" (p.98). Divine, like Teresa, will die many times over "a death more mysticall & high" before her final glorious consummation.

As in the case of the murderer, the saint's life is ordained by a higher power, and Divine is well aware of this fact, rediscovering it in every minute accident. Walking in the park, she spontaneously breaks into a dance step – which is instantly spoiled by the ugly dragging noise of her torn sole. This returns Divine to herself. Deliberately she cultivates the sense of her own poverty and shame, hanging her head and murmuring theatrically: "Lord, I am among Thy elect" (p.187). Poverty and meanness is the sign of her election. It is the sense of this which transforms her actions in the tawdry garret into angelic operations, operations of Fate or Providence. At the same time the appeal to Fate constitutes only a superficial similarity to the murderer, and this is amply illustrated by one of the finest episodes of the novel. Divine is in a bar frequented by pimps and fairies. On her head she wears a crown, a small tiara of false pearls. Suddenly she laughs, the tiara falls to the ground and is shattered. Ironic condolences pour in from every side: "The Divine in uncrowned!" At this point of humiliation Divine is possessed by a desperate courage: "then, Divine lets out a burst of strident laughter. Everyone pricks up his ears: it's her signal." She snatches her *false teeth* from her mouth and sets the new crown on her head to replace the old: "Dammit all, Ladies, I'll be queen anyhow!" (pp.181–2) This superbly grotesque act is Divine's triumph and it exemplifies all her victories. First there is the moment of shame, then that of glory, painfully realized through a *willed* deeper immersion in shame. In the terminology of *Saint Genet* Divine "wills her Fate". If abjection there must be, her glory will lie in a daring, perhaps extravagant gesture which places her above shame. If she cannot avoid a humiliation then she will go one better, she will intensify it and so demonstrate her ultimate inviolability. It is the masochist's solution to the problem of shame, an attempt to assert freedom and dignity in a situation in which they are not merely threatened but already lost. If I say "*let* them be lost, I *will* their loss" I have salvaged an essential minimum of my self-respect, I have outwitted Fate (God or the human Other, it doesn't matter which) and turned my passivity into an assault. This is Divine's approach.

Indeed, it is the basis of her entire life, finding particular expression in her relationship with her lover, Darling. The story is told with light irony and given the appearance of delightful fantasy. Yet the reader is not allowed to forget that Divine is a passive homosexual, willing to be maltreated by a thug. Darling, petty thief, informer and pimp, plays the role of master of the Look which reduces Divine to a thing of no consequence. As he goes by Genet comments: "the Eternal passed by in the form of a pimp" (p.62). This God does not even despise Divine. He scarcely knows of her existence, as Madame in *The Maids* scarcely dreams of her maids. At the same time, we are told, "but to Divine, Darling is everything" (p.104). Of course, Divine is abandoned by Darling. An ageing homosexual, she suffers loneliness and jealousy. Living with a negro and the youth Our Lady, she ministers to them from a position of abasement and anguish. There is a further complexity, though.

> Loue's passiues are his actiu'st part
> The wounded is the wounding heart,

Crashaw wrote of Teresa – and Genet's saint is no different in his own context. For Divine submits to her lovers only because she is in the final analysis stronger than they are, able to destroy them by her very submission. So just as her subtle and devious surrender is really one-upmanship, her love is a form of hate. Again and again she *allows* herself to be dominated by males whose banality and weakness she carefully conceals, submitting as it were not to the real lover but to an ideal, that is, to *herself*, to her own power over herself. Thus she imaginatively creates and preserves in being the status of supposedly heroic thugs whom she so much admires – she *must* create a hero if he is to dominate her and so give her the requisite opportunity of freely willing her subjection to him. This is not to say that Divine's predicament is merely a product of her imagination, far from it. It is precisely because Divine *is* a victim of society that she obsessively seeks a victory over society in the form of the dominant partner, who functions symbolically rather like the victim in the situation of murder already discussed. It must be said that, in this early novel, Genet is uncertain about who is to be his hero, the murderer Our Lady or the saint Divine. In spite of his choice of title, though, the direction in which he is moving is clear enough and it is favourable to Divine. Our Lady kills blindly, his is the glory of a dummy. Divine, on the other hand, exists throughout as a vital centre of consciousness, alert to every change in her situation. In order to see how favourably she compares not only with Our Lady but also with Darling and other supposedly dominant males it is enough to refer to a theme noted by Sartre, that of 'hollowness". Village, the killer, makes hollow tin soldiers while in prison (p.160). When Divine tempts God by rifling the tabernacle of a church, there is no lightning from heaven:

> God was hollow. Just a hole with any old thing around it. A pretty shape, like . . . the little soldiers, which were holes with a bit of thin lead around them. (p.164)

Genet adds: "thus I lived in the midst of an infinity of holes in the form of men" (p.164). This is his real comment on Darling, on all of Divine's lovers, and, above all, on the type of the murderer. They are all of them like God: hollow, *creux*. Fate itself, that power from above so revered by the killer, must share in this unmasking. Thus, Divine, the type of the saint, works assiduously – through her masochism – to undermine Fate, God, society, the Other, *any* power which threatens her embattled integrity. She is clearly comparable to Lefranc in *Deathwatch*, though her way is more obviously a Little Way, like that of St Thérèse of Lisieux, a lowly ascesis but with its own *Magnificat*, Divine's song of victory:

> She sings that she is buggered out of taste.
>
> She robs and betrays her friends.
>
> Everything concurs to establish about her – despite her – solitude. She lives simply in the privacy of her glory, of the glory she has made tiny and precious. (p.273)

Divine is the first of a line of similar characters, saints of abasement who, through love, insidiously undermine the authority of those they serve. In the autobiographical *The Thief's Journal*, and in novels like *Miracle of the Rose* and *Funeral Rites* (*Pompes Funèbres*, 1947) where Genet himself appears as the protagonist, the author's identification with the type of the masochist is complete. As he explains in the *Journal*:

> I have thus been that little wretch who knew only hunger, physical humiliation, poverty, fear and degradation. From such galling attitudes as these I have drawn reasons for glory. (p.92)

This could be a description of Divine. Genet too is a victim and he reacts to his situation by willing the worst, by living a life which is willed necessity, beginning with his decision at Mettray reformatory. At the institution he suffers all the indignities society heaps upon the young offender: the cropping of the hair, the uniform, the environment. In order to survive he elaborates a discipline. Whatever is done to him he will accept as merited, whatever accusation is brought against him, whether just or unjust, he will *assent* from the bottom of his heart:

> I suffered there. I felt the cruel shame of having my head shaved, of being dressed in unspeakable clothes, of being confined in that vile place . . . In order to weather my desolation . . . I worked out . . . a rigorous discipline . . . to every charge brought against me, unjust though it be, from the bottom of my heart I shall answer yes. Hardly had I uttered the word . . . than I felt within me the need to become what I had been accused of being . . . I owned to being the coward, traitor, thief and fairy they saw in me . . . I became abject . . . I had succeeded. But what torments I suffered! (p.145)

This austere code remains in force during his later life when he wanders throughout Europe, prostitute, thief and beggar, servile before his lovers – notably Stilitano. But of course there is the expected reversal: Stilitano, like Darling, is "hollow", a creation of Genet's superior intelligence, a coward and a liar and yet revered by Genet because, like Divine, Genet *needs* to be an object for someone. Towards the end of the book Stilitano's insignificance is clearly illustrated. He is caught in a maze of mirrors, screaming with frustration while the spectators laugh. Finally, he gives up sulkily and refuses to continue. The real glory has gone to the abject Genet who becomes, in the words attributed to him in Sartre's book, "Jean Genet, the weakest of all and the strongest".[6] A similar pattern informs *Miracle of the Rose*, in which Genet submits to criminals whom he greatly surpasses in intelligence and imagination, indeed whose mystique he carefully invents and preserves. This emerges clearly in the dream sequence which climaxes the novel, since it is Genet's dreams, not Harcamone's, which we witness. Genet, in his cell, informs the other's progress to the guillotine with splendour, controlling in his imagination every move he makes. Thus Harcamone's glory and his solitude are really Genet's. The saint reveres his master only to destroy him and to reassert his own initiative and this is the significance of the theme of betrayal which is highlighted in the novel. Genet betrays Harcamone, morally speaking, by sleeping with Divers, the man who gave Harcamone up to the police, even as Harcamone awaits his execution. Thus he becomes Divers' accomplice, one with his baseness, "the abjection in which Divers remained" (p.253). The betrayal is complex, and may be taken as a type of many subject–object relationships in Genet. Genet is betraying one whom he really loves, otherwise there would be no masochism in the act. At the same time, however, by despising himself for his betrayal, by accepting his abasement, he becomes larger than the hero he has betrayed, he emancipates himself from Harcamone's influence, that is, from his own love for Harcamone. Masochism now turns into sadism and servility into a proud assertion of freedom.

Nowhere is this strategy more grotesquely evident than in *Funeral Rites*, Genet's third novel. Genet's lover, a member of the *Résistance*, has been killed by a French militiaman fighting for the Germans and Genet is desolate. His solution to his grief is similar to that in *Miracle of the Rose*: he will transcend his love, that is, the power of his lover over him, by a betrayal. He finds a way while at the cinema. Paris has just been freed and the film is a documentary of the fighting. It shows a captured French traitor, one of the despised militia. As the audience hisses Genet spontaneously sees that this militiaman, whom he dubs Riton, may, to all intents and purposes, be regarded as his lover's killer. Genet will betray his dead lover, Jean Decarnin, by falling in love with Riton, his murderer. He will be a traitor to Decarnin as in the earlier novel he is a traitor to Harcamone, by joining his enemy. In this way he will be as gloriously abject as the defeated militia, hated and vilified by the whole of France. Thus the rest of the novel depicts Genet's spiritual participation in the life of the militia and the Germans, particularly during their last days in Paris, when their humiliation is at its peak. Clearly, Genet is betraying not only Decarnin but also France whom he loves as he lives out the story of Riton, above all, as he sides contemptibly with the Germans, sharing the abjection of Hitler, a hero of degradation and so of solitude, a saint of evil. Genet is *willing* the *unavoidable* rape of his country, as well as his personal loss. Decarnin is dead and France prostrate. In order to free himself of his grief, that is, of his love for Decarnin and France which enslaves him, Genet places himself on the other side, he *accepts* the loss, he becomes an accomplice to the other side, in short, he regains his freedom: it is as if *he* had killed Decarnin and raped France. At last he is self-sufficient, rid of those emotional chains, alone. A small incident in *Funeral Rites* illustrates the mechanism perfectly. Pierrot puts a maggot in his mouth by mistake. Instantly the choice presents itself: either to admit defeat and submit to disgust or to *savour* the experience, to will the inevitable which has already occurred. Pierrot chooses the latter:

> He found himself caught between fainting with disgust or mastering his situation by willing it. He willed it. He made his tongue . . . knowingly and patiently suffer the hideous contact.[7]

The saint who betrays the Other is in exactly this position.

The pattern is more complicated in Genet's last novel, *Querelle of Brest*, since in this case the distinction between murderer and saint has been blurred: Querelle is a murderer intelligent enough to transform himself into a saint. After he murders his companion, he avoids the Fate which leads the unthinking killer to his end and chooses the way of homosexual abjection and betrayal instead – and he is successful. In order to forestall his Fate, he wills it – in a different form, as a death to self rather than as a death beneath the guillotine. One other character in the novel is comparable to him: Madame Lysiane, a forerunner of Irma in *The Balcony*. She too rises above herself by allowing herself to be turned into an object of shame.

From Divine onwards, then, Genet's saint is one who sinks to depths unknown to the murderer or the aggressive thug, who searches for subjectivity in the very act of being an object of the Look. Now from a Sartrean standpoint this approach cannot succeed. It is impossible, in the terms of *Being and Nothingness*, to find oneself as subject in the situation of being an object. Either I *return* the Look and so reassert my subjectivity by objectifying the Other or I *remain* an object of the Look, in which case I cannot dominate the Other. Any other alternative is out of the question because it would necessitate the union in one person or in one act of subject and object, nothingness and being, freedom and determinism, *pour soi* and *en soi*. Of course it is precisely this union which the Genet saint seeks. He wishes to be free by means of submission, to *will* what is already *determined* by Fate or God or society: his degradation. In like manner, Sartre argues in *Saint Genet*, Genet *wills* to be the thief and outcast he already *is* in the eyes of society. But for Sartre the subject–object synthesis is an unrealizable dream. If these poles could be joined one would achieve a unity of activity and passivity, of freedom and determinism, one would *be* one's *nothingness*, in short, as Sartre puts it, one would be God. Sartre believes that this is impossible. To *be* and to *be conscious* are two separate things. In Genet, these two poles are identifiable as the murderer and the saint, the one an unthinking creature moved by Fate – a *something*, dense and passive like Yeux-Verts – the other a self-conscious, deliberate, active force, like Lefranc or Divine. But Genet would like to *combine* the characteristics of these opposed types in the single figure of the masochist saint. He is caught in what is termed in *Saint Genet* a *tourniquet* or whirligig. Sartre argues that the mechanism of willing one's Fate cannot really work, that one cannot hoodwink the Other by means of masochism, that one cannot will oneself an object: it would be like freely willing one's non-freedom. In spite of everything, the saint who tries to destroy the Other cannot possibly make any real progress.

What is impossible in a Sartrean context may, of course, be possible in Genet's work. Certainly Genet is aware of the problem, if not exactly in the straightforward terms proposed by the philosopher. After the four novels, the journal and *Deathwatch*, therefore, the question is raised anew: Is masochism a genuine way to solitude or does it fail as does the fake sadism of the killer? Genet is uncertain and summarizes his ambiguous conclusions in his second play, *The Maids*.

The Maids has already been discussed in terms of the Sartrean Look and it is clear now that the maids, Claire and Solange, belong to the second Genet category, that of the saint. They are alienated from themselves, masochists who love Madame and despise themselves. But there is more to their behaviour than this and we are now in a position to view their masochism not simply as an inert *given*, something the maids are forced to practise, but also as a deliberate choice, a *willed* degradation. Like other Genet saints, the maids submit to the Other, in this case Madame, and accept their inferior status. When Madame is out they dress in her clothes and act out the maid–mistress relationship, heaping upon themselves the abuse and scorn that represents Madame's, and society's, attitude to them. In short, they want to be, they work towards being, the dregs they are said to be, they further and aid the effect of Madame's Look upon themselves. Of course the game is supposed to end in the humiliation of the mistress – but it never does. The two are so obsessed with the preliminaries, which concern *their* humiliation, that they never reach the goal of their ritual. Yet it remains a fact that the game represents a way *out* of the situation, an act of self-assertion, an assault upon Madame, since the maids' search for abjection reveals a desire for transcendence and a resentment of their lot as servants. Eventually, Claire and Solange move to destroy the mistress openly. They scheme to get at her through her lover, the plot fails and necessitates an attempted poisoning of Madame. Not surprisingly, this does not come off either. The maids cannot escape the Look by direct, active means, they must do it by a form of activity-in-passivity, by the way of the masochist. So they return to their game. Solange, the dominant partner, will kill Claire dressed as Madame. In this way "Madame" will die, Solange, now a murderer, will achieve the glory of other Genet killers and Claire, as victim, the glory of the saint, a death of love: after all, she will die *as* Madame, identified *with* Madame. It is as if Genet were playing all his cards at once, testing once and for all both of his character types, the murderer and the saint. In Claire's words, "we shall be that eternal couple . . . of the criminal and the saint" (p.22). Solange looks forward to her apotheosis, anticipating, like all the killers, her judgement and execution. She mocks society – in the person of Madame, naturally – in advance: "now . . . I'm your equal. I wear the red garb of criminals . . . Madame now sees my loneliness . . ." (p.38) But Solange, a curious mixture of the passive saint and the aggressive thug, is, as we might expect, hollow, and Genet is relying on the true saint, Claire, after all. When the game turns into reality Solange loses courage. In the end she kills Claire but only because Claire insists so that Claire in effect commits suicide and reveals herself as the stronger of the two. The important thing, however, is not the comparison of the two Genet types but Claire's death, that is to say, her spiritual confrontation with Madame. "Madame is dead", Solange argues, "we are beautiful, joyous, drunk and free!" (pp.42–3) Does this in fact happen?

Claire dies, dressed as Madame. But it is by no means clear whether the maids' strategy has succeeded or not. Who has died, Claire or Madame? Madame has died symbolically, it is true. We may go further and say that Claire's love for Madame has died, that Claire has killed Madame's power over her, that is, *Madame-within-herself*, by asserting her own inalienable dignity – much as Genet kills Decarnin in *Funeral Rites* or Harcamone in *Miracle of the Rose*. But to kill *Madame-in-Claire* is not the same as killing Madame. Moreover, there is a real corpse, and it is Claire's. The question is unresolved. Claire's way is the masochist ascesis of all of Genet's saints and it involves an interior victory over the Other, a triumph of the spirit when, on the face of it, all is lost. We cannot deny that a victory of sorts is won. After all, the power of the Look is installed within the victim to alienate him from himself, to make him love the Other and despise himself. Claire appears to have disposed of this interior Madame, this Other at the heart of herself. But it is at the price of her own final destruction – as if, we may speculate, she and Madame were one, as if the masochist were unable to eradicate the Other from his own soul except by suicide. Thus the solution is more extreme than the problem. This ambiguity cannot be ignored and we must return to the facts: it is Claire who has died, *not* Madame, the victory of the saint is more than dubious. All that Claire has done is to *will* upon herself the worst that the Other could do to her. We are thrown back on the original equivocation: if I *will* my being an object, do I regain the initiative? Is the masochist solution a way to metaphysical solitude? Although Genet leaves the issue open, it seems that the saint's way is questionable. Doubt has been cast on the achievement of the murderer, from Our Lady to Solange. The killer fools himself. Convinced that his is the aggressive solution of the sadist, he is, in fact, a fake, a masochist in disguise. The saint fools other people. He pretends to be a masochist but he too is a fake since his masochism disguises an aggressive stand, a form of sadism. And yet in the final analysis he fools himself also. For all his efforts, he remains an object, a masochist whose only success is suicide. Divine, the Genet of the *Journal*, of *Miracle of the Rose* and *Funeral Rites* and, finally, Claire, all end on an equivocal note. It seems that fake sadism and fake masochism lead to the same impasse. Solitude remains an obscure goal yet to be reached. In Sartrean terms, it appears unattainable. Not surprisingly, at this point in his writing career, Genet begins to panic.

11 Genet and Sartre: the image and the revolutionary

I The image: real masochism, fake indifference

> The fight is no longer taking place in reality, but in the lists. . . It's the combat of allegories.[1]
>
> GENET

After the publication of the novels and plays so far discussed, as well as the journal and various minor works, Genet is silent for several years. The Gallimard edition of the Complete Works began in 1951, *Saint Genet* (oddly enough published as volume one of the Complete Works) came in 1952 and Genet's next play, *The Balcony*, only in 1956. The gap between *The Maids* (1947) and the journal (1948) on the one hand and *The Balcony* on the other represents a turning-point in the author's life. The crisis was obviously of some magnitude and to a large extent it must have been prompted by *Saint Genet*, whose revelations doubtless proved too much for a Genet unused to being the object of such sustained and merciless analysis – so much of it relating to Genet's private life as homosexual and criminal and all of it embarrassingly accurate. At the same time it is likely that the real crisis came from Genet himself. In 1948 he was liable to life imprisonment for his numerous petty crimes. Some of the most influential literary figures in France petitioned successfully for his release and he received a presidential pardon. It meant though that his life of vagabondage and theft was over, that a Genet who had been painfully constructed over many years had to die and a new Genet be born. Sartre wittily describes the funeral, with its empty grave and the culprit hiding behind a cypress, watching the mourners who include the representatives of Gallimard and Sartre himself delivering the oration. Genet has wept a little, now he will go off whistling, he will *live*. For the philosopher, he has at this point saved himself from the legacy of his early years and he has done so by becoming a writer: "ten years of literature ... equivalent to a psychoanalytic cure".[2] Beginning with the original situation of the Look, he has finally escaped being an object, as writer he now *acts*, he initiates, he has regained his subjectivity or freedom. Certainly, no one who has made a thorough study of Genet's work could doubt that Sartre's chart is at least very close to the truth. But *Saint Genet* follows Genet's progress only up to 1951 and, in Genet's later work, from 1956 onwards, it is clear that old preoccupations are still being aired, that the search for "solitude" is far from over.

Genet is obviously dissatisfied with the impasse of *The Maids*. Now he panics to the extent of questioning the possibility of a way out of his predicament. In *The Balcony* he reasons in the following way. Granted that the basic issue is one of retaining the initiative over the Other, is it not true that, even as I struggle with my opponent, I am in fact reliant on his being there? Solitude, if it is attainable, means complete autonomy. But there can be no autonomy in the relation of the Look since, even if I escape being object and objectify the Other instead, I cannot be a dominant subject without the existence of a corresponding object. The very struggle against the Other suggests that he is *necessary*, that I need him even as he needs me. This in turn suggests something more disquieting, that each side exists *only* in the other, that I *am* only in so far as I relate to the Other and that he *is* only as related to me, in short, that to *be* is *to act out a part*. Now the struggle of subject and object takes on the appearance of a ghostly duel, a battle of roles, each entirely dependent for its existence on a complementary opposite, a mirror. Thus I play the role of object made possible by the Other who plays the role of subject made possible by me – and so on, ad infinitum. The struggle for solitude has degenerated to a play of shadows, a Pirandellian *giuoco delle parti*. No *real* victory or defeat is possible because the rules of the game require two players. Solitude is by definition unattainable, either as an escape or as an affirmation of one's uniqueness, because one cannot eliminate either of the players or because, if one were to do so, one would be left with nothing at all. Genet has tried to free himself of the Other by recourse to the fake sadism of the murderer, then to the fake masochism of the saint. The former way has been discredited, the latter is also in doubt. As he attempts a third time Genet wonders if the project is not impossible. Thus the relationship of self and Other is now envisaged as a relation between two *images*, two mirrors, each existing only as a reflection of the other, and the struggle as fought not between society and the criminal individual but between illusion (or appearance) and reality. Actually, this formulation of the problem is already explicitly present in Genet's earlier work. In spite of this it remains true to say that the theme of the mirror really comes to the fore in *The Balcony* and it is in relation to this play that I wish to consider it.

The first few scenes of *The Balcony* illustrate Genet's new predicament. The point has already been made that Genet is here depicting an interdependence of opposites: subject and object, that is to say, bishop and sinner, judge and thief *need* each other. But there is more to it than this, for mutual need suggests to Genet a mirror game in which each term of the relation is no more than a reflection, exists *only* by virtue of the mirror. The bishop of the first scene of the play who comments "ornaments, laces, through you I re-enter myself" (p.13) knows that the mystery of his office owes nothing to what he does, least of all to personal attributes. It is a power he assumes. A bishop *is* his appearance, his mitre, his lace and so on, something one puts on as one puts on clothes. The same is true for judge and general and this explains why the judge sees himself as a dead man, along with those he condemns: "I, King of Hell, weigh those who are dead, like me" (p.17). He is dead in a Pirandellian sense because he has assumed a mask, because his life is frozen in an image, that of judge. Likewise the judged has become fixed in the role of thief. In the next scene, the general too dies to become no more than an appearance: "nothing, no contingent trails behind me. I appear, purely and simply" (p.26). This appearance could not exist without its complement, in this case the general's men who go to their deaths for him. And this is true for bishop and judge also. If the judge were that by virtue of something innate, he could be a judge by himself. But a judge, like a character in Sartre, is nothing at all in himself. He *is* only as a role and the role depends on someone else assuming an opposite role. It is not surprising that he has to beg the thief to steal. Without her he would not exist: "you'd deprive me of being!" (p.19) Moreover if the judge is a judge only because he gazes at the thief and sees that he is *not* that, the formula may be reversed. We could say that the thief is a thief only because she is not the judge. In that case the judge would be a judge *only* because he is not the thief who is herself *only* because she is not the judge. The difficulty is obvious. There are no people left, only mirrors. Of course, bishop, judge and general are in any case fakes. They are visitors at Madame Irma's establishment who wear elaborate costumes for the purpose of sexual titillation, in short, actors. Even as they play their parts machine-gun fire outside proclaims the reality they are trying to exclude. Later, a further complication is introduced. As the revolution proceeds and the chief religious, judicial and military figures are killed, it becomes necessary for the fake dignitaries of the brothel to assume the roles of *real* bishop, judge and general. In these new roles they are able to quell the revolt. Why not? If role is everything, then a fake bishop acting the part of a real bishop *is* a real bishop, since a real bishop is simply one who acts the part of bishop. Genet has made his point twice. First he presents us with a fake dignitary playing the part of a true one. Already the implication is that real dignitaries too are actors. To underline the conclusion, Genet goes further and actually demonstrates the interchangeability of true and false. As the envoy puts it: if the queen is dead – long live the queen. Since the queen is no more than a mask, Madame Irma can be queen as well as anyone else. A similar reasoning is assumed by the photographers in scene nine. When they take a picture of the (once fake, now real) dignitaries, it is the image they seek, the *ideal* dignitary, in short, the role. They want a picture of the new bishop taking communion. In the absence of a genuine wafer, they use the general's monocle. Does it matter, in a world where all is illusion?

Similar conclusions emerge from another major relationship of the play, that of the Chief of Police and Madame Irma. It is, in one sense, the old subject–object relation. The police, representatives of society, need the brothel as much as it needs them. But neither brothel nor police exist in themselves, each is an image, an appearance bolstering the other, and both Irma and the Chief accept this, taking their stand upon illusion. This is why the Chief longs for immortality in death and builds a giant mausoleum for himself – which is matched by Irma's temple, the brothel, a "house of illusions" (p.34), filled with mirrors, a "balcony," that is, a facade, a place of show, indeed a fake, nothing beside appearance – like the real world, its complement. Thus Irma can say: "I'm no longer playing", meaning that she is in earnest, and then add: "or, if you like, not the same role" (p.44). All behaviour is play-acting. Even the establishment's pimp, killed by a stray bullet on the day he is preparing to act the part of a corpse, has merely exchanged one appearance for another. With respect to the Chief, however, there is a special point to be noted. In contrast to those of bishop, judge and general, his role has little tradition behind it, it is historically recent. The Chief's power is very real, of course – it is he who leads the conservative forces against the rebels – whereas bishop, judge and general are merely figureheads. And yet it is thanks to the figurehead, to the dignitaries and to Irma in the role of queen, not to the Chief, that the revolution is crushed. Illusory power, power based on myth, is more effective than actual power. And the Chief knows it. He is aware that real power is worthless unless it is operative in the realm of appearances, that is, of fantasy, that what one must have is not actual power but a powerful *image*, a power-filled *role.* So whereas the bishop, judge and general find their fantasies become reality the chief, a *real* Chief of Police, wants to progress from reality to fantasy. His dream is to witness an impersonation of himself in the brothel: if men wish to impersonate him it means that the authority of the police image now extends to the mind. But, to begin with, he is disappointed: those who visit the brothel want to impersonate only traditional figures of power.

There is a third relationship to be considered in this play. In addition to that of bishop and sinner, judge and thief and so on and that of police and brothel *The Balcony* presents us with the conflict between revolutionaries and the establishment. Now the revolutionaries are not simply planning to destroy the old regime, the court, the church and so forth. Their primary aim is to do away with the game of roles, to substitute reality for illusion, and for this reason they are enemies of the brothel as well as of the police. Moreover, whereas the usual Genet rebel, from Divine to the maids, *accepts* the law he breaks, the revolutionary in seeking to go beyond all mere forms, all appearance, necessarily rejects the rules, customs and morality of the establishment. This means that the revolutionary, although an enemy of society in the tradition of the murderer and the saint, represents a new type in Genet's work. His way represents a *sadist* solution, not the fake sadism – submission in the guise of aggressiveness – of the killer, but a genuine attitude of Sartrean hate, a real attempt to overcome the Look of authority not by any form of submission but by a direct assault. The revolutionary tries to do what the killer fails to do, to transcend the Look, objectify the Other, and regain the initiative of the subject. In other words he tries to achieve Sartrean freedom by a direct confrontation. From the standpoint of the mechanism of willing one's Fate the change in tactics is simple: instead of adopting the masochist solution, the revolutionary seeks to *alter* his Destiny, not to submit to it, to alter what the Other has decreed, in short, to *will freedom*. This represents yet another Genet attempt to realize the ideal of solitude in a particular character type and I shall return to it in due course.

At this stage it must be said that the revolution in *The Balcony* is a failure. From the start the Chief of Police sees it as still another illusion and his scepticism is justified by the comments of Roger, one of the rebels, on Chantal, who has left the brothel to join the uprising:

> So she's no longer a woman . . . In order to fight against an image Chantal has frozen into an image. The fight is no longer taking place in reality, but in the lists . . . It's the combat of allegories. (p.57)

In order to defeat a symbol Chantal has herself become a symbol, Joan of Arc of the revolution. The struggle, then, is no longer between appearance and reality: one mystique has simply been replaced by another. It is a struggle of myths, old and new, a battle between two illusions, a contest of mirrors in which the revolutionaries are themselves acting out a part, like their enemies. In fact the uprising is a failure because Irma and her clients are able to impersonate the dead queen and her dignitaries. But this is beside the point. The revolution fails because it is betrayed from within. When the final confrontation takes place, the conflict is between Irma, the image of a queen, and the people's image, Chantal. In this contest of symbols, the old proves stronger, but even if the case had been reversed the revolution would have been defeated because its ideal of reality has been compromised. Once Chantal is frozen into an image she is already dead and the victory goes to the forces of illusion, the Chief of Police and the brothel, established society in its twin facets.

Genet now toys with the idea of a new solution to the problem of the Look. Since appearance has the victory, since all is illusion, perhaps one may go to solitude by way of appearance and illusion. If every action represents the acting out of a part it may be that there is an ultimate role to be assumed, that solitude itself is a role. Conceivably, one might retreat into *pure appearance*, one might become a symbol or an image, and, discarding all else, exist in a pure heaven of eternal Ideas. What if by this means one might reach a state of independence from the Other? An image is not a vulnerable human being, it is dead, a mere shell containing nothing. Perhaps it exists in an impregnable Platonic paradise, utterly alone, utterly perfect. Clearly the great symbol of the victorious establishment and of victorious illusion in *The Balcony* is the Chief of Police. Thus the Chief comes to represent a third Genet character type, following the murderer and the saint, and his way a third alternative for the attainment of solitude. Strictly speaking not a social outcast like his predecessors, he nevertheless seeks like them to detach himself from society and to discover himself in glory, a glory which, in this case, must be seen as residing only in death, since to be pure image, pure appearance, is to be immobilized and preserved against the pressures of time. We are returned to the Chief's splendid tomb, a maze of mirrors, each mirror reflecting another and all ultimately reflecting the Chief who is himself merely a reflection, living for ever in legend, that is, in death:

THE ENVOY: He who gets it will be there – dead – for eternity. The world will centre about it . . . mirrors will reflect to infinity . . .
THE CHIEF OF POLICE: O.K.!
THE ENVOY: . . . the image of a dead man. (p.69)

As we might expect this triumph is to be represented by a (giant) phallus and confirmed by the fact that millions will come to the mausoleum to impersonate the Chief, to reflect his glory by assuming his role, while he himself remains unique, the basis of all lesser illusions: "not the hundred-thousandth-reflection-within-a-reflection in a mirror, but the One and Only, into whom a hundred thousand want to merge" (p.80). Like the general earlier in the play, then, the Chief seeks his own ascesis, a dying to self to that he might live "not even for myself, but for my image, and my image for its image, and so on" (p.27).

And yet, in *The Balcony*, Genet is throwing us into confusion. Despairing of ever realizing his ideal of solitude he opts once more for a very dubious solution. The resemblance between the Chief as image and the murderer type should put us on our guard, since in each case we are concerned with a power that is essentially "hollow". Moreover the triumph of the Chief is the triumph of illusion, which as already argued, would seem to be incompatible with the realization of solitude. It is the triumph of the game of mirrors, the I-depend-on-you-and-you-depend-on-me relationship, a veritable *negation* of the possibility of solitude – and this could hardly be otherwise. Role implies the status of the object. A role, an image, an appearance, all these presuppose the Other. One *appears* in order to be *seen* – by someone else. The man who plays a role is making himself objective, a *something* others can point to and identify as, for example, a Chief of Police or a bawd. Thus one's role is a way of being-for-other-people, an exterior, something directed outwards: role-playing is a social pastime, not something one can do *for oneself.* And Genet sees this. What would be the point of impersonating a judge if there were no one to masquerade as sinner? For all his supposed glory, the Chief is simply objectifying himself and, since an object can only exist in relation to a subject, that is, since an image can only live on in other men's minds, making himself utterly dependent on the Other. If no one impersonates him, if there is no one to reflect his glory, the Chief ceases to be. As pure image he is entirely at the mercy of the Other, an absolute slave, there to be made use of for all eternity. Clearly there is a link here between the image and the murderer. In each case the attempted escape from the Other has led only to self-deception. The image in fact represents a new form of the masochist solution. Just as the killer dies to self to be reborn as an object, a passive instrument of society, so the image exists as a mere reflection of the Other's objectifying Look. The killer is a fake sadist, in reality a masochist. The Chief as image represents *pure* masochism: he is all object, a being who is nothing for himself, everything for the Other. It follows that his claim to solitude is even more questionable than the murderer's.

Thus the Chief–Irma relation must be referred back to the Darling–Divine, Harcamone–Genet and Solange–Claire couples. In each of these earlier cases the real search for solitude is associated not with the hollow dominant figure – who is inevitably revealed as a passive object in disguise – but with the saint, whose passivity conceals aggressive initiative. In *The Balcony* it should be Irma. In fact it is that other complement to the Chief, the revolutionary Roger. Now so far it seems that Genet has driven himself into a corner. In every respect the revolution and its ideal of reality have been defeated. What is left is the classical Pirandellian situation of the mask in which all men, whether on stage or not, are merely actors, men taking part in a crazy masquerade. One thinks of *Six Characters in Search of an Author*, where all the characters have made roles for themselves, what the author calls *costruirsi*. There are the actors, real actors playing the part of actors. There are the six characters, actors playing the part of characters who *are* themselves, that is, who are masks, literary creations. There is also the audience, of course, whose individuals play a role in everyday life. The question arises: who is *not* playing a role or attempting to fix life into a mask? The same question arises in *Henry IV* (*Enrico IV*). Enrico fears life and adopts a mask, that of a dead emperor, and in so doing hopes to withdraw into the fixity of history. His visitors are called upon to join the masquerade. But they are all of them play-actors in their own lives. Who then is *not* an actor? Only the madman, perhaps – although even madness may be turned into a mask – or the man who acts on impulse, as Enrico does when he kills Belcredi. Then again the effect of the killing is precisely to fix Enrico more than ever in a role: now he is required to pursue the pretence of being a lunatic for the rest of his life. To a degree, a similarity with Pirandello is also a similarity with Sartre (one could scarcely imagine *Kean* without *Six Characters* or *Henry IV*). Just as in Pirandello one is *nobody* in oneself and *somebody* as a mask, so in Sartre one is a nothingness, *pour soi*, until one *pretends* to be something, *en soi*. Since being and nothingness are incompatible one *fools oneself* that one is something. Thus all roles – even necessary ones – are acted in bad faith. The waiter who is conscious of it is not in fact a waiter, he is fooling himself. A dog does not play a part: it is self-identical, without consciousness *of* itself. To be conscious *of* onself is to admit that one is *not* self-identical. Consequently all human behaviour in so far as it depends on concepts is a game in bad faith, *mauvaise foi*. But it should be noted that it is possible to evade the role in Sartre's philosophy – by *doing*, when freedom, one's being-nothing, is exercised, as in Pirandello it is possible to perform a spontaneous act expressive of life and not of the mask. In *The Balcony* no way out of this sort is envisaged. Genet throws up his hands in exasperation and returns to the solution of the saint, in this case to the character Roger. Unfortunately Roger is no improvement on Claire of *The Maids*. At the end of the play, having lost all hope after the defeat of the revolution, he capitulates to the forces of illusion and arrives at the brothel to impersonate the Chief of Police, that is, to imaginatively *become* the Chief: "I've a right . . . of merging his destiny with mine . . ." (p.93). Then, at the crucial moment of the impersonation, he castrates himself. Like earlier Genet saints he *wills* his Fate, confirming by a free act what has already come about, namely, defeat. But the action raises the same problems as does the suicide of Claire: who is castrated, the Chief or Roger? One the one hand it looks like a final submission, a masochistic acknowledgement of failure, as if the revolution admitted the impossiblity of breaking out into reality and bowed to the sexual power of the Chief. On the other it may be interpreted as an act of self-assertion, that is, it may be said that Roger has emasculated himself *as* Chief, in short, emasculated the Chief in *himself* and so rid himself of the power of illusion – and the illusion of power. Of course the significance of the act is meant to remain ambiguous. Like the ending of *The Maids* which it so closely resembles, Roger's castration is a victory-in-defeat, something of a victory and something of a defeat. But the present argument has already questioned the validity of the masochist solution for Genet and it is clear that the author is even more dissatisfied with it in *The Balcony* than in the earlier play. Claire, after all, dies with dignity. Roger's act is surreptitious and sudden and there is little suggestion of glory about it. *The Balcony* ends on a note of despair. Reality has been overcome by the image, the revolt has been crushed and the rebel has turned to a solution already partly discredited in *The Maids*. At the end of the play a new revolution is under way and it seems no more likely to succeed than the other. Irma, the voice of relativism, has the last say.

In spite of overwhelming frustration and failure, however, something of a positive nature does occur in *The Balcony*. Genet's timid attempt to create a fourth character type – the revolutionary, a real sadist in the Sartrean sense of one who overcomes the Look – fails because the author undermines it by means of the theme of illusion and the image. This ensures a reversion to the doubtful masochist solution at the end of the play. And yet in one way Genet's preoccupation with the maze of mirrors *upholds* the sadist solution and the reason is as follows. If the subject–object relation established by the Look is such that each side plays a role, is nothing in itself but exists *only* in its complementary opposite, then of necessity there is a certain *parity* between subject and object. Where the maids and Madame have a one-sided relationship in which the subject, Madame, is *essential*, and the object, Solange – Claire, is simply a parasite or secondary phenomenon utterly contingent upon the first, relations in *The Balcony* presuppose an *equality* of terms. A judge needs a thief *as much as* a thief needs a judge. If this is so, then the masochist approach has lost its force. While neither partner in the equal relationship is *free of the relation itself*, the one who plays the role of object to the other's subjectivity is free of the disadvantages of being an object. He is no longer alienated from himself. How could he be? He *is* no longer an object, he *plays the part* of an object, just as the other plays the part of the subject. Whether one is subject or object begins to be a matter of indifference. The maids hate themselves and love Madame because Madame is absolute and they are relative to Madame. But the underdog in *The Balcony* is as necessary as his master and consequently he has his own kind of dignity in the relationship. Genet is beginning to transcend the masochist stance precisely because his insistence on the theme of illusion leads in the direction of relativism.

This is the positive achievement of *The Balcony*: that for the first time Genet is suggesting that the subject, master of the Look, is simply the object *in reverse*. The Genet of the novels and early plays accepts society: the murderer acknowledges the law he breaks and the saint is ambivalent about it. Now it becomes possible for Genet to visualize a character who does *not* acknowledge the power of the Other, in short, a true sadist, the revolutionary. That the sadist revolt is betrayed and crushed in *The Balcony* simply reflects the author's indecision, the fact that *The*

Balcony is a transition play. From now on Genet's work concentrates on the figure of the rebel, as willing-one's-Fate is replaced by the mechanism of willing-freedom, of forcibly *altering* one's situation.

But even as Genet works his way out of the masochist impasse he necessarily raises up a new obstacle to the search for solitude. If all existence is role-playing and all role-playing requires a partnership, then solitude is abolished. Out of the masochist's chamber of horrors, Genet finds himself in the maze of mirrors.

II The revolutionary : real sadism

> But what exactly is a black? First of all, what's his colour?[3]
>
> GENET

This is exactly the position in *The Blacks, a Clown Show* (*Les Nègres, Clownerie*, 1958), a play dominated by the – ultimately successful – revolt of black against white. Of course white denotes Sartrean subjectivity, the initiative of the Look. Thus:

> For two thousand years God has been white. He eats from a white table cloth. He wipes his white mouth with a white napkin. He picks at white meat with a white fork. (p.20)

God, who is white, watches the snow fall, "*il regarde tomber la neige*".[4] His representatives on earth are the white court, queen, governor, judge, missionary, and so on. On the other side is the victim of the Look, the Sartrean Us-object, Africa: "Africa of the millions of royal slaves . . . block of darkness, compact and evil, that holds its breath, but not its odour" (p.60). The blacks are engaged in yet another Genet ritual. They have killed a white woman, who stands for the enemy; she is lying in a catafalque and her murder is to be reenacted.

Genet calls upon his entire repertoire of ambiguities. There is, first of all, no escaping the fact that the ritual recalls the masochism of the murderer. Even if we overlook this, there remains a disturbing echo of the masochism of the saint. The blacks announce that their aim in committing and reenacting the crime is to *merit* the judgement the whites have *already* pronounced on them: "we must deserve their reprobation . . ." (p.26). In other words the blacks are acting in such a way as to become what the whites have already made them. This is the old mechanism of willing one's Fate and, indeed, the victims know it: "we are what they want us to be. We shall therefore be it to the very end . . ." (p.95). They are black. Very well, they will be more so, they will make themselves worthy of blackness. In keeping with this attitude, the blacks find it difficult to hate the enemy. In fact they feel a fascination which is dangerously close to love. Village, who has murdered the white woman, is accused of having done it because he loved her (p.23). "Invent not love but hatred" (p.22), is the cry of encouragement. Only true sadism can save the underdog and it seems necessary, at least for a time, to hate all things, to reject, in any sphere, the least show of love. Village is required to reject Africa itself: "darkness, stately mother of my race . . . you are Africa, oh monumental night, and I hate you" (p.30). Of course the ambiguity is still there: the maids also hated themselves – and so loved Madame. In spite of this, though, it can be stated that the overall tone of *The Blacks* is very different from that of earlier plays. It is as if the masochist forms were being perpetuated, but emptied of their previous contents. In fact the blacks' feeling for their masters is not as confusedly ambivalent as that of the maids for Madame or that of Roger for the Chief and we can reasonably argue that the love–hate relation of master and slave is giving way to a relationship of hate alone. But we have hardly begun to enumerate the complexities of *The Blacks*. When the murder is reenacted, a *black* (man, not woman) is chosen to represent the dead woman – who may in any case be black and not white. Diouf, the black victim of the ritual, has been converted to the white's religion of love and so qualifies as a representative of whiteness. The killing which is acted out, then, is not that of a white, only of a black who stands for the whites, that is, it represents the destruction of whiteness *in the negro*, just as Roger's castration represents the Chief's death in Roger and Claire's suicide the death of Madame in Claire. Nevertheless, a new element has been introduced into the Genet ceremony. In this case the purge is successful and without the need for an actual black sacrifice. Indeed, the tone of *The Blacks* is not at all defeatist. At the end it is the whites who are masochistically seeking suicide, fascinated by the darkness of Africa. As they proceed into its forests they fall into a trap. Expecting to condemn the blacks for the murder of a white woman they discover there is no corpse, the catafalque being a fake. This places them in the situation the judge in *The Balcony* is so anxious to avoid. If there is no crime, there can be no guilt. The white queen states her case: "in exchange for a crime, we were bringing the criminal pardon and absolution" (p.78). But the only crime is blackness, which is no crime at all: "that crime of mine, is all Africa!" (p.78). The whites surrender and die ceremonially one by one. It is true that they are actually blacks wearing white masks, a fact which has been apparent all along. But this merely confirms the sense that the play dramatizes a rejection of guilt rather than an actual struggle with the Other, that is, that it is concerned with the expulsion of the Other *from oneself.* The blacks are rejecting their status as object, in short, the masochist's desire to regain the initiative and to transform submission into aggression is in the process of being realized as the ritual of the saint gives way to that of the revolutionary.

There is a final complication. It appears that, while the ritual is going on, a *real* drama is being enacted elsewhere and one which is an exact counterpart of what is taking place on stage: a black traitor is being tried and executed. This once more underlines the message that black revolt consists essentially of the obliteration not of the enemy, but of the enemy-within-oneself. In this bewildering series of about-turns we are forced once more to the questions raised in parallel contexts by earlier plays: Who has paid, the victims or the oppressor? All that can be said here is that, in spite of Genet's game of boxes-within-boxes, *The Blacks* represents an advance beyond the old masochist solution, since whiteness is in the end defeated, since the blacks are able to free themselves of attachment to the enemy. Certainly, a black and not a white woman has been executed. To that extent we witness all over again the fate of Claire and Roger. But despite this, there is a new spirit in the rebel, a sense that alienation from oneself has been overcome, a baptism of hate. The blacks are Sartrean sadists, aggressive and confident. Not that *The Blacks* actually offers us a picture of the white man as object of the negro's Look. Still, the suggestion is that this is to happen and there seems little doubt that the blacks are on the way to becoming Sartrean subjects. In fact Genet's next play confirms this conclusion.

But we are still left with the problem of illusion, for if the *real* revolt of the blacks offstage exactly parallels the stage *ritual* of revolt, may it not be that both are fakes, that no clear distinction can be made between appearance and reality? "But what exactly is a black? First of all, what's his colour?" Genet pertinently asks. Blackness may in fact be any colour; it simply represents the oppressed. Then again, if blacks may wear white masks, whites may wear black ones. It is simply a question of role-playing. This returns us to the question raised in *The Balcony*. If both sides are acting out a part, then perhaps each side is relative to the other, that is, a mirror. Both whites and blacks in *The Blacks* believe this to be so. "Say to them that without us their revolt would be meaningless – wouldn't even exist" (p.93), the white queen argues. Likewise the black Felicity knows that whiteness cannot do without its complement. If the white queen were to obliterate blackness she would have nothing to define her:

> THE QUEEN: I'm going to have you exterminated.
> FELICITY: . . . You fool, just imagine how flat you'd be without that shade to set you off in high relief. (p.80)

Consequently, what the black revolutionary envisages is not the destruction of whiteness, which is not possible, but an *exchange of roles*. From now on black will be white and white, black:

> To you, black was the colour of priests and undertakers and orphans. But everything is changing. Whatever is gentle and kind and good and tender will be black. Milk will be black, sugar, rice, the sky, doves, hope, will be black. (p.81)

But in that case, what exactly is achieved by the sadist revolt? The oppressed have overcome the Look, subject and object have changed places. The two are still mutually dependent, only now with the black as master and the white as slave. Masochism did not lead to solitude, although it asserted the dignity of the individual in a roundabout way. Sadism asserts his dignity directly, but in so doing brings him no closer to solitude. Thus at the end of *The Blacks* Genet is uneasy. He is not satisfied with his triumphant blacks and feels the reality of their victory eluding him. It is *The Balcony* over again, with a ghostly failure now replaced by ghostly success. From a Sartrean viewpoint, of course, the attainment of subjectivity is the ultimate human achievement: *Saint Genet* depicts Genet himself as moving to this goal. For Sartre there is no way of avoiding the subject–object relationship, since it is part of the structure of human ontology. One may overcome the Look, certainly, but not escape human relationships altogether or transcend the opposition of subject and object, an opposition based on that of *pour soi* and *en soi*, nothingness and being. At this point it is evident, then, that for all its usefulness a Sartrean framework cannot adequately explain the pattern of Genet's imagination. The ascesis of the fourth Genet type, the revolutionary, leads to Sartrean freedom but no more suffices to encompass the dimension of solitude than that of murderer, saint and, it would seem, image. Genet's only alternative is to grope towards another type, as it happens, a development of a previous experiment. Significantly, we are drawn to the unknown black traitor of *The Blacks*, the one man who is said actually to die. In Genet's next play, *The Screens* (*Les Paravents*, 1961), this character is revived.

III The impossible nullity : real indifference

> To the old gal, to the soldiers, to all of you, I say shit.[5]
>
> GENET

Before considering this character we may note that *The Screens* clarifies other conclusions arrived at in earlier plays. It appears that the revolt of the blacks is a success and that, even as a success, it leads nowhere: *The Screens* confirms these two assumptions. Now the conflict is between French and Algerians, two sides which function as complements in the old master–slave relation, each allowing the other to stand out. "The fact is that the dirtier they are the cleaner I am" (p.159), says a colonial of the Arabs – and, of course, this works in both directions. The natives have run a comb over their masters, they take the dirt with them and leave respectability behind:

> As the sea recedes, in like manner they recede from us, carrying away with them and on them, – like treasures, all their wretchedness, their shame, their scabs . . . (p.159)

At the same time they are in a state of revolt, like the characters of *The Blacks*, animated by an intense and liberating hate. Eventually the revolt, which is completely free of even the masochist echoes of the previous play, is shown to be an unambiguous success. Of course it was a war of images, of revolutionary symbols against the old symbols of France, so that victory means a substitution of roles. Thus in the end the rebels are depicted as Sartrean subjects, conscious of their freedom and dignity which, however, makes them nothing more than a mirror reflection of the defeated colonials – as they themselves realize: "to be their reflection is already to be one of them" (p.119). The move, foreseen in *The Balcony* and *The Blacks*, is now out in the open. Having conquered their masters, the Algerians become masters in turn, requiring new creatures of abjection to provide a new complementary opposite. So the village, once united, divides in two. At the centre is the brothel, a place of sin; about it live the respectable: "round about is virtue. In the centre is hell" (p.153). Later, Warda the whore is killed, a victim of Arab righteousness; Sa'id, the outcast, is shot by the same forces of decency. In the end, then, little has been achieved by the success of the sadist revolt. In their special part of the stage, the dead – characters who have died in the course of the play – laugh at the spectacle. Among them Arabs and French mingle freely. It is clear that the entire conflict was utterly relative. Everything is a facade, a "screen", as suggested by the title of the play, and Genet's fourth character type finds solitude as unattainable as ever.

There is only one thing for Genet to do and that is to return to the abject hero once more with the insistence of a Beckett returning to his tramps. This time there are new combinations. Warda the whore, a development of Madame Irma, combines the abjection of the saint with the search for the ideal of the image characteristic of the Chief of Police. However, as saint she represents no progress beyond Divine of *Our Lady of the Flowers* and as image she fails because her being-a-whore is relative to the Other and so continues to serve an essentially social function. Indeed, her difficulty comments retrospectively on the situation of the Chief, himself at the mercy of his own mystique. Warda is an ideal whore, *putain totale*, "total whore down to the skeleton" (p.21), a mask representing the life of shame, with her bracelets and leaden weights in the hem of her skirts. She has worked very hard at what Pirandello calls *costruirsi*, the building up of an image of herself: "twenty-four years! A whore's not something you can improvise. She has to ripen" (p.18). Yet during the war she finds to her horror that she is unwittingly on the way to becoming respectable, a patriot, no less. Nothing could reveal more clearly – and humorously – the way in which the image escapes his own control. Before the war Warda is an image of shame, during the war she may become a patriot, she may perhaps cease to be an image at all and become a human being through no fault of her own. "I laboured . . . to be only a kind of gilded dummy" (p.115) she moans, and later: "I'm less and less someone" (p.123). As long as to be an Arab is to be a fighter for freedom, Warda is less and less a Pirandellian *qualcuno*, less and less a *someone*, an object, and more and more a free *pour soi*, nothingness. Fortunately the revolution ends and things return to normal. The point, however, has been made once again. Solitude cannot belong to the image. But there are other alternatives presented in the play. The Mother, for example, is both abject and aggressive, that is, a combination of saint and rebel. In the end, though, Genet pins his hopes on the true protagonists of *The Screens*, Sa'id and his wife Leila.

Sa'id is the very lowest of the low, driven to marry the poorest and the ugliest woman in the region. At times the family lives in the village dump. Sa'id steals and is ostracized by other Arabs, he moves in and out of the local prison. Of course it is deliberate: he wants his degradation since it is essential to the way he has chosen. So too with Leila who welcomes contempt, aiming to achieve the same glory as her husband "that of stinking more and more" (p.56). "I want you," Leila tells Sa'id, "to be without hope. I want you to choose evil and always evil. I want you to know only hatred . . ." (p.97). The reason is familiar: "we're here so that those who are sending us here realize that they're not here . . ." (p.97). Sa'id and Leila are what they are in order that society may define itself as respectable by means of the contrast. But although the rationale resembles that of the saint, we are dealing with something new in Genet's work. Sa'id's approach is not submissive in any sense, it does not involve an ethic of passivity, like that of Divine or Claire. His betrayal of his people to the French, for example, is not motivated by attachment to the colonials, as Genet's betrayal of Harcamone is motivated by masochistic love for him. Sa'id loves nobody, he is self-sufficient and herein differs from all earlier heroes of abjection. He steals, betrays, in the end mutilates his wife, for one reason only, to detach himself totally from other men. Thus he will have nothing to do with the French or with the Algerians. There is one last difficulty in this brutal and relentless ascesis, the temptation to desire becoming a legend, an image. Ommu, one of the women, sees his value as a sign to his people of that degradation from which they have risen. She wants him to be preserved in legend, afraid that the triumphant Arabs will forget their origins and, having expelled the French, turn to respectability. Thus "nothing must be protected so much as a little heap of rubbish" (p.168). Sa'id must be embalmed. Even as refuse he has the possibility of fulfilling a social function, for all eternity both dead and living, like the Chief of Police:

SA'ID: [furiously] That's leaving me dead alive! (p.170)

Another temptation is being offered at the same time. The victorious revolutionaries are prepared to forgive. Presumably Sa'id has the choice of being, like them, a free subject, an acceptable member of the newly established society. His final reply to Ommu and to the soldiers is categorical: "To the old gal, to the soldiers, to all of you, I say shit." He is shot as a traitor but does not enter the area on stage symbolically reserved for the dead. The dead themselves – his mother among them – wait in vain: neither Sa'id nor Leila will be seen again:

THE MOTHER: Then where is he? In a song? (p.176)

This question receives no answer, though in the original French version, the reply is *chez les morts*, among the dead. Either way, the play ends on an ambiguous note. Sa'id, being dead, is *chez les morts*, but it is evident that in fact he has not joined the other dead. It appears that he inhabits a region of death made only for him. From the point of view of all the other characters of *The Screens* he has simply vanished.

The significance of this strange conclusion to the play must not be lost. The first inescapable fact is that Sa'id's end is that of the image; in no other way can we explain his disappearance. Sa'id, is, as he complains, dead alive, "*mort pour vivant*", dead but not in the company of the dead, "*chez les morts*" in the way characteristic of types like the Chief of Police. His is a living death, the legendary end of a symbol or image of abjection – as Ommu foresees. But if this is so, Genet has merely returned to the untenable position of *The Balcony*. Yet *The Screens* ends on an optimistic note, as if Sa'id's being an image were no impediment to his attainment of solitude. In order to follow Genet's reasoning at this point we must first of all see that in Sa'id Genet has developed his concept of the image considerably beyond the examples offered in *The Balcony*. Sa'id, who grows out of that important character in *The Blacks* whom we never see, the black traitor who is judged and executed by his people, in fact represents what Genet has wished to depict from the beginning. He has remained an underdog to the end, yet without the masochism of the saint. If he does not hate, he does not love either and in this resembles the revolutionary. But unlike the revolutionary he has committed his crimes for no human motive, only in order to distance himself from other men, to be *alone*. He does not will his Fate, as does the saint, nor does he seek to alter it, as does the rebel. Simply, *he does not care*, he is indifferent – and this is the essential element of his achievement. It is also what clearly distinguishes him from Genet's earlier experiments with the image. We must see why this is so. So far all attempts to escape the subject–object relation have failed and they have all been based on an attitude of masochism or sadism, Sartrean love or Sartrean hate. Clearly as long as one takes a stand which depends on a social complement, one is playing the game of roles and neither the sadist attempt to destroy the Other nor the masochist attempt to surrender to him will succeed in realizing the ideal of solitude. But to be indifferent is to *refuse to play the game*: "To the old gal, to the soldiers, to all of you, I say shit." Through *indifference* Sa'id breaks out of the relationship of the Look, he moves out of the Other's reach and so becomes free, not in the Sartrean sense in which the Arab revolutionaries are free – they are free to act upon their complementary opposites and so not free of the relation itself – but free of both activity and passivity, neither acting nor being acted upon. Likewise he finds his way out of the maze of mirrors. For if he *does not care* he has in effect transcended (if not solved) the problem of appearance and reality by seeing the relativity of all things, *including the game of illusions.* To refuse a role in the ritual of love and hate is to cease to concern oneself with the distinction between the real and the imaginary, a distinction of necessity relevant only to those who continue, in one way or another, to seek to influence the Look. Of course indifference cannot obliterate the Other, nor can it do away with the relationship of roles. To that extent, Sa'id cannot escape. But it is not essential to remove the Other, indeed, if one is indifferent, it makes no difference at all. The Other may still be there, but Sa'id is alone; the maze of mirrors may be a fact, but it is of no interest to Sa'id. In this way Sa'id is sharply distinguished from the type of the image presented in *The Balcony* whose existence is dependent on the mirror. We recall that the aloofness of the Chief is a fake, disguising a complete reliance on the objectifying Look. The Chief emerges as the ultimate masochist, a creature existing only for the Other, avidly watching for the Other to approach him, to admire him and to perpetuate the legend through impersonation. But Sa'id's aloofness reflects real indifference and that is the meaning of his refusal to Ommu: the glory of the image does not tempt him. Of course he cannot avoid being turned into a symbol and to that extent being made relative to the Other. Still, it does not matter to him. Let others do what they will to Sa'id's image, Sa'id remains undisturbed. In that case, even as image, he can claim immunity to the Look, for it is not Sa'id who is being objectified, only a shell, the mask of Sa'id. Thus Sa'id manages to transform the image by ridding it of its major liability, its association with the masochist object. He performs the magician's disappearing act, once and for all illustrating "how one must lose oneself" (p.166), slipping behind the mask and vanishing while all eyes remain on the mask. As image he lives on, objectified for all time, as indifferent he turns his back on the Look, ignoring it and beyond its power. We are not surprised that, at the end of the play, he is not to be seen.

If Sa'id's mask is really empty, that is, empty not in the sense of being "hollow", as it was with the fake dignitaries and the Chief of *The Balcony*, but of denoting a genuine spiritual achievement, then it may well be that solitude and the image are by no means incompatible. It is simply a matter of *purifying* the image, of removing all trace of masochism which, in this context, must be seen as ultimately a preoccupation with self. It is true that the

Chief has his own ascesis, but we are now in a position to see that the only real dying to self and consequent living-in-the-image is one which goes by the way of indifference. Judge, bishop, Chief of Police, as depicted in *The Balcony*, merely represent a starting-point in the development of the type of the image. Even Warda the whore may best be regarded as a transition figure, one whose asceticism does not go as far as Sa'id's. In the end, then, Sa'id is the only character in Genet's plays to illustrate a way out of the dilemma of *The Balcony*. However repugnant when viewed outside the context of the author's desperate search for inward peace and integrity, he is the apotheosis not only of the image but of all the Genet types, an example of solitude achieved. As such he is to be related to those other types of solitude discussed at the beginning of these chapters – the statues and paintings of Giacometti and the tightrope walker. In each case solitude implies a dying, a fixing of life, a becoming a work of art, an *appearance* of life emptied of life itself. The tightrope walker diminishes himself in order to allow his image – that symbol inhabited by a corpse – to shine. *L'Atelier d'Alberto Giacometti* and *Le Funambule* came in 1958, *The Screens* in 1961. In those three years all that has changed is that the protagonist has ceased to show any signs of emotion. Otherwise Sa'id, like the tightrope walker, may be said to offer the public a complex performance which disguises the essential fact that there is no performer, only the wire, on the stage.

The entire Genet search as outlined in these chapters may now be summarized as follows. Everything begins with what Sartre calls *le regard*, the Look. The Genet character is a victim, objectified by the Other's gaze, searching frantically for a way out of his situation and at the same time for "solitude", a state understood not simply as a retreat, but a form of glory, an ultimate assertion of one's uniqueness which goes beyond mere self-assertion and involves a dying to self, an ascesis. The first attempt to achieve this goal is represented by the murderer. But his supposed challenge to a cruel society turns out to be submission in disguise, his sadism is not genuine. Genet's interest shifts to the saint, a character who *wills* submission and in so doing affirms his own threatened integrity. Again, however, the result is dubious, fake masochism offering no more of a way out than fake sadism. Now Genet despairs as the entire struggle begins to look like a game of roles. Characteristically, he wonders if he cann find a solution where it is least to be expected. But, to begin witl the type of the image fails to satisfy. Nor is the revolutionary success. If the real masochism of the image delivers one up to th power of the Other, the real sadism of the rebel merely ensures a exchange of roles. Genet's search therefore continues. Solitud it seems, is a kind of absence, a withdrawal from the subject object relationship. The emotional stance corresponding to absence is indifference. In the figure of Sa'id such ascetic detachment from all human ties is fully realized. The little hoodlu Genet is finally free, he has reached *himself.* Of course at thi point the comparison with Sartre breaks down completely. I *Being and Nothingness* indifference is regarded as a variant of hat Moreover it is in bad faith. I can *pretend* that I bear no relation t an Other, that the Other does not exist. But in fact no escape fro the subject–object relation is possible. Genet will not accept this although at the same time he cannot postulate an alternativ relationship, a *mitsein* or being-with, a human bond of genuin love untainted by masochism: it is something he has in all honest never encountered, though he *has* imagined the colloquy of tw demi-gods, each safe within his own uniqueness, solitude speaking to solitude on equal terms ("being what I am, and withou reservation, my solitude understands yours", *L'Atelier*, p.57). A any rate, the divergence from the philosophy of *pour soi* and *en so* does not come as a surprise. Sartre's universe is a secular one and if we are to believe *Saint Genet*, so is Genet's by about 1950. O this count, though, Sartre has been hasty: Genet's goal never wa the state of being-a-subject which Sartre identifies with freedom and his characters evade properly Sartrean categories to the ver end. From *Our Lady of the Flowers* to *The Screens* Genet envisage the ideal in metaphysical and religious terms: solitude is a approximation to divinity, it has an aura of the numinous about it.

Throughout his writing career Genet returns obsessively to hi double, the figure of the outcast, hoping, through a total rejectio of relationships which compromise individual autonomy, to ente a magical realm where revolt itself turns into an absolute, an are deep within the human being where revolt ceases to be a struggl *against* and becomes something in its own right, an affirmation o particularity, essential difference, singularity. Not unexpectedly at this point he is driven, like Beckett, to a language of negatives

In the early novels the criminal hero is rarely actually seen and this is also true of Madame in *The Maids*. Later, the tightrope walker strives to be "*bloc d'absence*" (p.183), a sign or symbol of a spiritual void. In *The Screens* this process reaches it climax with the disappearance of Sa'id, who vanishes behind the mask and dissolves into his own transparency. It is as if he had swallowed himself, as Genet tells us he would like to do:

> I wanted to swallow myself by opening my mouth very wide and turning it over my head so that it would take in my whole body, and then the Universe, until all that would remain of me would be a ball of eaten thing which little by little would be annihilated . . . (*Our Lady*, p.76)

There is a sense, then, in which solitude, like Beckett's Unnamable, is an impossibility, a blend of being and nothingness, as if Genet were to sever one after another all the bonds which link him to the Other: eventually he would reach a threshold, on one side, minimal relations, on the other, absolute particularity, a uniqueness of being indistinguishable from *nothing*. Solitude, as Genet conceives it, must be seen as residing in that no-man's-land which is the domain of irreducibles. It is here that spiritual presence expresses itself as a form of absence, an absence which is not mere nothing but a nothing which *is*: "the impossible Nothingness" (*Journal*, p.77). A goal of this kind is not only inconceivable for Sartre, it may be said to be un-existential to boot, since, as has been argued, the essence of the existential position is in the affirmation that man cannot *be* in a vacuum, without place, time and *other people*. Yet Genet, like Beckett and Ionesco, craves absolutes, in this case, absolute singularity. If existence is defined as a relation, then Genet, tracking down his own ultimate misfit or *alogon* – "that precious point where the human being would be led back to what is irreducible in him" (*L'Atelier*, pp.23–4) – seeks to break out of the existential net. Where Beckett coils *inwards* in order to disappear, where Ionesco makes his escape by *flying* out of the restrictive space, Genet makes a less exalted exit: with the likes of Sa'id, he will be *excreted* out of existence.

IV The approach to art

12 Beckett: the task of saying nothing

I

If I could speak and yet say nothing, really nothing?
(*The Unnamable*, p.305)

But that which remains, is established by the poets.[1]
HÖLDERLIN (quoted by Heidegger)

What are the implications for artistic theory and practice of the conclusions arrived at by a comparison of the work of Beckett, Ionesco and Genet with that of Sartre and Heidegger? The following chapters will examine some central aspects of this rather large topic, beginning with Beckett.

Beckett's approach to art is to some extent implicit in what has so far been said about the Beckett subject, the Irreducible. Art concerned with a being-nothing must be an art of *saying nothing*. This is why the painting of van Velde is inexpressive. Its says nothing at all, it is simply itself, which is as much as to say, of course, that it is nothing. If van Velde may be said to say nothing in his work, the same may be said of Beckett, who in naming the Unnamable, names nothing that is in any way positive. Saying nothing is not synonymous with silence, any more than being-nothing is synonymous with nothingness. Rather it is a tension, a constant reduction towards a silence which is never reached. Beckett does not stop speaking but his speaking is characterized by a perpetual tending towards cessation. This aspect of Beckett's work has already been analysed in terms of the Irreducible so that we may pass over it quickly here. From the point of view of Beckett's approach to art it may be defined as an attempt to make an end of words, an attempt which is never successful but always almost so. Thus the tramp groans, "how many hours to go, before the next silence, they are not hours, it will not be silence, how many hours still, before the next silence?" (*Texts*, p.100) – always anticipating the end, "my voice and silence, a voice of silence, the voice of my silence" (*Texts*, p.121). The Unnamable searches "for the means to put an end to things, an end to speech" (p.301), tantalized by the one thought: "If I could speak and yet say nothing, really nothing?" (p.305). Sometimes it seems easy: ". . . all you have to do is say you said nothing and so say nothing again" (*Texts*, p.99). In the words of the narrator of "The Calmative": "All I say cancels out, I'll have said nothing" (p.26). But it is a heartrending task. The Beckett subject is forced to deny every word he utters since it represents a betrayal of the silence. But to deny the word is to affirm it, to say "no" is to utter yet another word. Of course as we have seen this should not be interpreted as a pattern of failure and frustration. The Unnamable cannot be named, but its presence can be evoked as the substratum of silence without which there would be no words and to which all words point. Thus we return again to the essential paradox of the Beckett task, that the word is as unavoidable as the silence to which it refers. "Words have been my only loves, not many" (p.147), says the tramp of *From an Abandoned Work.* At times the word wearies and disgusts. It becomes that "convention that demands you either lie or hold your peace" (*Molloy*, p.88). "I use the words you taught me. If they don't mean anything any more, teach me others. Or let me be silent" (p.32), shouts Clov, and the Unnamable speculates: "Would it not be better if I were simply to keep on saying babababa . . .?" (p.310). In the end, however, the word is necessary, not to maintain a Tantalus condition, but to preserve in existence the mystery of Being and art, "drops of silence through the silence" (*The Unnamable*, p.386). So the panting of Lucky or the narrator of *How it is* or *Not I* mirrors the primary quality of art as Beckett conceives it, an art which stops to begin again and begins again to stop, preserving indefinitely the state of miracle.

It is immediately obvious that one cannot say nothing *deliberately*. I shall return to this subject later in this chapter but reference to it is necessary at this point. If art is to be inexpressive, a saying nothing, it cannot be *willed* – otherwise it becomes an expression of something, if only of a desire to say something. Thus Beckett pictures its genesis in the following terms: I cannot express, I fail to do it if I try and in any case I do not try. What then am I doing when I write? Duthuit might call it self-expression. But how could

I express myself when I am in no way involved? The work of art cannot be something created by the artist but only something wrenched from an unknown region through the artist's unwilling mediation. Beckett has said nothing, but nothing *has* been said, there is the proof of it, the non-event of the work of art. How did it happen, this failure of something to happen, and how did Beckett come to cooperate, when he remained passive? The only answer is the *fact* of the non-event, the existence of a nothingness, the working, the work of art – interpreted as a necessity, something undergone by the artist, thrust upon him. So it is not so much a matter of depicting a negative, a naming the Unnamable, as of accepting the fact that, impossibly, inexplicably, this *has occurred.* Beckett's notion of art is of an act no less incomprehensible than its subject, the Irreducible. Indeed, artistic creation and the work of art are precisely irreducibles, as Beckett explains to Duthuit:

> The situation is that of him who is helpless, cannot act, in the event cannot paint, since he is obliged to paint. The act is of him who, helpless, unable to act, acts, in the event paints, since he is obliged to paint. (p.119)

Or, as Molloy puts it:

> Not to want to say, not to know what you want to say, not to be able to say what you think you want to say, and never to stop saying . . . that is the thing to keep in mind, even in the heat of composition. (p.28)

The basic tenets of Beckett's art, then, are two: art is defined as a *saying nothing* and the artist relegated to the role of an amazed spectator, that is, reduced to *doing nothing.* Before considering in greater detail some of the implications of this position, however, we must return to the philosophers.

Sartre, when he talks about literature – as for example in *What is Literature?* (*Qu'est-ce que c'est que la littérature?* 1948) – insists on assigning to art and the artist an important social, indeed political, role. (The same is true for Camus.) Since this aspect of the question – the function of writing as *engagé* – is given overwhelming prominence, we may say at once that there is no parallel whatever with Beckett. Once again, it is more profitable to turn to

Heidegger, whose interest in art dominates the later thought.

Heidegger's theory of art centres on the notion of *erschlossenheit* or disclosedness which is elaborated in *Being and Time*. *Dasein* is a being-there and this implies an openness on its part, a power to embrace its "there", that is, its world, to take it up into itself and in so doing to reveal it or disclose it. *Dasein* is illuminated, it is its own light, lighting up the "there" which is a part of it. This notion of revelation is closely bound with what has already been said about being-in-the-world. If man is defined in terms of his milieu, it follows that the world is defined in human terms. From an epistemological point of view we could say that Heidegger inherits the legacy of Kant and, in a general sense, of the German Idealists and the Romantics. The mind is not passive in the act of perception; rather it helps to mould that which it perceives: in Heideggerian terms, it reveals it. Before man there is, strictly speaking, no "world", only an undifferentiated mass. Man's role is precisely to differentiate this mass, to illumine it, and this involves much more than mere perception of what was there before. Rather, man's disclosure of things, his power to confer *thereness* or presence on his world, is something without which the world would remain impoverished. The world is more itself, in other words, for being gathered up into the existence of man. Thus when I use wood to build a house, for example, I reveal the nature of wood. I disclose wood as hard or soft, rough or smooth, able to be shaped into planks and so forth. This is not mere subjectivity. The wood *is* those things which I perceive in utilizing it and it is only fully *itself* when I have utilized it. Thus man confers meaning on objects, that is, differentiates his world even as he acts to achieve his practical ends. None of this, however, is possible without language. In the essay "Hölderlin and the Essence of Poetry" Heidegger argues that being-there and language are synonymous. Man *is* language, he *is* his own speech, and it is speech which as it were *exposes* man to his world. Language is a form of action. It does not merely express an act, it is itself that. Thus we may say that man differentiates the world by *naming* it, he reveals it by language. It follows that the word is not a passive label, something *added* to an object. On the contrary, to name is to disclose, to cooperate creatively in the revelation of the nature of a thing. More precisely it is to situate the subject in relation to Being, since, in the words of the *Letter on Humanism*, "language is the house of Being",[2] a pledge of my nearness to Being, my kinship with it. In this context the naming of a thing *alters* that thing, a given object may be said to *be* its name. Of course a name may reveal the object falsely, it may disguise its true nature. Moreover as, by the power of habit, my grasp of the reality of things deteriorates and fades, I will more and more tend to obscure that reality by means of language. The word now becomes everyday, it loses the power of revealing and, as the reality of the world slips from it, so too does the reality of the ground of things, Being itself. Clearly this deterioration of the word is indistinguishable from the forgetfulness of Being which has been discussed already. Since man is language, inauthentic man becomes inauthentic language. The creative Word now becomes the Idle Talk of the "they". Two questions arise at this point: who originally reveals reality by naming it? Who rediscovers or renames it once it has been lost? The answer in both cases is the poet.

For Heidegger, language is rooted in poetry, it has its origins in it. Thus the poet is the first of men to speak:

> The poet names the gods and all things . . . This naming does not consist merely in something already known being supplied with a name; it is rather that when the poet speaks the essential word, the existent is by this naming nominated as what it is. So it becomes known *as* existent.[3]

The poet is an unacknowledged legislator, one who, by means of the word, opens man out towards the world and in turn enables the world to disclose itself to man. Poetry thus becomes identical with *dasein* or being-there. The essence of man is poetry, source of language. Poetry and language are not *expressions* of human reality, they *constitute* it: man is a poetic animal. In the words of Hölderlin quoted by Heidegger: "But that which remains, is established by the poets".[1] That which remains is, above all, Being itself, forgotten by the "they". The task of the poet is to awaken man to his poetic existence, to his *da-sein*, his place in the world and, beyond this, to his ultimate ground, *Sein*. It follows that, as Heidegger conceives it, the role of poetic utterance is rather like that of *angst*. "Remembrance of the Poet", another essay on the work of Hölderlin, illustrates the point. It proceeds as a philosophical commentary on the elegy "Homecoming" which describes Hölderlin's return to his native Swabia. For Heidegger the journey over Lake Constance is a return to man's true home, to Being itself. The imagination of the poet – and we must use the term "imagination" in the strong, the Romantic sense – reveals the lake for the first time, the *real* lake, in all its complex reality as gathered up into the world of man, the sphere of thought and feeling. This *is* the lake, the *geographical* lake is an indefinite, neutral thing, a non-lake called Constance, something analogous to the indefinite "they" which is everyone and no one. Only with the advent of the poet is the true, the individual lake disclosed, and this because in naming what he sees Hölderlin is referring nature to its origin, which is to say Being.

The poet, then, reveals things *as they are*, he does not merely give them an alien "human" colouring. In this he resembles the Heideggerian philosopher and indeed exemplifies the assumptions of Phenomenology. We recall the argument that the existential thinker mediates between the Idealist position and that of the empiricist. Man, who perceives reality, neither reduces it to thought, that is, to himself, nor does he stand passive in relation to it. He does something of both: he perceives actively in such a way as to disclose reality *as it really is in itself*, he both *perceives* and helps to *bring about* that which he perceives. Thus the phenomenon is defined in *Being and Time* as something manifest or revealed, "*that which shows itself in itself*".[4] Unlike many philosophers and, in a way, Husserl, Heidegger does not wish to distinguish between appearance and reality, between the thing as it is for me and as it is in itself, between the Kantian phenomenon and noumenon. Rather, a thing *is* its appearance. Phenomenology thus becomes "to let that which shows itself be seen".[5]

This "letting-be" is crucial. To reveal is not to manipulate reality but to stand back from it, to *allow* it to be itself. The question is examined at length in the essay "On the Essence of Truth", which argues against the notion of truth as *adaequatio*, the correspondence of the thing and the intellect, reality and one's idea of it. This concept is too static, too passive for Heidegger. Truth, he asserts, has more to do with human freedom, a choice to permit the world to unfold in the act of consciousness. Freedom means "letting beings be"[6] which in turn implies *alētheia*, unconcealment. In the very nature of disclosure, however, there is a tension. Man's opening out of the world is not such as to render it transparent. On the contrary, the mystery remains; what is revealed is revealed *as* obscure, concealed – and we are now speaking of Being itself. Years later, in "The End of Philosophy and the Task of Thinking", the same point is made in different words. *Alētheia* is now identified with *lichtung*, understood as an opening in a forest – clearing (of trees) which permits light to enter. Within this primal opening (the *urphänomen*, in Goethe's terminology), "presence" and "absence", disclosure and mystery are possible. It is here that Being and consciousness as it were meet and exchange gifts: Being offers itself, man accepts, is constituted as man, as existing – in Being. Again, the revelation keeps back as much as it gives, the opening is of "presence concealing itself".[7] All of this, of course, applies as much to art as to epistemology. In "The Origin of the Work of Art" (1936), Heidegger uses the example of Van Gogh's picture of peasant shoes. This picture tells the truth about its subject, it locates it in the truth, the disclosure of Being. Art "sets up" an entire world, but it does so discreetly, with reverence, since it has no intention of *making use* of this world. Rather the function of art is to bring to our attention its subject *as existing*, as *there*, nothing more. Consequently it presents it as "strange", "solitary". In short, the art object is, as Oscar Wilde put it, strictly useless. At the same time it has all the force of something utterly unique, as unique as the Being of beings. One may discern in all of this something fundamentally akin to Keatsian Negative Capability and indeed "The Origin of the Work of Art" could plausibly be represented as a philosophic gloss on the poet's identification of truth and beauty. The emphasis, however, is on the artist's preservation of the mystery of things as much as on his function of naming. We now return to the essay on Hölderlin's poem, "Homecoming". The poet reveals the landscape of the lake and mountains as mysterious because, ultimately, what he seeks to disclose is not simply the world of being but Being itself. To reveal things *as they are* is to evoke the presence of their mysterious ground. Thus the poet who names the world and its Being, who seeks to evoke the meaning of "home", that is, of the essential nature of things, reveals the truth *as* hidden, as poetic and allusive, not to mystify the reader but out of respect: ". . . we never get to know a mystery by unveiling or analysing it; we only get to know it by carefully guarding the mystery *as* mystery".[8] Being is the Reserved and the poet, like a cloud which filters the light down to the world beneath. The closer the poet comes to the light of being, the more intense the darkness becomes. It is the same situation depicted in "Conversation on a Country Path about Thinking" (*Discourse on Thinking*) where the image is one of three seekers after truth (scientist, scholar, teacher) walking into the starry night. In this poetic parable the path is philosophy, the night is Being itself, always encompassing, never attained, and the lights in the sky suggest the disclosure of individual beings. It is perhaps Heidegger's most evocative depiction of the process of revelation and the attitude of letting-be and it blurs once and for all any distinction between poetry and thought.

Now in its sense of dignified awe, the "Conversation on a Country Path" has no counterpart in Beckett's work. Reverence, however, may take many forms, some not easily identifiable. We recall that the voice of the tramp and of the Unnamable is that of consciousness itself. It is equally that of the artist, and from this point of view we can say truthfully that all of Beckett's work is about art. If the voice of art is identical with that of consciousness it follows that for Beckett as for Heidegger man *is* his own speech and that that speech is "poetic". To be is to be made of *words*, to exist is *to be a poet*:

> . . . the words are everywhere, inside me, outside me . . . I'm in words, made of words . . . the place too, the air, the walls, the floor, the ceiling, all words, the whole world is here with me . . .
> (p.390)

This comment is made in *The Unnamable*. Time and time again the Beckett narrator emerges as the Heideggerian poet who asks the Metaphysical Question and, supremely conscious, suffering the torments of *angst*, reveals the world of human reality. This issue has already been adequately discussed, though not in terms of art and the artist, and relatively little needs to be added. Beckett, like Heidegger, is a modern Romantic in his approach to art. His artist is a storyteller, one who, by an act of *consciousness*, brings into the light of day an existential world. In a sense, he invents or imagines this world, as the Unnamable, understood as an Idealist Absolute, invents the finite universe. But strictly speaking the voice of consciousness, which is that of the artist, is not identical, as we have seen, with the Unnamable. Rather, the role of the voice is that of an *agent*. The artist gives visible form to a mystery which envelops him and goads him into speech; he does not *create* but, like Heidegger's poet, *discloses* and, of course, he discloses his own situation, that of consciousness or existence and, *by implication*, the further sphere of Being, the Unnamable. In this way Molloy is an artist and so is Moran, writing his report. Malone writes in his room – with a blunt pencil – the voice of the Unnamable tells its endless stories, like the narrator of *How it is*. Pozzo's voice too is that of the artist, as is that of Hamm. More centrally, Lucky's outburst is an image of poetic creativity and Krapp appears as one who composes – and, it seems, whose compositions have the same excremental status as those of Shem the Penman in *Finnegans Wake*. Many more examples of the storyteller and the artist may be found in Beckett's work, from Henry of *Embers* to the narrator of *Company*. Even the tortured voices of *Play* are, from one point of view, illustrative of the artist's situation. In each case the voice is responsible for the revelation of an entire world of tramps with their bicycles, their crutches and so on. The Beckett artist shows us "how it is", in Heideggerian terms he *names* things. But of course he has no wish to name things. His whole task is to *deny* all positives and by this means to name the one important truth, the Unnamable. Thus the world is named by mistake: it is named as a result of the failure to name the Unnamable. In a way, though the context is more positive, something parallel happens in Heidegger, where the poet reveals the world only in the act of negating it in the experience of *angst*, that is, in the act of affirming the reality of Being, the ground of all things. We now return to the concept of art as a saying nothing. In the final analysis, the Beckett poet or storyteller is bound to argue that his stories are untrue, that the entire exercise in speech is a lie. So Moran explains: "Then I went back into the house and wrote, It is midnight. The rain is beating on the windows. It was not midnight. It was not raining" (*Molloy*, p.176). So also the narrators of *The Unnamable, How it is* and *Company* reject all that they have said. Art, in a way, is rubbish, like the heap in which Biddy the hen scratches in *Finnegans Wake*, "krapp", something utterly degrading, fit only for creatures like Shem the Penman or Malone. Why not? Beckett will have nothing to do with the limited aims of literary realism, "the penny-a-line vulgarity of a literature of notations" (*Proust*, p.76) and has only contempt for "the realists and naturalists worshipping the offal of experience, prostrate before the epidermis and the swift epilepsy, and content to transcribe the surface, the facade, behind which the Idea is prisoner" (*Proust*, pp.78–9). Art is not concerned with the surfaces of things. Its desire is to penetrate beneath the positive, to negate even itself, that is, to negate the word itself in order to attain a reality transcending all language. In this context the word becomes a hindrance, a sluggish and imperfect medium which serves to conceal rather than to reveal. If we are to say nothing art must rise above itself, language must, finally, be rejected, not in favour of silence but of a razor edge of statement and denial. Art thus becomes a lie by means of which truth is spoken. As in Heidegger, the word now reveals the truth *as* concealed, *as* mysterious, it reveals the Irreducible *as it really is* – like Heidegger's Being, Reserved, unknown, inexplicable. Beckett's tendency is exactly that of the Heideggerian poet: to speak the silence of Being without compromise, to preserve the negative *as* negative.

Such an approach necessarily implies an equivalent to Heideggerian "letting-be". Thus the work of art is not willed but simply happens. For Beckett, the artist does not force reality to yield its secrets, but vice versa. The trouble with the painter Masson, he tells Georges Duthuit, is that he *wants* to paint the void, he has "the malady of wanting to know what to do and the malady of wanting to be able to do it" (p.17). Beckett's logic is simple: How can I paint nothing deliberately? On the contrary, given that I desire nothing at all it may perhaps happen that in my passivity something will occur, the void will paint itself through me. The Romanticism of such an attitude is as obvious as in the case of Heidegger's "letting-be". In each case the artist does not *will*, he stands back and *allows* something to be revealed. Beckett sees this as a characteristic of Proust for whom the work of art is "neither created nor chosen, but discovered, uncovered, excavated" (*Proust*, p.84). Again, "Proust . . . is almost exempt from the impurity of will. He deplores his lack of will until he understands that will, being utilitarian, a servant of intelligence and habit, is not a condition of the artistic experience" (p.90). This is a description of Beckett himself who, like Macmann of *Malone Dies*, "in helplessness and will-lessness" (p.279), and like van

Velde, "who is helpless, cannot act", brings about creation without the least desire for control of the imaginative process. The Beckett artist, as we find him in the novels and plays, is indifferent, and this indifference, which derives partly from Geulincx and partly from the shock produced by *angst*, represents an openness, a wise passiveness towards the real. There is, of course, an element of compulsion in the act of artistic creation and to a large extent the question has already been discussed in chapter three under the heading of "freedom". Art offers a picture of the human condition. I do not desire to be conscious and yet I am, I do not desire to speak and yet I do. The facticity of existence operates also in the sphere of art and all art, like life, is an impossible, a miracle. Thus: "It is I who write, who cannot raise my hand . . . I am Matthew and I am the angel". (*The Unnamable*, p.303). The artist is possessed by the voice of inspiration as man in general is tyrannized by the anguished voice of consciousness. It is a state indistinguishable from that of insanity. Thus the lunatics of Murphy's asylum are "feverishly covering sheets of paper with . . . verbatim reports of their inner voices" (p.116). Watt hears voices, a mixed choir, no less. In due course the voice is identified as that of the muse, or at any rate as fulfilling the function of a muse. To the end, though, the act of creation involves a harsh disjunction of self from self, a kind of schizophrenia. There is the protagonist of *Not I*, clearly prompted by an unknown force (with whom she refuses to cooperate), a fact underlined by the image of division (between Mouth and Auditor) which is present on the stage throughout the performance. A similar image dominates *That Time*, which involves a passive Listener surrounded by his own voice, and *Rockaby*, where the female in the chair proclaims both her identity with and her separateness from her voice. Since this voice is recorded, the situation recalls the disjunction in *Krapp's Last Tape*. Likewise the voice remains distinct from the subject in *Company*. One of the most moving representations of the artist's predicament, however, is found in *Ohio Impromptu* (1981). On the stage Listener and Reader sit at a table. Listener knocks on the table to indicate stop and start, he functions, in short, as prompter. Reader then reads a tale, performing the role of the voice. The tale concerns a story of heartbreaking suffering and it too involves a double, the sufferer and his visitor who comes to read what amounts to the book of the sufferer's life. When the visitor has finished he leaves and, on stage, that is, in the story-containing-the-story, Reader comes to the end of his task. What has been achieved? A tale of sadness identical with reality has been read by a visitor who hardly speaks. On stage an image of the artist has read the tale – his own – as if it belonged to another, and he has done so *for* another, the Listener. Only at one point does this incredible mutiplicity (which must be regarded as existing within the chameleon artist) tremble on the verge of synthesis: at the end of the performance Reader and Listener exchange a look. But can it be any more than Murphy's gazing into the eyes of Mr Endon? If *Ohio Impromptu* offers a picture of the act of creativity, what is shown to us is, once again, something approaching the miraculous.

In the final analysis Beckett's artist is surprisingly analogous to Heidegger's. For the latter, the poet does not choose his vocation, he is chosen by Being. Poetry, like existence, is a "gift".[9] It entails suffering: "The poet is exposed to the divine lightnings . . . The excessive brightness has driven the poet into the dark."[10] " 'Cast out' . . . from everyday life",[11] standing uncomfortably in a no-man's-land, exposed to excessive light and detached from the inauthentic, the artist "intercepts" the signs of the gods and offers them to men.[12] In Hölderlin's words:

> . . . the bold spirit, like an eagle
> Before the tempests, flies prophesying
> In the path of his advancing gods.[13]

Thus the poet is a prophet, a man of vision, an Oedipus with "one/Eye too many perhaps",[14] driven to madness – like Hölderlin – "one who has been cast out – into that *Between*, between gods and men".[15] Beckett's unwilling artist adheres to this Romantic archetype. He is a madman, driven by an unknown force which gives no rest and separates him not only from other men but from all created things, a reject from society, a tramp or voice in solitude, cursed with the gift of vision and the burden of an obscure commission. In the words of a passage which is as applicable to Beckett's characters as to Proust's: "the artistic tendency is not expansive, but a contraction. And art is the apotheosis of solitude" (*Proust*, p.64). In so far as Beckett's artist is a prophet he is one possessed by a No. In the Hölderlin essays Heidegger conceives of the modern poet along just these lines.

We live in an age, he argues, when "Holy names are lacking", when a poem can only be "a song without words",[16] because this is an "age when the god is lacking".[17] God, in Nietzsche's words, has died, and man lives in a time of transition, a time when Being has been "forgotten" and has not yet been rediscovered:

> It is the time of the gods that have fled *and* of the god that is coming. It is the time *of need*, because it lies under a double lack and a double Not: the No-more of the gods that have fled and the Not-yet of the god that is coming.[18]

It follows that the vision of the modern poet, who stands between the no-more and the not-yet, can only be a negative one, that Being can only be experienced as Reserved:

> The time is needy and therefore the poet . . . would often like to relax in thoughts of those that have been and in eager waiting for that which is coming and would like only to sleep in this apparent emptiness. But he holds his ground in the Nothing of this night. Whilst the poet remains thus by himself in the supreme isolation of his mission, he fashions truth, vicariously . . . for his people.[19]

But this fashioning of truth is, for the time being, unrewarding, an exercise in patient endurance, and the poet is forced to "remain near the failure of the god, and wait".[20] Beckett's artist too is waiting, staying close to the No, a negative as austere as Heidegger's "double Not", and his only message concerns an impossible, an absence. He is not a pious prophet, like Heidegger's, but a complaining one, however, a rebellious and disheartened one, eager to avoid the imperative, like Jonah before Nineveh or Elijah in the desert when his morale is at its lowest. The tyrant is the Irreducible, truth, the muse, Being, Beckett does not care to specify. But his fidelity to his negative mission is extraordinary. Perhaps the short radio play, *Cascando*, sums up the nature of the task better than many more familiar works.

Cascando consists of an Opener who prompts Voice to tell the story of its search for the tramp Woburn. In an earlier chapter, this was described as the movement of the Irreducible out of itself, into the voice of consciousness and the figure of the tramp and, at the same time, as the Irreducible's attempt to return to itself through the voice's search for the tramp and the tramp's search for his own origins. From the point of view of the Beckett aesthetic, though, another interpretation of the play is possible. We may think of Opener as a prompter or muse and of Voice as the artist, or, again we may regard the Opener as artist and Voice as his (detached) utterance whose content is the story of Woburn. At any rate Opener, who appears to be in control, is in fact simply an agent (like Voice who is *his* agent): "There is nothing in my head . . . I open and close" (p.43). When he opens, Voice pants its confused speech, retelling the old story of the artist's burden, his attempt to define the most elusive reality of all:

> – story . . . if you could finish it . . . you could rest . . . not before . . . the ones I've finished . . . thousands and one . . . all I ever did . . . saying to myself . . . finish this one . . . then rest . . . no more stories . . . no more words . . . (p.39)

The *consummatum est* in this story of a search for a negative is never heard. If it could be uttered the Reduction would be completed, the task of the poet and philosopher done.

II

Everything that has been said about Beckett's approach to art naturally has its implications in the practical sphere of his writing. Now Reduction is Beckett's guiding principle and from the point of view of style it determines the essentials of the artist's use of language and his approach to larger structures such as plot. Reduction, however, leads not to a mere void but to a tension, an impossible. Thus the reduction of style leads, not unexpectedly, to a seeming paradox: the simpler Beckett's style grows, the more complex it becomes. This phenomenon exactly parallels the literary and philosophical patterns observable in Beckett's work. *Angst*, I have argued, involves the dual revelation of beings and of Being, of multiplicity and of unity, of complexity and simplicity. In different terms, the Reduction involves the dual revelation of the complex world of the tramps and of consciousness and, beneath this, of the sphere of simplicity itself, the Unnamable. It is important to see that the two aspects of this vision go together.

To reveal the transparent simplicity of the Irreducible is necessarily to highlight, by contrast, the endless and tormenting complexity of the life of consciousness. To affirm simplicity is to negate complexity; to negate complexity is to affirm it once again and, by an inexorable mechanism, to negate simplicity. Thus the pattern of affirmation and denial continues, alternately focussing on the Many and on the One, on words and on silence. It is therefore a characteristic of the Beckett style that the more one affirms the less one affirms and, more significant for the purpose of this chapter, the *less* one affirms, the *more* one does so: "I mean that on reflection, in the long run rather, my verbal profusion turned out to be penury, and inversely" (*Molloy*, p.34). But it is not only a question of more or less words. What Beckett achieves is a less and more within the word itself or rather within the basic unit of his speech. By the same token he manages to strike an extraordinary virtuoso balance of less and more in the unit of action or plot-construction. These will now be examined in turn under the respective headings of "saying nothing" and "doing nothing".

With respect to language the paradox of saying more by saying less is unmysterious. It simply means that, as it is pruned and simplified, Beckett's writing becomes more *poetic*. As poetry its range of suggestiveness is, of course, increased. Thus Beckett will use less and less words, simpler and simpler words and, at the same time, achieve in his units of language all the complex allusiveness that goes with the poetic.

The movement towards a simpler and more poetic prose begins in *Murphy*, where Beckett uses a style that is not unconventional and yet already prefigures later developments:

> At this moment Murphy would willingly have waived his expectation of Antepurgatory for five minutes in his chair, renounced the lee of Belacqua's rock and his embryonal repose, looking down at dawn across the reeds to the trembling of the austral sea and the sun obliquing to the north as it rose, immune from expiation until he should have dreamed it all through again, with the downright dreaming of an infant, from the spermarium to the crematorium. (p.56)

The rhythms of *Watt* also evoke the sense of the poetic though the style is still not Beckett's final and distinctive product:

> Watt had watched people smile and he thought he understood how it was done. And it was true that Watt's smile, when he smiled, resembled more a smile than a sneer, for example, or a yawn. But there was something wanting to Watt's smile, some little thing was lacking, and people who saw it for the first time, and most people who saw it saw it for the first time, were sometimes in doubt as to what expression exactly was intended. To many it seemed a simple sucking of the teeth. (p.23)

In the *Stories* and in *Molloy* and *Malone Dies* the characteristic panting, broken utterance begins:

> I am in my mother's room. It's I who live there now. I don't know how I got there. Perhaps an ambulance, certainly a vehicle of some kind. I was helped. I'd never have got there alone. (*Molloy*, p.7)

This is a new poetry of spareness, of fine juxtaposing of brief phrases which are used, in *Waiting for Godot*, as motifs:

VLADIMIR: Charming evening we're having.
ESTRAGON: Unforgettable.
VLADIMIR: And it's not over.
ESTRAGON: Apparently not.
VLADIMIR: It's only beginning.
ESTRAGON: It's awful.
VLADIMIR: Worse than the pantomime.
ESTRAGON: The circus.
VLADIMIR: The music-hall.
ESTRAGON: The circus. (p.34–5)

It reaches its first perfection in the tortured rhythms of *The Unnamable*:

> . . . you must go on, I can't go on, you must go on, I'll go on, you must say words, as long as there are any, until they find me, until they say me, strange pain, strange sin, you must go on . . . (p.418)

Here Beckett needs only the comma and even that is scarcely necessary, the pauses come so naturally between the self-contained units of his speech. It is a poetry whose effect is cumulative, like that of a symphony in which themes, here represented by verbal patterns, appear and reappear in various disguises, moving about the central stylistic pattern, the struggle of pause and speech, word and silence. This is the language – sometimes adapted for dialogue – of many of the plays, particularly *Endgame, Krapp's Last Tape* and *Happy Days*. The real line of development, though, is to the utterly simplified, unpunctuated – there is no need for punctuation – poetry of *How it is*:

> suddenly we are eating sandwiches alternate bites I mine she hers and exchanging endearments my sweet girl I bite she swallows my sweet boy she bites I swallow we don't yet coo with our bills full
>
> my darling girl I bite she swallows my darling boy she bites I swallow brief black and there we are again dwindling again across the pastures hand in hand arms swinging heads high towards the heights smaller and smaller out of sight first the dog then us the scene is shut of us (pp.33–4)

So much for a lovers' picnic. Beckett attempts variations of this kind of style, in *Imagination Dead Imagination, Ping* and *Lessness*, although nothing written after *How it is* has the same sustained inspiration, except perhaps *Not I* and *That Time*. At any rate simpler language than this could hardly be imagined. Yet the rhythmical virtuosity, the lucid beauty of Beckett's units of speech creates equally the sense of verbal richness, even extravagance, a complexity, a musical quality, an allusiveness which is normally associated with poetry. *Waiting for Godot, Malone Dies, The Unnamable, How it is*, no less than *Ulysses* and *Finnegans Wake*, very likely constitute the finest poetry this century has produced.

The unlikely union of less and more is as evident in the dramatic construction of the novels and plays as it is in the unit of language. Beckett simplifies his action and reduces it to a minimum and yet the movement towards doing nothing, like that to saying nothing, results in a new complexity. In this case Beckett combines seeming opposites by achieving a sense of *situation* rather than action, that is, by compressing the essentials of an action into a situation. The concept of the situation has already been examined in a philosophic context, but it is equally relevant in the context of a discussion of literary form.

The sense of situation, the reduction of succession to an instant, is often conveyed by an image of stasis, such as Winnie's sandpile, or of a closed space, such as Malone's room, but it does not rely on such obvious techniques. Likewise it is more explicit in novels and plays concerned with characters who are unable to move, but is equally present where Beckett's tramps are free to wander from one place to another. It does not exist from the first in Beckett's work. *Murphy*, for example, is concerned with a story, an action – if an uncomplicated one. Already in *Watt*, however, this approach is being more and more modified. Watt comes to Mr Knott's and then leaves but the reader is not really offered an image of progression. Rather, the entire novel, regardless of its plot sequence, registers as a single image, that of a man struggling to order his world or, more concisely, it offers us the single situation of "questioning", a protracted, agonized "what?" The trilogy moves away from even the minimal action of *Watt*. Strictly speaking, Molloy does not search, he is in a *situation* of eternal searching, he does not move but exists in a situation of motion. In *The Unnamable* there is no movement, no action, and we are left with the situation of existing, of being conscious or, if we prefer, of speaking. The single, utterly simple act is examined, varied like a musical theme until, without the *addition* of action, it acquires the richness, the allusive breadth of a poetic image, the structural complexity of a novel or play. In *Waiting for Godot* little or nothing happens yet, as Beckett simplifies the traditional plot to a point beyond which it would be difficult to go, he gains in complexity precisely because he has turned action into the poetic stasis of situation. The character *does* nothing, he simply *is*. This is ontological or existential theatre with a vengeance. Beckett does not develop his plot. He offers us an initial situation and then revolves it before our eyes so that we see it from all sides. As in *Malone Dies*, we begin and end with "waiting". Nothing has happened beyond that but the original situation has been enriched. Even the Pozzo and Lucky interludes add nothing to the flow of events – they simply help to pass the time *while we wait*. The only relief from pure stasis is the circularity of the structure and even this merely underlines the fact that there is no action, that the end returns us to the beginning or rather that we have not moved at all but are still keeping the same vigil. Similar comments could be made about more recent works. Thus the three moments of the past in *That Time* represent one present moment, *all* time being *one* time, *that* time, *the* time from which the play never strays. And in *Company* eighty-nine pages of sensitive prose reiterate the point, that it is all – for company. What is offered to the audience of *That Time* is simply the single situation of *time*, and to the readers of *Company* the single fact of *company*, the dialogue of self with self which is productive of multiplicity and yet amounts to *one* phenomenon, that of solitude.

To a greater or lesser degree in all the above cases nothing has happened, a situation has been elaborated, has revolved before our eyes like a many-faceted sphere so that its full dramatic potential has been revealed. Beckett has carried off another impossible, he has shown the situation *as* single, that is, he has reduced it to a unitary phenomenon, like a poetic image whose multiple connotations are grasped simultaneously. He has allowed us to read a novel or see a play *all at once*, as it were. In a way he has squared the literary circle and carried the Romantic principle of organic form, of the part in the whole and the whole in the part, to its logical conclusion. In some works, notably *Play, Krapp's Last Tape* and *Rockaby*, this concept of the all-at-once is given a uniquely concrete form. In *Play* Beckett achieves a new kind of simultaneity by orchestrating the voices of the three characters. At certain points the three actually speak at once so that three action strands are running simultaneously and dramactic language is treated with a freedom normally reserved for music. In *Krapp* – to take a less striking but equally ingenious example – Beckett does not run his characters together but divides the single character in two in order simultaneously to offer two views of one man by the simple yet theatrically brilliant device of the tape. Something comparable is done in *Rockaby*.

In the hands of Samuel Beckett, then, the work of art itself becomes an irreducible, an impossible which combines in an extraordinary equilibrium the contraries of less and more. From the point of view of language, the movement towards saying nothing leads to a poetic tension between speech and silence. From the point of view of dramatic structure the movement towards doing nothing leads to the theatre of situation or, more generally, to theatrical and novel *forms* which rely on the existential concept of situation. Here the tension is one of doing and nothing in a rhythm that reduces doing to nothing and elevates nothing to doing. In other words again, Beckett manages to combine the poles of succession and simultaneity, of time and timelessness, of multiplicity and unity. Of course perfect simultaneity of action, total unity of the work of art means the abolition of action and Beckett does not reach this extreme any more than he reaches that of silence. Rather he compresses everything to an irreducible zero, that unstable point of uncertain metamorphosis which in his hands becomes a reliable point of reference in defiance of every law. The situation is neither static nor dynamic but something of both. It represents a state of things such that, beyond a certain point, the tendency to stasis is transformed into action and vice versa. Each new angle, like a new camera shot of a single indivisible phenomenon, is a new negation of its irreducibility, of the organic unity of the novel or play, of stasis, a new affirmation of multiplicity and fragmentation, of what the work of art is *not*. Thus every word sins against silence, every act is a crime against the void. So Beckett denies the word and the action and so says and does nothing once more, he reaffirms the *situation*, the simplicity of the work of art. Thus the work unfolds by the familiar process of affirmation and negation, the more coiled in the heart of the less, that is, by an *action* that affirms the part and negates the whole, followed by a return to *situation* that negates the part and affirms the whole, an oscillation between the poles of extended temporality and simultaneity. In the final analysis the dynamism is not even an oscillation between two points but a paradox of motion and stasis, a *vibration* about a fixed point, a constant pull of expansion and contraction which resolves itself to a fine trembling. This pattern corresponds to the metaphysical or philosophical tension in Beckett's work between being and nothingness and it is, of course, the fundamental "shape" or "rhythm" of Beckett's inspiration. The work of art, by its very *form*, reveals the twofold reality of things, on the one hand the sphere of the Many, existence, on the other that of the One, Being – existence revealed only to be overwhelmed by the encroaching presence of Being, Being revealed even as existence reasserts itself and returns us to the inconceivable shore.

13 Genet and the Mass: sacrament as efficacious sign

> . . . the highest modern drama has expressed itself for two thousand years and every day in the sacrifice of the mass.[1]
>
> GENET

The close parallel which exists between Beckett and Heidegger cannot be drawn between Heidegger and Genet. Nevertheless, there are some basic similarities in the approach to art. Like Beckett, Genet is a modern Romantic where aesthetics are concerned, although in his case the Romantic quality is modified as a result of other influences. Moreover, as in the case of Beckett's work, we are justified in speaking of existential form in Genet, once again with the proviso that Genet derives his inspiration from a variety of sources. Genet's approach to art has little affinity with that of Sartre or Camus. Certainly, the Genet play or novel is envisaged as an act of revolt and Sartre and Camus tend to see the work of art primarily in these terms. On the other hand, where the latter regard revolt as a supremely human action and so exclude the numinous from the sphere of art, Genet emphasizes precisely the element of religious mystery.

Occasional comparison with Pirandello has so far helped to clarify Genet's position and this is also true where Genet's attitude to art is concerned. Pirandello's feelings about art are equivocal. On the one hand art is a form of death, a fixing of life, a limitation, so that the statue of Diana falls far short of its original, the model Tuda. On the other hand art may heighten life, it may discover unknown possibilities for man. This latter view, tending to neo-Platonism, is found in such late works as *The Mountain Giants* (*I Giganti della Montagna*). Genet is also somewhat ambiguous in his attitude. Much of *Our Lady*, for example, is treated as a disrespectful game in authorial asides. Of his first play Genet writes in 1967: "I find it hard to remember when and in what circumstances I wrote it. Probably in a state of boredom and by chance."[2] Of his second: "What could I possibly say about a play from which I felt detached even before it was finished?" (letter to Pauvert, p.142). Again, speaking of the same piece: "So my play was written out of vanity, but through boredom" (letter to Pauvert, p.144). There is the Pirandellian ending of *The Balcony*, in which Irma tells the audience that the show is over, that they are to go home "where everything – you can be quite sure – will be falser than here" (p.96). Art is a forgery, an appearance, like Irma's balcony. But these words may be read in another way. *Encore plus faux* may equally be taken to mean that the falsity of art is less than that of life. The way is open for a more positive assessment of the function of art.

In one fundamental respect Genet views art in Heideggerian terms, as a revelation, a disclosure. Art reveals the solitude of things, their particularity or uniqueness, that is to say, their hidden glory. The perfect example is the work of Giacometti as seen through Genet's eyes and also the art of the tightrope walker. We can therefore say of art all that has been said about the Image in earlier chapters. It is an appearance, masking the essential presence within, which withdraws into itself, perfect, alone. In one sense, then, the object of its revelation is a negative, as it is for Beckett. Speaking of Giacometti's work in *L'Atelier*, Genet stresses that it is not the line of a drawing which is beautiful but the space it contains: "It's not the line which has fullness, but the white" (p.42). Ultimately the glory of Giacometti's draughtsmanship is the blank page rather than the stroke of the pencil; the pencil is there simply to reveal an absence, to give sensible shape to a negative. Thus Giacometti shows as much respect for the mystery of the piece of paper as he does for the work he will produce:

> . . . Giacometti seeks to give sensible reality to something which was merely an absence – or if you prefer, indeterminate uniformity – that's to say, the white space, and even, in a deeper sense, the sheet of paper. It seems . . . that he has given himself the mission of ennobling a blank sheet of paper which, without his outlines, would never have existed.
>
> Moreover, once he has pinned the blank sheet in front of him, I've really the impression that he has as much respect and

> care before its mystery as he has before the object he is going to draw.
>
> Every work of the sculptor and the sketcher might be entitled: "invisible object". (pp.42–3)

Such a description fits Genet's own work and certainly recalls Heidegger, though its language is different. The artist's task is to ennoble, to thrust into the open, a white piece of paper – by his drawing. In the end, the drawing points to something beyond itself, an object which cannot be seen: *l'objet invisible*. Heidegger would say that by the act of poetic naming (which spotlights whiteness by differentiating it with black pencil marks) the artist has disclosed his subject – as Reserved, or withdrawn. An absent Sa'id, if we may put it this way, has been depicted by means of Sa'id's image. Thus Genet dreams of an art where nothing is said and everything is evoked (Pauvert, p.142). It would have to be an art of suggestion, not unlike that of the Symbolist poem. Obviously the solution offered through Sa'id, that of *actual* absence, cannot serve as a basis for Genet's practice any more than actual silence can serve as a basis for Beckett's art. Solitude may be a negative but the role of art is to reveal, that is, to suggest the negative by means of the positive. For Genet, as for Beckett, then, the achievement of the artist is necessarily always ambiguous. On the one hand art has the exalted role of opening the door to the unknown, on the other, it is simply an appearance. In terms of action and passivity the choice presents itself as follows. Either one opts for real, that is, *efficacious* solitude or for an *image* of solitude which, inevitably will have no active power, only the power of an appearance. Of course art represents a choice for the latter alternative. But Genet would like to have it *both* ways, he would like to offer us an image that *acts* upon us. We are returned to Beckett's predicament. If art is obsessed with a spiritual presence, an elusive negative reality, it must constantly fail, it must strive for an impossible goal. And Genet's impossible goal is to make *solitude communicable*, to show that, in spite of evidence to the contrary, the image or work of art is a living power and not simply an appearance or mask.

This involves Genet in an approach to art which is essentially sacramental. Genet's fascination for the Mass is well known. In *Our Lady* Divine reacts strongly to it:

> On Sunday, Divine and he [Darling] go to mass. Divine carries a gold-clasped missal . . . They arrive at the Madeleine . . . They believe in the bishops with gold ornaments. The mass fills Divine with wonder. (p.85)

A less pointedly equivocal statement occurs in the letter to Pauvert:

> . . . the highest modern drama has expressed itself for two thousand years and every day in the sacrifice of the mass . . . In the appearance of something as homely as a crust of bread a god is devoured. Theatrically, I know of nothing that works more effectively than the elevation. (pp.145–6)

From the point of view of the theatre, there is nothing more dramatic and moving than the lifting up of a piece of bread – which is a god to be eaten by men. Genet's dramas inevitably model themselves on this Christian ritual. Moreover, the Mass, as Genet realizes, is rooted in Eucharistic theology. A piece of bread becomes God. In the language of the Thomists its "accidents" remain unchanged – it continues to *look* like bread – its "substance" turns into divinity. In other words, God *appears* as bread but, because he *is* that bread, he is able to *act* through it. Thus a sacrament may be defined as a natural vehicle for divinity, nature unchanged in its appearance and radically altered in its substance. It is not merely a symbol in the usual sense of the word. A symbol is generally regarded as a passive sign. But a sacrament has the power to act upon the recipient: it is an "efficacious", a living sign. The transposition of these ideas to the Genet context is not difficult. Genet reveals solitude by appealing to the sacramental mentality. He does not choose between image and act: he combines these. Solitude is revealed in the work of art as pure *appearance* – which *works*, is efficacious. A play is a show, a facade with nothing behind it and yet it is expected to act miraculously upon the audience, to be an efficacious sign, "a profound intertwining of active symbols" (Pauvert, p.142). This is why Genet wants an audience of believers, not people who seek entertainment:

> A representation without effect on my spirit is useless. It is

> useless if I do not believe in what I am seeing . . .
> I spoke about a communion. The modern theatre is an entertainment. (Pauvert, p.146)

Under special conditions a true theatre might come into being, in the catacombs, for example, if only the participants were able to discover a *raison d'être* for their ritual of revolt:

> A clandestine theatre, to which one would come in secret, masked and by night, a theatre in the catacombs would still be possible. It would suffice to discover – or create – the common Enemy. (Pauvert, p.147)

This is exactly what Genet's work attempts to do. Genet offers us, in each of his novels and plays, in illegal ritual, a sacramental drama of love and hate. Its aim is to *effect* an emancipation from the power of the Other, as if it were a Mass for rebellious slaves, or – it amounts to the same thing – to realize the active presence of solitude, the individual's uniqueness. This effective movement, however, works through mere appearances, through gestures. Claire's sacrifice, for example, does not achieve a *real* liberation from Madame, at least not in one sense. The same may be said of the ritual of hate in *The Blacks*, which aims at the undermining of white authority, or of Roger's castration in *The Balcony* or of the ritual of betrayal in the novels. In *Miracle of the Rose* Harcamone is sacramentally devoured by Jean Genet, betrayed, deprived of his power. *Funeral Rites* is a similar celebration of Genet's cannibalism, the victim being the dead Jean Decarnin. In each case a *gesture* of self-assertion attempts to *effect* the presence of solitude, that is to say, to *exorcize* the Other, the figure of the beloved or of authority. It is a movement akin to the Christian concept of transubstantiation. Just as Christ's passion is reenacted and actualized once more in the Mass, so Genet reenacts in each of his works the archetypal struggle against the Look, the undermining and defeat of the Other – often through a symbolic sacrifice – and the victorious confirmation of the original victim's inalienable solitude. Of course Genet's sacramentalism suffers from the same ambiguity present in the ritual of the maids or the blacks or Roger. It has all been an empty show, Irma assures us at the end of *The Balcony*, nothing real has been achieved. The

Sartrean sceptic may well suggest that the sign cannot, as sign, be efficacious, that the work of art in presenting an *image* (*en soi*) necessarily sacrifices the living power of *action* (*pour soi*). Genet's position is secure, however. One must be a believer. If I believe in the gesture it becomes endowed with efficacy. Doubtless in the short run ritual achieves nothing. Claire dies, not Madame, Roger is sacrificed, not the Chief. But, indirectly, something is achieved and, impossibly, solitude *is* realized through the work of art. Thus the ritual reenactment of the struggle for liberation leads to eventual liberation, the saint takes us to the revolutionary, the maids to the blacks and these in turn to the Algerians, the "hollow" image leads to Sa'id. Moreover, if one is to accept Sartre's thesis that Genet's career has been "ten years of literature . . . equivalent to a psychoanalytic cure", it is clear that his own rituals have been Genet's salvation. Analogous things may be said of the childhood experience in which Genet is labelled a thief. Ultimately, perhaps, the Look is effective only because I believe in its power. Notwithstanding, it *is* effective, it has the sacramental power to *make* me a thief. So also with the work of art. No wonder, then, that Genet sees it as a form of crime. To name is to influence what is named. On this score Genet recalls not only the Pirandellian and Sartrean belief in the power of the label but also Heidegger's insistence that to name is to constitute reality.

In some important ways the artistic principle so far outlined resembles that of Antonin Artaud. It seems unlikely that there should be any question of an influence, as Roger Blin, one of Genet's first directors, emphasized in an interview with Bettina Knapp.[3] Nevertheless the similarity between the two writers is very great. The question has been investigated, notably by Robert Brustein in *The Theatre of Revolt*, but it is worth a brief reconsideration here. Artaud's famous definition of the theatre as a plague is at the centre of his influential *The Theatre and its Double* (*Le Théâtre et son Double*). Artaud sees European civilization as corrupt and repressive. Theatre is a way of bringing the disease to a crisis or, again, of draining the sore:

> It seems as though a colossal abcess, ethical as much as social, is drained by the plague. And like the plague, theatre is collectively made to drain abcesses.[4]

The theatre therefore serves a therapeutic function:

> Like the plague, theatre is a crisis resolved either by death or cure. The plague is a superior disease because it is an absolute crisis after which there is nothing left except death or drastic purification.[5]

In a sense, then, theatre is "cruel". It shocks man into a renewed contact with his inner life. Its working is analogous to magic and, if one is willing to believe, it has an efficacious power, it *alters*, it *acts*. The parallel with Genet is obvious. Moreover, for Artaud, the theatre reveals a "double" and this double is not a mere mirror, as realism would have it, but a non-human reality hidden within man, a metaphysical dimension: theatre reveals secret truths, mysteries of depth. We could be speaking of Genet and the revelation of man's hidden glory. In each case, of course, the approach is fundamentally Romantic, although its origins vary: where Genet turns to the Mass for inspiration, Artaud is impressed by the Balinese theatre. Either way necessitates a rejection of surface realism. As in Beckett, the concern is with metaphysical man, although Genet's interest in ritual stylization distinguishes him sharply from Beckett. Genet discards the realist convention from the start:

> Without being able to say exactly what the theatre is, I know what I will not have it be: a description of everyday actions seen from the outside. I go to the theatre so that I may see myself . . . as I could not, or would not dare, see or dream myself, and moreover as I know myself to be. (*Comment jouer Les Bonnes*, IV, p.269)

Consequently Genet has tried to achieve

> the abolition of characters – who exist in general only through a convention of psychology – in favour of signs . . . In short, to achieve the situation in which these characters are no more on stage than a metaphor of that which they represent. (Pauvert, p.144)

What is called for is a theatre of living signs, not men. All natural effects must be avoided, as in Artaud. In his stage direction for *Deathwatch* Genet states:

> The whole play must unfold as if in a dream. Give to the backdrop and costumes . . . violent colours . . . The actors will try to make their movements either heavy or incomprehensibly rapid. If they can, they will deaden the tone of their voices. (IV, p.181)

In *The Screens*, the acting must be precise, there must be no superfluous gestures (p.8). We are reminded of the tightrope walker's poise, the perfection of self-control which Genet conveys by his use of the term *bander* (to have an erection), of the celebrant in the Mass and the Balinese dancer.

The fact that Genet's imagination is influenced by the patterns of the Mass does not mean that, in the final analysis, his approach to artistic form differs radically from Beckett's. On the contrary, it leads to the same goal. In order to see this we must return to the idea of a work of art as an incarnation of the divine, as a making-present of the deity – solitude – in and through a theatrical performance. As a ritual, the Genet play (or novel) is not concerned with history, with events in secular time. Just as the moment of consecration in the Mass represents an intersection of the planes of eternity and time as God enters into the stream of history and becomes present to the believers, able to act out an *eternal* mission *in time*, so in Genet the dramatic moment is not of time but partakes of temporality and eternity. Genet calls it "dramatic time" (*L'Etrange mot d'* . . . , IV, p.10). While a play is being performed time has no beginning and no end: "from the start of the theatrical event the time which is going to pass belongs to no indexed calendar" (*L'Etrange mot d'* . . . , IV, p.10). Yet at the same time the ritual itself is an action and so temporal. If it were not there would be no point in repeating it. Like the Mass, Genet's drama presents us with an act which is both real and unreal, merely a gesture and yet active, a sign and a deed, in short, an eternal recurrence or a *recurrence in eternity*. Genet wants once again to combine opposites of action and passivity, reality and image. He wants, finally, to give an effect of static perfection and to combine this with movement. A stylized ritual is one way of doing it. Of course the approach derives all its power from the sense of tension, the simultaneous pull of stasis and dynamism, the timeless and time. We are surprisingly close to the inspiration of Samuel Beckett. After all, solitude is an irreducible, an impossible, like the Unnamable and like that other wonder (in Descartes' words), "the Man who is God".[6] Seeking to realize concretely an absence, a spiritual reality, Genet is driven, like Beckett, to an aesthetic of impossibility and to a form which mirrors this aesthetic. It is the dilemma of Christianity, a religion founded on the notion of an interplay of divinity and humanity. Not surprisingly, although he chooses a different road, Genet arrives at the same point as does Samuel Beckett. Again, the form of a work of art reflects a Romantic and existential tendency towards unity or rather towards unity-in-diversity. I have already termed this approach "situational". Like Beckett and for similar reasons – and this in spite of his different starting-point – Genet presents us not with action but with *situation*, that is, with a paradox of action and inaction. As in the Mass, nothing happens – it is mere show, ritual. But the ritual is *effective* and so nothing really *does* happen. In the Mass Christ's death is impossibly repeated; in *The Maids*, for example, the archetypal victory-in-defeat of the Genet saint is impossibly repeated, perhaps, as Sartre argues, the eternal crisis of Jean Genet, child hoodlum, is reenacted.[7] As in Artaud's work there is an appeal to "total" theatre, a theatre of organic unity. Artaud speaks of "breaking language in order to touch life", of a "physical language",[8] a language of signs and gestures, of "spatial poetry"[9] of *spectacle total*, a theatre in which words, actions, costumes, lighting, backdrops and music come together to express a vision of the whole man. All of this applies to Genet's work. The difference is that Artaud is a child of Freud and Jung who cannot see beyond the archetypal myth whereas Genet, for all his use of similar techniques, is after something more rarefied and philosophical. In the end the Genet play appears less as a series of events which have taken place than as a single event, a sign or metaphor, something which happened-in-eternity, that is, something which *happened all at once*. It is as if by "a profound intertwining of active symbols", a tangle of living signs, Genet hopes to link all the parts of his drama, to link everything so tightly that the sense of part is lost altogether, that, by means of an alchemic transformation, part and whole coalesce and the play appears as an indivisible unity. It is a matter of joining the parts so tightly that all movement comes to a halt – only to begin again, impossibly, with the cry of the Beckett hero: *e pur si muove.* So we progress by a series of alternations comparable to Beckett's, in this case the tension being one of realism and ritual, of event and non-event, of time and time abolished. In its simplicity born of extreme complexity, the Genet *situation* will evoke the presence of the paradoxical being, solitude. The existential has been reached by the unexpected route of the Mass.

A final aspect of Genet's approach to art must be considered: the role of the artist or the actor. The artist in Genet is a priest, as in Heidegger. He does not initiate, he transmits, and in this respect resembles the work of art itself. Just as the celebrant of the Mass possesses the power to transform bread into divinity not through personal merit but as an agent of the divine will, so the artist in Genet, whether a sculptor like Giacometti, a tightrope walker, an actor or a writer, is not himself responsible for his creation, at least not overtly. The artist, and this point needs no stressing since it is implicit in all that has been said of the image, is empty of self, at least in one way *passive.* Genet complains that European realism will not permit the actor such a role: "the western actor does not seek to become a sign charged with signs; he simply wants to identify himself with a dramatic or comic character" (Pauvert, p.143). The difficulty is the actor's habitual lack of discipline, his careless attitude to his art: "Instead of being recollected, theatre people live in a state of distraction" (Pauvert, p.145). Genet wants his actors to be recollected in the religious sense of the words implying a state of ingatheredness in prayer. This means, as in the case of the tightrope walker, a dying to self, not selfishness:

> You are an artist . . . But this is not a matter of coquetry, egoism or love of self. What if it were a matter of death itself? Dance then . . . it's your image which is going to dance for you.
>
> (pp.179–80)

It is not the tightrope walker but his sign which moves on the wire. In self-obliteration and passivity the artist becomes efficacious, as if an alien power – his solitude is that – were working through him. So with Giacometti:

> His dream would be to disappear completely behind his work. He would be still happier if the bronze had manifested itself without his help. (*L'Atelier*, p.36)

Giacometti, like the tightrope walker, leads an abject life, seeking not his own glory but that of his material. His drawings aim at setting off the beauty of the piece of paper, his statues, that of the original metal. If he could hide altogether behind the work of art, he would be satisfied. Genet's attitude to his own writing is similar, though such a view may appear surprising in view of the fact that it is so easy to discover Genet in every page of his work. And yet in the novels and plays a supremely personal vision is revealed by means of an ascesis away from self; Genet leaves himself to discover an alien identity within himself which he calls solitude. The protagonist of the novels and plays is therefore not Genet himself but the other Genet who rises to the surface when the author does not interfere:

> When, in the Santé prison, I began to write, it was never because I wanted to relive my emotions or to communicate them, but rather because I hoped, by expressing them in a form that they themselves imposed, to construct an order (a moral order) that was unknown (above all to me too). (*Journal*, p.142)

In his own words, Genet writes not in order to relive or to communicate experience but in order to step into the unknown. It is true that such a description of the creative process is more suited to his early work. But it applies to Genet even when he writes in a more self-conscious vein. Genet holds a theory of art which recalls Keats' Negative Capability, the Romantic attitude of passivity before inspiration. We are reminded not of Sartre but of Heidegger's analyses of Hölderlin and above all of the idea of "letting-be" which is at the centre of the notion of art as revelation, *erschlossenheit*.

Genet's attitude to art hinges on three things. Art is a revelation of solitude. The revelation is sacramental, that is, embodied in a ritual involving efficacious signs. It is effected through the passive artist. In his method Genet recalls Artaud and, even more obviously, the Catholic liturgy, although the end result is existential drama akin to Beckett's drama of situation. Like Beckett – and

Ionesco – Genet stands closer in his approach to art to Heidegger than to Sartre (or Camus). Where Beckett evokes irreducible Being as an absent presence, as the *ground* of the existential situation, Genet evokes irreducible solitude as a presence hidden *behind* the visible sign and paradoxically revealed in it, as divinity is revealed and made present in the Christian ritual. The religious bias is far more explicit in Genet than in Beckett and expresses itself in surprisingly conventional terms. If the gods are absent in the universe of Beckett and Heidegger they are very nearly present in Jean Genet's – along with certain demons.

14 Ionesco: The free imagination

> The free development of the powers of imagination must not be restricted. There must be no canalisation, no directives, no preconceived ideas, no limits.
>
> (*Notes and Counter-Notes*, p.128)

Where Beckett seeks to reveal the Unnamable and Genet the mystery of solitude, Ionesco sets out to reveal the wonder of things, the radiant experience that things *are*. "It's in order to talk about this light, in order to talk about this wonder . . . that I've created literature," he explains in *Découvertes* (p.60), and, in "Why do I write?" "that above all is why I write: to express my sense of wonder" (XI, p.122). This is what interested him in theatre, from the time he first watched *guignol*: not the meaning of the performance, but its ineluctable reality, "the brute fact of existence" (*Découvertes*, p.71). It is for this that he wishes to create, to be like God, by *adding* to being and, at the same time, by fighting death and oblivion in the act of *perpetuating* an otherwise transient being ("Why do I write?" XI, p.134). But the important thing is the note of wonder, what Heidegger terms the "uncanniness" of the world, and in this context it is not difficult to see why Ionesco's feelings about art revolve about the concept of the New, not in the sense of mere novelty but of vision, of authentic insight. Ionesco wants us to see the world as his protagonists see it, as too heavy or too light, as *unusual*. For Heidegger, art ultimately discloses what is normally "forgotten" or "covered over", the ground of things. Again and again Ionesco struggles to show us this ground in the terms in which he conceives it, either as frightening or intoxicating, as awesome, even monstrous, as impossible proliferation of things, a stifling void of matter, or as joy in a transfigured world, evanescence and plentitude. On the one hand this necessitates a struggle against conservative forces, against art which does not surprise and is based on preconceptions. On the other, it implies a continuing assertion of the value of the free imagination. For Ionesco, "the imagination is not arbitrary, it is revelatory" (*Notes*, p.47), "only it expresses the reality of man" (*Un Homme en Question*, p.60). Again, "what we imagine is revelatory. Imagination cannot lie since it . . . is an unveiling" (*Découvertes*, p.77). Imagination is not mere fantasy, but something to be trusted, something which cannot lie if it is allowed to express itself without interference. It is logic which becomes unreasonable if given free rein. As a character in *The Killer* put it, "reality, unlike dreams, can turn into a nightmare" (III, p.26). Dreams, unlike everyday consciousness, reveal the true nature of things. "When I dream", Ionesco explains, "I do not feel I am abdicating thought. On the contrary, I have the impression that . . . I see evident truths" (*Notes*, p.115). The same point is made to Claude Bonnefoy. Logic may turn into madness, dreams do not:

> The dream is natural, it's not mad. It's logic which is liable to turn mad; the dream, being the very expression of life in its complexity and its incoherences, cannot be mad. (*Entretiens*, p.129)

This is Ionesco's version of Romantic Negative Capability or of Heidegger's "letting-be" with the added perspective of Freud and the surrealists. Imagination, the dream, these pierce through the falsity of the everyday and demystify it.

It follows that the artist must not force his inspiration along predetermined lines but must bow before the authority of mystery, of spontaneity. The alternative is ideological art, the counterpart of rhinoceritis in the socio-political sphere. Ionesco dwells obsessively on this theme in *Notes and Counter-Notes*. Art is the realm of passion, not of pedagogy (p.31); the writer does not teach: "A writer is not a teacher but an inventor" (p.38). Practically, this stand implies a conflict between the New and the cliché: "a thing once spoken is already dead, reality lies . . . beyond it" (p.41). Only by producing something new is the author able to communicate in real terms; he is therefore committed to pure invention and also to the restoration of what has been disfigured. We are not far from the artist's "uncovering" of what is "forgotten" in Heidegger. Ionesco sums up his feelings about the freedom of the imagination as follows:

> The free development of the powers of imagination must not be restricted. There must be no canalisation, no directives, no preconceived ideas, no limits. I believe a genuine work of art is one in which the initial intentions of the artist have been surpassed; where the flood of imagination has swept through the barriers or out of the narrow channels in which he first tried to confine it: extending beyond messages, ideologies and the desire to prove or to teach. (*Notes*, p.128)

Of course the enemy here is the writer with a specific purpose. Ionesco records with indignation his meeting with an English critic – presumably Tynan – who congratulated him on being very nearly the greatest living playwright. "How can I become the greatest?" Ionesco facetiously asked. "It's very easy," was the answer, "we are only waiting for you to deliver us a message . . . Be a Marxist, be Brechtian!" (*Notes*, p.67). This is the burden of Tynan's and Ionesco's well-known critical exchange in *The Observer*. Ionesco's stand is that there is no point in repeating Brecht or Marx or anyone else and he takes frequent opportunity of saying so. Brecht is something of a butt in this context, as is Sartre – in *Notes and Counter-Notes* and, more recently, *Découvertes*. In every case art is regarded as free spontaneity: the rest is politics, ideology, moralizing (*Notes*, p.277). It follows that the best way to write a play is to allow the play to write itself. Will-lessness, as in Beckett, becomes a primary artistic virtue:

> Creation implies total liberty . . . When I write a play, I have no idea what it is going to be like. I have my ideas *afterwards*. At the start, there is nothing but an emotional state . . . For me art means the revelation of certain things that reason, everyday habits of thought, conceal from me. Art pierces everyday reality. (*Notes*, p.134)

Of course the muse is *angst*, as this passage clearly indicates, that state in which everydayness is transcended and the truth is revealed. Not surprisingly, the attack on everyday logic, on that kind of art which expresses only surface realities, becomes an attack on artistic realism. For Ionesco, "boulevard" theatre, which offers the audience what it expects, means any theatre which has recourse to the realist convention. It may be Broadway or socialist drama or any kind of theatre without novelty of form: "I have always considered imaginative truth to be more profound . . . than everyday reality. Realism, socialist or not, never looks beyond reality " (*Notes*, p.14). In the end realism kills the theatre because it is profoundly unreal, "bourgeois unreality on the one hand, so-called socialist unreality on the other" (*Notes*, p.158). And yet Ionesco's own work may, in this context, be regarded as realistic. Thus *Amédée* is "a slice of life" (*Notes*, p.203). If we object that this is hardly so in the accepted sense, the reply is categorical and places Ionesco beside Beckett and Genet: "I reject the kind of realism which is nothing but a sub-realism" (*Notes*, p.203). This is Ionesco's final defence of the imagination. The imagination is not everyday vision but reality itself, since it tells the truth about man's deepest fears and desires. Any drama which can ignore these in order to amuse or instruct the public is less than realism. We could say that in all of this Ionesco continues his fight against the collective, with its "already-done . . . already-said" (*Notes*, p.48). Where Beckett's artist is a cursed, insane prophet and Genet's a possessed, demonic priest, Ionesco's is a visionary and a rebel, against the past, the preconceived, the limiting. And yet, because he deals with the fundamentals of the human situation, his isolation is only apparent. Again and again in *Notes and Counter-Notes* the argument must be seen in the context of the eternal French debate between Classicism and Romanticism, between doctrines of social utility and variations of *l'art pour l'art*, between the rival claims of tradition and the *avant garde*, history and the ahistorical, popular and élitist theatre. It is ironic that his stand against ideology has, in the eyes of some, placed Ionesco in the reactionary camp.

Ionesco's feelings about art are given some expression in the plays. *Victims of Duty* is the first and most obvious example here, since Choubert's search amounts to a statement about drama. All plays ever written, argues the naive hero early in the play, are whodunits, realistic detective thrillers, stories about problem and solution: "you seek, and then you find" (II, p.269). Truth is an object to be appropriated as an object, or so the detective imagines as he sends Choubert in search of Mallot, an unknown whose identity is never revealed. Thus the artist's quest for Being is reduced to a crime drama. But Mallot is more elusive than is supposed. The detective, here representative of the realist or the

Brechtian, that is, of those who, in Ionesco's eyes, regard art as a medium for ideology and clichés, finds no simple answer to the riddle. At the same time Choubert proves Ionesco's point, that drama is indeed a search, but one which leads to man's mysterious depths, not to ideology. At one point the image of the theatre becomes concrete. Choubert is an actor, telling his audience – Madeleine and the detective – what Ionesco's protagonists always tell their audiences, the story of man's dreams, his fear of claustrophobia and his desire for liberation. Madeleine reacts with everyday common sense: it would be more entertaining, she tells the detective, to spend the evening in a cabaret (II, p.293). Later, when Choubert attempts to fly, she and the detective seek to restrain him with arguments which subordinate art to social criteria. Something similar is involved in Amédée's flight also. Amédée is a playwright and his embarrassment at his levitation is expressed as a conviction about Social Realism in art: "I like to be of use to my fellow men . . . I believe in social realism" (II, p.225). In this context the flight clearly represents the abandonment of realism and ideology for a more imaginative approach to art. But this is only partly the theme of *Amédée*, whereas it is central in *Victims*. After his escape is thwarted, Choubert is joined by Nicolas d'Eu who promises to be an ally, since his notions of art are substantially Ionesco's own. Significantly, however, the mood of the play remains oppressive. Nicolas argues against a theatre dominated by reason and for the validity of the dream. But as he speaks Choubert is being choked with dry bread. Later, Nicolas will kill the detective and take his place as Choubert's tormentor. Clearly Ionesco will accept no ideology at all, not even one which supports his own views. This is the point of *Improvisation or The Shepherd's Chameleon (L'Impromptu de l'Alma ou le caméléon du berger*, 1955), Ionesco's one play which is didactic, if facetiously so. Ionesco, writing at his desk, in interrupted by the entry of the critic Bartolomeus I, full of scientific theories about drama. Bartolomeus asks about the play which is being written and Ionesco gives evasive answers. It is coming of its own accord, Ionesco does not know quite where it is going; at any rate it hinges on a scene in which a shepherd embraces a chameleon. The shepherd is Ionesco embracing – the theatre. Bartolomeus is scornful and as Ionesco begins to read his play (it is a repetition of what is, in fact, taking place) a second, then a third Bartolomeus appears. Follows a long assault upon the playwright on the part of the (proliferating) critics who lecture Ionesco on themes of commitment with Sartrisms, leftist jargon, theories of theatre and general confusion. The critics, themselves divided on details, represent the view that art should be didactic, that it should reflect social norms. Luckily Ionesco is rescued by Marie the housekeeper – representing the theatre-goer – who hustles the critics out and, once alone, the playwright begins to air his so far repressed views about art, those views expressed so copiously in *Notes and Counter-Notes*. But as he continues, he forgets himself. The play has become didactic with a vengeance, Ionesco himself has become a pedagogue. He is rebuked by Marie and apologizes to the audience. The chameleon, we gather, should be left to change colour at will, the theatre must be bound by no rules, not even Ionesco's. This is Ionesco's pressing problem, of course, to defend himself from dogmatism without himself becoming dogmatic, and we find it in other plays. Bérenger of *A Stroll in the Air* is a playwright who does not want to offer his audience a message. Yet, at the end, that is more or less what he does. Jean of *Hunger and Thirst* becomes an unwilling witness at a frightening performance when brother Tarabas presents a play about freedom: the fact that one of the protagonists is called Brechtoll speaks for itself. The play comments not only on totalitarian politics but also on ideological art. But then it is precisely here that Ionesco is in real danger of preaching to his own audience and so of effectively negating his point. Perhaps it is just as well that the traveller of *The Man with the Luggage* has lost his third case, the one containing his writings: they might have included essays, commentaries and interviews.

It seems, then, that the polarity of euphoria and claustrophobia takes a new, though not unexpected form, in Ionesco's approach to art: the dualism is now that of creative imagination and ideology. In order to liberate art one must learn to see anew, and in Ionesco this is expressed as a dislocation of normality. The form of the work of art must reflect the strangeness of reality when seen as if for the first time, it must incarnate the vision of *angst*, with its radical rearrangement of the everyday:

> We need to be virtually bludgeoned into detachment from our daily lives . . . which conceal from us the strangeness of the

> world. Without a fresh virginity of mind . . . there can be no theatre and no art either; the real must be in a way dislocated, before it can be reintegrated. (*Notes*, p.25)

Ionesco's attitude emerges in his handling of the theatrical. In *Notes and Counter-Notes* he admits that he disliked theatre before he became a playwright. And yet he enjoyed *guignol*:

> I can still remember how my mother could not drag me away from the Punch and Judy show in the Luxembourg Gardens . . . It was the very image of the world that appeared to me, strange and improbable but true as true, in the profoundly simplified form of caricature . . . (p.18)

Here he found the solution to the problem of theatre. If the discrepancy between life and art is embarrassing, it is better to make it more so rather than to attempt to hide it. Realist theatre, with its carefully prepared replicas of the world outside, appears, to Ionesco, as an attempt to stifle a glaring truth – that there is something strange about the theatrical situation and, perhaps, about life itself. Ionesco's concern is to prick this bubble and Punch and Judy is one way of doing this. Art must evoke the Uncanny, not conceal it. Where Beckett reduces to a fine point, Ionesco sets out to amplify reality to monstrous and wonderful proportions: negative theology becomes superlative theology. Where Beckett underlines the inescapable concreteness of the human situation by his stress on the *fact* of being, Ionesco does it by daubing reality with garish colours. If, he argues, the value of theatre is its exaggeration, then this exaggeration must be even further accentuated, whatever is odd must be made to seem more so, everything must go to the point of paroxysm:

> So if the essence of the theatre lay in magnifying its effects, they had to be magnified still further, underlined and stressed to the maximum . . . go all out for caricature and the grotesque . . . No drawing-room comedies, but farce . . .
> (*Notes*, p.24)

Of course this is above all a description of the early plays, but it remains valid for the later work. In the Bonnefoy interview the author recounts his initial difficulties in making producers understand his formula. Peter Hall, who wanted to produce *The Lesson* in 1955, could swallow everything except the daily murder of forty pupils. He and Ionesco settled for four: "four was possible, forty wasn't possible" (*Entretiens*, p.111). In a similar spirit the first producer of *Rhinoceros* could accept a mass metamorphosis but insisted that Bérenger could not, in all politeness and making allowance for American custom, visit Jean in the second act without telephoning first – in act one (*Entretiens*, pp.111–12). In the original production of *The Chairs* the German producer refused to allow more than a dozen chairs on the stage. Ionesco wanted fifty and for obvious reasons (*Entretiens*, p.112). The dislocation and heightening of reality which Ionesco advocates in his comments about theatre are equally evident in his approach to language. If everyday speech disguises strangeness, then it must be broken down and reconstituted. Thus, like the Heideggerian poet, Ionesco sets out to restore words in order to restore man's relation to the wonder of Being. It is the old struggle against propaganda, the cliché. We must make the word theatrical, says Ionesco, which is to say that we must strain and exaggerate: "the whole tone should be as strained as possible, the language should almost break up or explode in its fruitless effort to contain so many meanings" (*Notes*, p.27). In *The Bald Prima Donna* this "disarticulation of language" (*Notes*, p.25) has the function of undermining the commonplace in a world where language falls apart: "language breaks down . . . words drop like stones or dead bodies" (*Notes*, p.170). "Yoghourt," Mme Smith tells us, "is very good for the stomach, the lumbar regions, appendicitis and apotheosis" (I, p.87). But already in this breakdown of speech we sense a restoration and in later plays this is marked. *Amédée, The Killer, A Stroll, Hunger and Thirst, Oh what a bloody circus* and *The Man with the Luggage* differ from the early work in that their use of language is more conventional. Mere dislocation turns into poetry. But the rationale is unchanged. Poetry is itself a dislocation and heightening of the commonplace, a freeing of language, a return to the truth. As in Heidegger, man lives poetically, poetry is simply the spontaneous expression of Being, language forever renewing itself.

But it is in Ionesco's approach to the structure of his plays that his bias is best exemplified. In order to escape the control of the rational mind with its petty restrictions, or, in Heideggerian terms, to allow the truth to be itself, to let-be, Ionesco turns to abstract dramatic patterns, he views plot as *shape* rather than as *story*. It is his long-standing grievance against the critics that this has been overlooked and that the plays have been judged according to inappropriate criteria. In the harangue of the critics depicted by *Improvisation* the work counts for nothing, only ideas are important: "I feel", Ionesco complains, "I have been judged not by literary critics . . . but by moralists" (*Notes*, pp.81–2). In fact his real concern has always been not for ideas but for artistic forms ("more likely . . . structure than . . . story", *Notes*, pp.126–7), not for a sequence of events but an abstract progression through various phases or states of mind. Thus Ionesco dreams of structures without specific content, of "abstract theatre. Pure drama" (*Notes*, p.188). In so far as it tells a story, a plot is liable to simplify, to rationalize unduly, to fix and stunt the immediate complexity of things. But if a play is treated like a symphony, if language, action, backdrop are all treated as components of a larger dynamism, the *shape* of the plot will allow for complexity, the sense of wonder will be preserved, the imagination will not be bound. The dynamism of a given play thus states very little and at the same time illustrates, in heightened form, the rhythms of life as Ionesco conceives it. Life is a tension of joy and claustrophobia, authenticity and inauthenticity, freedom and restraint, and so the play itself becomes an oscillation between these poles, a rhythm of *angst*, revealing different aspects of reality in turn and, ultimately, the poles of existence and being, the tension of the human situation and the desire to escape, the existential and the Ideal. Now ontological theatre, theatre which mirrors the structures and dynamisms of existential reality, is, for Beckett and Genet, theatre of *situation*. The same may be said for Ionesco. When the latter focusses on the abstract pattern of a play and, like Beckett and Genet, rejects the idea of plot as succession, he does so because he wants to capture reality as a whole. It is a Romantic and existential tendency towards the principle of organic unity. Thus, as in Beckett, nothing "happens" in a Ionesco play, there is no history to be recounted. Rather, the audience is offered an all-inclusive and, in a sense, static image: that of existential reality, the wonder of things. Within this image there is movement, of course, but, strictly speaking, no succession. We observe reality in terms of situation, that is, as a *state of affairs* rather than as a series of events. In order to capture the complexity of the situation we examine it from various angles – as dense or evanescent, as claustrophobic or euphoric, as too heavy or too light and so forth. While little happens, everything *is*. Once again the idea of the all-at-once, the idea of a work immediately grasped as a totality, dominates the approach to art. This point has been sufficiently stressed in earlier chapters, however, and needs no further amplification.

There is another sense in which we may speak of the form of Ionesco's work as existential. Once the Cartesian rift between subject and object, that is, between the mind and its object of knowledge – the world – is effected, it becomes extremely difficult to reassemble the epistemological Humpty Dumpty. One can give up in despair and adopt the Occasionalist stance: reality is then fundamentally twofold and nothing – except an outrageously interfering *deus ex machina* – can hold it together. Or one can emphasize the second term of the epistemological relation of subject and object, that is, adopt the empiricist solution in which the mind is regarded as somewhat passive before its objects of perception. Empiricism tends towards the neutralization of the subject in the search for truth, or towards what is more usually described as an elimination of subjectivity, the bias of the mind to colour reality. Subjectivity has become *mere* subjectivity, objectivity the only valid, if ever-receding, criterion of truth. Or one can choose to emphasize the active role of mind, the subject in the act of knowing. Suddenly the whole world, which the empiricist would like to reduce to matter and to mechanical processes, is reduced to mind and to spiritual processes. Instead of things, we speak of ideas expressing themselves in material form. For the Idealist, everything becomes the temporal and finite expression of an eternal and infinite thought. The surprising thing is that extremes are liable to meet, that both the empiricist and the Idealist postulate the possibility of a detachment from the world. Where the former attempts to take the point of view of a distinterested spectator, the latter attempts to take the God-like viewpoint of the Absolute. The existential approach, as I have argued, may be thought of as steering a middle course between philosophical extremes. This is already evident in Kierkegaard's reaction against Hegel and in his affirmation that man exists concretely in a concrete world. The new stance is best expressed in the famous definition of truth as passionate inwardness or subjectivity.[1] It now follows that the Idealist's Absolute is inconceivable, that the detachment of pure Thought is a Hegelian myth. Likewise, it follows that the objective detachment of the empiricist is quite unattainable. Of course the empiricist conceives of subjectivity and objectivity as distinct, even as opposed. To reach truth one must overcome the bias of the mind, what is disparagingly referred to as *mere* subjectivity. The Idealist goes to the opposite extreme: in his case objectivity is swallowed up and disappears in the gorge of the Absolute. Passionate subjectivity implies a respect for each term of the epistemological relation; here subjectivity and objectivity are not opposed, nor is the objective criterion discarded. Truth is grasped when one is deeply committed to it, not when one is neutral and detached. At the same time it is not ultimately a product of mind but of a harmony of mind and its world as object of knowledge. This is Heidegger's approach in "On the Essence of Truth". Speaking in a way that recalls Coleridge's description of the imagination, Heidegger wants to allow the mind active participation in the revealing of truth, not mere passive perception. And yet it is a question of revealing the world as it really is, independently of the mind. Truth becomes a cooperation of mind and world, of subject and object, in which neither term of the relation dominates the other. The mind *allows* the world to be as it *is*, it *lets it be*. One does not simply *see* the truth, one helps to *make* it, not by arbitrary invention but by revealing what is *there*. Such creative interaction between man and his environment is, of course, the essential viewpoint of all Existence philosophies. It is implied in the Heideggerian concept of being-in-the-world or being-there, in the Sartrean notion of *situation*, and, somewhat differently, in Husserl's insistence that consciousness is "intentional", that is, consciousness *of*. Husserl called his approach Phenomenological, and when Heidegger defines Phenomenology as "to the things themselves!"[2] he is being true to the original inspiration of Husserl and, further back and in another context, Kierkegaard. Passionate subjectivity implies a situation in which subjectivity and objectivity, mind and its object of knowledge, each equally real and equally active, are *one* in the moment of perception. The phenomenon of the world is encountered in man's committed *subjectivity* and encountered *objectively*, in keeping with its *true* nature. In short, I know a given truth not when I assume a disinterested stance but, on the contrary, when I *care* about it; truth belongs not to the neutral observer, empiricist or Idealist, but to the poet and the lover. To the objection that this is liable to lead to self-deception, the existential answer can only be that this may be so in fact, not in principle, and that neutrality, for its part, *necessarily* distorts the truth.

The relevance of this discussion to the form of a Ionesco play (or novel or short story) emerges when we consider what may be termed its point of view. Ionesco blurs the distinction between inner and outer reality, between what a character *feels* about an event and about the event as such. At any moment we are uncertain about the reality-status of a given action. A teacher murders his pupil. Actually, it is a verbal murder, not one in the empirical sense; yet there is no hesitation in presenting us with an actual murder, as if to underline the point that a murder at the level of *feeling* is a murder in *fact*. Ionesco gives us no external reference points for judging events: it is as if we were *inside* the plays, as if no outside view of things were possible. We cannot ask: are forty pupils actually murdered each day, do people actually turn into rhinoceroses, are the invisible guests actually present at the old couple's *soirée*, is the killer an actual individual haunting the radiant city, does Amédée actually evict a giant corpse – or does it happen as it were in the mind? Pupils *are* murdered, humans *do* turn into beasts – at the level of feeling – and what happens at the level of feeling, that is, of subjectivity is real enough, *objectively* so. What men feel to be true is existentially true for men. It may or may not be true for the neutral observer, empiricist or Idealist, but it is true for all beings involved in a given situation. We cannot shed our ontological skins, we cannot survey our world from above: *that* is the implication of the viewpoint of Ionesco's work, and it is an existential one.

At the same time this existential perspective takes a more specific form; it is coloured by the influence of the dream. In dreams, subjectivity – truth-for-me, truth as *I* experience it – is synonymous with objectivity, truth as independent of me. Clearly the existential and the oneiric are not necessarily and at all times related: if life, as Calderón put it, is a dream, it is after all a *corporate* one. In Ionesco's work, however, this distinction is not important. Of course Ionesco appeals to the oneiric because it enables him to reveal the everyday in a new light, as unexpected, mysterious and strange. He also does so because dreams, for him, tell the – existential, let us say – *truth*, they reveal freely and without the interference of the conscious mind, they do not lie. The original – in Ionesco's case, archetypal – dream pattern is that of release and claustrophobia, but there are other dream mechanisms such as the sudden metamorphosis, the tendency for characters to blur and merge, the phenomenon of repetition and the acceleration or slowing down of action. In *The Bald Prima Donna* the sense of growing anxiety seems inexplicable until its oneirical logic is recognized. *The Lesson* belongs to that class of dreams in which a sense of security is gradually turned into a nightmare, *The Chairs* to the class of wish-fulfilment dreams. The Jacques plays also contain strong dream elements, including specific Ionesco dreams such as those of the flaming horse and the guinea pig (*Entretiens*, p.85). Even the ludicrous formula of submission, "I love potatoes" etc., recalls dreams in which irrational statements are endowed with affective significance. Among other things *Jacques* is an erotic dream with overtones of nightmare. The oneiric pattern of later plays is more dynamic. Choubert's dream search is suggestive of an unconscious synthesis, the working out of a problem by means of dream symbolism. This is also the pattern of *Amédée* whose power of conviction stems from the fact that its action appears as a substitute, at the level of the unconscious, for a struggle in the conscious sphere. In short, the audience feels that the *real* action is going on somewhere else. So in silence and by moonlight Amédée and Madeleine evict the strange corpse that fills their home, working its huge bulk out of the window. The dream now becomes euphoric. Another play of the same period, *The Picture* (*Le Tableau, guignolade*, 1954), involves patterns of eroticism and wish-fulfilment and a mutiplication of identical characters, this last usually a sign of claustrophobic threat in Ionesco. *The Killer, A Stroll* and *Hunger and Thirst* are all euphoric dreams which turn into nightmares. *The Killer* in particular is characterized by a dream blockage, the desire one has in a dream to carry out an obscure task of great importance, matched by an inability to do it. And, most recently, *The Man with the Luggage* dramatizes a dream anxiety, that of the traveller who is frustrated at every turn. One might add that the "oneiric" viewpoint of all of these works could equally be referred to expressionist or, in some cases, surrealist influences. Ionesco is heir to a long tradition which includes the dreamlike distortions of reality of certain kinds of *commedia dell'arte* and *guignol*, of the creator of Ubu, of Büchner, Strindberg and the German dramatists who mirrored the visions of Grosz, Nolde and others, of Dali, de Chirico, Magritte, Delvaux, Ernst and their literary counterparts, of Duchamp, of the Dadaists. But if what I have described as existential is explicable in terms of the oneiric or the expressionist or the surreal, it may be objected, why not simply refer Ionesco's work to the latter? The point is that the appeal to the dream, as well as expressionist or surreal perspectives on reality all share a common ancestor: Romanticism. The same is true of existential thought. So the connection between the existential on the one hand and the oneiric, expressionist and surreal on the other, though complex, is not fortuitous.

The present chapter leads directly to a discussion of Harold Pinter's plays in the course of which what has here been said will be reaffirmed and elaborated. So far Heideggerian concepts such as those of art as revelation and "letting-be" have been shown to be of some relevance to the theory and practice of Beckett, Genet and Ionesco. Beckett's ideal of saying nothing leads to a notion of art as a revelation of an unknown: the Irreducible. In Genet art reveals sacramentally, as an efficacious sign, it makes the mystery of solitude present as the Mass makes present the historical sacrifice of Christ. In Ionesco art reveals the New, it affirms the transforming power of the imagination. Such an approach implies a notion of the artist as will-less, either a mouthpiece, or an officiating priest, or a dreamer of dreams. It also implies a rejection of literary realism and a movement towards what I have termed existential form and theatre of situation. In Beckett the aesthetic of the "all-at-once" is expressed as a curious drawing together of the opposites of simplicity and complexity, the result of which is poetry and the situational plot. In Genet it appears as a reduction of succession to simultaneity, a ritual bringing together of the poles of eternity and time. In Ionesco we find it in the stress on effects of dislocation and distortion which lead to abstract theatre, to theatre of situation and, above all, to a dream perspective which represents equally a phenomenological viewpoint. In order to complete this discussion we must now turn to Pinter and this because Pinter alone of those writers who are here considered develops an essentially phenomenological approach in an unlikely direction. The next three chapters will discuss Pinter in terms of existential thought and at the same time comment on the form of Pinter's plays. As in the present chapter, the analysis will be based on the concepts of subjectivity and objectivity.

V Pinter and the problem of verification

15 Pinter and phenomenology: the subjective–objective synthesis

> The desire for verification is understandable but cannot always be satisfied.[1]
>
> PINTER

Pinter's artistic search is for something less extraordinary than Beckett's Unnamable or Ionesco's experience of joy or Genet's solitude. It is simply a search for knowledge, a concern for verification. Of course it is possible to verify – to arrive at reliable knowledge of something – in various ways. Pinter's distinction, in the context of this argument, is that he has tried, at different times, to do it in widely divergent ways.

Writing in *Evergreen Review* in 1964 he sets out to make his position clear in terms reminiscent of Ionesco and, in the long run, Pirandello. Truth is not easily arrived at, the search for verification leads to varying points of view, to difficulties with simplistic labels, to the shifting basis of reality. "I'm not a theorist", Pinter begins,

> I'm not an authoritative or reliable commentator . . . knowing that there are at least twenty-four possible aspects of any single statement, depending on where you're standing at the time . . . A categorical statement, I find, will never stay where it is and be finite.[2]

As in Pirandello the great enemy is the label which fixes truth in a straitjacket: "We don't carry labels on our chests, and even though they are continually fixed to us by others, they convince nobody" (p.80). Follows a passage which is a restatement of Pinter's well-known manifesto – the programme sheet given to the audience who saw *The Room* and *The Dumb Waiter* at the Royal Court Theatre on 8 March 1960:

> The desire for verification is understandable but cannot always be satisfied. There are no hard distinctions between what is real and what is unreal, nor between what is true and what is false. The thing is not necessarily either true or false; it can be both true and false. The assumption that to verify . . . presents few problems I take to be inaccurate.

There is a forced quality in this writing which betrays the man who is not at home with ideas. And yet this very self-consciousness also gives Pinter his tone of conviction. This is no academic debate but a deeply personal commitment to the problem. Pinter applies his formulations to his own plays:

> A character on the stage who can present no convincing argument or information as to his past experience, his present behaviour or his aspirations, nor give a comprehensive analysis of his motives, is as legitimate and as worthy of attention as one who, alarmingly, can do all these things.

In the *Evergreen Review* version of the above argument the point is elaborated:

> Apart from any other consideration, we are faced with the immense difficulty, if not the impossibility, of verifying the past. I don't mean merely years ago, but yesterday, this morning. What took place, what was the nature of what took place, what happened? (p.81)

We are in the world of *Watt*, examining the fall of sand, or in *Endgame*, where "something is taking its course". There can be no doubt that Pinter's own profound curiosity becomes eloquent through contact with Beckett:

> If one can speak of the difficulty of knowing what in fact took place yesterday, one can I think treat the present in the same way. What's happening now? We won't know until tomorrow . . . and we won't know then, we'll have forgotten, or our imagination will have attributed quite false characteristics to today. A moment is sucked away and distorted, often even at the time of its birth. We will all interpret a common experience

> quite differently, though we prefer to subscribe to the view that there's a shared common ground . . . (p.81)

Pinter does not deny the existence of a criterion of truth, a "common ground", though, since this would be to undermine the search for verification and, indeed, to make nonsense of his own sustained concern for the truth. Thus he continues:

> I think there's a shared common ground all right, but that it's more like a quicksand. Because "reality" is quite a strong firm word we tend to think, or to hope, that the state to which it refers is equally firm, settled and unequivocal. (p.81)

Clearly, if by the truth we mean something forever immutable, a restricting of reality, there is no certainty possible in Pinter's world. But one may seek for verification of a different order and one may do so in various ways. Pinter, as we shall see, experiments with two or three. Like Beckett he will search for that shifting, elusive and yet very real point where *something* may be ascertained, a point between the incompatible areas of the namable and the unnamable:

> My characters tell me so much and no more, with reference to their experience, their aspirations, their motives, their history. Between my lack of autobiographical data about them and the ambiguity of what they say lies a territory which is not only worthy of exploration but which it is compulsory to explore. (pp.81–2)

The "territory worthy of exploration" is Pinter's sphere of operations, his no-man's-land. Here the phenomenon of reality is subjected to processes of verification in the course of which certain conclusions become possible.

In what follows, this strip of territory will be examined by means of a general comparison with existential thought and also in relation to a quite different philosophical approach. The *Evergreen Review* article after all recalls unmistakably in its formulations the scepticism and specific concern with verification of the scientific thinker. "Verification" itself is a term more likely found in the pages of a positivist than of an existential philosophy.

Pinter's interest in the present argument is that his work straddles the poles of the existential and the empiricist, that, at times more, at times less successfully, it brings together Sartre, Heidegger and Hume. The immediate inspiration is Beckett, however, and Pinter has made no secret of this.[3] Opening the Beckett exhibition at Reading University on 19 May 1971, he singled out *Watt* for comment and also admitted the keeping of a copy of *Murphy* borrowed from a library[4]. This stress on the novels is significant (the *Evergreen Review* article ends with a reference to *The Unnamable*), partly because it links the Beckett influence to the also acknowledged influence of Kafka: "when I read them [Beckett and Kafka] it rang a bell . . . within me. I thought: something is going on here which is going on in me too."[5] What Kafka and the Beckett of the novels, particularly *Watt* and *The Unnamable*, have in common is a concern with meaning and order. Pinter at times borrows the nightmarish quality from Kafka. From Beckett he derives the questioning doubt and the obsessive analytical drive towards truth. Of course Pinter lacks Beckett's fine intellectual lucidity, and moreover Beckett's aporia, that systematic doubt doubtfully proposed in the first page of *The Unnamable*, belongs to a very diverse and sophisticated tradition, owing much to Descartes, comparable to Husserl's radical beginning, to Heidegger's experience of the ground of things and, finally, to the *via negativa* of mystical theology. Pinter's scepticism and his search for true knowledge, in spite of its echoes of Beckett and the Continental tradition and of British empiricism, lacks this richness of association and this depth. Nevertheless the link with Beckett suggests the seriousness with which we must regard Pinter's quest.

Briefly, the search involves above all the question: how to arrive at the truth? But for the most part Pinter prefers to see the issue primarily in emotional terms, that is, not in terms of *knowledge* but of what relates closely to it: *security*. Security is linked to the question of human *identity*, which in turn, has to do with human *relationships*. Thus the quest for verification, the concern with security, human identity and relationships inevitably go together.

The Dwarfs was performed on the BBC in 1960 and serves to define something of a boundary between earlier and later Pinter styles. Here it is best to consider it first, since it furthers the understanding of other plays. Actually *The Dwarfs*, looking back as it does to the unfinished novel of the same name – a novel which preoccupied Pinter in the early and middle fifties – may be seen as underlying a great deal of Pinter's work. It depicts a rather cryptic relationship between three men, Pete, Mark and Len. Pete and Mark are unpleasant characters (this comes as a surprise in the case of Mark who is clearly reminiscent of the author). Len appears to be a victim. At the beginning of the play Mark is away, in a hospital or an asylum, at the end it is Len's turn. The scene shifts from one house to another as we alternate between Len's room and Mark's. Beneath the frequently casual conversation a fight for survival is taking place. The pattern of the action is simple and what we have come to expect from Pinter. We begin with an insecure man, threatened by others. Gradually, external pressures mount and we reach a point of crisis. It is not clear why Len is terrified, although his difficulties obviously relate to attitudes taken by his friends. In a brief soliloquy he expresses his anxiety: "There is my table. That is a table. There is my chair. There is my table. That is a bowl of fruit. There is my chair . . . This is my room."[6] Len is in the process of losing his grip on everyday certainties. More and more insecure, he clings to his room, image of safety:

> This is a journey and an ambush . . . This is the deep grass I keep to. This is the thicket in the centre of the night and the morning. There is my hundred watt bulb like a dagger. This room moves . . . It has reached . . . a dead halt. This is my fixture . . . I have my compartment. I am wedged. Here is my arrangement, and my kingdom. There are no voices. They make no hole in my side. (pp.94–7)

Only in his room is Len able to feel that a dangerous movement of reality is being arrested. The room is a fixture, a thicket in which one is safe from ambush. And yet there is an awareness of imminent danger, as if everything in the room were liable to be lost, drained away through a hole in Len's side. And indeed rooms have doors and doors let other people in. A moment later the doorbell rings and Mark enters. Everything reverts to an image of confusion and fear: "The rooms we live in . . . open and shut . . . They change shape at their own will" (p.99). As the play proceeds it becomes evident that in an obscure way Pete and Mark are in the process of destroying Len. Pete is the gull who swoops down on a rat by night: "Gull screams, tears, Pete, tears, digs, Pete cuts, breaks, Pete stretches the corpse, flaps his wings" (p.108). Mark's hatred is more stealthy and spider-like: "Mark lies, heavy, content . . . smiles at absent guests, sucks in all comers, arranges his web" (p.110). Inevitably, mysterious dwarfs stand and watch. They represent the scurrying, elusive resentments and insincere overtures of friendship which underlie the relations of the three men.

It is not surprising that Len's vision of horror and disintegration should go hand in hand with his own breakdown. His crisis of security ("Why haven't I got roots . . . Why haven't I got a home?" (p.111)) eventually expresses itself unambiguously as a crisis of identity. In an important passage, Len realizes that his apprehensions focus on the question of selfhood:

> LEN: The point is, who are you? . . . It's no use saying you know who you are just because you tell me you can fit your particular key into a particular slot, which will only receive your particular key because that's not foolproof and certainly not conclusive. (p.111)

At this point the face beneath the mask is revealed. Pete's dream of a world in which faces peel off and fall away (pp.101–2) is realized for Len. Beneath the everyday facade is something quite different: "Look at your face in the mirror. Look. It's a farce. Where are your features? You haven't got any features" (p.103). Len sees that beneath the social mask man has no simple, fixed identity. Human beings pretend to recognize each other in what amounts to "a joint pretence" (p.112):

> We depend on these . . . contrived accidents, to continue . . . What you are, or appear to be to me . . . changes so quickly, so horrifyingly, I certainly can't keep up with it and I'm damn sure you can't either. But who you are I can't even begin to recognize, and sometimes I recognize it so wholly, so forcibly, I can't look, and how can I be certain of what I see? You have no number. (p.112)

Pinter goes from a Pirandellian emphasis on the flux of life to a more explicit concern with verification:

> Where am I to look . . . so as to have some surety . . .? You're the sum of so many reflections. How many reflections? Whose reflections? Is that what you consist of? What scum does the tide leave? What happens to the scum? . . . I've seen what happens. But I can't speak when I see it. I can only point a finger. I can't even do that. The scum is broken and sucked back . . . What have I seen, the scum or the essence? (p.112)

Len goes to "hospital". Like Stanley of *The Birthday Party* and Aston of *The Caretaker*, he is utterly broken. The dwarfs have left, the yard is cleared of their rubbish, only images of sterility and defeat remain: "Now all is bare. All is clean. All is scrubbed. There is a lawn. There is a shrub. There is a flower." (p.117). Len's identity has been effectively lost. We have gone from insecurity provoked by human relationships to a crisis of identity. Significantly, a theme of verification, a concern with the truth – about human beings, their behaviour towards each other and their ultimate identification – parallels the action and echoes the arguments of Pinter's article in the *Evergreen Review*.

It is tempting to view Pinter's presentation of Len's crisis in the terminology of R.D. Laing, who, writing about certain kinds of schizophrenia in *The Divided Self*, argues as follows:

> . . . a basically *ontologically* secure person will encounter all the hazards of life . . . from a centrally firm sense of his own and other people's reality and identity. It is often difficult for a person with such a sense of his integral selfhood and personal identity, of the permanency of things, of the reliability of natural processes . . . of the substantiality of others, to transpose himself into the world of an individual whose experiences may be utterly lacking in any unquestionable self-validating certainties.[7]

I wish to refer to Laing's ideas not because some of them were fashionable for a time but because they are very definitely connected with existential philosophy and because there are real parallels with Pinter. The important notion, of course, is that of "ontological insecurity". Laing suggests that security is a phenomenon not of psychology but of ontology, such that its collapse represents a loss of *being*, of one's own being, a loss of Self or identity. Insanity is not an illness but an *ontological* state, in short, a way of *being* or *existing* – without an identity. The schizophrenic who assures me that he *is* nobody must be taken at his word, his statement must be regarded not as metaphorical but as statement of *fact*. The point to be stressed here is that the Pinter pattern of insecurity leading to crisis of identity – not simply to a psychological but to an ontological crisis in which selfhood may *actually* be lost – corresponds closely to Laing's theories. In so far as this is so, moreover, it becomes possible to say that Pinter's approach to the question of human identity in *The Dwarfs* is existential. If I am so made as to be liable to lose my Self, understood ontologically as my very being, I may be said to be ontologically *open*. In short, I *am* in such a way as to be exposed to an outside, *ontologically* exposed because it is possible for me to *lose* my very *being*. My identity is not something which closes me off from the outside, quite the contrary. I am not an Ego, something one may name or reify and set *against* the outside world. What I am reaches *out* to the outside world and at a certain point blends with it. If this were not so, how could I lose my being, how could it slip out of me? Like Laing, himself following Heidegger and Sartre, Pinter depicts Len's identity as a continuum of Len and his world. More precisely, he suggests that Len *is* a relationship, that he *is* his world about him. Just as Len's being reaches out to relate to the world, so the world reaches into the deepest part of Len. We recall that Heidegger refuses to use words like "man" or even "consciousness" because they suggest something self-contained and separate and defines man as *dasein* or being-in-the-world. Man is not a being who *happens* to exist in a world: his "there" is ontologically part of him. In Sartre, of course, there is the corresponding notion of situation. In each case the assumption is that we cannot regard man as a thing – even as a mental thing, a psyche or Ego. Laing follows Heidegger and Sartre here and of necessity breaks with the Freudian tradition. The two alternatives are mutually exclusive. Either I am an Ego, a creature determined largely by my past and a possible object of the science of psychology, or I am a being-there, a freedom thrusting my way into the future, a subject rather than an object, an *ontological* phenomenon rather than a *psycholo-*

gical one. Of course if we accept the existential approach and define man as being-in-the-world we must acknowledge that his world is largely made up of other people. To say that I am a being-there is to say that I *am* other people, that self-identity goes hand in hand with the fact of there being other people besides myself. This otherness is a part of me, the Other reaches deep inside me. Again, my name is legion, my "me" includes the being of other men. It is for this reason that Heidegger call *dasein mitsein* or being-with and makes it clear that the two terms are synonymous. Now for Pinter, Len is defined first in terms of *place*, then in terms of his *relationships*. Of course "place" in this context cannot be understood in a purely spatial sense. Len is indissolubly or organically linked to his room, his room is actually an extension of himself. The room is Len's area of operations, in short, his "there". This means that to leave the room or to lose it leads not simply to an emotional crisis, a crisis of ownership, but to a total loss of Self: if we separate Len from his room we undermine his sense of identity. In the light of this statement we may return to passages already quoted from the play. When Len clings to the objects in his room, seeking to define them by naming them, he is in effect clinging to his own identity: "There is my table. That is a table. There is my chair. There is my table . . . This is my room" (p.96). The room is a "fixture" (p.96), it guarantees one's selfhood: "Here is my arrangement, and my kingdom." (p.97) Unfortunately, rooms have doors. To *be* a relationship, a being-there, is very dangerous, it represents an *exposure*. As in Heidegger, to exist is to stand out or ex-sist, to be in the light, to stand *revealed*. Being-there leaves one open to threat or, in Sartrean terms, it gives one an *outside*. In Pinter language, "the rooms we live in . . . open and shut" (p.99). Thus Len, Christ-like, has a "hole in his side" through which the Other has ready access to his deepest being, through which the objects in the room and Len's very identity are liable to flow away. In other words Len is a place and because he is a place, a being-there, he is also a relation, being-with. It would be as inadequate to assert that Len *has* relations as it would be to say that he *has* a place. Len *is* these qualities. When Mark enters Len's room he enters Len, he installs himself within Len:

LEN: You're trying to buy and sell me . . . You've got me

> pinned to the wall before I open my mouth . . . Both of you bastards, you've made a hole in my side, I can't plug it . . . I've lost a kingdom . . . I can hide nothing. I can't lay anything aside. Nothing can be put aside, nothing can be hidden, nothing can be saved, it waits, it eats, it's voracious, you're in it, Pete's in it, you're all in my corner. There must be somewhere else! (p.107)

Of course, from the existential viewpoint, we are all in each others' corners and there is no somewhere else. Len is a public being, he is such as to be open to Mark and Pete, ontologically open. The Other is able to enter Len at will, through the hole in his side, to deprive him of his kingdom, of his room, of his identity, to reduce him to the state of schizophrenia or loss of Self described by R.D. Laing. The Sartrean echoes are strong. Len is object of the Look, "pinned to the wall", destroyed by the presence of the Other and, as in Beckett, "*l'enfer c'est les autres*", the hell of one's relationships is inescapable because it is part of one's very being. Of course what Mark and Pete can do to Len, Len can do to them. Indeed, earlier in the play it is Mark who is in "hospital". The point is that the characters of *The Dwarfs* cannot escape each other, that Pinter's assumptions about the nature of human identity in this play are those of Heidegger and Sartre.

Len's question – "The point is, who are you?" – has been answered, though not explicitly. Identity in *The Dwarfs* is being-in-the-world. In view of this it is not surprising that from the point of view of verification we are faced with difficulties. Selfhood is dynamic and elusive, like Len's room it is in a state of motion. But this is not to say that we need have recourse to the concept of the Absurd: it is enough to say that beneath the "joint pretence" (p.112) is a complex reality which can be defined in phenomenological terms. And yet a different point of view is put forward by Pete, one of the three protagonists of the play. When Len complains, "there is a different sky each time I look" (p.101), Pete warns of the dangers of subjectivity:

> You've got no idea how to preserve a distance between what you smell and what you think about it. You haven't got the faculty for making a simple distinction between one thing and another. Every time you walk out of this door you go straight

> over a cliff . . . How can you hope to assess and verify anything if you walk about with your nose stuck between your feet all day long? (p.101)

This is the voice of the empiricist arguing for objectivity and detachment. There can be no doubt that Pete's approach is not that of *The Dwarfs* as a whole. Pete is presented as a limited and destructive person and as one lacking in Len's insight. At the same time his viewpoint, that of the objective spectator rather than of the involved, existential subject, represents a valid alternative approach to the issue of identity and one which, as we shall see, is found acceptable in other Pinter plays.

I have spoken of "the approach of *The Dwarfs* as a whole", and this phrase requires further explanation. It refers, of course, to the implicitly existential treatment of human identity in the play, but is also refers to the *form* of the work. *The Dwarfs*, like the plays of Ionesco and, in a different context, those of Beckett and Genet, is situational theatre. This means that sequential action is replaced by the presentation of a total situation, that Pinter sets out to present not a series of events but a *state of affairs*. The situation is complete from the start. All that remains is for us to view its many facets. Once again, the operative principle is that of the "all at once". We are not concerned with particular actions performed by Pete, Mark and Len, only with an enduring state of tension, a state of human relationships, of insecurity, of threatened identity. The only real action of the play, the constant change of setting from Mark's room to Len's, merely emphasizes Pinter's formal approach: as in Ionesco, it is the pattern, the shape that counts, not the succession of events. The parallel with Ionesco is even closer, however, though it is not to be explained in terms of "influence". *The Dwarfs*, like *The Lesson*, may be termed a phenomenological play and for similar reasons. When Pete suggests that Len's point of view on reality is subjective and so inadequate he is putting forward an argument for objectivity which is not in keeping with the viewpoint of *The Dwarfs* itself. That is to say, the play as a whole has a phenomenological viewpoint. We cannot clearly distinguish between actual events and events which may be taking place within the mind – presumably Len's. Thus we cannot ask whether the threat to Len's identity is actual or imaginary. The fact is that there *is* a mental collapse and that Len's friends *are* inextricably bound up with it. Does it matter whether they are directly or indirectly responsible? In so far as Len *feels* threatened he *is* threatened: the rest is a quibble. *The Dwarfs* presents a total phenomenon, a single entity which can be examined in various ways but which cannot be divided into separate parts: the phenomenon of Len's-being-in-the-world or, better, Len's-having-relations-and-consequently-losing-his-identity. In other words, Pinter's presentation offers us the subjective and objective as *complements*, it stands with Kierkegaard's definition of truth as passionate subjectivity, not with the empiricist's definition of it as detached objectivity. This is not to say that the viewpoint of *The Dwarfs* is altogether dreamlike, although there are elements of nightmare in the play. Pinter differs a little from Ionesco here, but in essence the approach is similar. We see this when we reflect that in this play Pinter shows no interest in psychology, in patterns of motivation – the causes and effects which are the stuff of psychological drama. Broadly speaking, a psychological approach implies an objective standpoint. Pinter rejects psychology and – since psychology and the convention of literary realism are closely related – a realist viewpoint as well, and he does it because, like the existential thinker, he wishes to evoke the sense of a composite reality, a world in which man's feelings have objective validity. We return to the R.D. Laing approach to schizophrenia as a valid existential choice or to Kierkegaard: in each case it is a question of regarding a passionately subjective experience as compatible with objective truth, indeed, as a means of reaching the truth. The argument is simply summed up by saying that if we wish to verify the facts of the Mark, Pete and Len situation we do not refer ourselves to a detached empirical observer. On the contrary, we accept the committed viewpoint of the protagonists themselves – above all, the viewpoint of Len. Consequently, Pinter in *The Dwarfs* offers no *external* reference point according to which one might interpret or understand the play, he offers us, for example, no framework of psychological causes and effects. *The Dwarfs* must be taken as a whole, like one of Ionesco's plays, as consistent only with itself, as referrable only to itself. This is as much as to say once again that it offers a situation or subjective–objective totality. Certainly there is a great deal of surface realism – in the dialogue of the protagonists, for instance. But at the same time everything is modified by the sense of shifting reality, by the subjective or inward view implicit throughout. The characters are not viewed from the outside, in terms of psychology, but from the inside, in existential terms of freedom, the inexplicable and the unexpected. This is felt by the audience as an absence of reference point, as action oddly surreal or expressionist. *The Dwarfs* moves, like Len's room it will not submit to observation from a single philosophical angle. It places the audience in the same situation as Len, that is, in the situation of *dasein* which gazes at its world as one already *in* it, as one whose objective viewpoint is necessarily grounded in subjectivity. This is not simply to say that everything in the play is seen through Len's eyes. The point is that no detached explanation for events in *The Dwarfs* is forthcoming, that whatever objectivity is available is contained by the play and does not contain it.

A number of Pinter plays fall into the category of *The Dwarfs*, in particular the so-called "comedies of menace", where the central image is that of the room and the basic pattern the playing off of security and threat, inside and outside. In Pinter's words:

> Two people in a room – I am dealing a great deal of the time with this image . . . The curtain goes up on the stage, and I see it as a very potent question: What is going to happen to these two people in the room? Is someone going to open the door and come in?[8]

We are at once reminded of the closed spaces in Ionesco's plays and, even more strikingly, of Beckett's diminishing areas. Outside the room is a threatening presence: the Other, an unknown with power to destroy. With the hindsight provided by the analysis of *The Dwarfs* we may boldly state that the room represents one's identity, always a precarious possession in Pinter, that is, oneself as *dasein* or being-there. By the same token the door, avenue for the entry of the Other, represents oneself as *mitsein* or being-with. In the early plays the characters exist as ontologically exposed, then, and the door images a weakness built into the very structure of the personality. *The Room* (1957) is particularly reminiscent of Kafka with its small area of security surrounded by a great and mysterious house and by the darkness and the cold. As Rose, fussing around Bert, puts it: "it's very cold out, I can tell you. It's murder . . . Just now I looked out of the window. It was enough for me."[9] Rose is in a state of total ignorance as regards what is outside her room: "I've never seen who it is. Who is it? Who lives down there?" "Whoever it is," she adds conclusively, "it can't be too cosy" (p.8). With the room, on the other hand, "you know where you are" (p.8), "you stand a chance" (p.11). The moment of tension comes when someone is at the door, that source of uncertainty and uneasiness. It turns out to be the landlord. Again the sense of threat is suggested by the lack of information about things. It is as if no one were able to verify what obtains in the strange house:

> ROSE: How many floors you got in this house?
> MR KIDD: Floors. [*He laughs.*] Ah, we had a good few of them in the old days. (p.14)

Mr Kidd's knowledge of things is as fragmentary as Rose's. He "wouldn't be surprised" to learn that his mother was a Jewess (p.15). Later in the play Rose's anxiety grows when other visitors arrive. As always, uncertainty and confusion add to the tension. The visiting couple are looking for the landlord but his name is not Mr. Kidd. "Maybe there are two landlords" (p.19), someone suggests. Inside the room Rose and the newcomers rapidly move to resentment, and a moment later the issue is out in the open:

> ROSE: This room is occupied. (p.24)

In *The Dumb Waiter* (written in 1957) two thugs, awaiting orders in a room, are startled by the demands introduced by the dumb waiter, an obvious variant of Pinter's door. Gus, the more insecure of the two, keeps asking questions about the job to be done. When the dumb waiter begins its impossible demands Gus's insecurity grows. The situation in *The Birthday Party* (1958) is reversed. Ben and Gus, now the aggressors, have become Goldberg and McCann. Petey, Meg and Stanley make up the timid inhabitants of the room – in this case a dingy seaside boarding house. Meg has made the place as "cosy" as Rose's. Moreover, she mothers Stanley as Rose does Bert. In each case the room is both secure and claustrophobic. Stanley is a run-down individual who refuses to face the threatening outside world, in need of

Meg's haven and yet hating Meg in so far as she encourages his weakness. Whatever else one makes of them – and mystery is essential to their power to terrify – Goldberg and McCann stand for the world which rejected Stanley and which he left behind to crawl into his shelter. Clearly, Stanley's effort to construct a small world from which the threatening Other is excluded can only fail. The coming of strangers is as inevitable as the opening of a door.

One of Pinter's poems, dated 1953, speaks of "the stranger/ That strangered the calm".[10] It is tempting to see the element of fear in the early plays as something akin to *angst*. Unease – as in *The Dwarfs* – makes the environment appear alien and uncanny and this takes the characteristic Pinter form of a juxtaposition of normality and the abnormal, of Meg's breakfast cereals and the sense of underlying horror. A toy drum becomes a mysterious object, a dumb waiter, a threat. But the striking thing about Pinter's characters is not their *angst* but their inauthenticity. If we wish to see them in relation to Heidegger we must stress that they stand on the edge of the void but never quite go over. They are all of them experts at evading the experience which is the normal state of Beckett's and Ionesco's characters. This means that, while they cannot escape simple facts, they work hard to render this knowledge inoffensive. It is true that they are exposed, beings-in-a-room which is accessible to the Other. But it is possible to manoeuvre in such a way as to avoid any real communication with the outside, to allow the Other no glimpse of oneself, in Heideggerian terms to seek refuge in Idle Talk, speech whose function it is not to reveal but to conceal, to confuse. Pinter characterizes the speech of his creations in these terms in the *Evergreen Review* article:

> Language, under these conditions, is a highly ambiguous business. So often, below the word spoken, is the thing known and unspoken . . . you and I, the characters which grow on a page, most of the time we're inexpressive, giving little away, unreliable, elusive, evasive, obstructive, unwilling. (pp.81–2)

Evasion, the article continues, may involve silence or a mass of words calculated to fill the void of things:

> There are two silences. One when no word is spoken. The

> other when perhaps a torrent of language is being employed. This speech is speaking of a language locked beneath it . . . The speech we hear is an indication of that which we don't hear. It is a . . . smoke screen which keeps the other in its place . . . One way of looking at speech is to say that it is a constant strategem to cover nakedness. (p.82)

We recall Rose's compulsive chatter to a silent Bert at the beginning of *The Room* and Meg's prattle to an uncommunicative Petey, very like Rose's and yet closer, in its arrangement of recurring phrase motifs, to the poetry of *Waiting for Godot*. Comparable to this is the confrontation of anxious talkativeness and grim reticence in *The Dumb Waiter*. In each case, as Pinter suggests in his article, it is not a question of failure of communication, that favourite theme of early criticism, but of evasion:

> I think that we communicate only too well, in our silence . . . and that what takes place is a continual evasion, desperate rear guard attempts to keep ourselves to ourselves. Communication is too alarming. (p.82)

But, as Heidegger argues, the truth cannot be concealed. It can be revealed either as it is or as disguised but either way it needs must be revealed. This is precisely what happens in Pinter. The more one tries to hide one's insecurity and fear, the more evident it becomes. Gus of *The Dumb Waiter*, Rose of *The Room* and Meg of *The Birthday Party* all simultaneously disguise and lay bare their anxiety by their speech. In *The Dumb Waiter* an argument about the correctness of the expression "light the kettle" threatens to reveal the tension in the two men. In *The Birthday Party* Meg, unable to face the truth about her relationship with Stanley, is nonetheless embarrassingly revealing:

> MEG: You shouldn't say that word.
> STANLEY: What word?
> MEG: That word you said.
> STANLEY: What, succulent—?
> MEG: Don't say it!
> STANLEY: What's the matter with it?
> MEG: You shouldn't say that word to a married woman.[11]

Meg, like Stanley, is a master of illusion. Just as the latter boasts of his success as a pianist and tries, unconvincingly, to account for his failure, she lives in a world of fairy tale and birthday parties. Yet her very insistence on unrealities, her belief that the house is "on the list", that she is the "belle of the ball" and so forth, betrays her.

In any case fantasy and escapism cannot ward off the inevitable Pinter threat for very long. At the end of *The Room*, Rose's fears materialize in the mysterious visitor from the basement. The blind negro has little to say: "Come home, Sal" (p.30). Bert returns to beat him, Rose goes blind. As in *The Dwarfs* the pattern is from insecurity to crisis and the crisis is provoked by the entry of the Other into the room. Also as in *The Dwarfs* there is a clear suggestion that the crisis is one of identity: who is Rose, perhaps Sal? This is not to say that the blind negro may be regarded as an aggressor, as the Other who breaks into the room to rob its inmates of their identity. It seems likely that his function is rather to recall Rose to her true Self, to her past life, perhaps – as Sal. This fact explains his symbolic quality as a figure arising from the depths of darkness, like the Freudian Id or the Jungian Shadow, that is to say, the repressed side of the personality. If the situation depicted in *The Room* is slightly different from that in *The Dwarfs*, the pattern of an external threat to one's identity leading to a crisis is given unambiguous expression in *The Birthday Party*. Stanley, previously threatened by Meg's motherliness, is now subject to a sadistic assault from the outside. Goldberg, the aggressor, is a more complex version of Pete in *The Dwarfs* and his strength lies in his identifying himself with normality and objectivity. Overwhelmingly paternal, giving all the appearance of confidence, sentimental, brimming with platitudes, he immediately takes control of Meg's house. His "True? Of course it's true. It's more than true. It's a fact" (p.28) could well be the motto of the Heideggerian "they". Goldberg stands for conventional things but normality disguises many horrors and Stanley's party becomes the setting for the victim's total collapse, a game like the game of corners in *The Dwarfs* in which one is liable to lose one's Self. Of course Stanley loses his identity, as in *The Dwarfs* insecurity is a matter of one's very being. At this point the room, or rather the house, emerges clearly as an image of Stanley's Self. When the visitors enter it is to effect the victim's mental collapse, to reduce Stanley to Len's position. Thus Stanley, like Len, may be said to be ontologically *placed*, ontologically *exposed* to the Other, in short, *dasein* and *mitsein*. Stanley is hardly the only insecure person in the play. Even Goldberg and McCann mask their deep anxiety with a show of force. But it is Stanley who is most open to assault and whose loss of identity is complete. Significantly, his glasses are broken. If there is doubt about the exact meaning of Rose's blindness, there can be none here. We are not surprised to find that in a 1958 poem entitled "A View of the Party" Pinter speaks not of a dislocation of the personality – that is understood – but of a dislocation of the *room*. Again, the last stanza of the poem sees the whole struggle for identity as a contest for the room. Stanley has lost his eyes, or, if we prefer, the light of reason, his Self; Goldberg has taken possession:

> A man they never knew
> In the centre of the room,
> And Stanley's final eyes
> Broken my McCann.[12]

We must recognize the full significance of the victim's being led away at the end. In leaving his room, Stanley takes leave of himself. Like Lulu, whose fate comments on his, he has been seduced. The threat to Gus in *The Dumb Waiter* differs in details, in the manner of a variation on a theme. Gus too is in the dark as the waiter proceeds with its outrageous demands, he too is dominated, this time by Ben. The real crisis is the one we hardly see: Gus's realization in the final scene that he is the victim. It is not exactly a crisis of identity, of course, since it seems that Gus is to be killed. But the pattern follows closely that of other plays. At the heart of each of the early "comedies of menace" is Len's question: "the point is, who are you?"

Let us add that the viewpoint of *The Room, The Dumb Waiter* and *The Birthday Party* is that of *The Dwarfs*, the viewpoint of Phenomenology. While it is possible to point to realism of detail in all these plays – there is the dialogue, for example, notably in the breakfast scene of *The Birthday Party* – Pinter rejects any possibility of a detached viewpoint on the action. Rather, we are presented with a *total* situation, the phenomenon as a whole and as self-sufficient. In other words Pinter offers us reality as a conjunction of inwardness and outwardness, subjectivity and objectivity. In so far as an objective viewpoint exists it is contained by the plays and not vice versa. Thus while we may discern psychological patterns in the relations of Pinter's characters we cannot explain the given play *as a whole* in these terms. Put differently again this means that Pinter sees the truth of a given situation as embedded in that situation so that if one wishes to verify it one can only do so from the inside, that is, from within the situation itself. And of course one *can* verify certain facts in *The Room, The Dumb Waiter* and *The Birthday Party*, objectivity is possible – but not independently of its complement, subjectivity. For this reason *simple* explanations are unavailable, there are no answers supplied from above to the many questions which arise. *The Birthday Party*, for example, presents us with action viewed from the involved and emotional viewpoint of its protagonists. More precisely, what we see is an action in which *external events and externalized emotional responses to these events are indistinguishable* – as in *The Dwarfs* or Ionesco's *The Lesson*. Under these circumstances we cannot be certain that much or all of it is actual; it may be taking place in Stanley's mind, or Meg's. We may be witnessing not an actual confrontation but a parable or, better still, a projection of Stanley's insecurity and fear. But then we are not concerned to distinguish between subjective and objective truth. The truth is that Stanley *is* in danger of being destroyed by a force from his world, that Stanley's insecurity and his loss of identity are *real*. As in Kierkegaard, truth – objective truth – cannot be separated from human emotions, from the committed human being, that existential being-*there*. If this is the case in *The Birthday Party* is it equally the case in *The Room* and *The Dumb Waiter*. Is the blind negro, for example, a distinct personality or simply a projection of Rose's conscience? Are we to regard the room in all of these plays as an actual space or as an area within the mind, as the *inner* space of the human being? We must conclude that such questions are here irrelevant. What is in the mind, what is true in one's emotional life, is also factually or objectively true. At the same time the effect of the dual lens is, as in *The Dwarfs*, specifically surreal or expressionist. Even when the pattern of Pinter's dialogue and action appears to correspond to patterns of everyday life, there is something odd about it and the audience feels that it is not quite in realist focus. Sometimes the symbolic intrudes as it does at the end of *The Room* with the entry of the negro. Yet it is not the glaring symbol which militates against realism in these plays but the surreal juxtaposition of normality and the abnormal which is the result of a *simultaneous* presentation of inner and outer reality. Dali will paint a realistic giraffe – but set its neck on fire, or a realistic leg where one would expect to find an arm, and so on. If the comparison with the surrealist breaks down we may think of an expressionist landscape in which the colour is unnaturally bright and betrays the emotional or spiritual lens through which external nature is being examined. Pinter offers us a breakfast scene or a birthday party and then turns it into a nightmare; or he offers us the image of a dumb waiter sending down orders – to a pair of thugs who have no way of executing their orders; again, he presents us with an interrogation not "all that surrealistic and curious because surely *this thing . . . has been happening in Europe in the last twenty years*"[13] – and yet word the interrogation in a way that recalls the chaotic use of language in *The Bald Prima Donna*. In each case it is not the content of speech but the emotion which counts and this because the phenomenon is being examined from the inside. The interrogation is real, it is an objective fact, but it is a fact of subjectivity, a matter of feeling. What interests Pinter is the objectivity of the interrogation process as registered on the subjectivity of the victim such that the interrogation and its impact on the victim are presented as a single, total phenomenon.

Not surprisingly, the author's concern with truth and its presentation affects his own approach to the writing of the plays. Like Ionesco, Pinter rejects the art of propaganda ("To supply an explicit moral tag to an evolving and compulsive dramatic image seems to be false, impertinent and dishonest," *Evergreen Review*, p.81) and, more fundamentally, excessive authorial control: "Given characters who possess a momentum of their own, my job is not to impose on them . . . The relationship between author and characters should be a highly respectful one, both ways" (*Evergreen Review*, p.82). Again:

> . . . the explicit form which is so often taken in twentieth-century drama is . . . cheating. The playwright assumes that we have a great deal of information about all his characters, who

> explain themselves to the audience. In fact, what they are doing . . . is conforming to the author's own ideology. They don't create themselves as they go along . . .[14]

At times this *laissez-faire* is taken to extremes which the unsympathetic will interpret as affectation. Speaking to Laurence Kitchin, Pinter stresses that his plays are as obscure to him as to anyone else.[15] Inevitably, he explains the genesis of his work as follows:

> I start off with people, who come into a particular situation. I certainly don't write from any kind of abstract idea.[16]

> All I know is that blank sheet of paper in front of me, and then, when it's filled, I can't believe it.[17]

The problem may be phrased in the terms of the foregoing discussion of the plays: if subjectivity (in this case the author's) is to be objective, if it is not to distort, it must be seen as performing the function of "revealing" or, again, as the condition in which things are *allowed* to be what they *are*. We recall Heidegger's poet at Lake Constance, which, like Wordsworth's Tintern Abbey, is incomplete, unable to be itself, without an observer who perceives and half creates what he perceives. In this vein Pinter explains in the *Evergreen Review* that his method is by no means totally uncontrolled:

> The function of selection and arrangement is mine . . . But . . . a double thing happens. You arrange *and* you listen, following the clues you leave for yourself, through the characters. (p.82)

Arranging *and* listening means adapting oneself to the autonomous object: "If I write about a lamp, I apply myself to the demands of that lamp. If I write about a flower, I apply myself to the demands of that flower . . . I do not intend to impose or distort."[18] From a phenomenological standpoint this is the strength and objectivity of Pinter's method. Of course from a different standpoint the method, as applied in plays like *The Dwarfs* and *The Birthday Party*, looks like a strange *refusal* to look at things as they are – as if, rather arbitrarily, Pinter chose to withhold information from the audience. If his approach is accepted as valid, however, it is evident that the author is not withholding anything, that everything is *there*, out in the open, that there is nothing to *add*. In short, there is no merely objective viewpoint, the mystery is essential. But we need not conclude from this that an approach to writing consistent with Heidegger's theory of "letting-be" necessarily results in plays whose perspectives are phenomenological or whose form is expressionist. Pinter's comments about composition hold good for all his work, from the early plays so far considered to the very different work of later periods.

Two other plays ought to be mentioned in the same category as *The Dwarfs*. *The Hothouse* (1958) was written in the year of *The Birthday Party*, though it was only performed in 1980 – with "a few cuts but no changes".[19] In the setting of what appears to be an asylum, it poses a variety of questions, some of which are answered, though we cannot always verify the answers: why did inmate 6457 die? Who seduced 6459? Who released the rioting inmates? Where exactly and under what authority is all of this taking place? Underlying this is the fundamental question of identity in an establishment where human beings are denoted by numbers. Three times in the course of the play we hear detailed (and at times contradictory) descriptions of characters. Not unexpectedly, it is all in the context of a game of mutual threat: Roote, the head of the institution (who may well be the cause of 6457's death and 6459's pregnancy) is menaced by his subordinates (themselves at odds); Gibbs, with the help of Miss Cutts, menaces the naively well-meaning Lamb, as well as Miss Cutts. Gradually both Roote and Lamb, the strongest and the weakest of the staff, are destroyed, while in the background unrest grows among the inmates, whose function resembles that of the ubiquitous dwarfs in the other play. Lamb is broken, like Stanley of *The Birthday Party* (though in a way which anticipates *The Caretaker*). Roote loses his security, his sexual power is queried, he fails to make a speech when first required – significantly – his eyesight becomes an issue ("vision's very important", p.87). Although we are in winter, it is warm, indeed we are in a "hothouse", another claustrophobic Pinter space, crammed with creatures whose energy is constantly spilling over as it were into another's ontological area. As in *The Room*, there are symbolic touches – it is Christmas, one inmate had died, another given birth, a "lamb" has been destroyed – but the nightmarish quality which dominates is not dependent on these. Gradually, action becomes strange with the multiplication of inexplicable violence. Aggression is externalized in unexpected ways. In the end *everyone* except Gibbs is killed by the rioting inmates. By this stage surface realism has been completely overwhelmed, as in *The Birthday Party*, violence of feeling has become indistinguishable from actual violence. The same dual focus is evident in *A Slight Ache*, first performed on the BBC, then on stage two years later in 1961. Edward, the protagonist, has a vague awareness of something wrong: the irritating wasp which he kills and the unknown matchseller outside his gate both image this unease. His insecurity is heightened by uncertainty regarding the matchseller's identity and intentions. Inside his affluent country house – another of Pinter's rooms – Edward, troubled by an eye affliction, becomes increasingly anxious and the situation is not improved by his wife, Flora, who mothers him as Meg does Stanley. Eventually Edward calls the matchseller inside in an attempt to exorcize him. What happens is that the decrepit old man has nothing to say and, as elsewhere in Pinter (or as in the final scene of *The Killer*), insecurity, faced with silence, degenerates into panic. Babbling compulsively, Edward breaks down. Husband and matchseller change places and Flora goes off with the old man. Like Len, Edward is broken and deprived of his identity by an outside force and once again the question of truth and of its perception is uppermost, particularly in view of the fact that Edward is a philosopher and has a Kantian interest in space and time (p.17). Later, he explains his collapse in these terms:

> . . . it was not so much any deficiency in my sight as the airs between me and my object . . . the change of air, the currents obtaining in the space between me and my object, the shades they make, the shapes they take, the quivering . . . Sometimes . . . I would take shelter, shelter to compose myself . . . Nothing entered, nothing left my nook. (p.38)

The poetry of this is very like that of *Watt* and the subject is also similar: the breakdown of everyday modes of perception. We are also reminded of Len's statements in *The Dwarfs*. Edward, like other Pinter victims, has crawled into a small shelter which defines him, which provides him with an identity, a nook or room gained "after . . . long struggling against all kinds of usurpers" (p.35). But the room is open to the Other who enters in the form of the matchseller and, in destroying Edward's security, destroys his identity. The existential pattern is identical to that of other plays already discussed. Like Edward, the audience cannot verify the action from an outside standpoint. We cannot ask whether the matchseller is a real character or merely a projection of Edward's fears. Edward interprets the old man's movements in terms of his own expectations and Flora too sees the matchseller in terms of her situation, that of a sexually frustrated woman, so that where the intruder appears menacing to Edward he appears as repulsively desirable to Flora. The existential truth, of course, is that the old man *is* what others *feel* him to be.

In all the plays so far discussed Pinter seeks to define a "territory worthy of exploration", to discover a criterion for verification. He finds it in the implicit and existential conclusion that truth is grasped only in deeply subjective experience. But what of Pete's diagnosis of Len's trouble as "mere" subjectivity, or Edward's tendency to suggest that his crisis involves a failure of empirical objectivity, a loss of objective vision?

16 Pinter: psychological realism and the scientific approach

SOLTO: I got hold of this photo of you, see? So I got hold of the photographer. He told me what club it was, and here I am.[1]

PINTER

Where phenomenology regards subjectivity and objectivity as complementary terms, the positivist or empiricist view declares them to be opposed. The result of this shift is that subjectivity now implies a limitation, and objectivity – understood as its contradiction – becomes the sole criterion of truth. In this transition we have gone, let us say, from Kierkegaard to the British tradition of philosophy, from the committed subject of existential thought to the dispassionate outside observer. At the same time we have profoundly modified the existential definition of human identity as being-in-the-world. We have postulated the possibility of non-involvement in the world and so effectively split the entity being-in-the-world into its component parts. Man and his world no longer imply each other. Certainly, we do not find the one without the other but we are able to consider each as ontologically distinct. Having isolated the phenomenon man, moreover, we are able to objectify him, to name him in terms not of his situation but of his own distinctness. Man becomes, for example, an Ego, as in the Freudian system, or, more generally, a Self – whether defined in purely material and deterministic terms or not. The link between empiricism and the science of psychology points to a further link between empiricism and literary realism, that is to say, between the objective approach and psychological realism. This pattern of relationships is especially obvious in the nineteenth-century novel, of course – *The Mill on the Floss* provides the best example in English – but it is also observable in the drama from the naturalism of *Miss Julie* and the realism of Ibsen's middle period to the present day. Just as psychology, regarded as a science, presupposes that a human being may be studied objectively as part of a large framework of causes and effects, so realism in art presupposes the objective viewpoint. Of course literary realism does not do away with subjectivity or freedom. It merely keeps it from usurping the place of honour and upsetting the objective focus. Where the line between subject and object begins to blur, on the other hand, we move from the world of Maggie Tulliver to that of Leopold Bloom – the latter encompassing a whole range, from realism to the expressionist. Pinter reverses this movement by beginning with a form of expressionism and moving back towards a more empirical approach; he does so because a tendency to objectivity exists in his work from the start. In the terms of the present argument, the plays begin by depicting subjective and objective viewpoints as complementary, then go on to oppose them. This has been noted by some critics as a movement towards realism, but the point has been confused by inadequate definitions of the term. John Russell Taylor argues for what we might call "incomplete" realism ("it is not that the motives are unknowable, but simply that the author will not permit *us* to know them").[2] To the view that motivation in the Pinter character is unavailable *in fact*, Esslin replies that it is unavailable *in principle*. Does not life itself withhold information from us? I see two men arguing in the street; I know nothing about them yet the scene is perfectly transparent to me.[3] *Ergo* when Pinter refuses to motivate his characters he is being a realist. Now it may be that life itself is (for example) surreal. To conclude from this that surrealist writing is realist is quite misleading. Realism in art has, strictly speaking, nothing to do with life "as it is", it is, like expressionism or surrealism, a way of seeing things, a convention. Above all, it is a convention which presupposes availability of certain data – so that we cannot legitimately argue for it when such data is withheld. We *can* argue for it in plays in which Pinter transforms the existential phenomenon into an empiricist one.

Albert, the insecure and timid protagonist of *A Night Out* (1960), is the victim of a possessive mother. He wants to go to a party and the mother wants to keep him at home. When he does go he is unjustly accused of making indecent advances to one of the girls. Humiliated before other people, he leaves the party and eventually ends in a prostitute's flat. But the prostitute obviously recalls Albert's mother with her domineering ways. Albert asserts himself, winning a vicarious triumph over the mother figure represented by the whore. Soon after, he is home again and probably once more submissive to his mother. The themes which we find in *The Birthday Party* and *The Dwarfs* are unchanged. There is the insecure victim, the crisis followed by probable capitulation. The crisis is one of identity, moreover, since *A Night Out* poses the question: how autonomous an individual is Albert? As before, the crisis is provoked by the pressure of the Other, in this case the mother. But while the themes are unchanged, their treatment is no longer existential. Albert is identified with a room or rather, a house, and the play concerns his going *out*. But leaving the room does not mean loss of identity in this case. Albert is not a being-there, his relation to his home is largely spatial; the home is simply an important area where certain things happen. Likewise Albert is not a being-with. His mother is a power within him, certainly, but she does not exist within him as Mark and Pete exist within Len, that is, Albert is not *defined* by his mother any more than he is by his room, he is conceivable *without* his mother and his room. Albert is an empiricist individual: he is first himself and only *subsequently* engaged in human relationships. His relations are external to him, distinct from his being. Unlike Len or Stanley, Albert meets the Other in empirical space rather than in the space of his own inner world. Hence the crisis cannot involve a loss of identity. The Other does not *enter* Albert and Albert does not become insane – he simply suffers emotionally. We have gone from the sphere of the existential and the ontological to that of the *psychological. A Night Out* is psychological drama; in it human identity is no longer defined in terms of situation. The single unit being-in-the-world is now divided into two parts: on the one hand the human being, on the other, the world. There is commerce between these, but subject and object are conceived of as separate.

The implications of this attitude to the form of the play are many. To begin with, there exists now an external point of view, that is, a reference point situated outside the play itself. We may ask certain types of questions with regard to *The Dwarfs* but without expecting to find answers: it does not *matter* whether the action is real or a projection of interior neuroses, for example. But we *can* expect answers to questions raised by *A Night Out*. While a certain kind of complexity is compatible with the approach of this play, the fact remains that there are explanations for every character's behaviour in terms, broadly, of Freudian interpretations of reality. These explanations are objective in the scientific sense, they are objectively verifiable, there is no unknown. The mother's insistence that Albert remain at home is clearly motivated in the terms of her Oedipal relation to her son. The latter's two-mindedness about going is equally so: on the one hand he would like to escape, on the other, he is confused and guilty about his duty to his mother. The problem is focussed on in conversation such as this:

MOTHER: . . . Albert!

ALBERT: What?

MOTHER: I want to ask you a question.

ALBERT: What?

MOTHER: Are you leading a clean life?

ALBERT: A clean life?

MOTHER: You're not leading an unclean life, are you?

ALBERT: What are you talking about?

MOTHER: You're not messing about with girls, are you? You're not going to go messing about with girls tonight?

(p.47)

With a mother–son relationship of this kind of course there will be consequences. Albert will fear women and feel guilty about sex. He will become a social failure and his failure will constantly drive him back to the original stifling Oedipal situation. If he is accused of making indecent advances to an office girl he will be humiliated in an area in which he is most vulnerable. If he threatens violence to a prostitute it is because he seeks to overcome his mother in a symbolic way. Naturally he has no difficulty in identifying the maternal and the sexual in the figure of the whore because the two roles are blurred in his own mind. One does not need to analyse this play in detail to see how fundamentally it differs in its viewpoint from a work like *The Dwarfs*. While the *issue* of verification is still a vital one, the *difficulty* of verification has been removed with the separation of the levels of action and feeling. What is true – emotionally true – for Albert is not confused with external reality. The two are related, obviously, but distinct. In philosophical terms, subject and object are distinguished. Neither is over-emphasized, each sphere, that of subjectivity and feeling and that of objectivity and facts, is given its due. And it is precisely this which makes psychological realism possible as an art form. Because inward and outward reality blur in *The Dwarfs* there is no possibility of sorting out causes and effects: everything is equally cause *and* effect, it is a question of the chicken and the egg, there is no point in asking what comes first. Once we detach the subject from his world, however, and speak of him as, for example, an Ego, we are in a position to observe the way in which he acts upon the world or, more likely, the way in which the world acts upon him. The way is open for the interpretation of reality in the empiricist and determinist terms of a Freud: we may now speak of psychological cause and effects, that is, of motivated rather than free behaviour. The existential, ontological and expressionist approach of *The Dwarfs* has been replaced by the empirical, the psychological and the realist.

What has been said of *A Night Out* is applicable to *Night School*, a television play produced in the same year. Walter, released from jail, returns home to find that his room has been let to a young and attractive schoolteacher. Like any Pinter character, he is uneasy about this and takes a special interest in the girl. Very little is known about her. Walter, using a photograph, sets out to verify her story. The photo, taken from Sally's room, shows a girl in a nightclub. If this is Sally then the supposed schoolteacher is in fact a club hostess. Walter gives the photo to an older man, Solto, with instructions to trace the club and the girl but Solto, once he does so and confirms Sally's position as a hostess, becomes interested in the girl himself and does not reveal the truth to Walter. Finally, Sally, afraid of being discovered, leaves Walter's room. Walter is now alone, completely in the dark about the facts of the whole situation. Parallels with other plays so far discussed are easy to find. Sally recalls Albert's respectable prostitute, a woman leading a double life. Walter, who loses his room and then Sally, recalls the insecure victim. The whole play is concerned with the truth and the truth in question relates to identity: who is Sally? Is she the girl in the photo, is she a teacher or a stripper? The characters, all of whom are adept at playing roles, are reminiscent of other Pinter characters who are anxious to avoid communication for fear of revealing themselves. But it is clear that there is no mystery in *Night School*, as there is in the phenomenological plays. We begin by being in the dark about certain facts and we end by verifying them completely. As Solto tells Sally when he finds her, "I got hold of this photo of you, see? So I got hold of the photographer. He told me what club it was, and here I am."[1] Moreover, as in *A Night Out*, verification simply means *objective* explanation. To the simple question regarding Sally's identity we may reply that she is a club hostess. This being so, Sally's evasive behaviour towards Walter is clearly motivated, as is Walter's reaction to the loss of his room or his interest in Sally, as is Solto's suppression of the facts. *Night School* is a brief, realist analysis of a group of people and it offers us unambiguous criteria for truth. Obviously, by comparison with the phenomenological plays, something has been lost. Our sights are set on the surfaces of things, since psychology cannot represent the whole man, only the play of his thoughts and feelings. Thus, while there are now psychological or scientific answers to psychological questions we may well object that these answers reveal very little. The reason for this is evident. Psychology weighs motives as physics weighs particles. It provides answers but these answers can only be *probable* ones because science does not deal with certainties. Science is concerned with the probable and the approximate because it relies on experiment and measurement and no experiment is ever conclusive, no measurement ever final. One may add to one's information and so to one's accuracy but one cannot expect a definitive statement. As a result of this, literary realism, in so far as it adopts the scientific viewpoint, turns into a process of accumulation. The realist novel of the nineteenth century becomes longer and longer, indeed, a *series* of novels becomes a necessity for a Balzac or a Zola. The field is infinite, like that of the scientist's, psychological motivation exists as a never-ending chain of causes and effects representing an immeasurably complex pattern, and evidence is always, inevitably, provisional. In order to understand Dorothea we must come to terms with nothing less than what George Eliot refers to as "that tempting range of relevancies called the universe". In the drama, where time is limited, we must be satisfied with a slice of life, with a small cross-section. But, whether in the novel or the play, we can expect only probable, and in this sense partial or limiting, answers to the questions we wish to ask about reality. The advantage of the existential approach of *The Birthday Party*, for example, is that it achieves finality. Passionate subjectivity yields absolute certainty. Of course the truth *escapes objectification*, it cannot be given a name, it is known from the inside, as *experienced*. We understand *The Dwarfs* intuitively and as a whole because as a work of art it folds back into itself, it is self-sufficient, complete. In other words, the very distinction between a question and its answer is blurred in this case, the play is both question and its own answer, it must be taken as a single, total entity. As already stressed, there is no point in questioning Len's view of reality, or Stanley's. Within its phenomenological context it must be true, it *cannot* be false, the very question of its possible falsity is irrelevant. The empiricist, however, is not satisfied with this approach. Insisting on an objective or external reference point, he by the same token has to settle for probabilities. If I experience a given situation as my own, I am in no doubt as to its actuality-status. If I observe it from the outside I must weigh the chances of my judgement being correct or not. Thus the verification of truth in *A Night Out* or *Night School* is partial and incomplete, not in the sense that it leaves us without objective answers to our questions about the identity or motivation of a given character, but in the sense that its questions and their answers are strictly limited by an empirical criterion of truth.

In order to realize how difficult it is to categorize Pinter's plays neatly, we need only recall that *The Caretaker* belongs to the same year as *A Night Out*, *Night School* and *The Dwarfs*. This play, probably Pinter's best, is amenable to psychological interpretation, yet also suggests an existential perspective, though without the element of nightmarish distortion of earlier plays. (Clearly, the phenomenological viewpoint, though compatible with the expressionist, is not dependent on it.) At the level of realism we can see that Aston acts with shy reserve because of his hospital experience, that Mick is concerned about him, that Davies, standing between the brothers, arouses Mick's jealousy. Mick leads Davies on until the latter loses Aston's friendship and then helps to turn him out. It seems a straightforward enough story about a threefold relationship involving a gentle lunatic, an aggressive, jealous brother and an insecure tramp, anxious to establish himself in a room and yet unable to adjust to other men. However, this psychological element in *The Caretaker* is contained within a larger framework. Like the characters of *The Dwarfs* and *The Birthday Party*, Davies, Aston and Mick do not emerge as three separate Egos, three psychic and material objects reacting to each other in objective space. On the contrary, the play suggests a poetic presence and interaction which is best defined as existential. The three are organically bound – that is, bound absolutely and finally, not by a web of external, psychological connections but simply, once and for all, in their very *being* – with each other and with the space in which they exist, the room. They *are* their room, they *are* each other, in short, beings-there, beings-with. Only an assumption of this kind can explain the richness of this simple play. The realist novelist requires hundreds of pages to evoke the complexity of life; the realist playwright, with less time at his disposal, offers a *tranche de vie*. But Pinter's method here is not dependent on addition and subtraction. Rather it depends on the evocation of an added dimension, more or less suppressed in realist art, a dimension of density or depth best likened to poetic vision. Thus what we are offered in *The Caretaker* is not, strictly speaking, an action but a situation. Davies, Aston and Mick have very little to *do*: they are not characters – in the usual sense – enacting a plot, but three men existing, living out the implications of their situation.

Of course the three are faced with the issue of their identity and, like many Pinter characters, they are anxious to avoid it. This is true in a special way of Davies for whom Sidcup is that legendary place where all questions are answered and where one knows who one is. Davies' life may be summed up as a going to Sidcup in such a way as never to get there:

ASTON: Why do you want to get down to Sidcup?

DAVIES: I got my papers there![4]

The rush of absurdly improbable explanations recalls earlier Pinter characters, avoiding communication in a quantity of words:

> DAVIES: A man I know has got them. I left them with him. You see? They prove who I am! I can't move without them papers. They tell you who I am. You see! I'm stuck without them.
>
> ASTON: Why's that?
>
> DAVIES: You see, what it is, you see, I changed my name! Years ago. I been going around under an assumed name! That's not my real name. (p.20)

But Mick's accusing "I can take nothing you say at face value" (p.73) is as true of Mick and Aston as of Davies. Aston does not actually lie, yet his search for himself is as unreal and inauthentic as Davies', based as it is on projects which are unlikely to be carried out. Mick, quite apart from his devious, alternately violent and cajoling treatment of Davies, is adept at evasion and disguise. His dream of modernizing the house is as theoretic as Davies' journey or Aston's shed. Clearly, like the inmates of Meg's boarding-house, these three are living in a world of illusions, intent on keeping the reality of *angst* at a distance. Identity, which in this case, as elsewhere in Pinter, involves a particular settlement of relationships and of the issue of the room, is never faced. It is partly the horror of the truth which drives the three to torment each other, and which results in ever greater insecurity. Aston hides in his cluttered room, seeking solace among objects, recalling with resigned terror his experience of shock treatment. Like Len or Stanley or Lamb he has been broken, the Other has robbed him of his Self. And Pinter wishes to stress this. By focussing on Aston's long speech at the end of act two he goes a long way towards turning the whole play about this point in the action and so, thematically, about the experience of depersonalization which is at the heart of earlier plays. Unlike his brother, Mick reveals his insecurity by his aggressive behaviour. In his case the point of crisis has not been reached. Davies, of course, himself not a broken man like Aston, is the most insecure of all.

This emerges in all that he says and does, the fear that the authorities are after him –

> They might be there after my card, I mean look at it, here I am, I only got four stamps, on this card, here it is, look, four stamps, that's all I got, I ain't got any more, that's all I got, they ring the bell called Caretaker, they'd have me in, that's what they'd do, I wouldn't stand a chance. (p.44)

– the unconscious projection of his inferiority upon the "blacks", the neurotic inability to be honest, to accept a gift without in the same breath masochistically rejecting it. Aston offers a cigarette, Davies refuses, then, unable to resist, asks for tobacco; he wants a room but complains of the draught; demands shoes ("Shoes? It's life and death to me", p.13), refuses Aston's on the dubious grounds of a bad fit, is offered a new pair, refuses on the old grounds, weakens, accepts them – then argues that there are no laces. Davies is in terror not only of the authorities and of Mick but also of Aston. The final result of fear, of course, is that all lose by it, Davies his room, Aston companionship, Mick his brother's possible return to normality. The three fight because the insecurity of each brings out the same insecurity in others. Like Len, Pete and Mark of *The Dwarfs*, they drive each other to a point of crisis. It follows from what has already been said that this crisis, though unambiguously motivated, cannot be regarded solely in psychological terms: Aston, Mick and Davies do not simply express their particular reactions to particular problems, their struggle is an expression of their existence, it is the *form* taken by their existence. Of course verification of the ambiguities of motives along objective psychological lines is possible and it leads to reasonable answers. The drawback is that these answers fail to take stock of the overall effect of the play. It does not help a great deal to say that Davies is strictly explicable as a tramp, Mick as a jealous brother and Aston as a lunatic. These are not the central issues of *The Caretaker*. What is involved is a special way of approaching human identity and also verification such that, at the end, the objective answer to the objective problem is unsatisfactory. Here, as in the early plays, answers are tied to the teasing complexity of questions, the known and the unknown, the knowable and the unknowable are both *absolute* – and complementary, not opposed.

After 1960, the year of *The Dwarfs, The Caretaker* and *A Night Out*, Pinter's movement away from the phenomenological continues, although by fits and starts. *The Collection*, televised in 1961, is of particular interest in that it represents one of Pinter's most explicit references to the problem of verification. James accuses Bill of sleeping with his wife, Stella, claiming that Stella has confessed. Bill denies it, then admits to an indiscretion and, finally, to the whole story. In a scene with her huband, Stella sticks to her story but differs from Bill in the details. Understandably confused, James complains: "I can see it both ways, three ways, all ways . . . every way."[5] His relationship with his wife's seducer is becoming complicated through a sense of respect he feels for Bill. While the two men are together, Bill's friend goes to see Stella who tells him that the whole story has been fabricated by her husband. He returns to face Bill and James with this. Bill now agrees: the seduction never took place. Finally he promises: "I'll . . . tell you . . . the truth." (p.44) He met Stella and *talked* to her about making love. The seduction was only imagined. James now goes home to Stella:

> JAMES: . . . You just sat and talked . . . That's what you did.
> *Pause.*
> Didn't you?
> *Pause.*
> That's the truth . . . isn't it?
> STELLA: *looks at him neither confirming nor denying.* (p.45)

It is impossible not to be reminded of Mrs Ponza in the final scene of *Cosí è (se vi pare)*. The issue is the same: what exactly is the truth? It is also, as in Pirandello, closely tied to the question of identity – in this case Stella's – since we may ask of Stella, as of the schoolteacher in *Night School*: is she respectable or not? As in *Cosí è* the method is to alternate points of view, to offer a "collection" of opinions. The suggestion of a theme of identity is visually underlined in Pinter. There are two houses and the action switches from one to the other, emphasizing not only that there are two (or more) explanations of things but also that an explanation amounts to a personality, that what is at stake is a choice of identities. As one might expect, the question of security relates to that of truth and much of the play involves characteristically Pinteresque patterns of relationships of evasion and disguise, of defensive and offensive expressions of insecurity. James threatens Bill by entering his house, Bill's friend retaliates by entering James's home. Of course the concepts of *dasein, mitsein* and ontological insecurity are irrelevant here. *The Collection* offers us a single, external, objective point of view on the action as a whole. It stresses the complexity of the truth and the difficulty of objective verification without, however, deviating from a realist and psychological perspective. Truth is sought as if it were a matter of accumulation of evidence, a matter not of passionate subjectivity but of aggregates, of more and less, in short, of opinions. The fact that no objective answer is immediately available may seem to suggest a lack of confidence in the empirical approach, but this is not the case. On the contrary, the suggestion is the empiricist one already described, that truth is a matter of approximation and probability. The empiricist asks for as many opinions as possible and adds these up – statistical method applied to the sphere of the personal would have horrified Kierkegaard – in order to arrive at the truth. Naturally this truth does not pretend to certainty and the scientist is satisfied with a probability. In *The Collection* Pinter accepts the limitations of this approach. James never discovers the truth but he begins the long journey to objectivity. If this were an existential play he would have to see that truth is not in itself merely objective, merely a matter of facts. As it is, he has only to carry his investigations further, to uncover more and more facts in order to know the truth about Stella with greater and greater certainty. It is true that, like the scientist's, or the realist novelist's, this field is infinite, so that in one sense the truth remains a will-o'-the-wisp. But there is no suggestion in *The Collection* of an alternative approach to verification. The same may be said of *The Lover* (1963), Pinter's next television play. Once again there are echoes of Pirandello and, in this case, also of Genet. It is a game of roles, a *giuoco delle parti*, with a twist reminiscent in a small way of *The Maids* and *The Balcony*. Like the first scenes of Genet's plays, Pinter's opening deceives the audience:

RICHARD [*amiably*]: Is your lover coming today?

SARAH: Mmnn. (p.49)

Of course the lover is Richard himself. Husband and wife live a fantasy in which they become different people, lover and whore. The play poses a clear issue of identity with the added Pirandellian and Genet emphasis on role-playing: who is the real Richard, the lover or the husband, who is the real Sarah, the mistress or the wife? As usual, identity is a question which relates to a small space – the room in which all the action is set – and to a relationship. As well it relates to the more general question of truth. Richard, as Max the lover, tells Sarah that his wife does not know of his affair. Sarah objects that if the wife knew she would not mind:

MAX: She'd mind if she knew the truth, wouldn't she?
SARAH: What truth? What are you talking about? (p.70)

We are in Irma's *maison d'illusions*, asking the speaker to specify *which* truth he is referring to. As Richard and Sarah act out their parts, however, certain truths do emerge and, not unexpectedly, they involve feelings of insecurity. The pathos of Sarah's insistence on the pretence is directly related to her fear that without the role of whore she has no hold on her husband. As it happens, the play ends on a note of triumph for her, although there is no guarantee that this will last. The pretence goes on, the truth remains hidden beneath a mask. In spite of ambiguities, though, in spite of the play's insistence at one level on the elusiveness of the truth about human identity, *The Lover*, like *The Collection*, is closer to psychological realism than to the phenomenological plays.

The present argument has linked the work of Beckett, Ionesco and Genet to a philosophical tradition which includes Descartes, the Idealists and existential thought. In the case of Pinter we must stress that in important ways he stands within a native British tradition – in spite of his family origins – that tradition which is characterized by a bias towards experimental knowledge and which has dominated English thought at least from the days of Newton, Locke and the Royal Society, if not longer. The significance of Pinter in the present context is that he helps to clarify the relation between two philosophical lines, above all shedding fresh light on the existential approach as it is contrasted with its modern alternative, positivism. By the same token, tensions within his work help to define both psychological realism and the more avant-garde forms used by Beckett, Ionesco and Genet. In Pinter the existential gradually gives way to the empiricist. Yet Beckett, Ionesco and Genet also seem anxious to leave the existential behind, as if motivated by a desire to escape the limits of the human situation. Where they seek to avoid the existential sense of enclosure by an appeal to the transcendental, a return to the historical origins of the existential *Weltanschauung*, Idealism and Romanticism, or a movement towards a new Romanticism, Pinter makes a quite different escape by another philosophical door. The change in the plays is neither sudden nor clearcut and there are exceptions to the rule. Broadly speaking, though, it is possible to speak of three phases in Pinter's work. The first and second have already been characterized, the third remains to be discussed.

17 Pinter: the lure of objectivity

> RUTH: . . . Look at me. I . . . move my leg. That's all it is. But I wear . . . underwear . . . which moves with me . . . it . . . captures your attention. Perhaps you misinterpret. The action is simple. It's a leg . . . moving.[1]
>
> PINTER

It is not till we reach *The Homecoming* that another phase of Pinter's development becomes apparent. Performed in 1965, this play ranks with *The Birthday Party* and *The Caretaker* as one of Pinter's finest works. It has met with some criticism. Ronald Hayman sees aspects of the plot as gratuitous ("unexplained, arbitrary and structurally functionless") and feels that the behaviour of the characters consists of "a series of unexpected, separate actions, each one either disconnected from the last or at a tangent with it".[2] Martin Esslin and John Russell Taylor convincingly refute these conclusions. The background of the characters in *The Homecoming* is one of violence and prostitution; Ruth, wife of Lenny's brother – the academic Teddy – has been a model, perhaps a whore. It is not surprising that her visit to Teddy's family should become *her* homecoming, that she should steer her way through the rivalries of the men and return to prostitution under the protection of the family, leaving Teddy to return to respectability on his own. Far from behaving arbitrarily, the characters act as we would expect and the struggle is that of an educated man and his family past. There is no immediate reason to quarrel with this view of the play. If we compare it with the early plays the differences are striking, although the original issues remain unchanged. *The Homecoming*, focussing on Teddy and Ruth who have, in different ways, come "home", poses the question of identity and does so in terms of place and relationships. "The point is, who are you?" may be rephrased as: "Where is your home, your family?" Ironically, Ruth, who has a dubious background, very like that of Teddy's family, belongs with them in a way in which Teddy himself does not. Teddy, passive in the face of attack, is one of the line of insecure Pinter victims. Far from being the emancipated observer he would like to be, he is deeply involved with the others and has to escape to avoid being crushed – leaving his wife behind, a prize for the family. The issue is not presented in intellectual terms, of course, although it is true that Teddy, who is after all a philosopher, is concerned with the correct approach to truth: "to see, to be able to *see*!" (p.62). On the whole the problem is one of security, a struggle between Teddy and the others for possession of Ruth. Teddy does not have a crisis of identity, like Stanley, he merely loses his wife (an extension of himself) who plans to work as a prostitute for the family, taking the place of the dead mother, herself a whore. In order to realize Teddy's helplessness we need only recall some of the more striking examples of the family's animal aggressiveness: Lenny's story of how he beat the woman who approached him; Max's arguments with Sam; the flow of ready insults from one character to another; the ironic references to the dead mother; the easy cynicism with which Ruth is set up as a whore; the fight in which Joey and Sam are casualties; above all, the inexorable logic of the brothers' undisguised advances to Ruth while Teddy looks on. But while the thematic patterns are those of the early plays, the action of *The Homecoming* is clearly motivated from a realist viewpoint. As in *The Lover*, there is no mystery once we see the nature of the forces set against each other. Nor is there any question of a phenomenological link between the space of the action, the room or house, and the protagonists or between the protagonists themselves.

And yet even at first viewing one cannot accept the realism of *The Homecoming* at face value; there is something strange about it, and this strangeness relates to Pinter's obsessive surface treatment of reality. In order to comprehend the nature of the method it is useful to turn to that scene of the play in which a philosophic issue is explicitly raised. Lenny is taunting Teddy, the academic philosopher who cannot discuss philosophic ideas:

LENNY: Well, for instance, take a table. Philosophically speaking. What is it?

TEDDY: A table.

> LENNY: Ah. You mean it's nothing else but a table. Well, some people would envy your certainty . . . For instance, I've got a couple of friends . . . and they're always saying things like that, you know, things like: Take a table, take it. (p.52)

Ruth enters the argument:

> RUTH: Don't be too sure though. You've forgot something. Look at me. I . . . move my leg. That's all it is. But I wear . . . underwear . . . which moves with me . . . it . . . captures your attention. Perhaps you misinterpret. The action is simple. It's a leg . . . moving. (pp.52–3)

It is all the more vital to follow the argument here in view of Esslin's mistaken rendering of it in *The Peopled Wound*.[3] Esslin believes that Pinter is here concerned with the reality behind the words we utter, with the *way* we take a table rather than with the word "table". He overlooks the fact that Ruth is *disagreeing* with Lenny and supporting her husband and therefore misinterprets Ruth's example of the moving leg. What Ruth is saying is simple and empirical and it is quite the opposite of what Esslin suggests. She moves her beautiful leg and all males present gape. Do they see a mere leg, a mere physical object? Certainly not, they see an entire sexual metaphysics. But it only a moving leg, the sexual interpretation is irrelevant, let us even say *subjective* in the sense in which the term is used by the empiricist. *Objectively* speaking there is nothing there to make anyone gape. In other words Ruth is saying what Teddy has said: a table is just a table, Lenny's complex metaphysics "takes" the table nowhere. Things, whether tables or moving legs, are just things. Why foist human interpretations, subjective emotions on them? Why not just accept the simple, natural material presence of things? The relevance of this passage to the rather unrealistic quality of a seemingly realist play now begins to emerge. *The Homecoming* represents a new phase in Pinter and the Lenny–Ruth argument provides a vital clue about the philosophic point of view taken by the author and indeed about the form of the play as a whole, a clue which explains why Pinter's realism does not ring true at this stage. In this play, Pinter focusses obsessively on *things*. If one describes a tea party in realist terms one does not concentrate on a moving hand, a cup passing from the table to someone's mouth, a mouth sipping tea. One concentrates on the *psychology* of the situation, taking certain things for granted. Of course at a tea party there are cups, there are hands holding cups, there are mouths. But realism demands that one gloss over this and take it for granted that, for example, everyone has a hand and a mouth and so forth. If one focusses on the cup or the hand or the mouth as a pure material presence, an absolute object, realism is lost and the effect is surreal. Likewise if one thinks of the moving leg as an attractive part of Ruth the effect is realist, if one thinks of it as a pure presence, a moving object utterly without human connotations, the effect is surreal. The leg is suddenly strange. It could do anything, turn into a scorpion for example or, most mysterious of all, it could just go on being its own inconceivable self, a thing, an object, something quite impervious to reason. I want to suggest that Pinter's approach in *The Homecoming* as a whole is comparable to Ruth's attitude to her leg or to the table, that in this play Pinter's emphasis on the external goes so far as to work *against* the realist convention. Every character in *The Homecoming* is reduced to a material presence, every utterance to a vibration of particles, every action to a change in the arrangement of incomprehensible objects. This is not to deny the realist framework of the play. On the one hand the psychological structure, the human significance is *there*, on the other, Pinter approaches it in such a way as to make it appear strange. Every act or speech is seen *in itself* as it were and this is why Hayman reacts as he does to *The Homecoming*. Everything seems gratuitous, unexpected, violently disjointed – not because psychological explanations are lacking, as in *The Birthday Party* or *The Dwarfs*, but because Pinter shrugs his shoulders at these explanations. A character strikes another, two people chat during the night: we know why, yet we are encouraged to observe as if watching a strange ballet. In spite of the obvious realist placing of the events within a comprehensive structure, the effect is gratuitous because Pinter looks at it from a viewpoint of total detachment in a way no realist will do.

Of course in this context the very notion of human identity is lost. People are just material presences and that is all. Neither the existential nor the realist definition of identity remains, Ruth is neither a being-in-the-world nor an Ego, only a mysterious *res*. In terms of subjectivity and objectivity what has happened is that

Pinter has totally divorced the subject from the object and then obliterated the subject. There are no human beings, no *minds*, only things, objects which argue and fight and suffer, incomprehensibly. In one sense there are no relationships. How can there be, when one term of the subject–object pair is missing? There are *collisions*, of course, but no *meetings*. Objects are totally alone, self-contained in a world of atomic particles, each particle supremely itself and only itself, inexplicable, *there*. In his search for truth Pinter has adopted the point of view of the object and has taken empirical objectivity to its logical conclusion. The result is that we know tables as tables know themselves, that is to say, we know *nothing at all*, verification has come up against a wall. Things are there and we look at them in a world emptied of subjectivity, of mind and feeling and, indeed, of significance, since meaning is something conferred by the mind upon the object of knowledge. Superficially, *The Homecoming* suggests a return to earlier expressionist or surreal styles, but this is not the case at all. Rather it is a play of the kind David Hume might have advocated and this because in it Pinter takes empiricism, the apotheosis of the object, to a Humean point. Hume saw that if we take a truly objective point of view we cannot justify the law of cause and effect. A is always followed by B but this does not mean that A causes B, simply that A is always followed by B. Thus fire does not cause a burn. It is simply the case that the act of holding my hand in the fire is always followed by the sensation of burning. Empiricism, taken far enough, leads to philosophical scepticism and this is certainly the case in Pinter. Just as Hume reduces cause to proximity and by the same token human identity to a collection of sensations, so Pinter reduces his characters to pure presences and their actions to an impossible ballet. In each case too the quest for truth leads to a point where the possibility of verification is lost. If I focus obsessively on the objective and eliminate totally the element of subjectivity then knowledge is no longer conceivable. The world becomes an incomprehensible Newtonian body. Things no longer hold together. Relations, connections, human intercourse, psychological structures, meanings conferred upon reality – all dependent on concepts like that of causality – these fall apart along with the atomic universe. We have returned to Leibniz's monads or even to that distant cousin of British empiricism, Continental Occasionalism. Of course Hume will not go so far. But the entire process is visible in Pinter in whose work we see clearly the way in which a *limited* empiricism leads to psychological realism and a *total* empiricism beyond realism, to the pure materiality of things. It is a curious return to something like Heidegger's Uncanny by an unexpected philosophical route and also an oblique acknowledgement of Beckett's influence in an un-Beckettian context:

> But when the object is perceived as particular and unique and not merely the member of a family, when it appears independent of any general notion and detached from the sanity of a cause, isolated and inexplicable in the light of ignorance . . . (*Proust*, pp.22–3)

Pinter's *reductio ad absurdum* of the empirical search for objectivity recalls the collapse of causality in *Watt*. But that took place in an existential context, whereas Pinter's does not. Pinter pursues his quest for truth in a way quite unlike that of Beckett or Ionesco or Genet: he begins by accepting the existential or phenomenological postulate of truth as passionate subjectivity, as subjectivity made objective, then, by moving steadily in the direction of the empirical, completes the circle by returning to the impossibility of objective verification. But the final phase is very different from the phenomenological; it represents Pinter's version of a Humean scepticism and it recalls the work of another writer who seeks to be *objectif*, Robbe-Grillet. Indeed the Robbe-Grillet aesthetic of *chosisme* broadly describes Pinter's position and underlines the distance Pinter has travelled between *The Birthday Party* and *The Homecoming*. If we were to adopt an analogy with postwar styles in the visual arts, we could say that the difference between these two plays is that between Abstract Expressionism and a Hard-Edge approach, between the flux of intense emotion registered on a Pollock canvas and the precise definitions of the Geometric Abstractionists.

The change is by no means sudden, though. A peculiarly *chosiste* focus exists embryonically in the early work, then gradually takes over in works one would otherwise term realist – to the extent that, by *The Homecoming*, one is bound to speak of a more or less distinct third phase in Pinter's formal development. But it is in the screenplays that the movement to an aesthetic of objectivity is most pronounced and for an obvious reason: the medium of film itself, a medium which is intrinsically suited to an emphasis on the outside of things, the visual, uninterpreted aspect of reality. From 1962 onwards Pinter has written a number of screenplays (in addition to his adaptation of *The Caretaker*, *The Birthday Party* and *The Homecoming* for the screen), including *The Servant*, *The Pumpkin Eater*, *The Quiller Memorandum*, *Accident*, *The Go-Between*, *A la Recherche du Temps Perdu*, *Langrishe*, *Go Down* and *The Last Tycoon*; he also directed the film version of Simon Gray's *Butley*. Although the originals are not his own, he obviously chooses what is congenial to him and makes his presence felt in the final result. *The Servant* is a Pinteresque story involving a struggle of assertion and a change of identities and, in different ways, other screenplays explore the theme. There is Jo in *The Pumpkin Eater*, searching for herself in the context of motherhood, Leo in *The Go-Between*, who discovers himself in the transition from Innocence to Experience, and, notably, Marcel of the Proust screenplay, in search of identity as an artist, in search of sexual identity in a bewilderingly complex world of homosexual, lesbian and heterosexual relationships, above all, in search of the past. This last, and dominant, concern of course links the Proust screenplay, which was written in 1972, to Pinter's later plays and their concentration on the phenomenon of time. Here the point to stress is that, to a greater or lesser extent, and in a way which is by no means incompatible with lyrical and poetic effects, the screenplays exploit the objectivity of the camera. If, at times, they possess a somewhat surreal quality it is precisely because Pinter's emphasis, and the director's, is empirical to an extreme degree, because the camera lingers on the object and the entire treatment of character, plot and dialogue is designed to give precedence to the visual. The result is that at the end one feels that one knows everything and, at the same time, that there is nothing to know, or, like Lenny, that one asks what is a table only to be told, a table. Pinter has commented on this with regard to Joseph Losey's treatment of *Accident*:

> I do so hate the becauses of drama. Who are we to say that this happens because that happened, that one thing is the consequence of another . . . The most we know for sure is that the things which have happened have happened in a certain

> order: any connections we think we see, or choose to make, are pure guesswork.[4]

A statement such as this is illuminating with regard to many of the plays. It explains how at times Pinter can provide the psychological chain of causes and effects which is the essence of the realist convention and yet subtly undermine it at the same time. The chain is there but, as Hume asserts, the links are "pure guesswork". Teddy and Ruth behave according to a meaningful pattern in so far as the *order* in which things happen explains their meaning, but this is as far as objective certainty can go. Speaking of *Accident*, Pinter continues:

> In this film everything happens, nothing is explained . . . I think you'll be surprised at the directness . . . Just a level, intense look at people, at things. As though if you look at them hard enough they will give up their secrets. Not that they will . . .[5]

Clearly, mystery is far from ruled out by such concentration on the object. In *The Birthday Party* the psychological framework is vague and yet we know a great deal about Stanley. In *The Homecoming* and the films the psychological context is carefully delineated and yet at the end we frequently know very little about the characters. We note their behaviour, as we note that of Skinner's rats, but their inward life, their subjectivity, is out of reach.

One play in particular illustrates Pinter's new treatment of the subjective. Pinter's characters are always vulnerable in the eyes, that is, in their faculty of "seeing" the truth. The examples of Rose and Stanley come to mind, as well as those of Roote, Edward, Len and Teddy in *The Homecoming* (who is preoccupied with vision). In *Tea Party* (1965), a television play based on a short story, Disson, a businessman, asserts: "I like clarity. Clear intention. Precise execution" (p.19). Not surprisingly, his confidence masks a deep insecurity. Disson is afraid, threatened by his environment, afraid of the Other, of a loss of self-control. As the play proceeds, he feels that everyone is conspiring against him, undermining his authority, even his virility. At the end he collapses, broken by his fears. But the point to be stressed is that he loses his sight as he approaches the moment of crisis and, even more significantly, that he begins to see double. Pinter's handling of the phenomenon perfectly illustrates the shift to an empirical definition of subjectivity. Disson is playing ping-pong. Suddenly the camera sees two balls instead of one. Then it returns us to normal. Disson is gazing lecherously at his secretary. Suddenly her body swells threateningly. Then all is as before. There is only one possible explanation. *Tea Party*, for all its expressionist effects, is not an expressionist play. It is not reality which is grotesque but Disson's *subjective* view of it. Pinter is suggesting, by the simple use of double camera shots, that objective reality is unchanged and, at the same time, that Disson's imagination is responsible for the rest. We have come a long way from the phenomenological plays. In *Tea Party* the scientific downgrading of subjective truth is taken for granted and this is especially evident at the climax of the play where the camera alternates continuously from Disson's to the general and objective point of view. No plainer example of the empirical approach to truth could be imagined. Subjective and objective have drawn apart, the camera moves from one point of view to the other, underlining their fundamental incompatibility.

But it is in the plays written after 1965 and concerned with memory and the effects of time that Pinter's fascination for the empirical phenomenon, the naked presence, emerges with special force. The theme is Proustian, the tone that of Samuel Beckett, yet everything is dominated by the old obsession with verification: "apart from any other consideration, we are faced with the immense difficulty, if not the impossibility, of verifying the past" (*Evergreen Review*, article, p.81). Beth and Duff of *Landscape* (performed on the BBC in 1968, then on stage the following year) talk at cross purposes, Duff addressing his remarks to Beth but not noticing hers, Beth neither addressing him nor listening to him. It is the Pinter situation of evasion, with its consequence, solitude. Each character broods on past events, Beth returning in her mind to a beach, Duff to a rainy day, a visit to a pub and so on. Questions are posed for the audience: who is the man with Beth on the beach, Duff or someone else? Given Duff's infidelity, has Beth too had a lover, perhaps Sykes? But these questions require no answers, other than *probable* ones. The point is that none of this can be verified. Even Beth may be confused about something that happened in the past, as if it happened to another: "Of course when I'm older I won't be the same as I am, I won't be what I am".[6] Identity disintegrates like everything else: "I drew a face in the sand . . . The sand kept on slipping, mixing the contours" (p.20). What then remains of the truth? What remains is a series of memories, subjective in the positivist sense, of a series of *experiences*, solitary, discrete, like single atomic particles or monads. In this lies the essentially empirical scepticism of the play. Beth remembers specific statements she made, she returns to the issue of "touch" – in a way recalling the love motif of *Happy Days* – adding that in a touch, or a look, is her "meaning" (p.24). Of course she is longing for communication and affection, but the significant thing is that it is all expressed for her as a single, concrete *event*, a soundless gesture of love. Duff too focusses on the specific image, Beth at the window, for example, her reflection on the glass, the lucid sound of raindrops, "smacking on the glass" (p.27). Like Beth's drawing, the image is ambiguous, but not for an *intrinsic* reason. It is not that we cannot objectify the event, the image, simply that any given object is rendered inexplicable by time, or rather that, as object, it was never properly explicable and is now less than ever so. The result of all this is that *Landscape*, while not suggestive of the surreal element in the early plays, has a feeling of strangeness about it. Like Beth, we may touch the object (of memory) but it resists penetration, it remains a *sensation*, it both repels us with its density and disappears into air. Objective concreteness has led, predictably, to transience, the empirical phenomenon has proved *less*, not *more*, stable than the existential. Everything evaporates, but not into the world of the ideal, the world of the subject: the object *itself* has become a hole through which everything flows away. In short, extreme objectivity has metamorphosed into its antithesis, subjectivity understood not as the truth of feeling, that is, the truth about how *we* experience life, but as relativity, doubt. Maybe Beth's companion was Duff, maybe not. The only reliable given is the event – but what of its meaning? *That* varies with point of view, the passage of time. We have lost the human participants in the event, and so the event's *significance*: only the brute given remains, a "landscape" empty of mind. By a positivist route, and with a poetic appeal to Beckett, we have come in the most roundabout way to Pinter's own version of *Ukiyo-e*, an image of the floating world.

This point is reiterated in *Silence* and *Night* (1969), *Monologue* (written 1972), and, at greater length, *Old Times* (1971). *Silence* involves three characters reminiscing, a woman and two men. Ellen seems to want Rumsay who does not want her and to reject Bates who does want her: "there are two. I turn to them and speak. I look them in their eyes . . . and touch them as I turn" (p.35). As in *Landscape* the touch or meeting never eventuates. In Rumsay's words: "sometimes I see people. They walk towards me, no, not so, walk in my direction, but never reaching me, turning left, or disappearing" (p.40). The play offers few certainties, only queries. Ellen's past is dark, perhaps like Ruth she was a whore (p.36), but her relationship with the two men is not spelt out and appears, moreover, to be complicated by the possibility that the play dramatizes several, confused, time sequences: "I'm never sure that what I remember is of today or of yesterday or of a long time ago" (p.46). We are left with images of disputable status before which only "silence" is appropriate, Bates' memory of something in a tree, a vague, shadowy shape, or Ellen's and Rumsay's of the reflection in the window – rather like that in *Landscape*. Reality is impenetrable: "such a silence. Is it me? Am I silent or speaking? How can I know? Can I know such things? No-one has ever told me". (p.43) It seems that in plays like this a Beckettian influence on Pinter's style has softened the hard-edge inspiration of the later work. In spite of the dreamy poetry of the plays dealing with memory, this is by no means so. Beckett gazes at the object – let us say the lovers of *That Time* – with a contemplative eye, seeing it *sub specie aeternitatis*, Pinter's eye is halted by surfaces; both artists see only transience, but they do so from very different standpoints. The example of *Night*, a fine short piece which recalls the methodology of *Tea Party*, is instructive. A couple recall their first evening together, but each remembers it differently. The stress on sense perception does not help: "I felt the railings . . . behind me. You were facing me . . . My coat was closed. It was cold" (p.60). But in the end everything is unsure: "another night perhaps. Another girl" (p.59). Both versions of the story (did they stand on a bridge or against railings? Did he undo her coat or not?) are subjective, neither is verifiable. What interests Pinter, of course, is not the relation of lovers, though there is pathos in their loss of the past, but the brute event – whatever it was. And that is the point: under the pressure of time, or of personal feelings, the event has crumbled. It has done so not in spite of its objectivity but *because* of it. A similar disintegration is evident in *Monologue*, where, however, we are concerned not with conflicting perspectives but with the dubious recollections of a single individual. "Man" is talking to an empty chair as if it were his old friend. To begin with his tone is aggressive, involving a challenge to a game of ping-pong which carries the same connotations it did in *Tea Party* and alerts us not only to the theme of menace but also to that of subjectivity, Disson's problem with the balls. Soon aggressiveness reveals itself as bluster, then falters in the face of implacable silence from the chair. Silence, after all, is strength ("the ones that keep silence are the best off").[7] Gradually we piece the story together. It is, as usual, one of rivalry, here, a contest for the love of a woman, a black girl. The speaker lost her to his friend who subsequently probably lost interest in her. His anguish on this score is complex, however, since he both hates his friend and admires him. In a twist which looks back to *Old Times*, Pinter's fullest treatment of the issue of time lost and therefore left till last in this discussion of the memory plays, Man would like to blacken his friend's face, ostensibly to make him identical to the girl in question. There is of course a subtle degradation in this – Man would like to metaphorically "blacken" the other – but at the same time it is a way of *offering* the friend to the girl by as it were "making them alike". In short there is an element of masochistic *giving up* of the girl to the one who has in any case *taken* her. Naturally, one thinks of the mechanism employed by Genet's "saints". At the end this element dominates: Man, imagining his friend married to the girl (clearly no such thing took place), sentimentalizes over the possibility of children resulting from this union: he would then be an "uncle" of sorts. There were no children, in fact, yet the speaker casually makes the transition from possible to actual. "I'd have been their uncle", he comments, then, decisively: "I am their uncle" (p.276). Such a statement functions as an explosive, quietly introduced into the narrative to reduce the whole structure to ruins. If non-existent children may be called up as evidence, then the entire case is suspect. Maybe there never was a black girl or even a friend. Maybe the whole story is an exercise in masochistic daydreaming. All those details, evoked so empirically in the course of the play, in the manner of *Landscape* and *Night* – the day "she" was tired, the visit to the pub (over a bridge, as in *Night*), the "touch" (recalling *Landscape*), the visit to the friend's home, the "farewell" – may or may not have happened. Everything is subjective. Instead of the double bias of *Night*, we have a single, unreliable account of reality.

Comparable conclusions may be drawn from the situation of *Old Times*, a play which gives the lengthiest treatment to the memory theme but which tends too much towards mannerism by comparison with *Landscape*, *Silence*, *Night* and *Monologue*. Deeley and Kate are visited by Kate's old friend, Anna. Deeley is attracted to both women, who in some respects blur in his mind, and also threatened by the possibility that their friendship was a lesbian one. Kate, a passive, dreamy character, feels disgust at Anna (she appears to kill and bury Anna symbolically in the story she tells of Anna's dirty – it would seem, decomposing – face, which contrasts with her own cleanliness), and also, presumably, at Deeley, whose face she smudges with dirt. But then we are not sure it is Deeley. Indeed the entire play is full of unanswered questions. It actually begins, in the manner of *The Hothouse*, with a description (of Kate), which is promptly queried. We are never sure about Kate's identity (is she married, living in Sicily, etc.). More important: did Deeley know Kate in the past, or has he just met her? What exactly was the relationship of the two women? Did they – the usual Pinter inference – lead promiscuous lives, in short, were they perhaps prostitutes? Some events, it seems, *did* take place: these constitute our data. There was a film, a party, a scene in the girls' flat. But whatever it was, it happened long ago, and, in any case, objectivity could not even be guaranteed at the time, since all the participants were biased in their interpretation of the facts. Did Deeley meet Kate when he went to see the (ominously titled) picture, *Odd Man Out*? Or did Kate and Anna see the film, "almost alone",[8] as Anna puts it? And what of Deeley's usherettes, clearly suggestive of Anna and Kate? Deeley claims to have seen Kate and Anna at the party. Anna's version is that she had borrowed Kate's underwear (Kate's story is that she stole it), so that in looking up her skirt Deeley was looking, at least in a manner of speaking, at Kate, not Anna. Or are Kate and Anna scarcely distinguishable in Deeley's mind? Is everything we witness in the play talking place in someone's mind, Deeley's perhaps? Anna tells the story of the man who visited the flat and sobbed; in the final scene of *Old Times* Deeley seems to reenact the event, weeping, odd man out, broken by the one sure truth which emerges, that of his insecurity. Apart from that, everything is suggestion, like Kate's face, it is something we stare at, uncomprehending, unable to possess: "Yes, I look at it, holding it in my hands. Then I . . . take my hands away, leave it floating" (p.24). Present and past are light, like a balloon or a bubble, and as easily pricked. After all, even the status of the brute event is doubtful: "there are things I remember which may never have happened but as I recall them so they take place" (p.32). And yet we have not returned to the shifting world of *The Dwarfs*. In *Old Times* everything remains explicable, at least in terms of probability – until all explanations falter before the elusiveness of objectivity itself.

However, Pinter is quite capable of reverting to an earlier inspiration. After the realism of *A Night Out* and other plays he returned to the nightmare-focus of the comedies of menace in *The Basement*, which was written in 1964 and televised three years later. *The Basement* looks to the prose fragment *Kullus*, written as far back as 1949 but unpublished till 1968 and to a short story which shows the influence of *Watt*: *The Examination*, dated 1955. Law allows Stott and his girl Jane to enter his home. They quickly take over but while Law loses his room his rivalry with Stott results in his taking Jane from him. At the end we begin again: Stott owns the room and allows Law and Jane to enter. The pattern will doubtless repeat itself, with variations. But the important thing is that the treatment of this film returns us to the combination of inward and outward viewpoints characteristic of the phenomenological plays. After *Old Times* there is a similar return with *No Man's Land* (1975), which tackles all the issues of the memory plays, but with a backward glance at *The Dwarfs* and the pre-1960 works. Unfortunately *No Man's Land* is more mannered than *Old Times* and indeed represents a trivialized, parody Pinter – a fact which may have been obscured by the performances of Ralph Richardson and Gielgud. Pinter is dealing with the issues of time and verification, though the tone is often dreamlike, the action ritualized ("I have known this before. The door unlocked. The entrance of a stranger.").[9] Although the situation of four men (Hirst, Spooner, Foster, Briggs) involves reminiscence in a context of realism, the absence of an objective viewpoint is quickly felt and in due course reality takes on expressionist colouring. Hirst, like Len or Stanley, breaks down, morning comes, indistinguishable from night, above all, there is a Ionesco multiplication which, in this context, has the appearance of a farce, if a grim one. Soon everyone is a poet. Spooner accuses Hirst of seducing Stella (whom he loved), only to imply that he may have seduced Arabella (whom Hirst loved); then again, Hirst has seduced Emily, Spooner's wife, not to mention Muriel, Doren and Geoffrey Ramsden at Oxford. At the end of a tirade, Hirst calmly refers to Spooner as Wetherby. We may try to sort all of this out, to make sense of the relationship of Spooner and Hirst along psychological lines, but the attempt will not succeed, partly because, in so far as we are in the world of *Old Times*, factual truth is distorted by personalities and by time, and because, in so far as we have returned to *The Dwarfs*, truth is once again beyond the range of empirical investigation. The trouble is that *No Man's Land* does not work well, either as a phenomenological or as a positivist enquiry: its final effect is simply whimsical.

The same cannot be said of *Betrayal* (1978), which in some respects combines the evanescence of *Old Times* with the concreteness of *The Homecoming*, although it lacks the power of the latter play. *Betrayal* also looks back to *The Collection*. In this case, however, the problem of verification is not acute. Emma lies to Jerry, her lover, when she explains that she told Robert, her husband, about the affair in 1977; in fact she told him four years earlier. It is *demonstrably* a lie, the play is quite clear on this. Moreover the reason for the lie is equally straightforward. What mystery there is here has nothing to do with the ascertainment of facts or with the complexities of motivation. It is true that Robert's behaviour is problematical. He knows about the affair but makes no move to stop it. Perhaps, as when he discovers Emma and Jerry kissing in the final scene, he is even willing to advance it. At times Robert appears to be seeking to exclude Emma from his relationship with Jerry. He repeatedly asks Jerry to play squash with him. Are we to take this as a veiled masculine threat or as a form of wooing? Could it be that Robert's interest in Jerry is sexual? Why was he so happy at Torcello, after he found out about the affair? (Unless he is lying about being happy.) There are no simple answers to all of this, yet the play does not concentrate on such imponderables. And in a way it is enough to say that Robert feels ambivalently about both his wife and his friend. Everyone in *Betrayal* is a stranger to everyone else, as Robert suggests,[10] everyone to a degree lives an unreal life, like the man "writing a novel about a man who leaves his wife and three children and goes to live alone on the other side of London to write a novel about a man who leaves his wife and three children" (p.66). The real core of the play is elsewhere. Emma is unfaithful to Robert, himself unfaithful, and later she leaves Jerry for Casey who has left Susannah; Jerry has betrayed Robert and his own wife Judith, who may well be having an affair with a doctor; finally, Robert's insincerity may be the greatest of all. The subject is betrayal *per se*, betrayal considered abstractly. While the play is transparently realist in its handling of details, Pinter seems less concerned with psychology than with the *fact* of betrayal, that is, less with who is doing it and why than with the brute given, *that* it is being done. Once this is recognized, other elements of the play fall into place. Betrayal is Pinter's object under examination, something one needs to look at from different angles, like a hard gemstone. The time-span of the action is nine years, covered in nine scenes – suggestive of a natural cycle, the natural course of a series of relationships. In this context time itself becomes an object. *Betrayal* depicts the action in *reverse* order: we begin in 1977 and end in 1968, that is, we open with a post-mortem of the affair and close with its inception. At the same time some scenes are played in chronological order, *within* the larger, anti-chronological scheme. This is no mere gimmick on Pinter's part. *Betrayal* is no longer seeking, like the memory plays, to demonstrate the destructive effects of temporality. Rather time is now objectified, it has become a *thing*, a static phenomenon, something which, like a film, can be run forwards or backwards at will and, in the process, regarded coldly, objectively. In a sense time has been neutralized. Where *Landscape*, *Silence*, *Night* and *Old Times* evoke a sense of sadness or, at times, anguish at the uncertainty of experience, *Betrayal* remains cool. It is like that last scene of Orwell's *1984*: Pinter's lovers have grown apart, separated not by an existential void but by the holes in experience produced by the analytic eye.

Family Voices (1981), first performed as a radio, then a stage play, is Pinter's most recent work and, in part, it confirms the trend towards objectivity traced in this argument. But there is much more to it than that. In this fine work, more reminiscent than ever of Beckett yet totally Pinteresque in its handling of the drama, the author succeeds in achieving what he could not achieve in *No Man's Land*, a genuine synthesis of styles and approaches. *Family Voices* takes up all the old concerns, returns to all the obsessive images, in a way which appears to review, *da capo*, every phase of Pinter's development, like a symphonic climax. The room is there, with all its rich associations, derived from the early plays; so is the Oedipal situation of *A Night Out*, the most representative of the realist plays; likewise there is the aggressive family environment so vividly evoked in *The Homecoming*, the work of Pinter's hard-edge phase; then there is the evanescence, the poetry of the memory plays, from *Landscape* to *Old Times*. Three voices tell a story, in bits and pieces. The first is that of the protagonist who has left home for a large city and lives in an establishment rather like that into which Ruth was introduced. The second, alternately loving, pleading, bitter, resentful, rejecting, is his mother's. That voice calls him back home, but it does so ambivalently. Voice three is that of the father, sharp, destructive. Like Ruth the protagonist has found a new home, a new family. "Little did I ever dream I could know such happiness" (p.290), he gushes unconvincingly, with a stilted rhetoric indicative of emotional precariousness, unbalance. In fact the place is very dubious indeed. It contains Mrs Withers, a vulgar woman whose relationship to the protagonist combines sexuality with mothering oppressiveness ("sometimes she gives me a cuddle, as if she were my mother" (p.286). There are also Lady Withers, the woman in red – the "scarlet" woman, if we prefer – and Jane, the archetypal schoolgirl of the male imagination, who does not seem to go to school but is busy with work at home, homework, that is. Jane makes advances to the protagonist. All in all we would not be surprised to find that she is, with Lady Withers, "on the game". Then there are Riley, an unlikely policeman, who offers the protagonist a seedy homosexual relationship, and Mr Withers, an eccentric who keeps to his "room" and whose cryptic comments and burning eyes unsettle the young man. As the mother's voice calls the protagonist "home", it explains that the father has died. But at the end the father's voice, that of the living dead, is also heard. The young man, who has at this point clearly undergone a traumatic experience either as a result of his guilt-ridden memories or of his sojourn in the strange house or both, prepares to rejoin his parents – only to be told by the mother's voice that she too is dead. Pintersque questions abound. What do the unusual noises in the house mean? That it is a brothel? More pertinently, who *are* these people, all, or most of them, called Withers? Riley says he is a relation, adding, "of a sort" (p.293). "Bewildered" (like, according to *one* account, his dying father), "anxious, confused, uncertain and afraid" (p.293), the protagonist asks: what kind of relation? Is Lady Withers Jane's mother, in which case Mrs Withers, otherwise her mother, could be her grandmother? And who is Mr Withers? But for the audience all this is hardly the beginning. What we need to know is the status in reality of statements made by the three voices of the play. Is the father, who speaks, dead or not? Is the mother dead too, or is her reported death at the end merely a comment expressive of her hardening attitude to her wayward son, in short, a rejection of him? Why is the youth refusing to return? If we are to believe his report of Riley's story, the mother came looking for him, but was refused entry into the Withers house. Did that happen? Of course we need not simply query details. There is the *entire* play to question, since it might all be taking place in someone's mind, the young man's, presumably. Now totally new issues arise: there is a crisis, but what exactly is its nature? Are we witness to an inner conflict – located either entirely in the mind or partly in the mind, partly in a real situation involving the Withers – in the course of which the protagonist decides to "return", either actually or metaphorically? If the conflict take place in a particular social context, may we assume he has been broken, like so many Pinter victims? He has, we gather, been given a name, that is, a new *identity*, by the household: he is now Bobo. Does the clownish name indicate some obscure degradation? Or is it the case, as the mother's voice asserts, that her son has been turned into a male prostitute? Finally, assuming a home to return to *exists*, can the protagonist return if his mother is dead? Questions multiply, levels blur, at least at first sight. This is not to say one cannot make a positive effort to explain the complexities of *Family Voices* along psychological lines. In that case we may choose to overlook certain ambiguities and to assert that this is a drama of a black sheep whose relation with his mother is both loving and unhappy and who seeks to escape, only to find that, following the death of his father, he is bound to respond to his mother's call. As far as it goes, this is satisfactory, although it fails to explain away some problems, notably the mother's final statement about her own death. If we tackle *Family Voices* in the context of the later, *chosiste*, plays, we could add that, after all, it is all a question of point of view, that is, of subjective interpretation of reality. There is no empirical evidence offered for most of the assertions made by the play's voices. Indeed, most assertions are at some stage contradicted. The father, supposedly dead, materializes; he says he is not dead, then admits he is; his last words are variously reported by the mother, who also asserts that *she* is dead; the protagonist lies about the time (p.288), says he is drunk, then that he is not; he appears to be wording letters to the mother which, however, she claims not to receive. Clearly none of these are reliable, scientific witnesses. Significantly, the word "decide" recurs in the play to suggest a mental construction of reality – the protagonist, for example, "decides" Jane is Mrs Withers' grand-daughter, or that Lady Withers' dress is not red but pink. Is he simply *inventing*? If the entire story exists in his mind, then the whole play represents a dramatization of "mere" subjectivity, like *Monologue*. But we cannot stop here, any more than at a purely realist interpretation, because *Family Voices* unmistakably echoes the early plays too. In point of view it is, at least at times, dreamlike, surreal. We need only recall the odd multiplication of Withers, or the peculiarly unrealistic interlude with Jane. The young man is invited into a sensually overwhelming atmosphere. Even as he focusses, strangely, on Lady Withers' not red but pink dress, Jane's green outfit and her black toes, the latter is introducing her feet into his lap. Everyone now eats buns, indeed the place is full of buns, some soft, some astonishingly hard. A bun, too hard to chew, falls in the youth's lap where it is picked up by Jane's agitated toes – and so on. Obviously it is the logic of an anxious sexual dream. Later, the protagonist's crisis will be suggested with the same strangeness, though with expressionist force, such that the ridiculous name Bobo takes on overtones of terror. The fact is that we are, in part, in the world of the phenomenological plays. Truth cannot be ascertained in objective terms alone. Voices – that of the father and mother– live *for*, are real *to* the protagonist, so that we need not, in the final analysis, ask: Are the parents (one or both) alive or dead? They exist for the son and that is enough – the rest is a matter of scientific probability, that is, conjecture. The real question has to do with the crisis, not with the reality-status (its details, its context. And to the question of the *nature* of th crisis we may reply: *whatever* its empirical context (the exact an unverifiable nature of the facts), this is a crisis of *mitsein*, being with. The young man is *choking*, he is full of other people, of th past, of his over-possessive mother and his brutal father. *That* i what he needs to escape, but cannot, since the Other ha insinuated itself into the very structures of consciousness. *That* i why there can be no "homecoming", no "going back". At thi level of interpretation it makes no difference if details – the entir Withers interlude, the death or otherwise of one or both parents represents an invention. Indeed at one point the young ma suggests he *is* at his parents' house, searching for the fathei whom he cannot find. Place, in short, is immaterial, reality bein unverifiable. But there is *no doubting* the keenness of the crisis. T that extent too, we are far from the positivist sphere of th probable. Someone, it makes no difference who, *is suffering*, an the suffering relates to need for and revulsion against the Othei Can one live *alone*, Pinter asks, only to reply in the negative. Th terror of otherness is not as great as the terror of solitude Whether the crisis relates to the situation of the Withers or occur in the mind of an obsessive individual scarcely matters. Th Withers after all repeat with nightmare precision most or all of th original family problems. It is all *one* crisis, indeed, *one* family, *one* not two, sets of family "voices". Incredibly, in this last play, all o Pinter's cards are played at once, the point of view is that of th complex lens of phenomenology and the surreal, and, simul-taneously, that of the psychological realist – even that of th extreme empiricist illustrated in the memory plays or *The Home-coming*. Somehow the final effect is whole.

This argument has sought to define three approaches t verification discernible in the work of Harold Pinter, two of whicl – the phenomenological and the empiricist – are philosophicall incompatible, and two – the empiricist-realist and the extreme empiricist – philosophically related. In general the trend in th plays is towards objectivity, to the point where existential im-ponderables are replaced by even deeper mysteries, those stem-ming from the sceptical relativism inherent in any philosoph which takes its epistemological stand on the object rather than the subject. Of course the process of change is discontinuous, i involves frequent returns to earlier styles, and, in some plays, extraordinary mixtures. Moreover the old concerns, with truth, with security, with relationships, with identity, remain throughout. In spite of this it is clear that Pinter's inspiration changes gradually so that we can say, in the terms proposed by this discussion, that we begin with the phenomenological assumption that subjective and objective viewpoints are reconcilable, then proceed to draw subjectivity and objectivity apart until the two face each other as adversaries. By the time the process is complete, subjectivity has been obliterated, only the object remains and the victory of the empirical is absolute. And yet the lure of objectivity has brought about a curious reversal. Whereas in the phenomenological plays truth, defined as passionate subjectivity, may be immediately grasped in its dynamic totality, known in all its mystery with utter certainty, and whereas in the psychological plays objective truth is attainable in a context of approximation and probability, truth in one sense ceases to be an issue in plays like *The Homecoming*. We may put it as follows: whereas in *The Dwarfs* questions and answers are confounded and in *A Night Out* objective answers are available to objective questions, in *The Homecoming* and in plays like it Pinter has assumed the viewpoint of the object to the extent that knowledge is scarcely possible, since mind has been all but annihilated. In terms of the quest for human identity the threefold shift may be described as a movement from an ontological perspective where man is defined as *dasein* and *mitsein*, one with his room and with the Other, to a psychological one where he becomes an Ego related to the Other not in his very being but externally, in a web of causes and effects, to, finally, a perspective in which empiricism empties the notion of identity of any meaning and reduces man to an unrelated presence, stumbling across the Other in a series of inexplicable motions reminiscent of the Occasionalist dynamism. Of course Pinter's altered philosophic stance cannot but be reflected in the form of the plays. Thus the movement towards objectivity is imaged in a gradual shift from expressionism to psychological realism to something resembling Robbe-Grillet's *chosisme*.

Pinter's unique importance in this discussion is his ability to span two widely divergent world views, the poles of the existential and the empirical, in a way none of the other writers here considered are able to do – moving, as one of his poems puts it, "in a hostile pause in a no man's time".[11] Pinter does not have the stature of Beckett or Genet, and perhaps, in the final analysis, not that of Ionesco either. The fact remains that he is the only significant writer of the period to have managed the leap across the Channel.

Conclusion

The present work has not attempted to isolate the motif of imprisonment in the writings of Beckett, Ionesco, Genet and Pinter, or to focus on it as such. It is obtrusive enough, though it takes varied forms. In Beckett images of constriction and closed spaces run the gamut of possibilities, from the institution – generally an asylum for the insane – to the small private room, the cripple's chair, the bed, a bin, a sandpile, the womb and the grave, the region of the skull, the mind-within-the-mind, identity-within-identity. In Ionesco rooms close around their occupants, matter proliferates, food chokes, sex appears as a marsh into which one sinks, words, like furniture or corpses, cause blockages, the world's embrace is that of a tomb. For Genet, of course, prison is no mere image, though the worst captivity may not be that of *Deathwatch* or *Miracle of the Rose* but Stilitano's maze of mirrors. And in Pinter too, the room, the flat, the house stifles and oppresses, though here prison appears safer than liberty. We are returned, by complicated routes, to the prisoner of the Introduction to this book, Richard with memories of kingship, Monte Cristo scheming for exit. Four situations of containment generate four – or more – masterplans for escape.

Beckett, like his characters, is a sufferer. Pain, supremely real, is the goad, and it drives one away from the cruel eye of the world, to a refuge of peace which, on the face of it, appears unattainable. Because Beckett, in the time-honoured tradition of the *via negativa*, withdraws into inwardness, further and further until every imaginable stage in the process seems gross, requiring yet another move, towards a more and more refined point, where every trace of consciousness itself, the ultimate *esse* and *percipi*, is removed and only stillness and silence remain. But this drive into the void at the heart of being cannot be seen merely as escape. Even in the act of withdrawing from pain, Beckett observes his own situation, cool in his assessment of its possibilities for discovery. Escape from hurt turns into a search for the one necessary reality, that of the unnamable. Beckett is an intellectual, spurred by the need to *know*, to *name* – the ultimate without name, his self's self, the one who is silent in Beckett's speech. Prison, in this situation, means the inability to be *one*, to be the unnamable, to coincide with non-being, to vanish not negatively but as it were *positively*. The prisoner has opted to make his exit by an impossible route, through deeper and deeper entry into imprisonment, that is, from cell to cell-within-cell to cell-within-cell-within-cell, right up to that point which is innermost and where enclosure itself metamorphoses into its opposite, freedom. Such freedom can only exist as a paradox, freedom-in-chains, as an act which relentlessly seeks out hope where there should be none. It is, as I have argued, a New Romanticism, single-minded in its refusal to dream of a way out except by means of the way in. The prisoner has once and for all acknowledged that he cannot break out, the wall is, in its way, absolute. All that remains is to break *in*, to create space where there is no space. Within the limits of the exercise, Beckett's prisoner succeeds; sceptical, unsatisfied, doomed to fail, he makes his getaway.

For Ionesco, the jail is the astonishing, yet banal bordello of the world, age, dying, finitude. Ionesco is a frightened individual in a foreign country, haunted by nightmare memories, less an intellectual, like Beckett, than a man of feeling, a *sentimentalist*. Heart-broken, he weeps for his own failures and those of others, overwhelmed in turn by regret, nostalgia and by concern for the state of society. Here the prisoner hungers unashamedly for the Caspar David Friedrich paradise he has left behind. The only means of escape is the dream, the fantasy. The prisoner *flies* out of jail, no less, a Romantic as it were *by night*, soaring towards the fulfilment of absolutes, absolute freedom, absolute being. Inevitably the dream escape turns into the nightmare that is reality: the prisoner wakes to find himself once more hemmed in. Ionesco's exit fails, and, even as he attempts it, Ionesco knows it. If Beckett's Truth is unattainably attained, Ionesco's Good for which human beings yearn and to which they have primordial right is always out of reach.

On the other hand Beauty is everywhere in Genet's world, something as casual as a cigarette butt or a used contraceptive in the gutter. However, the Beautiful is generated by relationships of power, it is, initially, power to overcome, in the final analysis, power to resist, to retain one's virginity in the situation of rape. If we return to the metaphor of the prison we must insist that Genet's jail is his own self, and the jailer the Other installed within, the one who controls the Look. Where Beckett's characters shrink inwardly from the penetrating eye, Genet's are confused, disoriented: they have no inside, there is nowhere to withdraw, the more they turn towards self the more they are plunged into otherness. It is as if Genet, the aesthete to Beckett's intellectual and Ionesco's man of sentiment, were not one but many beings, all of them alien, a protean, mercurial creature of uncertainty. Here the prisoner at least half believes he really is a criminal. Consequently he trusts no one, not even himself. Rather he tell fibs, knowingly, playing a most complex game, planning escapes which he does not take seriously or which, alternatively, assume complete credibility. In his long internment, he endlessly elaborates such plans, partly to pass the time, partly because he *wants* to get out. Should he murder the jailer – and then suffer the consequences? Or should he *seduce* him, destroy him *lovingly*, that is? Or should he organize a revolt of the entire prisoner population, overthrow the prison establishment? Or, when all this fails, *pretend* not to care by transforming himself, exquisitely, into a work of art? What if, when the jailer comes to beat him, he were able *genuinely* not to care, if he could withdraw into indifference, so that the brutal guard would be tormenting a mask, a dummy, while he himself would be absent, having slipped away somewhere behind the disguise, inviolate? In this prodigal series of transformations, it becomes difficult to say whether or not Genet's New Romantic successfully evades the jailer within. Apparently, real indifference represents an escape of sorts, since the prisoner no longer cares about the walls and bars of his cell; to that extent he has created a somewhere else, another, and a free, interior space. But, like Giacometti's art, this surely represents a minimalist solution to the problem.

In Pinter's world, as in Genet's, power is the central issue. But Pinter, like Beckett, also wants to *know*, although, unlike Beckett, he approaches knowledge as a means to power. Pinter's jail resembles Genet's to the extent that its jailer is established within the prisoner. Escape therefore implies a deadening or hardening of one's responses, something closer to Genet's indifference than to Beckett's inwardness, yet complicated by Pinter's uncertainty about what exactly it is he is doing. Indeed the prison might well be defined as Pinter's inability to understand, to "see". Pinter lives in a dangerous world, haunted by nightmares, as does Ionesco, but he lacks the confidence to admit any desire for relief, just as he lacks the confidence to pursue truth to the end. His prisoner adopts a tough stance, impassive, choosing *not to feel*, or again, to *become one of the stones in the prison wall*, an object among other objects. In this way Pinter's problem of knowledge vanishes into scepticism about all knowledge, and the prisoner, an anti-Romantic, turns away from any possibility of freedom, freedom which no longer even seems desirable, since if one is to be a stone one may as well be part of the Château d'If as of a Caspar David Friedrich peak. As the prisoner objectifies himself and his surroundings everything begins to dissolve, the more solid the cell the more transparent it becomes. But the real problem has been sidestepped, since the prisoner remains where he always was, inside a dungeon.

Of the four master plans for escape, then, one succeeds (impossibly), one fails, one succeeds (minimally), one avoids the alternatives of failure and success. In a hopelessly difficult situation this constitutes, as Vladimir would say, a reasonable percentage. However we regard the prisoner of the existential, we are bound to admit his tenacity and his ingenuity. Existential consciousness is like a straitjacket; it is, quite simply, *insufferable.* However, in Beckett's world, in Ionesco's or Genet's or Pinter's, there appears to be no other alternative. Something comparable may be said about the worlds of Heidegger and Sartre, although the quasi-mystical recluse of the Black Forest is at least as successful in the philosophic sphere as Beckett is in the literary in envisaging a way out of the impasse. Of course the bourgeois intellectual of St Germain des Prés refuses to allow for the *possibility* of exit. Like his saint Genet he plays superlatively clever games whose rules have been carefully established in advance to forestall paradox or surprise. Where Genet, driven by intense need, finally breaks all the rules, Sartre maintains middle-class decorum to the end. It seems scarcely necessary at this stage to reaffirm that comparison across supposed disciplinary boundaries helps to place the work of Beckett, Ionesco, Genet and Pinter in focus and that, by the same token, such a procedure illuminates at least some of the major questions dominating modern existential philosophy and, in some instances, questions dominating European thought from Descartes to the present. Although this book is not ambitious enough to propose any conclusions about the relation of philosophy and art as such, it may be that a judgement emerges from it nonetheless: that the relation of the two disciplines is much more intimate than we are normally given to understand, either by philosophers or artists. We are returned to those philosophical comments quoted in the Introduction, Descartes' "It might seem strange that opinions of weight are found in the works of poets rather than philosophers . . . there are in us seeds of knowledge, as [of fire] in a flint; philosophers extract them by way of reason, but poets strike them out by imagination, and then they shine more bright" and Martin Heidegger's belief, increasingly expressed in the later work: "Out of long-guarded speechlessness and the careful clarification of the field thus cleared, comes the utterance of the thinker. Of like origin is the naming of the poet."

Source references

A single complete reference is given to all works by Beckett, Ionesco, Genet and Pinter. All subsequent references for quotations from these works are to the edition originally cited and are given in the text. All references are to editions published in London, unless otherwise indicated.

Introduction

1 René Descartes, *Descartes, Philosophical Writings*, trans. and ed. E. Anscombe and P. T. Geach (Edinburgh, 1954), p.4.
2 Martin Heidegger, "What is Metaphysics?", trans. R. F. C. Hull and A. Crick, in *Existence and Being*, ed. Werner Brock (1956), p.391.

Chapter 1 Beckett: the Reduction

1 Samuel Beckett, *Three Dialogues* in *Proust and Three Dialogues* (1965), pp. 22–3.
2 *Proust* in *Proust and Three Dialogues*, pp. 65–6.
3 Samuel Beckett, *More Pricks than Kicks* (1970), p. 148.
4 Samuel Beckett, *Murphy* (1963), p. 59.
5 Samuel Beckett, *Watt* (1963), p. 140.
6 Jacqueline Hoefer, "Watt", in *Samuel Beckett: a Collection of Critical Essays*, ed. Martin Esslin (Englewood Cliffs, NJ, 1965), pp. 62–76.
7 Deirdre Bair, *Samuel Beckett: a Biography* (1978).
8 Samuel Beckett, *Molloy* in *Molloy, Malone Dies, The Unnamable*, trans. Samuel Beckett and Patrick Bowles (1959), p. 18.
9 *Malone Dies* in *Molloy, Malone Dies, The Unnamable*, p. 255.
10 *The Unnamable* in *Molloy, Malone Dies, The Unnamable*, p. 319.
11 Samuel Beckett, *Texts for Nothing* in *No's Knife: Collected Shorter Prose, 1945–1966*, trans. Samuel Beckett and Richard Seaver (1967), p. 71.

12 Samuel Beckett, *Waiting for Godot: a Tragicomedy in Two Acts* (1965), p. 9.
13 Samuel Beckett, *Endgame: a Play in One Act, followed by Act Without Words: a Mime for One Player* (1964), p. 25.
14 Samuel Beckett, *Krapp's Last Tape* in *Krapp's Last Tape, and Embers* (1959), p. 18.
15 Samuel Beckett, *Happy Days: a Play in Two Acts* (1966), p. 40.
16 Samuel Beckett, *Footfalls* in *Ends and Odds: Plays and Sketches* (1977), p. 34.
17 Samuel Beckett, *A Piece of Monologue* in *Rockaby and Other Short Pieces* (New York, 1981), p. 76.
18 *Rockaby* in *Rockaby and other Short Pieces*, p. 20.
19 Samuel Beckett, *That Time* (1976), p. 10.
20 *Not I* in *Ends and Odds*, p. 19.
21 Samuel Beckett, *How it is* (1964), p. 12.
22 *All Strange Away* in *Rockaby and other Short Pieces*, p. 42.
23 *Ping* in *No's Knife*, p. 166.
24 Samuel Beckett, *The Lost Ones* (1972), p. 60.
25 Samuel Beckett, *Lessness* (1970), p. 8.
26 Samuel Beckett, *Company* (1980), p. 7.

Chapter 2 Beckett: the philosophical tradition

1 Martin Heidegger, *Being and Time*, trans. J. Macquarrie and E. Robinson (Oxford, 1967), p. 67.
2 Edmund Husserl, *Ideas: General Introduction to Pure Phenomenology*, trans. W. R. Boyce Gibson (1931), p. 183.
3 P. 27.
4 P. 80.
5 Edmund Husserl, *Cartesian Meditations: an Introduction to Phenomenology*, trans. D. Cairns (The Hague, 1960), p. 1.
6 *Ideas*, p. 20.
7 P. 86.
8 S. A. Kierkegaard, *Concluding Unscientific Postscript*, trans. D. F. Swenson and W. Lowrie (1941), p. 296.
9 *Cartesian Meditations*, p. 19.
10 P. 32.
11 *Ideas*, p. 109.
12 *Cartesian Meditations*, p.41.
13 P. 33.
14 *Ideas*, p. 21.

15 P. 103.
16 Martin Heidegger, "The End of Philosophy and the Task of Thinking" in *Martin Heidegger: Basic Writings*, ed. D. F. Krell (1978), p. 383.
17 *Basic Writings*, p. 381.
18 *Being and Time*, p. 67.
19 Martin Heidegger, "Letter on Humanism" in *Basic Writings*, p. 213.
20 P. 221.
21 *Being and Time*, p. 61.

Chapter 3 Beckett and Sartre: the Unnamable and the pour soi

1 Jean-Paul Sartre, *Being and Nothingness: an Essay on Phenomenological Ontology*, trans. Hazel E. Barnes (1958), p. 21.
2 P. xxxvii.
3 P. xli.
4 P. xlii.
5 P. 79.
6 P. 615.
7 P. 480.
8 P. 338.
9 Albert Camus, *The Myth of Sisyphus*, trans. J. O'Brien (Harmondsworth, Middx, 1975), p. 13.
10 P. 26.
11 P. 52.
12 P. 61.
13 P. 111.
14 *Being and Nothingness*, p. 623.

Chapter 4 Beckett and Heidegger: being-in-the-world and the concept of angst

1 Heidegger, *Being and Time*, p. 164.
2 Beckett, *Embers*, in *Krapp's Last Tape and Embers*, p. 39.
3 Beckett, *Ohio Impromptu* in *Rockaby and Other Short Pieces*, p. 31.

Chapter 5 Beckett and Heidegger: Existence, nothingness and Being

1 Martin Heidegger, "The Way Back into the Ground of Metaphysics" in *Existentialism from Dostoevsky to Sartre*, trans. and ed. W. Kaufmann (New York, 1956), p, 214. This is the introduction to "What is Metaphysics?" added in 1949.
2 Heidegger, "What is Metaphysics?" in *Existence and Being*, pp. 384–5.
3 Heidegger, *Being and Time*, p. 19.
4 Heidegger, "Letter on Humanism" in *Basic Writings*, p. 216.
5 Martin Heidegger, *Identity and Difference*, trans. J. Stambaugh (New York, 1969), p. 29.
6 P. 31
7 P. 39.
8 P. 63.
9 P. 65.
10 Martin Heidegger, *An Introduction to Metaphysics*, trans. R. Manheim (New Haven, Conn., 1959), pp. 5 and 6.
11 P. 4.
12 *Identity*, p. 33.
13 Heidegger, "On the Essence of Truth" in *Basic Writings*, p. 141.
14 "Letter on Humanism", p. 194.
15 P. 196.
16 P. 223.
17 P. 236.
18 "What is Metaphysics?", p. 306.
19 *Being and Time*, p. 331.
20 "What is Metaphysics?", p. 386.
21 P. 389.
22 P. 389.
23 P. 389.
24 "Letter on Humanism", p. 210.
25 P. 222.
26 P. 212.
27 P. 199.
28 *The Complete Works of Saint John of the Cross, Doctor of the Church*, trans. and ed. E Allison Peers (1964), I, p. 59.
29 *John of the Cross*, frontispiece to Peers edition.
30 "Letter on Humanism", p. 215.
31 George Berkeley, "Three Dialogues between Hylas and Philonous" in *The Principles of Human Knowledge, and Three Dialogues between Hylas and Philonous*, ed. G. J. Warnock (1962), p. 220.

32 *The Ethics* in *The Chief Works of Benedict de Spinoza*, trans. R. H. M. Elwes (New York, 1955), pp. 59, 66 and 77.
33 Arthur Schopenhauer, *The World as Will and Representation*, trans. E. F. J. Payne (New York, 1958), p. xxi.
34 Samuel Beckett, *Cascando* in *Play and Two Short Pieces for Radio* (1964), pp. 39 and 45.
35 Samuel Beckett, *For to End Yet Again*, in *For to End Yet Again and Other Fizzles* (1976), pp. 12 and 15.
36 *The World as Will*, I, p. 309.
37 I, p. 310.
38 II, p. 583.
39 I. p. 312.
40 II, p. 603.
41 II, p. 605.
42 I, p. 153.
43 I, p. 196.
44 I, p. 390.
45 I, pp. 411–12.
46 II, p. 612.

Chapter 6 Ionesco: claustrophobia and euphoria

1 Eugène Ionesco, *Notes and Counter-Notes*, trans. Donald Watson (1964), p. 169.
2 Claude Bonnefoy, *Entretiens avec Eugène Ionesco* (Paris, 1966), p. 145. This will be treated as a Ionesco work in all following references. My translation.
3 Eugène Ionesco, *Plays* (1958, 1960, 1963, 1965, 1968, 1971, 1973, 1976 and 1979), II, p. 157. All following references to the plays given in the text are to this eleven-volume edition, (vols.. 1–3, 5–10 translated by Donald Watson, vol. 4 by Derek Prouse and vol. 11 by Donald Watson and Clifford Adams).
4 Eugène Ionesco, *Fragments of a Journal*, trans. Jean Stewart (1968), and *Present Past, Past Present*, trans. Helen R. Lane (New York, 1971), I, p. 68, *Present Past* is volume II of the *Journal*.
5 Eugène Ionesco, *The Hermit*, trans. Richard Seaver (New York, 1974), p. 169.

Chapter 7 Ionesco and Heidegger: authenticity and the collective

1 Heidegger, *Being and Time*, p. 164.

2 P. 222.
3 Eugène Ionesco, *Découvertes* (Geneva, 1969), p. 47. My translation.

Chapter 8 Ionesco and Heidegger: authenticity, death and the search for Being

1 Heidegger, *Being and Time*, p. 294.
2 Eugène Ionesco, *Entre la Vie et le Rêve: Entretiens avec Claude Bonnefoy* (Paris, 1966, and 1977), p. 160. This and following references in the text are my translation.
3 Eugène Ionesco, *Un Homme en Question* (Paris, 1979), p. 189. My translation.
4 Martin Esslin, *The Theatre of the Absurd* (Harmondsworth, Middx, 1968), p. 153.
5 Eugène Ionesco, *The Colonel's Photograph*, trans. Jean Stewart (1967), p. 120. French version from *La Photo du Colonel* (Paris, 1962), p. 159.

Chapter 9 Genet: solitude and the Sartrean Look

1 Jean Genet, *L'Atelier d'Alberto Giacometti, Les Bonnes (suivi d'une lettre), L'Enfant Criminel, Le Funambule* (Décines-Charpieu, 1958), p. 26. My translation.
2 Jean Genet, *The Thief's Journal*, trans. Bernard Frechtman (Harmondsworth, Middx, 1975), p. 55.
3 Sartre, *Being and Nothingness*, p. 256.
4 P. 257.
5 P. 263.
6 Jean-Paul Sartre, *Saint Genet, Actor and Martyr* (New York, 1971), p. 2.
7 P. 8.
8 P. 17.
9 P. 18.
10 P. 45.
11 Jean Genet, *The Maids*, trans. Bernard Frechtman (1957), p. 39.
12 Jean Genet, *The Balcony*, trans. Bernard Frechtman (1958), p. 15.
13 *Being and Nothingness*, Part III, ch. 3, section III.
14 Jean Genet, *Oeuvres Complètes* (Paris, 1968), IV, p. 168.
15 Richard N. Coe, *The Vision of Jean Genet* (1968).

Chapter 10 Genet and Sartre: the murderer and the saint

1 Jean Genet, *Our Lady of the Flowers*, trans. Bernard Frechtman (1966), p. 116.
2 Jean Genet, *Miracle of the Rose*, trans, Bernard Frechtman (Harmondsworth, Middx, 1971), p. 273.
3 Bettina L. Knapp, *Jean Genet* (New York, 1968), ch. 3.
4 Jean Genet, *Deathwatch*, trans. Bernard Frechtman (1961), p. 19.
5 Sartre, *Saint Genet*, p. 90.
6 Quoted in *Saint Genet*, p. 120.
7 Jean Genet, *Funeral Rites*, trans. Bernard Frechtman (1971), p. 94.

Chapter 11 Genet and Sartre: the image and the revolutionary

1 Genet, *The Balcony*, p. 57.
2 Sartre, *Saint Genet*, p. 544.
3 Jean Genet, *The Blacks*, trans. Bernard Frechtman (1960), p. 5.
4 Jean Genet, *Les Nègres* (Décines-Charpieu, 1958), p. 31.
5 Jean Genet, *The Screens*, trans. Bernard Frechtman (1963), p. 173.

Chapter 12 Beckett: the task of saying nothing

1 Martin Heidegger, "Hölderlin and the Essence of Poetry", trans. D. Scott, in *Existence and Being*, p. 304.
2 Heidegger, "Letter on Humanism", p. 213.
3 Heidegger, *Existence and Being*, p. 304.
4 Heidegger, *Being and Time*, p. 51.
5 P. 58.
6 Heidegger, "On the Essence of Truth" in *Basic Writings*, p. 127.
7 Heidegger, "The End of Philosophy and the Task of Thinking" in *Basic Writings*, p. 391.
8 Martin Heidegger, "Remembrance of the Poet", trans. D. Scott, in *Existence and Being*, p. 279.
9 P. 306.
10 Pp. 308–9.
11 P. 309.
12 P. 311.
13 P. 311.

14 P. 313.
15 P. 312.
16 P. 284.
17 P. 285.
18 P. 313.
19 P. 314.
20 Pp. 285–6.

Chapter 13 Genet and the Mass: sacrament as efficacious sign

1 Jean Genet, letter to Jean-Jacques Pauvert in *L'Atelier d'Alberto Giacometti*, etc., p. 145. My translation.
2 Genet, *Oeuvres Complètes*, IV, p. 179.
3 Bettina Knapp, "An Interview with Roger Blin" in *Genet/Ionesco: the Theatre of the Double, a Critical Anthology*, ed. K. Morris (New York, 1969), p. 71.
4 Antonin Artaud, *The Theatre and its Double* (1970), pp. 21–2.
5 P. 22.
6 *Descartes, Philosophical Writings*, p. 4.
7 Sartre, *Saint Genet*, p. 5.
8 P. 27.
9 P. 28.

Chapter 14 Ionesco: the free imagination

1 Kierkegaard, *Concluding Unscientific Postscript*, book 2, part 2, ch. 2.
2 Heidegger, *Being and Time*, p. 58,

Chapter 15 Pinter and phenomenology: the subjective-objective synthesis

1 Harold Pinter, programme sheet for Royal Court Theatre performance of *The Room* and *The Dumb Waiter*, 8 March 1960.
2 Harold Pinter, "Writing for Theatre", *Evergreen Review*, VIII, no. 33, 1964, p. 80.
3 Harold Pinter, "Harold Pinter Replies", *New Theatre Magazine*, II, no. 2, 1961, pp. 8–9.
4 Harold Pinter, "Pinter on Beckett", *New Theatre Magazine*, XI, no. 3, 1971, p. 3.

5 Harold Pinter, interview with John Sherwood, BBC European Service, 3 March 1960, quoted in Martin Esslin, *The Peopled Wound: the Plays of Harold Pinter* (1970), p. 36.
6 Harold Pinter, *The Dwarfs*, in *A Slight Ache and Other Plays* (1968), p. 96. References to *A Slight Ache* and *A Night Out* are to this volume.
7 R. D. Laing, *The Divided Self: an Existential Study in Sanity and Madness* (Harmondsworth, 1965), p. 39.
8 Harold Pinter, Interview with H. Tennyson, BBC General Overseas Service, 2 August 1960, quoted in *The Theatre of the Absurd*, pp. 265–6.
9 Harold Pinter, *The Room*, in *The Room and The Dumb Waiter*, (1966), p. 7.
10 Harold Pinter, "Stranger" in *Poems* (1968), p. 11. Reprinted in *Poems* (1971) and in *Poems and Prose 1949–1977* (1978).
11 Harold Pinter, *The Birthday Party* (1965), p. 17.
12 Pinter, *Poems* (1968), p. 19.
13 Interview with John Sherwood, *The Peopled Wound*, p. 36.
14 P. 38.
15 Arnold Hinchliffe, *Harold Pinter* (New York, 1967), p. 8.
16 Harold Pinter, "Writing for Myself", *The Twentieth Century*, CLXIX, no. 1008, 1961, p. 174.
17 Harold Pinter, interview for *The New Yorker*, 25 February 1967, in *The Peopled Wound*, p. 52.
18 Harold Pinter, letter, quoted in *The Peopled Wound*, p. 227.
19 Harold Pinter's note to *The Hothouse* (1980).

Chapter 16 Pinter: psychological realism and the scientific approach

1 Harold Pinter, *Night School*, in *Tea Party and Other Plays* (1970), p. 111. References to *Tea Party* are to this volume.
2 John Russell Taylor, *Anger and After: a Guide to the New British Drama* (1969), p. 326.
3 Martin Esslin, *The Peopled Wound*, p. 42.
4 Harold Pinter, *The Caretaker* (1962), p. 19.
5 Harold Pinter, *The Collection*, in *The Collection and The Lover* (1966), pp. 31–2. References to *The Lover* are to this volume.

Chapter 17 Pinter: the lure of objectivity

1 Harold Pinter, *The Homecoming* (1968), pp. 52–3.

2 Ronald Hayman (ed.), *Contemporary Playwrights: Harold Pinter* (1969), pp. 65 and 67.
3 P. 212.
4 Harold Pinter, interview with J. R. Taylor, *Sight and Sound*, Autumn, 1966, quoted in Hinchliffe, *Harold Pinter*, p. 127.
5 Interview with J. R. Taylor, p. 127.
6 Harold Pinter, *Landscape* in *Landscape and Silence* (1969), p. 24. References to *Silence* and *Night* are to this volume.
7 Harold Pinter, *Monologue*, in *Complete Works: Four* (New York, 1981), p. 275. References to *Family Voices* are to this volume.
8 Harold Pinter, *Old Times* (1971), p. 38.
9 Harold Pinter, *No Man's Land* (1975), p. 60.
10 Harold Pinter, *Betrayal* (1978), p. 80.
11 Harold Pinter, "I shall tear off my terrible cap", *Poems* (1968), p. 4.

Index